At the Altar of Lynching

The story of a black day-laborer called Sam Hose killing his white employer in a workplace dispute ended in a lynching of enormous religious significance. For many deeply religious communities in the Jim Crow South, killing those like Sam Hose restored balance to a moral cosmos upended by a heinous crime. A religious intensity in the mood and morality of segregation surpassed law, and in times of social crisis could justify illegal white violence – even to the extreme act of lynching. In *At the Altar of Lynching*, distinguished historian Donald G. Mathews offers a new interpretation of the murder of Sam Hose, which places the religious culture of the evangelical South at its center. He considers how Southern Protestants, especially men, came to support or accept lynching, and give the act religious meaning and justification.

DONALD G. MATHEWS has taught at Duke and Princeton Universities, as well as at the University of North Carolina at Chapel Hill. He has studied and written about religion and the South for more than fifty years, publishing three books and more than thirty articles. He is the author of *Religion in the Old South* (1977) and coauthor of *Sex, Gender, and the Politics of ERA* (1990).

Cambridge Studies on the American South

Series Editors

Mark M. Smith, *University of South Carolina, Columbia*
Peter Coclanis, *University of North Carolina at Chapel Hill*

Interdisciplinary in its scope and intent, this series builds upon and extends Cambridge University Press's longstanding commitment to studies on the American South. The series offers the best new work on the South's distinctive institutional, social, economic, and cultural history and also features works in a national, comparative, and transnational perspective.

Titles in the Series

Robert E. Bonner, *Mastering America: Southern Slaveholders and the Crisis of American Nationhood*

Ras Michael Brown, *African-Atlantic Cultures and the South Carolina Lowcountry*

Christopher Michael Curtis, *Jefferson's Freeholders and the Politics of Ownership in the Old Dominion*

Louis A. Ferleger and John D. Metz, *Cultivating Success in the South: Farm Households in Postbellum Georgia*

Craig Friend and Lorri Glover, eds., *Death and the American South*

Sarah Gardner, *Reviewing the South: The Literary Marketplace and the Southern Renaissance, 1920–1941*

Eugene D. Genovese and Douglas Ambrose, *The Sweetness of Life: Southern Planters at Home*

Luke E. Harlow, *Religion, Race, and the Making of Confederate Kentucky, 1830–1880*

Ari Helo, *Thomas Jefferson's Ethics and the Politics of Human Progress: The Morality of a Slaveholder*

Karlos K. Hill, *Beyond the Rope: The Impact of Lynching on Black Culture and Memory*

Katherine Rye Jewell, *Dollars for Dixie: Business and the Transformation of Conservatism in the Twentieth Century*

William A. Link and James J. Broomall, eds., *Rethinking American Emancipation: Legacies of Slavery and the Quest for Black Freedom*

Keri Leigh Merritt, *Masterless Men: Poor Whites and Slavery in the Antebellum South*

Susanna Michele Lee, *Claiming the Union: Citizenship in the Post-Civil War South*

Scott P. Marler, *The Merchants' Capital: New Orleans and the Political Economy of the Nineteenth-Century South*

Peter McCandless, *Slavery, Disease, and Suffering in the Southern Lowcountry*

James Van Horn Melton, *Religion, Community, and Slavery on the Colonial Southern Frontier*

Barton A. Myers, *Rebels against the Confederacy: North Carolina's Unionists*

Thomas Okie, *The Georgia Peach: Culture, Agriculture, and Environment in the American South*

Johanna Nicol Shields, *Freedom in a Slave Society: Stories from the Antebellum South*

Damian Alan Pargas, *Slavery and Forced Migration in the Antebellum South*

Brian Steele, *Thomas Jefferson and American Nationhood*

Jonathan Daniel Wells, *Women Writers and Journalists in the Nineteenth-Century South*

At the Altar of Lynching

Burning Sam Hose in the American South

DONALD G. MATHEWS

University of North Carolina, Chapel Hill (emeritus)

CAMBRIDGE
UNIVERSITY PRESS

CAMBRIDGE
UNIVERSITY PRESS

One Liberty Plaza, 20th Floor, New York, NY 10006, USA

Cambridge University Press is part of the University of Cambridge.

It furthers the University's mission by disseminating knowledge in the pursuit of education, learning, and research at the highest international levels of excellence.

www.cambridge.org
Information on this title: www.cambridge.org/9781316633984
DOI: 10.1017/9781316863510

© Donald G. Mathews 2018

First published 2018

Printed in the United States of America by Sheridan Books, Inc.

A catalogue record for this publication is available from the British Library.

Library of Congress Cataloging-in-Publication Data
NAMES: Mathews, Donald G., author.
TITLE: At the altar of lynching : burning Sam Hose in the American South / Donald G. Mathews (University of North Carolina, Chapel Hill).
DESCRIPTION: New York, NY : Cambridge University Press, 2018. | Series: Cambridge studies on the American South | Includes bibliographical references and index.
IDENTIFIERS: LCCN 2017019541| ISBN 9781107182974 (Hardback : alkaline paper) | ISBN 9781316633984 (Paperback : alkaline paper)
SUBJECTS: LCSH: Lynching–Georgia–Coweta County–History. | Hose, Sam, 1875-1899. | African Americans–Violence against–Georgia–Coweta County–History. | Coweta County (Ga.)–Race relations–History. | Lynching–Southern States–Religious aspects–History. | Evangelicalism–Social aspects–Southern States–History. | Altars–Social aspects–Southern States–History. | Southern States–Religious life and customs. | Southern States–Race relations–History. | Racism–Southern States–History. | BISAC: HISTORY / United States / 19th Century.
CLASSIFICATION: LCC HV6465.G4 M37 2018 | DDC 364.1/34–DC23
LC record available at https://lccn.loc.gov/2017019541

ISBN 978-1-107-18297-4 Hardback
ISBN 978-1-316-63398-4 Paperback

For

Betsy

Elizabeth Farrior Buford

Contents

Introduction   Lynching and Altars: Family Memory   1
1   Before the Burning: Southern Mastery   14
2   Sex, Danger, and Religion: Facing a "Savage Fury"   55
3   Kindling for the Fire   92
4   Burning Sam Hose   139
5   After the Fury: Rape and History   178
6   After the Fury: The Blind and the Sighted   219
7   At the Altar: Crucifixion   259

Notes   285
Index   333

Introduction: Lynching and Altars

Family Memory

"Now these are the judgments which you shall set before them: ... You shall not circulate a false report. Do not put your hand with the wicked to be an unrighteous witness. You shall not follow a crowd to do evil; nor shall you testify in a dispute so as to turn aside after many to pervert justice."
Christian Bible, KJV, Exodus 21:1, 23: 1–2

"Pilate ... said to them again, 'What then do you want me to do with Him whom you call the King of the Jews?' So they cried out again, 'Crucify Him!' Then Pilate said to them, 'Why, what evil has he done?' But they cried out all the more, 'Crucify Him!' So Pilate wanting to gratify the crowd ... delivered Jesus, after he had scourged him, to be crucified."
Christian Bible, KJV, St. Mark, 15:11–15

"And after they had mocked him, they took the robe off from him, and led him away to crucify him. And as they came out, they found a man of Cyrene, Simon by name: him they compelled to bear his cross."
Christian Bible, KJV, Matthew, 27: 31–32.

***

On the third Sunday after Easter in 1899 about forty miles southwest of Atlanta near Newnan, Georgia, a white crowd burned to death a black laborer known as Sam Hose. The atrocity blended anger, contempt, brutality, festivity, and satisfaction into a mood just beyond comprehension. "Glory!" shouted an excited man enraptured by the intensity of the moment, "Glory be to God!!"

The cry erupted from the depths of human desire. It was familiar to both white and black worshippers in the evangelical South as it celebrated one of the most notorious lynchings in American history. Praising God during such an event may seem bizarre to those who think lynching and religion do not blend well. The former is an illegal act by groups that kill someone for doing something they believe disrupts community life so radically that it demands swift and deadly retribution. Religion is a way of acting and thinking that imagines humans enmeshed in webs of sacred meaning and obligation that authoritatively explain and manage life. The spontaneous shout of "Glory!" that Sunday afternoon gushed from within a drama of good and evil as an expletive of wonder and satisfaction.

The crowd insisted their victim had committed such evil that his hideous death was a perfect killing that restored balance to the moral cosmos after his crimes had disrupted it. Their acts transformed punishment for a specific crime into a sacrificial act. "Sacrifice," Robert Jay Lifton and Greg Mitchell point out, means that an action is sacred, which is why the old man shouted "Glory." The shout had been a familiar expression of realization and release within the language and rituals of religion for well over 135 years in the evangelical South. The excited participants in this sanctified vengeance sensed that religious excitement and a ritualized death by fire affirmed the moral order as they converged to generate community solidarity. Religion did not cause lynching; lynching *was* religion.[1] Such a statement demands explanation.

LYNCHING DISCOVERED

Lynching is an American institution. Thousands of men, women, and children have been assaulted, raped, or killed by vengeful crowds, vigilantes, and other self-appointed judge-executioners. Native peoples, Hispanics, immigrants, strangers, neighbors, blacks, and whites have all been casualties. An accurate tally of victims and incidents is beyond reckoning; many incidents are lost to the public record. John, for example, was a white man whose story is known only to a few members of his family. He was born in Elmira, New York, in 1872; his father moved the family to Kansas while John was an infant and then to Oklahoma. By 1900, his father was working in a farm with his two sons. Frank was unmarried but John had wed fourteen-year-old Nancy Lula, who had given birth to William and Herman before 1900; Leo and Lucille came shortly thereafter. By 1910, John's father had moved west to Kingfisher County; Herman had been killed by swine and Frank disappeared from family memory and the census. John remained on the farm in Lincoln County; he was fairly well-off if not prosperous and employed a man to help manage seasonal laborers. John's sons remembered playing with the man's children; they were of African descent.

John ran afoul of his white neighbors probably in 1910 amid rumors of riots in Kansas City when Jack Johnson, an African American, beat a white, Jim Jeffries, for the world's heavyweight boxing championship. In response, whites mobbed blacks throughout the United States.[2] The contagion spread to rural Oklahoma, to Lincoln County, McKinley Township, and to the home of John's foreman. One evening, after chores, John, Lula, and the children sat down to supper when John's black assistant and his family crashed through the door: "John, John," Leo remembered the man having cried, "They've burned us out. They'll kill us!" John did not ask who "they" were; from exchanges with his neighbors he would already have known who and what they held in contempt. Eastern Oklahoma had not been immune to racial violence. In 1898, about thirty-five miles to the south of Lincoln County, a crowd of white men and boys, after prayer by a Christian layman, had burned to death two Seminole teenagers for killing a woman. The crowd ignored testimony by the only witness to the crime that they were innocent.[3]

John told the black family to run for their lives while he held off the mob he knew was coming. He then parceled out his firearms and turned a utility wagon on its side in front of the porch and waited. The neighbors came. As they broke into the yard, John fired a shot. There was a moment of silence; Leo, his second son, remembered it as an eternity. "We want the niggers!" someone shouted. Silence. "Who'll die first?" John supposedly shouted. No one volunteered. Then silence reigned once again. The family remained on alert throughout the night but by morning the crowd had disappeared, still angry with *God Damned "niggerlovers!"* John had allowed their prey to escape! Shunning and danger enshrouded the community. Attempts to kill John failed and gradually a welcome quiet settled on the household. In thanksgiving for having been spared the penalty for flouting racial etiquette, Lula thought that it would be a good idea for her husband to come with her and the children to prayer meeting. This was not John's favorite pastime but he went. Afterward, as the family were leaving the meeting house, a group of men who would not have expected him at prayer, seized him; they spirited him to a wooded grove. There, they detached the oak and iron single-trees from the traces of a wagon and beat John mercilessly, leaving him for dead.

John was my grandfather, John Demarest Mathews. His story became my father's story, his children's story, and profoundly burdened our mother. The consequences of that night in the grove were longlasting, malignant, and generative. They disclose how acts of violence can affect families far beyond the immediate damages inflicted. They have shaped the bias through which I discovered lynching and came to think about it in the language of religion. Because those effects sent me into the South, where family histories are highly valued, friends urged me to tell the story that brought me to the immolation of Tom Wilkes, whom his killers knew as Sam Hose.[4] While studying religion in the New South, I discovered Hose in an essay written by a woman who defended his lynching. At the same time, I was asked to write an essay on why I, having grown up in western Idaho, had chosen to write about religion in the South.[5]

In retracing my journey into Dixie, I realized that descent from religious abolitionists in New Jersey whom I had discovered in 1964[6] had not led me to pursue Southern history so much as had the violence that dramatically affected my father's family. The brief answer to "Why study religion in the South?" was overly dramatic: "Because my grandfather was lynched."[7] That answer forced me radically to change the focus of my study of church life in the New South as I tried to reclaim the story my father had told many times. It was an obsession that haunted him because the story did not end with John's being seized by the mob; it began then because John survived.

The trigger for my first encounter with John's story was the casual use of a word that stains American history: "nigger." It had been mentioned in conversation to which I was an unwitting witness. The exchange was possible because once a month my father took the family to visit his parents and neighboring siblings after attending church. My grandfather sat alone and silent in an armchair: baffled and distracted. Unlike my mother's father, who was a vigorous and hardworking farmer, my father's father was an inactive man who intimidated me with a strange gaze and unexpected comments. Sometimes he was afflicted with violent shaking of hands and head. During most visits, I played outside with my rough-housing cousins but on this occasion I came through the front door and heard my mother say, "I don't ever want to hear that word again!" Why she had heard "that word" I did not know. At the time I was unaware of living near any African Americans. Mrs. Wilson lived next door; she was of African descent, but my parents never referred to her as a "Negro;" and she was no darker than my father's friend, Mr. Ruiz. My mother must have been thinking of Mrs. Wilson when she lashed out.

There was some sputtering, and then my grandfather seemingly out of nowhere announced: "I had a good friend once. And *he* was a 'nigger'." My grandmother broke into hysterical weeping and fled the room; my aunt followed. There was a hush; I left the house in confusion.

After we returned home, my father told me *the story* for the first time, emphasizing the damage done by his father that terrible night. John couldn't make appropriate decisions about running the farm, which gradually deteriorated. Sometimes he could not work, and at other times he would lash out at his family in a hideous rage. Lula tried to manage the farm, but then came a traumatic day when, as Leo recalled it even from the fathoms of his dementia, "my father tried to kill me." John had raised a heavy chair high above his head to crash it down on his second son. Escaping his father's rage, Leo fled to the home of a Methodist minister who settled him with a foster family until he could secure a fellowship for Leo at Francis Asbury Academy in Wilmore, Kentucky. In this haven of Methodist piety, Leo escaped his father's fury, but not the psychic effects that haunted him for the rest of his life. As disease began to destroy his mind many years later, he'd often shudder and shout, "Why?" In trying to explain each outburst before he lost his reason, he'd confess that he had imagined his father's attempt to kill him. Once, his mind having all but disappeared, three nurses answered when, in a hospital room absent forty-eight hours of sleep, he cried out "Why?"

Leo's nightmares were not the only consequence of the mob's brutality. The family that was shunned and damaged was also exiled. Lula pleaded with Leo to leave Asbury and join her, his father, and his siblings in Idaho, where he became head of household at age fifteen. Family life was toxic: Lucille was sent to another family and Bill simply left. Leo remained, but was frequently crushed by terrible bouts of depression. After marrying, his private anguish often spilled over into emotional violence against his own family; three times he even attacked my mother physically. He was often furious with her, my sister, and me for a failure of warmth within the family, which probably resulted from our trying to resist his unrelenting emotional blackmail. The trait undoubtedly reflected a longing for love in compensation for the chaos of his early life but he never found peace. He tried to be the best father and husband he could be and was profoundly saddened by his failures and haunted by the ever-descending chair.

If there were no chair in my own emotional life, my grandfather's rage was sifted through my father's impact on me and sank into the nether regions of my subconscious. It shaped assumptions about authority and personal relationships and led to consequences partially healed in therapy. Surprisingly, John's defiance became a source of pride within the family because it taught my sister and me that popular opinion was always suspect and "majorities" all too frequently wrong. This counter-balance partially compensated for the effects of John's wounds, but it could not conceal the fact that acts inflicted on the fathers' fathers and mothers could take their toll on the descendants.

Indelible as it was, however, *that toll is not what is important in telling the "story."* My sister and I – privileged but profoundly limited, too, by being born *white* in a culture of *white* – were blessed in countless ways. The story merely displays how one act of brutality could spawn violence, pain, dysfunction, and transgression far *beyond the immediate impact* of the mythologized but *real* original crime. This affliction forces me to reflect, well beyond my own family's experiences, in dismay, grief, and awe at the enormity of the emotional and cultural cost of violence inflicted by *thousands* of lynchings, beatings, rapes, and murders in the United States by *whites* against those unlike themselves. The pain and emotional distress that affected my father and through him my sister, mother, and me was absolutely *nothing* compared to the horror of hideous acts against the thousands of documented black lynching victims and their families, or the undocumented tens of thousands. The torture, terror, and shame of having a loved one butchered affected those families in ways impossible, at least for me, to imagine. We know that black nuclear families could be destroyed, the survivors scattered, their wealth seized, and most evidence of their ever having lived obliterated. But these immediate damages were only the first stages of a *multiplier effect* that has spread a sinister virus into perhaps millions of American families. The contagion, hidden though it may be, is as much a part of US history as the Emancipation Proclamation; its effects are far-reaching and contemporary.[8]

SACRIFICE AT THE ALTAR

The story of the damage done my grandfather eventually disposed me to think of salvation through sacrifice. Much of my youthful meditation on the Christian message had wondered at the crucifixion and ultimate defeat that became the ultimate victory through resurrection.[9] I came to treasure the hymn, "In the cross of Christ I glory, Tow'ring O'er the Wrecks of Time." The cross is the symbol as well as the means of atonement for Christians. Formally, in the atonement, that is, the death of what Anselm, Archbishop of Canterbury in the Middle Ages, called *Deus homo* [the God-man], Christ pays the penalty for human sin. He takes on humanity's burden vicariously even though he is innocent, thus satisfying the demand of the divine judge that sin be punished.[10]

To be sure, there are several ways of describing the drama of atonement other than Anselm's, but his is the one against which most other theories are called on to engage. There is always judgment. There is always condemnation. There is always blood. There is frequently the substitution of Jesus for fallen humanity (as in Anselm), and there is always a selfless death, which becomes the [possible] salvation of humanity [or a select few] – depending on which theory of atonement is embraced. There is always the love of God in Christ, balanced or unbalanced by divine wrath; the measure of balance is a major issue. There is, as well, always a carnivalesque mob, pretending innocence and insisting on death.

It was not the theological explanation of atonement that affected my imagination so much as the "frenzy" and narcissistic delusions of the mob that cries "Crucify Him!" I never historicized the mob as Jewish; it was rather a taunting, fevered, and self-righteous rabble – that is, *humanity*. It signified my grandfather's assailants. The rabble could very easily be "Christian," as my pastor once pointed out, because in later western history it had been "Christian." Medieval pogroms against Jews erupted from within Christian communities that became furtive "democracies" of punitive hatred. Through history, scripture, and family memory, I imagined the crowd before Pilate as transforming their deference to tradition and self-satisfaction into a demand for blood. This sacrificial drama at the center of the Christian imagination suggested the nature of every killing inflicted by a group acting under the delusion of its purity and righteousness. "Crucify Him" as a cry of rage prefigured the accusation: "Damn nigger-lover!" That reference explained my grandfather's fate, but was surpassed in significance when "Burn, Nigger, burn!" became the cry in horrendous lynchings such as that of Sam Hose.

For a long time, I suppressed the mystery of that awful night in Oklahoma, but eventually I came to wonder where my grandfather's defenders had been. In the fog of naïveté best suited to a third grade Sunday school class, I asked, "Where were the *Christians*?" How could a community, in which the sacredness of human life was supposedly valued according to a gospel presumably preached to offer redemption, allow a mob to punish a man who protected those for whom their Christ had supposedly died? The formulaic narrative of sacrifice is honored in even the most elementary of Christian imaginations, but I had conceded too much rectitude to the designation of "Christian." I had forgotten the pogroms and the hymn-singing Christians who legalized African slavery. I had forgotten that Christians bought Africans from slavers and created American capitalism. I had forgotten that if some Christians had fought to abolish slavery, others had prayed to transcend it, and still others had defended it by ignoring Paul's appeal to Philemon that he accept Onesimus, once a slave, as a brother "*in Christ*."

Later, in their commitment to white supremacy, Christians had denied freed people the benefits of Emancipation, imposed segregation as a guarantor of racial purity and supremacy, and instigated small-scale pogroms of their own.[11] The mob in Lincoln County, Oklahoma, formed naturally among those professing Christian faith. A sense of white collective solidarity demanded action against an alien "other." It was action that broke secular rules through a sacrifice that resolved the tension created by racial heresy and black resistance. Transgression became sacred. Violence became peace.

Christians selected John Mathews for sacrifice because he thought and acted differently, and worse, *defiantly*. He was not necessarily committed to "racial equality" when he confronted the mob, but to common sense and the integrity of personal relationships. No crowd would make him betray people who relied on him. No crowd would tell him to sacrifice a family because they were black. In the everyday affairs of work and family life, where he could defend himself, Mathews had been relatively safe. When he went to a Christian prayer meeting, he was brutally punished – not for an affront to God, but for failing to worship at the idol of race. One should imagine his enemies kneeling in Christian prayer with him that night because if they had come from outside the congregation they would have expected a man of his reputed lack of religious sensibility to be at home. They had been able to take him seemingly without serious objection from within the community of believers because they were part of that community.

Those who seized Mathews cannot be defined as *false* rather than *true* Christians because their commitments must be inferred from the fact that they were at a Christian meeting doing Christian things. They did what they did because they believed themselves to be justified. Otherwise they would have gone home absent blood on their hands. My grandfather deserved death not because he had murdered anyone, raped a woman, menaced his neighbors, stolen property, frightened little children, or voted – violations for which African Americans were killed by mobs at the time. Christians had seized and brutalized Mathews for *lese majeste* and *blasphemy*.

The first crime lay in Mathews' challenging the authority of the sovereign people. Those who validated community violence insisted by the end of the 1890s that lynching was not a breach of law but merely it's quickening. Lynchers were the same people who made up juries, it was said, and if in this case John Mathews had not broken any law, he had nonetheless thwarted the will of the people. That he had identified himself briefly with black people meant that he had challenged the whiteness of authority and had himself become in effect a "nigger." This primal violation of the ruling ideology transformed him into the personification of everything that threatened democracy.

John's second crime was blasphemy. Sacrifice was demanded because the ultimate concern[12] of pious white people was the purity of race. When they bowed in prayer, they brought all their values and loyalties as offerings to the divine. They had created a syncretism of folk tradition, ethnic loyalty, private prejudice, political commitment, gender identity, class distinction, ignorance, and stupidity. They worshipped at the altar of race, which meant they were willing to sacrifice another human being to sustain the transcendent meaning of whiteness. The faith of those who punished John Mathews was very much like that of nearby neighborhoods that had fed their men and boys into the crowd that had burned the two Seminole teenagers and would slaughter African Americans in Tulsa almost a decade later.[13] The aura of this faith was not one of mere bigotry or ethnic conceit but the narcissism of a people who could not imagine they were subject to the same death they inflicted.[14] They were gods. A crowd of people punishing those who challenged the moral economy of racial purity was enacting its version of what Christianity and Democracy meant. Most of those who tried to kill John Mathews may not have done so *because* they were Christian, but their Christianity did not prevent their doing it.

John Mathews' story helped make me susceptible to thinking about the emotional, intellectual, and spiritual linkage of religion and lynching. The story sent me to the South because one of its strangest consequences had been to transform my father into a Southerner. His siblings never claimed that distinction. Southerners had not been kind to Leo's family and yet at Asbury Academy he discovered that he was a Southerner. Most students there were "Southerners," and among them, in the camaraderie of work, learning, prayer, and association, he found a sense of well-being lost to his father's violence. The Wesleyan pietism of love, trust, and acceptance personified by his pastoral mentor – an elder of the Cherokee nation – had given him a second birth. It was, of course, difficult to fathom just what kind of Southerner he was, but he insisted, and when I began considering graduate programs in history I thought it was time to find out.

When I arrived at Duke University for postgraduate work, however, I found that there were many Souths, and more than one Christianity. I was drawn to the efforts of Southern black and white believers to map out a religious life for themselves within slavery where Christian mission justified exploitation, and Christian hope promised "liberty to the captives." By embracing a suffering Christ and anticipating Exodus, enslaved Christians, I thought, had enacted an authentic gospel. I came to think of the agonistic trajectory of religious life in the Old South as one of atonement. That I had come to think of religion in terms of sacrifice and victory of the dispossessed seemed to be confirmed by the stories I found. I imagined Christ in praise houses where worshippers became aware of the Spirit in apocalyptic anticipation: "King Jesus rides on a milk-white horse, no man can hinder him."

If the effect of the story on me became clearer through the passageways of faith and therapy, it was not until I heard an incidental question at a conference that my musings became insistent. "What role had religion played in the lynching of African Americans," someone asked. The responses were completely unsatisfactory; so was my silence. I had recently discovered the article in which Corra Harris defended the lynching of Sam Hose in *The Independent* magazine. She condemned African Americans as brutish men and sluttish women who drenched the South in sexual danger.[15] Harris came from deep within Southern religious culture. Her husband had been a Methodist preacher and most of her intimates were ministers or their wives. Musing on her fusion of religion and lynching, I remembered what W. J. Cash had written about Southern religion in *The Mind of the South*. Scholars now distance themselves from Cash for his tendency to sacrifice accuracy on the altar of meaning, and he is faulted for a flawed understanding of race, gender, and class. But there is one phrase that arrested me despite lacerations of his work; he branded Southern religion as "primitive frenzy and the blood sacrifice."[16]

The phrase flowed easily from Cash's early experience of heated Baptist preaching and meant something to a generation that remembered Confederate grandfathers as having been "baptized in blood."[17] The idea of "blood sacrifice" had been indelibly imprinted on the religious consciousness of most white Southern Protestants. Adding Cash's insight to my own predispositions about atonement, I began to think about sacrificial religion and the punitive violence of lawless mobs. Then, I reread W. E. B. DuBois' classic, *The Souls of Black Folk*, for the umpteenth time. Du Bois thought Sam Hose had been "crucified." The event had shaken him as had nothing else during his tenure at Atlanta University. Later, he imagined a Black Christ crucified by whites when they realize who he really is. African Americans at the time knew that Hose's burning was not simply a local atrocity. Its international notoriety encouraged Filipino commanders to ask black soldiers why they were fighting an imperialist war for the United States in the Philippines. The blood of their "brother," Sam Hose, cried out. Why fight for the people who had lynched him, and who would happily lynch *them*?

The burning of Sam Hose represented "America."

ACKNOWLEDGMENTS

David Moltke-Hansen has been a cheerleader, a pusher, an adviser, and a censor ("NO! You cannot say that, Don"). He has been the editor I needed; the colleague I needed; the friend I needed to complete this project. He believed in what I should have been doing when I didn't. We were engaged together in a joint project, but he is not responsible for the mistakes and unfortunate remarks I slipped past him. I owe him more than I can adequately say.

Lew Bateman heard of my research long ago and enticed me into the orbit of Cambridge University Press. His enthusiasm and support were more than welcome. I hope I have not disappointed him. His and David Moltke-Hansen's faith in the project ensured its completion. I am grateful to Deborah Gershenowitz for her help, approval, encouragement, and commitment to the project; she has been very generous indeed. Kristina Deutsch has been patient with me when I was more difficult than I had intended to be, or worse: obtuse. Thank you.

Mark Smith and Peter Coclanis as coeditors of the series read the text and made invaluable critical comments for which I am most grateful. Mark signed off on the final manuscript. Neither of them could prevent me from making errors of fact or judgment. I am sorry that Bertram Wyatt Brown is not here to see how our conversations and his scholarship helped me, although he would still be critical of some of my ideas. Skeptics in the Southern Intellectual History Circle helped clarify certain issues. A few thought I "let Christianity off the hook," but more positive critics sent me to Michael Bakhtin for his insights and thus enriched the argument and analyses.

Long ago, The Louisville Institute – funded by the Lilly Endowment, and situated in Louisville Theological Seminary – invested in the project that produced this book. I wish it had not taken me so long to complete it; I am sure my patrons do, too. The University of North Carolina at Chapel Hill supported me with a Kenan Leave and the opportunity to use my research in several undergraduate seminars. My students – none more creative than Matthew Leatherman – helped me immeasurably.

Whenever we write, we are not alone; colleagues, friends, and associates are present, too. Two of those who have aided me immeasurably have passed. John Hope Franklin told me, among other things, to include my grandfather's story in this book. Robert Francis Engs has been essential to my education. In this project he was gentle but honest in helping me see things I could not have seen without his help. Conversations in person or via the internet with Gavin Campbell, Michael Trotti, Regina Sullivan, David Ball, Kurt Berends, Cheryl Junk, Leslie Banner, Monte Hampton, Walt Conser, Ruth Doan, Lauren Winner, Emily Bingham, Sylvia Hoffert, Eric Millin, David Kelsey, Bruce Baker, Beth Schweiger, Nancy Schoonmaker, and Kathryn Lofton were all exceptionally helpful. Katie, Cheryl, Kurt, Regina, Ruth, Gavin, and Susan Donaldson read or heard portions of the manuscript and enriched it. Katie, like David Moltke-Hansen, helped solve problems that stumped me. Long ago, Fitzhugh Brundage was kind enough to criticize my first article, "Southern Rite," in a way that spurred me to continue the project. It seems impossible to list or thank everyone who inspired, helped, or prodded me. I almost forgot that Mary Lu Wooten asked questions, when I was beginning to write, that helped me think about my task. Katherine White was always encouraging – especially on New Year's Day: "Is this the year?"

The result of my thinking about the fusion of lynching and religion first appeared in 2000 in the online *Journal of Southern Religion* under the title, "The Southern Rite of Human Sacrifice." I am grateful to the editors for their allowing me to include many of the ideas and insights that I developed first in that article. I received permission from the University of North Carolina Press for the same largess with regard to "Lynching Is Part of the Religion of Our People: Faith in the Christian South," in *Religion in the American South: Protestants and Others in History and Culture,* ed. Beth Barton Schweiger and Mathews (2004). And I received permission also with regard to insights offered in "Lynching Religion: Why the Old Man Shouted, 'Glory!'" in *Southern Crossroads: Perspectives on Religion and Culture,* ed. Walter H. Conser, Jr. and Rodger M. Payne (2008).

The project took much longer than I thought it would. I followed too many tangents (death penalty and suicide) and I flatlined on the operating table unexpectedly. Dying even for ninety seconds puts things in perspective; it alerts you to how much you owe surgeons, physicians, and pharmacists. David Tate and Paul Mounsey saved my life in different ways; Frank Angotti followed Tom Curtis in helping me manage it. Raquel Daley-Placide and Jena Ivey Burkhardt have done the same; Dr. D-P has the healing touch that far surpasses her training. She, Dr. Tate, and Dr. Ivey persistently asked about the project so I had to finish it.

I am not sure that I could have written this book without having read studies by W. Fitzhugh Brundage, Jacquelyn Dowd Hall, and Timothy Gorringe.[18] The research and arguments of historians Brundage and Hall provided models of excellence and insight; the discernment and analyses of theologian Gorringe were especially thought-provoking and liberating.

Elizabeth Farrior Buford not only made the book possible; she has made my life possible. She allowed me to steal time to finish what I sometimes believed was beyond me. She also gave me an extended family in Frances, Gilbert, Margie, Frank, Janice, Michael, David, Abigail, Bryan, Sonya, Connor, and Adrienne. Her greatest gift was to marry and put up with me. Our conversations at the end of the journey have been essential; she read everything I asked her to many times. I needed her approval. It seems awkward to dedicate a book about lynching and moral failure to someone you love, but I do.

Donald G. Mathews
Epiphany 2017
Historic Oakwood, Raleigh

Before the Burning

Southern Mastery

"There is a generation that are pure in their own eyes, and yet is not washed from their filthiness."

Christian Bible, KJV, Proverbs 30:12.

"The Lord's voice crieth unto the city, and the man of wisdom shall see thy name: hear ye the rod and who hath appointed it ... For the rich men thereof are full of violence and the inhabitants thereof have spoken lies, and their tongue is deceitful in their mouth."

Christian Bible, KJV, Micah 6: 9, 12.

"Now these are the judgments which you shall set before them: ... You shall not circulate a false report. Do not put your hand with the wicked to be an unrighteous witness. You shall not follow a crowd to do evil; nor shall you testify in a dispute so as to turn aside after many to pervert justice."

Christian Bible, KJV, Exodus 21:1, 23: 1–2

**

On the third Sunday after Easter in 1899 about forty miles southwest of Atlanta near Newnan, Georgia, a white crowd burned to death a black laborer known as Sam Hose. The atrocity blended anger, contempt, brutality, festivity, and satisfaction into a mood just beyond comprehension. "Glory!" shouted an excited man enraptured by the intensity of the moment, "Glory be to God!!"

Sam Hose was accused of having killed Alfred Cranford and *ravishing* his wife, Mattie. He confessed to the first charge and denied the second.

The crowd, according to partisans, represented an enraged community that demanded swift and brutal action. The accusation of rape was standard fare in the folklore of Southern lynching, but students of collective violence have offered other explanations. Beyond the specific excuses for this event, perhaps it was – from within the long perspective of history – one of many recurring outbursts of brutality inherent in the ways whites had ruled blacks since enslaving them. Or perhaps the act was an atavistic remnant of rural culture untouched by the progress of industrializing America. Or it was the exact opposite: that is, action consistent with the "cultural logic" of a modernizing nation.[1] Or it was a celebration of what it meant to be "white." Or it was democracy in action. Whatever it was, the lynching was not unexpected and not without precedent.

Of available explanations, the protection of dependents from rape is the least persuasive. Historians agree that allegations of "rape" triggered lynching, but they know that only between 25 and 30 percent of lynching victims were ever accused much less actually guilty of the crime. In some areas, to be sure, mob murder for alleged assaults could range above 40 percent, but whites leveled false charges against blacks whenever they saw fit. The cry of "Rape!" could erupt from something as innocent as a careless touch, a muddled comment, a fleeting glance, or an artless request. Many blacks near Newnan could not believe Hose had ravished Mrs. Cranford. They thought the laborer had killed Cranford in self-defense during a workplace dispute; but whites believed they burned a rapist. Southern white men had long conflated sex, gender, power, and offense when relations between black and white were as tense as they were near Newnan in the spring of 1899. Whites' anxiety about their ability to control black people was elevated into alarm at the news of murder and rape. The three people at the core of the incident then became symbols of race and danger.

Over the thirty-four years almost to a day between Robert E. Lee's surrender to US forces and Hose's murder, Southerners had wrestled with new ways to work, transport, invest, and think. The most troubling of those ways for whites had been African Americans' drive after Emancipation for economic viability, personal independence, and citizenship. After the spring of 1865, blacks followed leadership cadres in religion, education, business, journalism, and politics to establish institutions through which to resist whites' continuous attempts to exploit them. The freed people were in a weak position. Most were still landless farm workers; most were reliant on whites for economic security; all were subject to laws designed to control them; voters were subject to intimidation and violence. During the brief period of Reconstruction between 1868 and the middle 1870s, blacks' aspirations seemed to be attainable until they lost their political viability by violence, fraud, and law.

Whites were always wary of blacks' collective action; even religious revivals could be considered seditious. By the late 1890s, crimes by a single black man could even be imagined as evidence of a widespread political conspiracy. A few imaginative whites even went so far as to claim Hose's killing Cranford was a political act that avenged a recent lynching. The accusation of rape, however, had greater emotional power. Confronted in the 1860s with a newly emancipated people, whites had claimed blacks' demands for civic equality amounted to rape. By the 1890s the cry had become a standard watchword of white power; it flowed from antecedents established long before by slaveholders who expected two things of black people – obedience and deference.[2]

PAIN, PENALTY, AND THE CROSS

The Old South, writes Bertram Wyatt Brown, was ruled by men bonded by honor under the rubrics of responsibility and command. The ideal was captured by a visiting Northern clergyman before the Civil War who believed the South was committed "to the proprieties and courtesies of life, which I have failed to observe in other parts of the Union – a reverence for age, deference to childhood, a polite regard for equals, a kind tone to the poor, treatment of the negro [sic] as if he were one of the family, and a truly chivalrous bearing toward women." The reverend visitor imagined a concord without variations created by geography, demography, commerce, politics, or class.[3] He also ignored the most important features that unified the region wherever slaveholding was dominant: the demands for obedience and deference issued by the master classes to the enslaved and the implicit violence that enforced them. He did not understand that the threat of pain sustained social discipline and power, which were based on wealth and warranted by reputation.

Wealth was established by land and slaves, as well as success in respected occupations, but reputation was less clearly defined. The criteria were subjective and rested on one's personal carriage, public persona, and way of acting within a community of like-minded people. Honor depended on one's ability, style, and success in commanding and protecting dependents – wife, family, neighbors, relatives, and slaves. It rested on one's integrity, courage, affability, hospitality, and the esteem of others.

For those who owned slaves, honor required men to be known as capable of violence if necessary. Necessity was learned by mimesis. "Honor," writes Wyatt Brown, was "self-regarding in character. Ones neighbors serve[d] as mirrors that return[ed] the image of oneself." Southerners seemed constantly to gaze "in the looking glass of communal approval," writes Gary Ciuba. "The result was that the community of honor was a network in which each member was at once a model for everyone else and a disciple for everyone else."[4]

White elites did not, however, rule by naked threats, loaded guns, or brandished whips. Indeed, they developed ways to avoid violence. The duelists' code, for example, was not designed to guide offended white men into fatal exchanges, but to avoid them. Careful negotiations allowed adversaries to explain, qualify, or deny offensive intentions for unfortunate words or acts and find a peaceful resolution of differences. The studied avoidance of violence, however, revealed just how much it shadowed imaginations. If at all possible, violence was also to be avoided in relations with people without honor. The enslaved had to learn how to evade violent punishment by their work, speech, attitude, and demeanor.

Unlike the mannered negotiations between men of honor, the dynamic between masters and slaves placed responsibility for amity only on the latter. The enslaved had to work as commanded and avoid direct eye contact while interacting with authoritative whites. They had to tell whites what the latter wanted to hear and agree with whites absent reason or reality. They had to obey! And they had to defer! They knew how painful the penalty for not doing so could be. As an African American bishop remembered many years after the Civil War, "Even under the most humane master," the slave "was still subject to the lash." The ever present threat was not, however, merely the implied reality behind every effort to avoid it, nor was it the brutality of "acts of individual aggression," in the words of Jon Pahl. Violence, this student of the phenomenon insists, is inherent in all "systems of exclusion and collective coercion, degradation, or destruction."[5] His description fits slavery all too well.

In this culture of continuous comparison, black people were the model of what white men were not. If the enslaved had the temerity to imply they were not without honor, they could be painfully reminded of their mistake, although rarely burned alive. If statutory law as well as custom approved the masters' resort to physical punishment, wise men ruled by allowing servants privileges such as trapping game, growing gardens, visiting spouses, and worshipping God. These concessions could nourish social space within which blacks constructed resistant localized cultures shaped by memory, religion, and social relations. Even behind the soft measures of *noblesse oblige* lay a menacing violence should transgressions occur. Former slaves interviewed in the 1930s recalled that good masters sometimes *needed* to whip them. This jarring concession called to mind a dramatic example of how necessity functioned. A respected black foreman once refused a senseless order by an angry overseer who in retaliation almost killed him. His master, a professing Christian, privately conceded that the overseer's attack had been vicious and criminal. It had been nonetheless necessary, the master insisted, to maintain the racial order. The foreman had not obeyed! When the other workers fled the overseer's fury, securing the racial order required the master to have them all whipped.[6] The entire workforce had been guilty of triggering the violence inflicted on them. Self-preservation was a crime.

Pain and penalty were written into the white Southern moral universe. The ultimate drama of salvation, imagined in the Christian piety of the region, rested on what a former missionary remembered as "belief in someone's right to punish you." Faith cannot be accurately reduced to such a simple formula, to be sure; but Lillian Smith's memory of the religion in which she had been immersed was profoundly affected by emphasis on sin, penalty, and sacrifice. Christianity had been birthed in an act of violence. Christ had had to die, preachers claimed, to satisfy God's just wrath with humanity. In submitting himself to a human tribunal, a Calvinist minister insisted, Christ had declared the punishment he shared with thieves on Golgotha was as just for him as it was for them [Luke 23:39–41).

The cleric was not alone. "Death is the penalty of sin," wrote a preeminent Southern Baptist theologian of the late nineteenth century; it was imposed, wrote a future bishop, by the "wrath of Almighty God," whose very nature, warned a fellow Methodist, was to "punish the guilty." As another theologian insisted, "Vindicatory Justice [is] Essential to God"; faith and penitence demanded the "blood of a victim." Congregations sang of Christ who died "to purchase our pardon with blood." Familiar references to him as the "dying, risen Jesus," the "redeeming Lord," all referred to a supernatural sacrificial act in which Christ "tasted death for me." By "appeasing the wrath of God" in blood, he could take "his ransomed people home."[7] Every white Southerner within the evangelical mood knew salvation came through blood. Some sang of a "Fountain Filled with Blood."

Pain and blood also affected the religious insights of Africans who accepted Christ as slain upon the cross for them. A spiritual sung from within the ethos of slavery declared that what had happened on the "tree" forced believers to "tremble, tremble, tremble" at the mystery of that sacrificial act. But contrary to the dominant theme of whites' views, black Christians believed the crucifixion was unjust; it did not fend off the wrath of God so much as place the Divine within the suffering of people who believed. God had been with Daniel in the lion's den; with the chosen in Egypt; with them as they fled with Moses; with Jesus as he walked the path of pain and suffering. Since they lived under a regime of obedience and penalty absent justice and equity, enslaved blacks understood the injustice of the cross. Christ suffered with them and promised a future freed of whites and punishment. The earnest of that hope was a profound experience of surrender, release, and anticipation that had its counterpart in white evangelicals' conversion experience but also resembled, writes Albert Raboteau, "the spirit-empowered ceremonies of the African ancestors." Such ceremonies, replicated in worship, created emotional space for distancing enslaved believers from the rigors of white dominion. Ecstatic worship, spirituals, and prophetic promises of judgment were liberating. They helped create a Christianity based on the insight that, contrary to the rules of white power and supremacy, God was "no respecter of persons."[8]

White ministers knew the laity could not always understand the theology of crucifixion. Yet, there were many ways to make the point. For people seeking to receive salvation in a dialectic between faith and hope, self-consciousness and doctrine could clash. When, however, it was time publicly to repeat the Creed or renew the Covenant or sing about "amazing grace," the sound of one's own voice uniting with others could, at least for the moment, confirm trust in Christ's sacrifice. Worshippers heard countless ritualistic sermons designed to make them feel Christ's wrenching wounds as the cross was plunged into the earth with a searing jolt. The message of guilt and punishment was conveyed by exhortations, prayers, hymns, maternal tears, and patriarchal discipline. Even tepid or rebellious believers learned that religion was punishment: they endured or remembered or heard about the connection in church trials, heated sermons, and the anguished pleasure of awakening sexuality. All these things, when crowned by the righteousness of God, taught children of Christians that punishment was essential to religion. W. J. Cash grasped the vernacular meaning of faith as "primitive frenzy and the blood sacrifice."[9]

Since punishment was vital in sustaining honor and mastery as well as religion, Christian slaveholders could easily meld the former with the latter. In a society sensitive to the polarities of free and slave, obedience and disobedience, male and female, honor and dishonor, a religion so clearly defined by conflict between good and evil helped validate a culture of constant vigilance. And masters had help. Most tax-paying adult white males participated in the matrix of command and control in patrols that policed slaves and troublesome whites.[10] The possibility of servile insurrection sustained the consensual accord that violence against blacks was legitimate. This understanding endured long after masters lost their rebellion against the US government. They may have lost slavery, but not, they insisted, their slaves.

DISMANTLING RECONSTRUCTION: SEX, VIOLENCE, AND DISFRANCHISEMENT

The moral validity of punitive violence against black people was challenged when the Thirteenth Amendment to the US Constitution abolished slavery; but the master classes regrouped. Southern legislatures passed Black Codes to help former masters maintain control of their workforce. White urban riots punctuated the widespread anger at freed people among whites who had never been slaveholders. In response, the Republican-controlled Congress passed Reconstruction Acts and submitted for ratification additional constitutional amendments designed to guarantee freed people rights shared by white men. The results proved traumatic to whites, for Congress seemed to be confirming the ways in which black people embraced the meaning of their Emancipation; they were pretending to be white. Many sloughed off the names ascribed to them by masters; others insisted on being addressed as Mr., Mrs., or Miss. On the street they frequently refused to doff their hats or bow; and they touched, even jostled, white men and women on crowded sidewalks. They frequently looked white people in the eye and brought charges against them in court.

They testified against white people in trials; some sat on juries. They challenged white peoples' version of events, in effect calling whites' lies "lies." All too many were sloughing off the deference that had signified servility. They moved about without whites' approval and refused to work according to traditional rules; they could even sometimes call a strike and meet in conventions to plan collective action. Some would not obey! The master class seemed to be teetering on the brink of chaos as habits of deference were slipping away.[11] The response of Southern white men was violent; their culture had been challenged, not changed. Having lost a war, they were determined not to lose the peace.

They would crush African Americans' attempts to gain citizenship.[12] Secret societies in most Southern states renewed hostilities against the United States within 30 months after Robert E. Lee surrendered in April 1865. These groups chose white and black Republicans and their women folk as surrogates for the US government and abolitionists that had humiliated them. They whipped, raped, tortured, and killed their enemies in campaigns of terror.[13] Many groups came to be identified as a Ku Klux Klan, although there was no single region-wide guerilla force. Rather, resistant groups in each Southern state armed themselves during the late 1860s and early 1870s to defeat their opposition by following the example of Confederate forces, which during the war had committed crimes, writes Michael Fellman, that "amounted to a policy of race warfare."[14] If violence was uneven across the South, it was nonetheless a pervasive possibility. "The path of resistance to Reconstruction in several states," writes George Rable, was "strewn with dead bodies, both black and white." In some areas, whites engaged in pitched battles against outgunned blacks.[15]

Partisans insisted violence protected women. By gaining the ballot under the Fifteenth Amendment, Martha Hodes points out, black men "unmasked the connection between political rights and black manhood." The connection was humiliating to Southern white men, many of whom had been disfranchised for rebelling against the United States. Because voting was the political expression of being a man, black men who did so, it was claimed, would demand other privileges of manhood. Chief among these, whites warned, was intimate association with white women. This alarmist theme, Hodes writes, spawned the "sexualization of Reconstruction politics." When African Americans helped elect Republican state governments and write new constitutions, white elites fused sex, race, politics, and pride into an ideology of white supremacy. They transformed the word "rape" from an act of brutality against women into a metaphor of black empowerment.

They fumed against Republican-led conventions as rape; they condemned African American voting as sexual dominance. They claimed that black men's forging into places where they were not wanted – government, public transportation, public gatherings, and white schools – was, in effect, rape! Public space and office were understood as the extension of domestic arrangements based on the power of fathers and husbands. Private gendered power relations flowed into social relations, thence into politics, and back again into the family. Thus the next venue to be invaded by black men, wailed clever patriots, would be the home. Such men claimed whites could lose the ability to protect their women, a condition condemned as "social equality." The phrase, Hannah Rosen observes, signified that blacks denied that race determined legitimacy;[16] for whites it implied interracial sexual intercourse, even rape, and thus became a "crime."

By the middle 1870s, Southern whites gained the aid of the US government. Most Northern voters never embraced racial equality and resented having to spend tax money to protect Southern blacks, especially after the financial panic of 1873. Rather swiftly, the US Supreme Court began to chip away at the legal foundations of Reconstruction designed to protect black citizens. With the *Slaughterhouse Cases*, the Court began to ignore, misinterpret, or reject the purposes of the Fourteenth and Fifteenth Amendments to the Constitution. These cases covered a dispute between New Orleans butchers and the state of Louisiana. The former claimed protection under the Fourteenth Amendment because it had expanded the "definition of national citizenship for all Americans." Not so, replied a 5-4 majority of the Court: the Amendment had not "altered traditional federalism" in any way. The Court thus ignored one of the clearly stated goals of the amendment and restricted the power of the federal government to protect American citizens. The result was confirmed in *United States v. Cruikshank* after the US attorney for the southern district of Louisiana indicted William J. Cruikshank for leading the massacre of over 100 blacks in 1873. He was charged under the Enforcement Act of 1870 with feloniously hindering citizens "of African descent" from assembling "for a peaceable and lawful purpose." Cruikshank appealed his conviction to the Supreme Court, which in 1876 decided he had been indicted illegally because the Federal government could not protect American citizens; only the states could do so.

This view ignored the fact that both proponents and opponents of the Fourteenth Amendment had agreed that Congress intended to "apply federal guarantees of citizenship to the states." The case, writes Lawrence Goldstone, represented "the most blatant attempt since the Reconstruction Acts ... to contort the spirit, and sometimes the letter, of both congressional prerogative and the United States Constitution." By relegating civil rights cases to state courts, the Supreme Court condemned blacks to the mercies of hostile white juries; it continued the trend in the *Civil Rights Cases* (1883). Then, the Court voided the Civil Rights Act of 1875, which had prohibited segregation in most public facilities and accommodations. The Court claimed that any law *protecting* black Americans elevated them above white citizens, contrary to the "equal protection" clause of the Fourteenth Amendment.[17] The amendment written to guarantee equality to blacks was now used to deny it.

These decisions confirmed the power of Southern elites to control politically active African Americans through three different kinds of statutory law. The first criminalized African Americans in ways that transformed offenders into unpaid laborers subject to abuses similar to or worse than slavery. The Black Codes passed before Reconstruction had since been rescinded. Yet by the 1880s, white elites were gradually expanding methods similar to those in the Codes to limit the mobility and exploit the labor of African Americans. They did so by legislation supported by judicial decisions and private management practices. Eventually, every Southern state leased prisoners to private persons or corporations instead of relying on jails and prisons to punish convicts. Conservative legislatures passed laws punishing people for a wide range of crimes. These included leaving employment without permission or appearing to have no job; each violation was determined by the subjective discretion of a peace officer in service to men who needed cheap labor.

Police arrested black men for insolence, debt, theft, loitering, or "speaking loudly in the presence of white women." Since most of those arrested were poverty stricken African Americans unable to pay even a fifty cent fine, they were at the mercy of what came to be known as a convict lease system. By law, a local planter, industrialist, or mine owner could pay the fine imposed on an offender in exchange for labor. Men convicted of felonies were in danger of spending the rest of their lives at forced labor for private contractors. Even those consigned to private parties for relatively minor offences could find their terms stretching into infinity by being charged for their food, beds, and the utensils they had presumably broken. The result, Douglas Blackmon points out, was to force people into "compliance with a social order" characterized by "complete domination by whites." Whites had found a way once again to make black workers obey. Within the convict lease system, Blackmon points out, violence was the means of control; outside it the threat of being forced into that system could tame an unruly people.[18]

"Debt peonage" complemented the laws establishing the convict lease system. White planters, farmers, and merchants who had extra funds or imaginative accounting techniques could extend credit to black tenant farmers or sharecroppers for buying tools, seed, fertilizer, or other necessities. Debtors could repay lenders when crops were harvested; but

creditors kept the books. They set and calculated interest; they stipulated
the worth of produce after harvest. Creditors decided whether or not
debtors had actually repaid the loans of the current or previous years
with appropriate interest. Fraud and low market prices drove black
families ever further into debt and despair. Those who calculated debt
on their own could face whipping or death; in certain cases, those who
tried to sell their crop independently of the landlord could face the same
penalties. Those who accepted the creditor's decisions could find themselves permanently indebted, i.e., enslaved. Debt peonage created a vast
resource of unfree labor; under its rules the Reconstruction Amendments
were effectively voided for large numbers of Southern black people.[19]

Southern whites passed a second set of laws designed to control African
Americans. The legislation was passed over a generation starting in the
late 1880s, and virtually eliminated blacks from electoral politics. The
political mantra chanted by Democratic activists was "Negro Domination." The phrase had once referred to a mythic Reconstruction past
when Republican legislatures adopted policies – falsely remembered as
entirely corrupt – benefiting blacks and poor whites. The slogan came to
mean that if black men voted, politicians would be obligated to act on their
behalf.[20] The danger loomed after the election of 1888 when a Republican
Congress convened to govern once again with a Republican president. In
his first message to Congress, Benjamin Harrison asked when the black
man would actually gain the "civil rights which have so long been his in
law?" He encouraged legislators to protect blacks' voting rights.

Soon, radicals tried to do so by appointing monitors to supervise
federal elections. A few senators even resurrected previous attempts to
reduce Southern representation in Congress as punishment for restricting
the black vote. Although they failed, Radical Republicans' goal of protecting citizenship rights was denounced as tyranny; an attempt to secure
education for Southern blacks was labelled a *Force Bill*. Southerners
warned of a new Reconstruction.[21] Alarmed at what Republicans wanted
to do and encouraged by what the Federal government could not do,
Southern Democrats scurried to disfranchise black men. The process
began first in Tennessee, Arkansas, and Florida through statutory law
and in Mississippi by a constitutional convention. After federal elections
that swept Democrats back into power in 1892, Southerners and their
Northern allies repealed legislation designed to guarantee black men's
voting rights.[22] Disfranchisement thereafter proceeded for a generation.
South Carolina disfranchised African Americans by constitutional convention in 1895 and Louisiana did so in 1898. During the next decade,

Alabama (1901), North Carolina (1900), Virginia (1901–1902), Texas (1901–1905), and Georgia (1905–1908) followed suit.[23]

REFORM, POPULISM, AND DANGER

Events in Virginia, Georgia, and North Carolina during the 1880s and 1890s revealed how political operatives dealt with threats to white supremacy that erupted also in such states as Alabama, Arkansas, and Texas.[24] Democratic reform could be crushed by campaigns based on gendered anxiety, sexualized politics, and racial contempt. Clever Conservatives blanketed economic distress, social inequality, and political fraud with a fog of racial *identity*, social *purity*, and masculine *honor*. The result was a beautifully crafted political *paranoia* that settled on Virginia after 1883, on Georgia after 1890, and on North Carolina after 1896.

In Virginia between 1879 and 1883, Republicans and dissident white Democrats assembled a coalition to solve problems Conservative authorities had ignored. The cooperating parties agreed to honor each other's agendas in order to improve their chances of success.[25] The issue that united reformers was how to "readjust" the state debt. In February 1879, white dissidents called 175 delegates to Richmond "without distinction of color" to found the Readjuster Party. It was clear that Conservatives would lose control of the legislature if the new party gained the support of black Republicans. "We must," wrote a white Readjuster, "let [blacks] know that we are their friends." Friendship involved cooperation and theoretically common values but it was easier sought than honored by whites, long subject to the alarm of "Negro Domination."

After losing the election of 1880, chastened white Readjusters reaffirmed their "friendship" with black activists and in the 1881 campaign celebrated equal rights. This meant, in the words of their leader, Senator William Mahone, rejecting "race prejudices" and affirming equality before the law. Readjusters and black Republicans then united to win both houses of the state legislature and the governor's mansion. Democratic hysteria about "Negro Domination" had failed to swing the election at least this one time;[26] but the test of the biracial coalition was whether or not the Readjuster government could survive attacks on it for cooperating with blacks. The new governor claimed his "liberal revolution" was committed to equality, but, as Jane Dailey points out, equality meant "different things to different people."

Blacks saw liberalism as the parity of manhood rights; whites believed some rights could be separated from others. The latter distinguished private rights from public rights; but blacks objected. They claimed citizenship was based on all, not *selected* rights. This claim meant to a Colored Citizens Convention in 1879, for example, that laws forbidding racial intermarriage should be rescinded; but when black assemblymen attempted to do so in 1880 and 1881 they failed. It is nonsense to believe that most black men wanted to marry white women; it is nonsense also to believe that Southern white men could not be swayed by hysterical claims that black men wanted to do so. Failing to find interracial couples to validate their claim, Conservatives discovered that Readjusters had allowed black school board members to "supervise" white women teachers! Thus in the electoral campaign of 1883 Democrats insisted Virginians faced the danger of *mixed* school boards, *mixed* schools, and *mixed* marriages.

Mixed *sidewalks* were also dangerous. When a white clerk stumbled over a black foot in Danville, an apology preceded a row that escalated into gunfire, leaving one white and four black men dead. Conservatives claimed that whites had acted in self-defense because two years of Readjuster rule had made blacks "rude, insolent and intolerant." The Readjuster coalition could never again mount a successful challenge to Conservatives who, as the Democratic Party, ruled Virginia for well over the next two generations by denying black men the ballot first by fraud and then by law.[27] Reform that required cooperation between black and white was lost to the clever manipulation of gendered fear, sexual fantasy, and hateful disdain for people whom, whites believed, they should be free to command.

In Georgia, a rickety interracial coalition for reform also lost out to a combination of fraud, violence, and clever political maneuvering justified by shrieks of "Negro Domination" and Rape! As the depression of the late 1880s deepened, a Farmers Alliance enlisted agrarians and their allies in the South, Southwest, and bordering states in a movement to improve purchasing power, farming methods, marketing skills, and political savvy. Alliance ideology took on a partisan cast as activists began to think government should serve popular interests. The movement entered Georgia in 1887 and birthed black and white Alliances. The former wanted more equitable cooperation than the latter could bear, which led to resentment on the part of African Americans. The Alliances did cooperate to elect a presumably friendly legislature in 1890, but it was more show than substance according to many farmers who turned to the newly formed People's Party in 1892.

Not all Alliance men in Georgia favored the Populists but the organization had encouraged enough of its members to consider radical political action that many of them left the Democratic Party for a while. One of the attractions of the third party was the clarity of its Ocala (Florida) Demands issued in 1890: Populists wanted banking and currency reform, government regulation (and perhaps ownership) of the railroads, direct election of US senators, and a plan to facilitate the sale of agricultural products at a profit.[28] Georgia Populists found in Congressman Thomas Edward Watson (D-Georgia) a brilliant editor, wordsmith, and speaker who insisted that Populists enlist black voters in the cause of reform. He spoke from the same platform as black Populists, explaining that the "colored tenant" was in "the same boat as the white tenant; the colored laborer with the white laborer." Black and white alike had been hurt by the depression; bankers, merchants, and railroad magnates seemed to fare much better than tenants, sharecroppers, and farmers of both races. Watson renounced the Democratic Party for abandoning "the people" – black and white, and hiding the crime by screaming, "Negro Domination!"

The Georgia elections of 1892, 1894, and 1896 tested the interracial coalition. It collapsed in the face of Democratic organization, rhetoric, and fraud as well as black-white enmity within the People's Party itself. In 1892, William Yates Atkinson of Newnan, chair of the Democratic state executive committee, warned voters that the third party's leader, C. C. Post, believed in neither democracy nor God. True to form, other Democrats predicted a Populist victory would result in destroying "our wives and daughters" under a hateful "negro supremacy." A circular warned landowners they would be prevented from dealing with tenants, workers, or croppers as they wished if the People's Party won. Each accusation represented themes repeated throughout the best-organized Democratic campaign since Reconstruction.

The youthful and energetic Atkinson was charged with re-electing Governor William J. Northen and defeating the People's Party. He could dispatch a large number of able orators throughout the large state far more efficiently than the Populists, many of whom were political novices. The campaign was also violent on a scale from heckling and silencing Populist speakers to riot and murder. In the election itself, fraud was an effective weapon; counties controlled by Democrats reported more votes for their candidates than there were voters. The same pattern appeared in a few Populist-controlled areas.

Congressman Tom Watson, now running as a Populist, lost his seat to Democrat James C. C. Black through bribery, intimidation, whiskey, and creative computation. In Augusta, twice as many men voted for Black as were registered. Populists did better in the election of 1894 as Atkinson won nomination for governor against the old guard of the Democratic Party. He had used his appointing powers as Speaker of the Georgia House of Representatives to create a network of supporters by appointing them to local offices throughout the state. When Atkinson won the general election by only 20,000 votes of the 218,500 cast, the People's Party seemed to have gained considerable strength even though they lost the elections to Congress. Watson once again lost to Black who received 2500 more votes in Richmond County than there were registered voters. [29]

In beating conservative Democrats' favorite for governor, Atkinson made enemies as well as friends. Allies of the new governor in the General Assembly were younger and more receptive to reform than the old guard; they often cooperated with Populists over the next four years in innovative legislation such as that which made appointive offices elective. They cooperated in supporting an end to the convict-lease system, but they lost. Populist legislators never included more than 24 per cent of the General Assembly, so they could achieve something only if the younger Democrats supported them and even then both could lose. Some younger Democrats' proposals were more "radical" than those of the Populists, especially when it came to passing child labor laws, which the third party resisted. Populists never tried to pass anything that resembled the Ocala Demands of 1890 primarily because only Congress had the power to do so. Populists' rhetoric was often more "radical" than their actions.

When it came to anti-lynching legislation, which was dear to African Americans, Democrats under the persistent scolding and pushing of Governor Atkinson were more assertive than Populists. Blacks had welcomed Tom Watson's invitation to cooperate with whites in the People's Party, but whites' relations with black Populists were always problematic. Too many white Populists came from counties ruled earlier by the Ku Klux Klan; too many white Populists assaulted or killed blacks insufficiently committed to the Party; too many whites offended too many blacks when the latter tried to work with them; too many whites scolded too many blacks about "social equality," insolence, and unwarranted ambition.

Then Adolphus Duncan, a black teenager, and the grandson of an affluent black businessman, was arrested and charged with attempted rape. After two defective trials based on perjured testimony, Duncan was found guilty and condemned to be hanged. Atkinson conferred with the leading attorneys in Atlanta and a private investigator; they claimed the youth was innocent. The governor pardoned him. In the election of

1896, the pardon was politicized. Democrats appealed to black voters on the basis of the pardon; Populists responded by accusing Atkinson of inviting the rape of every white woman in Georgia. In reply, Atkinson announced that if Georgians wanted a governor who would allow "an innocent man to be hanged just because a heinous crime is charged against him, then you should elect another man." Thousands of Democrats refused to vote for Atkinson; but thousands of blacks gave him a greater majority than he had had in 1894.[30] Political cooperation between black and white dissolved once again in the acidulous mixture of suspicion, arrogance, and "rape."

In North Carolina, as in Virginia and Georgia, interracial politics became possible when white men became aggrieved enough with Conservatives to cooperate with blacks. To be sure, appeals warning of African American political power had peppered Democratic rhetoric since the state's brief and modest Reconstruction; but as long as they won, Democrats had appealed to black voters. In the election of 1888, Conservatives' anxiety spawned a campaign against Negro Domination and they won, but fissures in Tar Heel society had not been addressed, and the Farmers' Alliance counter-attacked. The Alliance began to battle what it called a "centralized tyranny," writes Joe Creech. In arenas "economic, political, and religious," evangelical speakers energized the movement through a "clear-cut economic and political agenda backed by revivalistic zeal."[31]

In 1890, the Alliance sent enough reform Democrats to the General Assembly to create a regulatory railroad commission and create ways to prevent fraud. The reformers funded new institutions of higher learning for white women and African Americans. They devised ways to fight trusts and support economic development in farm, factory, and forest. North Carolina seemed to bask for a short while in a vibrant democracy not replicated in most other areas of the South. In those areas, frustrated dissidents joined the People's Party as the only successful engine of reform. When in 1893 the Democratic legislature of the Tar Heel state turned against reform and the Alliance, dissidents decided to cooperate with Republicans, blacks, and the new party.[32] In 1894, North Carolina Populists and Republicans agreed on the "Fusion" of their electioneering efforts that overwhelmed Democrats in the fall. The first Fusion legislature continued reform and protected democracy by providing for the election of county officials rather than their appointment by the state. A second Fusion legislature, elected in 1896, was able to improve legislation passed previously.[33] North Carolina politics had been democratized when white men rejected the politics of racial paranoia. Populists and Alliancemen were much more successful in North Carolina than in Georgia.

Conservatives regrouped. For the next three years they ramped up a campaign against "Negro Domination." They chanted the mantra into an anthem to white supremacy. White Populists were not egalitarians; like their Georgia counterparts, many accepted cooperation only as a way of gaining power. They were uneasy when the election law of 1895 increased the black vote in eastern North Carolina. White Populists began to chafe under "Negro rule." Eleven black legislators in the 1897 General Assembly signaled "Negro rule"; a black man on the Board of Directors of state-sponsored institutions indicated "Negro rule." The term applied to listing a black man's name on a cornerstone and to the election of blacks to minor political offices.[34] In 1897, Democrats followed former Congressman Furnifold Simmons and editor Josephus Daniels of Raleigh's *News and Observer*, into the wonderland of political paranoia. They created from myth, lies, and psychological projection a demonic force that endangered white women, that is, civilization. "Negro rule" was Rape!

The charge was not metaphorical. Conservatives complained Fusion had encouraged "social equality"; they accused Republican and Populist authorities of refusing to punish black rapists. They invented a fake surge of black violence that led one white man to warn that his people might be forced to "re-enslave, kill or export the bulk of the negro [sic] population." Killing then became public policy. In August of 1898, Alex Manly, the African American editor of the Wilmington *Daily Record*, poohpoohed rumors of black rape. He argued that in some cases the charge of rape was a mere pretext for punishing black men's involvement with willing white women. Our "experience," he wrote, "among poor white women in the country teaches us that the women of that race are not any more particular in the matter of clandestine meetings with colored men, than are the white men with colored women."

In response, Josephus Daniels warned "A RACE RIOT IMMINENT," but the "RIOT" was the white supremacy campaign itself. *Black men over white women* as the meaning of "Negro rule" dominated discourse associated with cartoons depicting white women trembling under the gaze of black magistrates. Charles Brantley Aycock prepared for his election as governor in 1900 by stumping the state to promise the redemption of North Carolina if "men who love their wives and daughters, and ... mothers" rallied to the Conservatives. Mounted Red Shirt militia led supremacist parades and invaded black churches. One Democrat predicted black men would be shot in eastern North Carolina if they tried to vote. Alfred Moore Waddell in the port city of Wilmington announced that he and his minions would destroy Negro rule "if we have to choke the current of the Cape Fear [River] with carcasses." White-clad white women on parade and aboard majestic floats personified the desires of wistful white men. Purity demanded protection! Through intimidation, hysteria, and fantasy, Conservatives obliterated the Populist-Republican majority in the General Assembly. Not content with "legal" means, an armed insurrectionary force led by Waddell removed Wilmington's Republican administration, murdering scores of blacks, burning Manly's press, and driving the black bourgeoisie into exile.

In Raleigh, the new legislature abolished democratic reforms passed by Fusionists. They segregated railway cars and reduced funding for blacks' education. They submitted to the electorate an amendment to the state constitution disfranchising most African American voters.[35] It passed in 1900. The "Revolution of '98" had saved civilization! The legislative assaults on blacks and democracy were the legal complement to the violence in Wilmington. Assemblymen and mobs embodied the resolve of Southern elites to eliminate black people as citizens. In doing so, whites not only established boundaries between white and black people in public, but by implication heightened a division within the Southern public between the lawful and the lawless. These acts stigmatized African Americans as immature, dangerous, and unworthy of citizenship. The implications of mistrust, danger, and worthlessness, however, flowed beyond the political realm. The continuous repetition of horrendous sexual danger from black men plunging ballots into boxes was beyond political theatre. The cartoons and hateful threats in some cases to anni-hilate black people to protect civilization could remind readers of the horrors imagined in the Revelation of St. John. Less dramatic but no less distorting of reality was the way whites passed laws to push African Americans to margins horizontal, vertical, and moral. Whites made blacks an abomination.[36] Racial arrogance and hysteria trumped democracy.

SEGREGATION AS LAW

When North Carolinians foreclosed electoral politics and restricted public space for blacks, they were joining the rest of the South. They were passing a third range of laws complementing those that created the convict lease system and disfranchised black men. They legalized segregation. Separating blacks from whites was not originally an exclusively Southern enterprise, to be sure. Before 1865 non-slaveholding states had reinforced the customary separation of black and white begun in churches, schools, cemeteries, and voluntary societies. On the other hand, in the South before Emancipation both white and black Christians had worshipped together in the same space, although within clear boundaries dictated by the masters. They pushed the enslaved as well as free blacks to the side or back of the sanctuary or consigned them to the gallery. Marginalization within proximity sustained mastery. Thus, at Emancipation, separation from white churches under the leadership of black preachers allowed African Americans to conduct their own affairs.

After Reconstruction, when whites began their campaigns against blacks' citizenship, forced separation of blacks from whites in public space paralleled their separation from the ballot. Segregation was a way of ensuring that being white meant being able to tell black people what to do and where to do it. If historians have debated the origins of segregation, they agree that it was always a function of white power.[37] By 1875, when white Southerners refused to obey the Federal Civil Rights Act prohibiting segregation of the races in public facilities, the practice was already considered essential to white supremacy. Sam Hose grew up with that fact. When in 1883 the Supreme Court declared prohibiting segregation unconstitutional, a Southern newspaper announced "A TRIUMPH OF LAW AND SENSE."[38]

Even before passage of the Civil Rights Act in 1875 Republicans had conceded that segregation in some cases would be the price for achieving desirable goals. Struggling to create public school systems for black people, educators knew they would fail unless they agreed to separate black and white students. To be sure, there were a few areas such as New Orleans where black and white were schooled together during radical Reconstruction, but these were exceptions. Most Southern whites believed that children simply could not be trusted to be suspicious of others unlike themselves when it came to forming friendships. Such intimacies had to be prevented. The same goal dictated laws forbidding interracial marriage. Neither the wild curiosity of innocent school children nor the amorous compulsion of undisciplined adults could be allowed to affect Southern life as gender and sex became the shibboleths of white supremacy.

These watchwords warned of pollution; and pollution implied danger if boundaries could be breached. Reflecting in 1911 on the necessity of separating black and white after the Civil War, Virginia historian Philip

Alexander Bruce celebrated the "statesmen" who had *consecrated* themselves to preventing "contamination" and discouraging "social equality." When he had examined post-Emancipation African-Virginians twenty-three years earlier, Bruce had emphasized their "uncleanness and moral infirmities"; bonding whites meant protecting purity. The feeling was essential to religion as well as white supremacy. Cleanliness is after all next to Godliness.[39]

Initial decisions to segregate education and marriage did not lead to widespread or immediate action everywhere. There were two stages in the process; the first evolved from the same sensibility among whites that had forced white Republicans to agree that "integrated" schools were dangerous because of their potential as nurseries of "social equality." Long before the disfranchising campaigns of the 1890s, whites' "race-related" assumptions, tastes, and irritations affected the ways in which they related to African Americans. Distance and boundary enforced deference on blacks and established mastery for whites. The next stage in the process was the result of decisions made by modernizing politicians and manufacturers who wanted a tractable labor force and political professionals who wanted safe elections. They believed they were threatened not only by an unruly black electorate but also by the knowledge and aspirations of a small but growing black middle class. Cities and towns with industry and relatively close living quarters required boundaries and distancing. Segregation was an urban and capitalist phenomenon. In the countryside, separation of black and white was impossible; roads, country stores, cotton 'gins, hunting, and fishing were not segregated. Exchanges between different groups continued relations based on proximity and tradition. White farmers needed black labor to be close by.[40]

By the 1880s, although a few affluent African Americans lived in posh districts among whites, neighborhoods in New South cities were becoming black or white. Segregation was at first partially a function of class; and the churches, schools, and businesses, which African Americans built to serve their vicinities, confirmed the legitimacy of some form of racial separation. But a new class of professionals and business people refused to remain in their neighborhoods both literally and figuratively. They wanted to travel in the first class sections of railway cars and claim seats in the orchestras of theatres because they could afford to do so.[41] A black person with money to buy a first class theatre or railway ticket would be able to dress like middle class whites. She might speak in clear and correct English and write forceful newspaper articles about equity, equality, and justice. She might disagree with white officials, editors, and railway conductors; she might object to being thrown off a railway car because of her race. That is, she might be Ida B. Wells.

Born into a Mississippi artisan's family, Wells had been orphaned by yellow fever as a teenager, but she was tough, intelligent, and determined. Well-read, independent, and intellectually aggressive, the diminutive and energetic woman became a teacher in Memphis amid a politically active and literate community. Her personality, ambition, talent, and intelligence won notice from a publisher who invited her to write for his newspaper. Through her essays, she became progressively active among African Americans committed to creating civic space for themselves and developing a political presence. As she entered public life and attracted negative as well as positive responses to her activism, she learned that being a New Woman elicited scandalous accusations of impropriety tinged with salacious innuendo. The lesson that sex and gender were as potent as race in public discourse and policy would eventually lead Wells to condemn the justification of lynching black men for rape as a "thread-bare lie." But the first political lesson she learned in 1883 was made abundantly clear when she was forced off a train for sitting in the first class railway car for which she had a ticket.

Wells sued for damages, claiming the "colored" car was not equal to the "ladies'" car. She won. Wells' presence in the ladies' car personified claims to equality and respect that black people expressed in newspapers, meetings, and behavior. For many whites, such claims were outrageous impudence, which suggested revolution. Wells was not merely one black woman: she was all those ambitious black people who were acquiring the benefits of a modernizing society along with middle class whites. Creating a middle class among black people was as revolutionary as voting; they were establishing a social base with a discourse that belied commonplace justifications for white supremacy. Blacks were beginning to exemplify characteristics that white leaders in their "language of merit" had argued would qualify men for public office: knowledge, respectability, "benevolence, fair mindedness, and gentility."[42] When it became clear that black men and women could approach this ideal, white politicians became convinced more than ever of the need to buttress white supremacy. They insisted on reminding black people that no matter what their accomplishments, wealth, or ability they were still inferior to whites. Forcibly removing Ida Wells from a railway car was a way of using pain to enforce a social distance that was the corollary of political homicide.

According to supremacists, Wells should not have been allowed to behave as if she were white or, worse, better than not a few whites.

Manners, attitude, bearing, clothing, knowledge, cash, and language suggested that black people like Wells were becoming less deferential. When in 1887 the Supreme Court of Tennessee voided her earlier victory over the railroad,[43] it was clear that she and people like her were to be denied equity and respect as well as first class seats. The Court's decision was not only specific to one case but symbolic. The decision extended the logic that justified the convict lease system and foreshadowed disfranchisement of blacks in Tennessee the next year, after the congressional elections of 1888. Soon, the legislatures of Florida, Mississippi, and Texas passed laws segregating railway passenger cars.

The issue was not new, for in 1877 the US Supreme Court had overturned a Louisiana law passed by Republicans in 1869 to prohibit segregation in public transportation. Since that time the court had decided that the federal government could not protect the citizenship rights of African Americans. Yet a few optimists still remained. When in 1890, Louisiana demanded "separate accommodations for the white and colored races" by either separate cars or sections, a group of New Orleans African Americans, guided by Louis Martinet, created a test case to take to the Supreme Court. Martinet and his ally, Albion Tourgée, decided that Homer Adolphe Plessy should challenge the Separate Car Law. Martinet had studied law and medicine and now edited a New Orleans newspaper; Tourgée was a well-known white Northern attorney and advocate for African American civil rights. Plessy was an African American who could have passed as white.

On June 7, 1892 he boarded a train in New Orleans and easily settled into the car reserved for whites; he then informed the conductor that he was in fact of African descent. He was arrested and in October appeared before Judge John Ferguson who upheld his conviction, as did the Louisiana Supreme Court on appeal. In January 1893, Plessy's lawyers appealed to the US Supreme Court. In April 1896, the appeal was finally heard. Tourgée's brief attacked the Louisiana law "on the very grounds," argues Lawrence Goldstone, "that offered the least chance of success: that the law was a violation of both the Thirteenth and Fourteenth Amendments of the United States Constitution." Tourgée knew that the Court had already restricted the meaning of those amendments in *Cruikshank* and the *Slaughterhouse* and *Civil Rights Cases*, but he nevertheless plunged ahead. Because the Thirteenth Amendment, he argued, had abolished slavery, such vestiges of servitude as restricting blacks to a designated space had also been abolished. In addition, the Fourteenth Amendment had guaranteed "equal protection of the laws," which Plessy had been denied. The Court might have been swayed by an appeal to the "right of contract," writes Goldstone, but Tourgée "wanted a moral statement or nothing. As a result he got nothing."[44]

This harsh indictment may be true enough, but Tourgée was attempting to reestablish the revolutionary nature of the Fourteenth Amendment. Its passage, he claimed, had stripped the states of "all control over citizenship." The result was a "new citizenship" that expanded the power of the federal government to guarantee the "personal rights on which our government is based." The Court, however, had repeatedly held otherwise; all save one of the justices could not, as Tourgée requested, imagine themselves as black people before white law.[45] Tourgée appealed for empathy; the Court was impervious; its response was a seven to one decision against Plessy, one justice having recused himself.

Writing for the Court, Henry Billings Brown of Massachusetts declared that plaintiff's claim was nonsense and unnatural. The Separate Car Act could not be unconstitutional because the men who wrote the Fourteenth Amendment never "intended to abolish distinctions based upon color." They would never have expected to "enforce social, as distinguished from political equality, or a commingling of the two races on terms unsatisfactory to either." Normal people did not ignore race. Although segregation of railway cars was an innovation of the previous eight years, Brown argued that its wisdom had been "established by [ancient] usages, customs, and traditions" based on "racial instincts."[46] Such instincts did not assume "a badge of inferiority," he wrote. Then he contradicted himself. "If one race be inferior to the other socially," referring to black people, Brown concluded "the Constitution of the United States cannot put them upon the same plane."[47] Race trumped Justice.

One justice disagreed. John Marshall Harlan of Kentucky had been raised in a slaveholding family and as an adult had opposed the Thirteenth and Fourteenth Amendments. He had, however, changed his mind. In one electoral campaign he even insisted that any "colored" man "has the same right that any white man possesses" to ride in a railway car. With regard to the Separate Car Law: its intent was clear, Harlan wrote. Contrary to his colleagues, he saw its purpose, "under the guise of giving equal accommodation," was to distance blacks from whites. This intent, he insisted, was clearly what Brown had denied it was, "a badge of servitude wholly inconsistent" with the Constitution. This was Tourgee's point exactly. Harlan went on to predict that the majority's decision would "stimulate aggressions, more or less brutal and irritating upon the admitted rights of colored citizens." The decision would encourage states to "defeat the beneficent purposes" of the Reconstruction Amendments. Despite the current preeminence of the white race in "prestige, achievements, in education, or wealth and in power," the Constitution itself, Harlan stated, knows no "dominant, ruling class of citizens. There is no caste here. Our Constitution is color-blind."[48]

Harlan read the Constitution differently than did the majority. Ignorant of the actual intentions of those who wrote the Fourteenth Amendment, the justices had deferred to Southern elites. Harlan's prediction as to the baleful effects of their decision described what Southerners were already doing by leasing convicts, disfranchising blacks, and segregating public facilities. Two years later the Court intensified its repudiation of the Fourteenth Amendment in *Williams v. Mississippi* when it indicated that laws designed to disfranchise black men could withstand scrutiny under the Constitution. The Mississippi constitution of 1890, which was under review, allowed electoral officials to disqualify voters at their own discretion; "race" and "color" were not mentioned. The Court, however, understood the constitution's purpose. Blacks were "clearly distinguished" from whites; they lacked "forethought, and [their] criminal members given to furtive offenses."[49]

The *Plessy* and *Williams* decisions confirmed what Southern elites had been doing for thirty years. Over a generation before a mob burned Sam Hose near Newnan, Georgia, Southern politicians had begun to use the law to bludgeon black people into submission. Law, in the person of peace officers and judges, made black men criminals so that they might be transformed into an unpaid labor force to service private enterprise. Law deprived black men of their citizenship rights to vote, hold office, or sit on juries; it restricted their ability to participate in public life. Law assigned black people to spaces where whites decided to put and keep them. Law made black people into objects to be distanced, disregarded, and degraded rather than persons to be conceded the courtesy, civility, and respect a civilized people are expected to express in public discourse. In short, whites owned the judges, the lawyers, the juries, and the law.[50] They made African Americans *outlaws* if they acted like white people.

The US Supreme Court's misreading of the Fourteenth Amendment permitted local jurisdictions throughout the South to apply law differently to blacks and whites. Leon Litwack, in his study of life under segregation, recounted comments by a Mississippi lawyer who observed that his colleagues needed to know "the common law, the civil law, and statutory law but also 'negro [sic] law'." The reference was to the complicated ways in which the legal system treated non-whites. The complexities of "negro law" differed from locale to locale, judge to judge, and possibly day to day; practice depended on the prosecutor's discretion. Black on black crime was punished less rigorously than black on white; white on black crime might not be punished at all. African American testimony could be accepted in trials but ignored if it reflected badly on the wrong white person. Well-known blacks, who could count on a white man to work the criminal justice system on their behalf, would fare better than strangers bereft of white support. Black women who had been assaulted could be denied justice if juries believed a black woman could not be raped.[51] When Law was designed to control one class of people in ways not applied to obviously favored people, it had become, in the words of Jon Pahl, a "system of exclusion and collective coercion";[52] that is, *law was violence.*

SEGREGATION AND RELIGION

Segregation was not merely law, or the creature of law; it was also culture. It came to have the force of religion. Nineteenth-century white Americans, as heirs to Europeans, were legatees also to centuries of suspicion or contempt of peoples markedly unlike themselves. Conquered nations at the periphery of Europe were especially subject to disdain that was not, George Fredrickson has argued, *racism* until "ethnic discrimination" bred a "worldview" that justified it. Anti-Semitism, by casting Jews as "Malevolent beings in league with the Devil" (John 8:44), for example, provided such an ideology. Jews became demonic simply by being Jews. To the "essentialist version of anti-Semitism" was then added a "color-coded white supremacist" ideology that justified enslaving Africans and Native Americans in the fifteenth and sixteenth centuries as Europeans began to reflect on the differences between themselves and the peoples of Africa, Asia, and America.

As one scholar points out, "Black bodies [became] the ever-visible counterweight of a usually invisible white identity." Thus stigmatized, blacks could be enslaved as capitalist development and the Atlantic slave trade merged with the displacement of native peoples to confirm the reality of Race. Europeans who believed that Christianity had superseded the Jewish people as the Chosen, now began to extend the idea of being chosen to being white, which "deeply affected the African," as W. J. Jennings explains. "In fact," he observes, "mercantile and theological interests . . . converged on the African at this moment, not only vivifying the idea of perpetual slavery, but also drawing African bodies onto a plane of existence that involved constant spiritual and material comparison with white bodies." By the 1720s in British America the fact that most Africans were slaves imposed a double imprint of inferiority. When the Atlantic Enlightenment then provided the impetus for classifying human differences according to race, the classifiers realized that reason indicated they were superior to all others.[53]

That superiority was confirmed in the United States by appeals to Christian scripture. After the War for American Independence, defenders of Southern slavery relied on the commonplace assumption that racial slavery was justified by the inferiority of Africans and the fact that Old Testament patriarchs owned slaves (or perhaps servants). Probably more important, St. Paul had commanded servants to obey their masters. Since many slaveholders were Christians, their privileged religious status seemed to confirm the morality of their power. The claim that sacred writ justified slaveholding allowed Christians to argue that the region was about to become a bastion of Christian orthodoxy. There were, to be sure, a great many masters who were still to be converted, but when they understood the social benefits of embracing the faith, they would do so. Consistent with this expectation, Southern Christians pointed out that Northern abolitionists were infidels who dismissed biblical defenses of slaveholding and wielded weapons from an armory of non-Christian values that resembled those of the French Enlightenment and Revolution. In defending slavery, Southerners were defending Christian civilization and fulfilling their Christian duty by converting the enslaved to Christianity. White Christians could sometimes concede it was possible to "civilize" Africans, but the radical transformation required in each case reinforced the assumption of inferiority by emphasizing the difference that had yet to be overcome.[54]

After Emancipation, Mark Smith points out, remnants of proslavery ideology encouraged "an emotional, visceral, and febrile understanding of racial identity. It was an understanding immune to logic, impervious to thought, and, as such, a perfect foundation for segregation." Blackness, white supremacists believed, could be "smelled, heard, and felt,"[55] a dogma that justified whites in herding and commanding blacks to the former's advantage. For some hysterical whites the difference was so great as to allow them to insist scripture and science together revealed that African Americans were not even human. The year before Sam Hose's fiery death, Charles Carroll declared *"the Negro"* a *"Beast."* As such, s/he lacked a soul and was thus outside the Christian plan of salvation.

The man whose writings were frequently published by a Christian press imagined *the Negro* in the Garden of Eden as the serpent that tempted Eve into the act that beguiled Adam into disobedience and cast humanity into sin. Worse, *the Negro* caused humankind to fall once again through "amalgamation" when Cain took a black female to wife. This second fall from grace would have made all subsequent humans mulattoes, and therefore beasts, if Carroll could have been held to consistency; but his excessively long outbursts were less argument than exclamation. His obsession was purity-and-danger; his fear was pollution by a satanic Other.[56] Such claims reflected something other than the grotesque blustering of childish fantasists. Exceeding the bounds of rhetorical license, such revisions of Genesis seemed to erupt from the night terrors of white believers who feared the Beast of Revelation [13:1–16] was the "Negro." Carroll seemed to be putting into expository prose the pictorial imagination of white supremacists whose cartoonists represented black men as incubi who seduced white women as they slept.[57]

Carroll was extreme; many supremacists dismissed him as a "crackpot." Decrying him did not, however, require repudiating belief in blacks' inferiority. Many who insisted on African Americans' humanity shared Carroll's obsession with "social equality" and "amalgamation." If Carroll believed that *the Negro*'s bestiality was exemplified by smell, color, physiognomy, musculature, licentiousness, and cranium, his critics agreed that these things also indicated racial inferiority, which was, alas, becoming much worse. The difference between Carroll and his detractors was of degree not kind. Carroll and his opponents agreed that crime, disease, intemperance, insolence, and superstition proved that black people were degenerating. If a scholar such as Franz Boas rejected the idea of superior peoples and civilizations, as he did in 1894, whites who believed that they knew African Americans better than a Jewish professor could scoff that only an inferior "race" would have allowed itself to be enslaved. In the modulated tones of civilized discourse an author could insist, "There is no hope whatever for any organic improvement of any race betterment of the Negro." Caucasians are an imperial race, wrote a publicist, and nothing could protect blacks from them. This was the language of violence; and far too many whites thought it appropriate.[58]

The society constructed through segregating and criminalizing black people was at the same time experiencing a resurgence and reordering of religious life. If Southerners were sloughing off the rule of local church discipline in many ways,[59] many were also demanding that that discipline be applied through prohibition to public life during the 1880s. People were joining the church then in ever-greater numbers. To be sure, southern white communities of faithful people had been devastated physically and psychologically by the Civil war. Their buildings had been damaged or destroyed; their colleges ruined; their periodicals silenced; their young men slaughtered; their leaders demoralized. Gradually, however, churchmen and women rebuilt local churches and colleges, bought new presses, and prepared to secure the faith through Sunday schools.

During the 1890s, new and wide-reaching denominational bodies could report that their renewed facilities were producing more members than ever before although percentages of church members in the general population did not yet surpass 50 per cent. Membership rolls alone, however, cannot capture the numbers of people who came under the influence of formal religious institutions. That influence included a majority of people because women were a majority of church members and all sources demonstrate that they lived up to cultural expectations by influencing both their children and husbands who were not on the rolls. In fact, women were becoming so assertive in some churches that they inspired a few sisters in rural Baptist churches miraculously to work for the "equal right" to vote on matters ecclesiastical. [60]

As opponents of enfranchising women feared, such concessions were not the end but the beginning. Despite prophecies of "confusion, intrusion, strife, error, and scandal,"[61] women forged ahead. They began forming their own societies, first among Methodists on behalf of foreign missions (1878) and then for domestic venues (1882ff). They were conducting their own gendered religious awakening. When challenged by men who feared this impulse would get out of hand, they pointed out that they had been inspired by the Holy Spirit and encouraged by the teachings of Christ Jesus. The contagion spread to Baptist women as well when they were stirred by the words, action, and life of Charlotte Digges ("Lottie") Moon to form the Woman's Missionary Union (1888). Women embraced a new solidarity through collective action expressed in expansive rhetoric that celebrated "the sweet ring of sisterhood."[62] And sisterhood, as feminists in a later generation insisted, was powerful. It motivated women to bring the Christian values of self-discipline, chastity, responsibility, and familial care, into the public forum.

This movement from the family and the church into the civic life of men was an invasion almost as disruptive to besieged manhood as that of black soldiers during the Civil War. If the temperance and prohibition movements were affected by the political calculation and class imperialism of men after the 1880s, they received a dramatic and innovative push from the Woman's Christian Temperance Union.[63] If politicking preachers were a serious departure from religious tradition, the actions of women leaving home to petition legislators on behalf of public policy in public places were even more disturbing. One of the axioms of Southern Honor – the dependence of women – was being impaired: by redefining womanhood women were challenging white men's understanding of manhood. It is not surprising that the latter should sound an alarm against lustful black men in order to remind women of just how much they owed their menfolk.[64]

Religion may be understood as the complex symbolic representation of the social order through which we learn transcendence. To be sure, believers and students will insist that religion is far more than this abbreviated definition – and it is; but it does reflect the important insight of Emile Durkheim. A founder of the sociology of religion, the renowned French scholar pointed out that the concept of God is birthed from within our social consciousness in our *awareness of group*. Through this awareness, society arouses a "sensation of the divine" and fosters a "sense of perpetual dependence" that allows "all sorts of restraints, privations, and sacrifices without which social life would be impossible." This sensation of the divine creates intensity in the "form of a moral power that, while immanent in us, also represents something in us that is other than ourselves." And this Otherness elicits a "mental state" in which we perceive a sacred world that we honor through consecrating things, people, or ideas.[65]

Acknowledging the Holy in such ways reflects our attempt to imagine an ideal world where everything is in its proper place and actions are designed to sustain the purity of the ideal and the symbols associated with it. The "distinguishing marks of the sacred," Durkheim insisted, were seen best in "rules of separation." These "ideas about separating, purifying, demarcating, and punishing transgression," Mary Douglas points out, function "to impose system on an inherently untidy experience."[66] Such an imposition, the Frenchman noted, was never "more in evidence than during the first years of the [French] Revolution" when a Cult of Reason and the Supreme Being was invented through "dogma, symbols, altars, and feast days."[67] The cultural inventiveness of white Southerners after the Civil War also birthed a cult, which was not opposed to Christianity, but presumed to be complementary to it. Southern patriots blended Christian hymns, rhetoric, and mood into a syncretic civic religiosity that valorized sacrifice that led to victory over Reconstruction,

Federal tyranny, and Negro Domination. Charles Wilson called this political resurrection the civil religion of the Lost Cause.[68]

If skeptics insist that the Lost Cause was not a religion, it was certainly imagined within a Christian ethos. The Confederacy became not a government so much as an ideal for which a sacred host had died just as Christ Jesus had sacrificed himself to redeem fallen humanity. The South may have been overwhelmed by the forces of evil on its own Golgotha, but like Christ it was rising from the crypt of defeat to spread the Good News associated with its highest aspirations. In explaining the meaning of Appomattox, partisans fashioned a mythology masquerading as history. Clever writers denied Southerners had seceded to defend slavery, thus ignoring forty years of partisan conflict in church and state and the sentiments expressed in ordinances of secession.

The North, ideologues insisted, had forced slavery on an unsuspecting and Edenic South. It was not our fault, Southern apologists wailed; we created a society far superior to the materialistic North. We created a Christian workforce that would never have tried to rise above its aptly servile state without the backing of hypocritical Yankees who, at Emancipation, taught blacks to believe they were equal to the Southern white man. Redeeming the South from the ravages of Reconstruction and the threat of Populism, the Democratic Party had secured the South through white supremacy. In this sacred history [*Heilsgeschichte*], Jefferson Davis could become, even for men who disliked him, a Christ figure "bleeding for his people." Like women at the Cross and Tomb, white women became the sentimental personification of Southern faith and purity.[69] It is not surprising that in this mix of ideology, myth, and sentimentality, Lost Cause partisans had created a way of thinking that saw, felt, and heard RAPE as a call to self-justifying violence.

As activist women and Lost Cause partisans expanded the meanings of religious life after the Civil War, they did so within an evangelical mood. The mood, which had shaped religious life in the South before the War continued to do so afterward within a conflicted discourse about who was "evangelical" enough. Most believers still conceded the theology of Crucifixion and punishment and imagined a distinct polarity between those who were saved and those who were not. Authenticity was established by the transforming experience of conversion in which one was saved from "careless" and "stupid" living and given a new life in Christ. He was imagined by many to have redeemed not a people who through him would enter the Kingdom of God, but the individual who had been "born again." The phrase, although rarely found in the Bible,[70] was the prevailing theme of "conversion" in the early nineteenth century. By the 1890s, having been "born again" was so familiar a sign of impending adulthood that suspicious traditionalists were becoming restive. But both reformers and their complacent coreligionists still valued a radical sense of before-and-after; evil and good; unsaved and saved; alienation and acceptance. The old self – now rejected as sinful, clueless, ignorant, and stupid – was contrasted with the prayerful, alert, new self, empowered with ways of thinking foreign to the old.[71]

This sanctified individualism meant that it was exceptionally difficult (but not impossible) for the "born again" to think of themselves as somehow complicit in the "sins" or failures inherent in the social order. Such an ethic, a theologian points out, cannot accept the "collective and social nature of sin and redemption." The peril of pious narcissism was obvious and could inspire rudeness in an evangelical braggart, such as the one who announced at dinner one night that he had never known a "religious Episcopalian" as he sat next to one.[72] Despite such inanity, the evangelical ideal could privilege the language of humility and deference to Christ while nourishing gratitude that one was quite unlike other people whose difference could be identified with the old and stupid self. At its best, Evangelical self-consciousness could open a person to a reality that granted a fulfilling life *beyond the power of context* to restrict her or him; at its worst, it could encourage a self-effacing and pious arrogance.

The polarity of unsaved and saved in the white Southern Christian ethos lent an intensely moralistic aura to racial difference. This was especially true in matters affected by gender. Evangelical taboo was particularly strict when it came to sex – witty and light-hearted conversation between the sexes was taboo. This mood was magnified into primal fears of pollution and danger[73] when difference was defined by race. Southern politicians had transformed African American expectations of full citizenship into "social equality," i.e., rape. Political campaigns enhanced and intensified an unassailable "awareness of the group," which is the source of religion. An obsession with the white "group" inspired Southern white elites and their mimetic constituencies as they fashioned white supremacy.

The ways in which law and violence distanced human beings from each other, established boundaries, and made dangerous their breach were the ways of religion. If Segregation was a political-economic system with laws to control workers essential to a modernizing New South,[74] its emotional power flowed from the fusion of purity and danger. Virginia historian Philip Alexander Bruce had long ago warned against blacks' "personal uncleanness and moral infirmities." These signified, he wrote, a "descent into the unmeasurable depth of degradation" that could not be cured from within the blacks' community because their religion was so defective. Their worship was "physical drunkenness" expressed as "ecstatic laughter and boisterous singing." Their religion had no moral discipline, Bruce insisted. There were, he sniffed in ignorance, no black Episcopalians.[75]

Feelings of pollution and danger at the proximity of an anomalous "other" supported the "sexual alibi" for segregation. Observers have long noted the hold of the "rape complex" on southern whites when justifying lynching.[76] But to assign the mental patterns behind this connection to a neurotic obsession unsupported by statistics is beside the point. In the cases of both lynching and segregation, the bodies of white females symbolized the social body. They did so whether as little girls in grammar school or as women in erotic fantasy. Symbolically coupling white females with black males underscored the danger of crossing boundaries. A culture that already made women religious surrogates or mediators for men, as well as the fount of purity, made it right to push black men to the margin of society. The blending of chastity and racial superiority combined with aversive custom and political will to fabricate a system that had the tone and imperative of certainty based on fact. The result approached holiness because it demanded individuals "conform to the class to which they belong.... Holiness means keeping distinct," Mary Douglas has written, "the categories of creation."[77]

Lillian Smith certainly remembered segregation as sacred. In *Killers of the Dream*, she mused about the ways in which "sin and sex and segregation" suffused the lives of Southerners.[78] She could not separate the motifs. Although as an adult she believed that Christian love impugned segregation, as a child she had been taught "to love God, to love [my] white skin and to believe in the sanctity of both." She had learned sin and guilt within the incubation of a "warm, moist evangelism and racial segregation" sanctified by a religion "too narcissistic to be concerned with anything but a man's body and a man's soul." The body was the "essence of morality" based on the "mysterious matter of entrances and exits" with sin hovering "over all doors."

Segregation, Smith argued, pushed "everything dark, dangerous, and evil" to the margins where danger lurked. Evil was thought to have been purged from the sin-distressed self so that whites became fascinated with other people's sins rather than their own and found personal salvation in the death of Christ without carrying a cross. Their narcissistic purity had shriven them of the capacity for understanding religion as service. Smith understood the power of values taught by God-like parents who fused the spectrum of white-purity-god-aversion into a powerful compound of holiness. Critics consigned her to the "shame and guilt" school of Southern writers. She was too critical, too heretical.[79]

The cultural patterns connecting law, practice, morality, and meaning often varied by locale but those who were separated and those who did the separating never varied. The moods and motivation of distance and boundary suffused the South. If legal patterns of separation fabricated with regard to transportation after 1890 were new, they merely replicated the sensibility that segregated education from the earliest days of Emancipation. There were few white dissenters from this demanding faith of purity, hierarchy, separation, and distance. If there was a theoretical dichotomy between racial "conservatives" and "radicals," with the latter representing the pole of racial hatred, the distinctions were of degree rather than kind.

With the passing of each year after the economic depression of the early nineties, separation-and-purity became ever more pervasive in public discourse enhanced by the widespread drive for prohibition. The white ribbons of women's temperance symbolized a ubiquitous "purity" associated with white supremacy, self-discipline, and female chastity. The crusade was all too often imagined as a contest between Christian sobriety and drunken black men; it reflected the cosmic struggle between good and evil that clad white supremacy in righteousness. Defending white purity against black danger justified the contempt and rage with which white confronted black.[80] Segregation was not merely law or sex; it was also religion.

For black people, segregation also revealed the sacred as well as the power of Evil. If whites learned the emotional power of segregation through the ethos of "purity and danger," African Americans learned its emotional power through violence and caution. Thinking of his life under the "ravages of segregation," Howard Thurman pointed out that "the human spirit [had to] accommodate itself to desolation." Black people did so by building a "thick wall" psychologically and emotionally against "perilous involvement with white persons." Thurman and his people had to remain as invisible as possible behind that wall, which meant that whites were never part of the "magnetic field" of African American morality. The perilous were "out of bounds" to the imperiled, that is, beyond the wall. Whites did not behave as moral beings; they had no religion; their behavior proved it. They could, like the Devil, breach the wall at any time. Their ability to do so without rule or reason demonstrated their lack of religion and therefore absolved blacks of relating to them as Christians. It was, Thurman confessed, "a rigid narrowing" of the Christian ethic.

In justifying "an immoral exercise of power of the strong over the weak" and enforcing it through violence, whites never had to answer to blacks or (in the view of the latter) to God. The primary dynamic of segregation as blacks understood it – that is, the truth behind its laws, traditions, and images and the engine that sustained it – was violence. Violence, Thurman points out, was not constant warfare or daily violation, at least so long as blacks avoided "perilous involvement" with whites. Violence was not always manifest; yet, much worse, it was always *possible*. It was a constant threat that nurtured an ethos of fear that "was always current and always active." The "power and tools of violence [were] all on one side," Thurman recalled. The "fact that there [was] no available and recognized protection from violence [made] the resulting fear deeply terrifying." He added that "the cost to the perpetrator of segregation is a corrosion of the spirit and the slow deadly corruption of the soul. It is to be overcome by evil."[81] Evil for Christian blacks was not an abstraction played out only in personal failures that one called sins. Evil was the truth enveloping black people in the American South, and affecting them beyond.

Segregation allowed whites to invade the personal and social lives of blacks with impunity. Unless one were protected or championed by a well-known white man who would brave the contempt for "nigger-lovers," few blacks found ways to hold whites accountable for broken promises, broken faith, fraud, murder, or rape, that is, the ever-present possibility of violence. When asked about their lives under "Jim Crow," people remembered a house burned by whites, a sister raped, a man whipped, a garden raided, produce stolen, a man murdered for a pearl-handled revolver. They remembered that for these and other violations, whites had never been called to account. People remembered insult, injury, and humiliation. They remembered stories of struggle and achievement and parents and grandparents who constantly reminded them "You are just as good as anybody" when whites acted as if they weren't. They remembered the solidarity and support of the black community and how much psychic and physical energy it took simply to navigate among whites when people left the haven of their community to engage whites in the latter's space.[82]

Entering that arena, as Thurman pointed out, was perilous. Sam Hose did so when he asked Alfred Cranford for a favor and wages; the request somehow implied obligation and equity, which enraged the white man. Law and culture had made the black man Cranford's inferior even before he approached his employer; the effrontery of soliciting special consideration was insufferable. When danger erupted into violence, the white God's justice gave white people license to light the fire that consumed Sam Hose.

LYNCHING AS A WAY OF LIFE

Such a statement is offensive; but offensive statements are frequently true. To be sure, no law allowed white men to torture and burn black people. In fact, it was definitely illegal for them to do so; but whites tended to believe that the only criminals in lynching dramas were black. Scholars helped them understand the extent of African American criminality. In 1884, Philip Alexander Bruce had warned Northerners through the *New York Post* that freed people were becoming less civilized. He was joined in his analysis throughout the 1880s and 1890s by a broad range of writers, social scientists, and journalists who exposed what they thought was the devolution of African Americans into savagery. Statisticians such as Frederick L. Hoffman and Walter F. Willcox famously supported Bruce's argument. As scholars, Bruce, Hoffman, and Willcox did not reach as many citizens as journalists and newsmen who sent their ideas throughout the nation and helped generate a widespread disquiet that could in some venues become an alarm.

By the mid-1890s, even a casual reader of *The* [Atlanta] *Constitution*, for example, could become aware that black men were committing crimes from Seattle to Boston, and from Miami to Los Angeles, as well as in Atlanta and Griffin. A small town newspaper such as the Newnan, Georgia, *Herald and Advertiser* marveled at how easy it was now to find news from across the entire country. By 1901, one could glean stories of African American criminality from Indiana, Ohio, Tennessee, North Carolina, Louisiana, South Carolina, and Florida simply by selecting at random five issues of a local Georgia daily. Almost any rumor of crimes committed by blacks could be believed. Even men who had reputations for defending African Americans could repeat as "fact" in 1893 the lie that black men had raped 300 white women in the previous three months.[83] Such alarmist rhetoric verged on creating what sociologists call a "moral panic" that encouraged whites to imagine young black men as "folk devils."[84] Their rumored crimes could justify something happening in the South that the *Chicago Tribune* described as relatively new.

In 1887, the newspaper reported white mobs were lynching more blacks than whites. Lynching was not new. A crowd's taking the law "into their own hands," that is, "lynching" someone, was based on the legendary actions of Squire Charles Lynch of Bedford County, Virginia. During the War for American Independence, he and his neighbors constituted a court for punishing suspected Tories whom the law could not touch. After the war, Christopher Waldrep points out, the words *"lynch"* and *"lynching"* traveled west and were applied to a community's punishment of crimes committed beyond the reach of law. By 1835, when a lynching in Vicksburg, Mississippi attracted national attention, Waldrep explains, the word and act were widely recognized throughout the United States. During the first two decades after Emancipation, more whites than blacks were lynched in the United States; violence against Southern blacks took other forms. In 1882, the *Tribune*'s editors, who had been printing statistics on such things as executions, suicides, and train wrecks, now added lynching.

The *Tribune*'s research, Waldrep points out, was not rigorous. Lynching was not defined; the size of crowds was not indicated; incidents were counted more than once; many events were not reported. The *Tribune*'s statistics, however, remain significant indicators of a trend. Its genesis was noticed as Southern legislators began disfranchising blacks amid the political paranoia triggered by the election of 1888 and proved, it was claimed, by the widespread danger of black rapists. The antecedents of Southern lynching were imbedded in patrols that policed slaves and in the nightriders, Klansmen, and vigilantes who thereafter punished blacks and dissident whites as elites redeemed the South from "Negro Domination." From 1889 to 1899, about 188 people a year were lynched in the South; from 1900 to 1909 the average was ninety-three. In the next decade it was sixty-two and from 1920 to 1924 it was forty-six. By 1929 it was seventeen. A map designed by the National Association for the Advancement of Colored People (NAACP) to depict lynching between 1889 and 1922 indicates one incident in Delaware, seventeen in Maryland, and fewer than one hundred in Virginia, North Carolina, Missouri, and Oklahoma. Kentucky, South Carolina, and Tennessee reported between 130 and 200 events; Texas, Arkansas, Louisiana, and Alabama recorded between 200 and 370 each; Georgia (451) and Mississippi (413) topped the list. Lynching was rare in most other states; Maine (1) was the only New England state to suffer the crime; but Northern cities could sometimes explode in riots that took many black lives.

By the 1890s, lynching had become a property of the South. Incidents were, however, not evenly distributed, as statistics indicated; some areas never suffered such crimes, others seemed fertile ground, and the two areas could be contiguous. The varied histories of states could also shape different patterns of violence. W. Fitzhugh Brundage, for example, found in his model study of lynching in Virginia and Georgia that the former state endured far fewer incidents than the latter because it had ended Reconstruction with less violence: The states' political histories were different. Moreover, Virginia had been selling slaves to the west and lower South for decades before the Civil War and, as a result, the "race" problem appeared to be less threatening in the Commonwealth than much farther south. Danger zones could also vary according to the ratio of black to white populations. In South Carolina, for example, the Piedmont with a large white population suffered many lynchings, but the overwhelmingly black low country supported relatively few of them, as did coastal Georgia.

Brundage observes that between 1880 and 1930 Georgians staged at least 451 lynchings; nineteen victims were white, the rest were black. During that time, 185 men were accused of murder or attempted murder; 138 were accused of rape or attempted rape; 128 men died for defying white supremacy in some way. Most Georgia mobs gathered in the vast territory between the Piedmont and coastal counties. The area surrounding Newnan endured relatively few mob killings; a lynching in Palmetto during the late winter of 1899, which preceded the burning of Sam Hose, was anomalous for the area. The two events erupted from within a social crisis imagined by whites disturbed by the presence of African American soldiers stationed in Georgia during the Spanish American War. The fact that Sam Hose's burning was so irregular to the vicinity in which it occurred is cautionary.

The immediate cause of every lynching was affected by specific relationships among specific people in specific conditions triggered by a specific incident in a specific place and time. Terence Finnegan, for example, found that most lynching in Mississippi and South Carolina had erupted from specific disputes between white farmers and black dependents. This was certainly the case when Sam Hose thought Cranford was about to kill him. In such situations, exchanges would be affected by the nature of personal relationships. Hose was merely a relatively recent hire living under an alias: he was a stranger. Transient laborers like Hose could be in special danger even for seemingly innocent infractions, as Edward Ayres points out.

If variations of lynching generally resulted from differences in agricultural production and population volatility, density, and distribution, the fact cannot account for specific incidents. Stewart E. Tolnay and E. M. Beck found that "gains in the real price of cotton," especially between 1883 and 1906, were generally "associated with years of reduced lynching activity against blacks." That trend, however, is irrelevant to understanding what happened between Hose and Cranford. A specific exchange erupted in tragedy. And it may have resulted from the fact that racial etiquette could vary from locale to locale. Acts thought inoffensive in one town could be dangerous in another. Hose – reared one hundred miles away – certainly violated Cranford's rules of acceptable behavior, but he may not have known what they were. The ambiguity and variations of racial etiquette nourished by local history should have made Hose cautious. Eternal vigilance was the price of white supremacy for both white and black; and both Cranford and Hose paid the highest price imaginable when Hose forgot that fact.

Lynching was not merely a public event that partisans could claim was a community-sanctioned execution. Crowds responsible for lynching varied in size (but included more than three people), composition, and motivation. Brundage suggests four types. The first he characterizes as *terrorist*. Groups that spread terror were more likely to have an enduring organization than others. Georgia's tradition of extra-legal violence included gangs of White-cappers that punished improper personal conduct, those who opposed moonshiners, or blacks who seemed to stand in the way of whites' economic self-interest. *Private* mobs were made up of friends, relatives, or neighbors acting without community approval and meting vengeance for personal offenses. There were mobs acting as *posses* and there were *mass crowds* of many hundreds, possibly thousands claiming to act with communal sanction. The latter were especially rooted in the cotton growing belt of Georgia and the contiguous area to the south. The need to control a large and sometimes restive labor force accounted for the high rate of lynching.

The historical, demographic, and economic features of a region were as important as the gender, age, and race of both the alleged victim and the accused. Locale, season, and the nature of relationships between the mob and the offender were also important. Executing a black man could be a way of displacing anger from prominent white men in what would literally serve as a vicarious sacrifice. Where there were divisions in the white community, too, mobs would be smaller and recruited primarily for personal reasons, as Brundage also points out. In the Yazoo Delta of

Mississippi, for example, Finnegan believes mobs were smaller for demographic and cultural reasons. Planters could discipline workers on their own authority absent collective action. But, conceding the need to complicate a quadrilateral typology, there is agreement on a significant difference between lynching by a large crowd and one committed by a posse; between one that exacted personal revenge and one that erupted from the desire to terrorize the black community. Mobs such as the one that burned Sam Hose were significantly different from the others not only for their large mass, but also for their celebration of white cohesion.

Such lynching and the solidarity it signified were secured by the social distancing of segregation. Roberta Senechal de la Roche orders her understanding of the "likelihood and lethality of lynching" by applying a "general theory of social control" based on that distancing by race (class, caste). "Who does what to whom" depends on the status relations between the parties involved. The calculus includes multiple factors: the lower the status of the accused (Hose) and the greater the status of his/her victim (Cranford), the greater the solidarity of the crowd and the isolation of the accused, the more likely the violence. Further, the possibility of lynching increased the stranger the accused and the closer to consensus the crowd. Sam Hose's fate was sealed by a ten-day sensationalist campaign by newspapers that created a public commitment to burning him.

In a culture that exercised power through distancing and boundaries, and made a fetish of race, lynching was not an anomaly; but neither were other forms of violence. Gilles Vandal points out that vigilantism – similar to Brundage's terrorist mobs – complemented lynching. He distinguishes between the relatively swift response to a specific act that characterized most lynching, and the well-planned operations of vigilance committees. Such groups obeyed specific rules, kept membership lists, and planned campaigns against blacks most likely to challenge white supremacy. If African Americans seemed to be doing well economically or were favored by planters or merchants, Whitecappers drove them from their homes, or in rare instances killed them. In September 1888, for example, white vigilantes massacred blacks in Free Town, Louisiana, with impunity. Driving out African Americans, however, was not unique to the region; venues above the Mason and Dixon line did so as well.[85]

It is clear that many Southern whites were not willing to enforce their rule by overt, illegal, and extreme violence. Partisans of mass lynching declared they acted on behalf of their communities and race, and their numbers sometimes seemed to certify their claim; but many Southern whites objected. They often objected, as well, to Whitecappers; and popular antipathy to private mobs accounts for the secrecy clothing the latter. Many whites feared mobs could turn on them, which accounts for silence that was claimed as approval when it was actually fear. Authorities in Georgia cities like Savannah and leading white citizens of towns like Darien were furious with outlaws, "savages," or anarchists that stained the reputation of their region or locale, hindered progress, and terrorized law-abiding blacks. Lynching could be abetted by local peace officers or prevented by them. Black men could sometimes find ways to prevent lynching or become casualties for trying to do so.

An entire community did not kill Hose. A few leading citizens tried to prevent even more leading citizens from murdering him. In Newnan, as throughout the region, there were always whites the vicious would contemptuously label as "nigger lovers." Vigilantes killed whites as well as blacks during Reconstruction. Conservative politicians lost or quashed ballots of whites as well as blacks; and because dissidents of both peoples cooperated in challenging the undemocratic policies of Conservatives, the latter shrank the political nation. White politicians could either tacitly support lynching or oppose it. Governor and Senator "Pitchfork" Ben Tillman of South Carolina was notorious for celebrating such violence;[86] the governors of Georgia during the decade when Hose was killed – William J. Northen, William Yates Atkinson, and Allen D. Candler – all publicly condemned [most] lynching and sometimes took action to prevent it. One of them even tried to face down the mob that burned Sam Hose.

Atkinson had been out of office for almost six months when he learned that Sam Hose had been captured. Alarmed, he hurried to the courthouse to address the crowd that had seized the man from jail. The former governor was well-known and controversial. He had used his powers as Speaker of the Georgia House of Representatives to appoint allies to important posts that established a well-positioned base. He had chaired the executive committee of the state Democratic Party to secure the reelection of Governor William J. Northen in 1892 and defeat an insurgent Populist Party. In the Democratic primary of 1894, he had handily beaten a political novice supported by the Old Guard; in the general election he defeated the Populist candidate, James K. Hines. Atkinson knew how to use the political system he inherited to gain advantage.

By the time he left office, however, he had also earned the respect of African Americans for his many attempts to prevent lynching. In addition, he had used his pardoning power to save Adolphus Duncan from execution. His reputation for racial justice had driven thousands of Democratic voters to forsake him when he won reelection in 1896. In 1898, his successor, Allen Candler, accused the young upstart of "raping" the party. Thus tainted by his popularity among blacks, Atkinson had little authority with the raucous crowd on that horrendous April Sunday afternoon in 1899. If he knew enough about the culture of honor to realize how easily it unleashed violence by a cry of "Rape," he felt compelled by his own sense of honor to stand against chaos and savagery. The mob howled him down as he entreated them to allow the court to pass judgment on their captive. Atkinson had the very best of intentions in this confrontation. He was a markedly principled man; but he had also been a champion athlete in the games of white supremacy. [87] Bearing no malice at all toward black people, he was nonetheless a creature of rules that secured political success in Georgia at the time. He had helped beget the monster he now tried so bravely to subdue.

2

Sex, Danger, and Religion

Facing a "Savage Fury"

"And I, brethren, could not speak unto you as spiritual, but as unto carnal, even as to babes in Christ ... For ye are yet carnal: for whereas there is among you envying, and strife, and divisions, are ye not carnal, and walk as men?"

Christian Bible, KJV, I Corinthians 3:1, 3.

"Within, out of the heart of men, proceed evil thoughts, adulteries, fornications, murders ... All these evil things come from within and defile the man."

Christian Bible, KJV, Mark 7:21, 23.

"Blessed are they which do hunger and thirst after righteousness, for they shall be filled. Blessed are the merciful: For they shall obtain mercy. Blessed are the pure in heart for they shall see God; Blessed are the peacemakers for they shall be called the children of God. Blessed are they which are persecuted for righteousness sake, for theirs is the kingdom of Heaven."

Christian Bible, KJV, Matthew 5:6–10.

***

On the third Sunday after Easter in 1899 about forty miles southwest of Atlanta near Newnan, Georgia, a white crowd burned to death a black laborer known as Sam Hose. The atrocity blended anger, contempt, brutality, festivity, and satisfaction into a mood just beyond comprehension. "Glory!" shouted an excited man enraptured by the intensity of the moment, "Glory be to God!!"

A few weeks after the burning, the Reverend T. G. Steward wrestled with the meaning of this ecstatic moment. He had heard the shout of "Glory" before, he told readers of *The Independent*. Devout people alert to expressions of religious enthusiasm would easily recognize it from having attended revivals. The cry that erupted near Newnan, however, struck the shaken minister as a grotesque perversion of religion. Those presiding over this savagery had cut the victim's body into relics through which to remember what they did. From one perspective, participants bonded with each other to perform the perfect killing that would solve the problem of intractable evil. Steward, however, could not concede this meaning, for the contagion of killing had spread. Other avengers murdered two more African American men who were innocent of any crime save that of being black. Evil had flowed from this carnival of blood. Steward was shocked at the ferocity. He hoped the American public would respond by establishing "the reign of justice and humanity over every foot of land beneath the sway of its flag." But in private, reflecting on his own experiences as a minister in Macon, Georgia, and as a chaplain to black troops of the US Army, Steward certainly knew better. He did hope, nonetheless, that his readers would agree that "the recent outrages in Georgia ought to shock the whole country, and will shock all right thinking people who are made acquainted with the facts."[1]

The Independent had long been condemning such outrages in their support of equal rights for African Americans. These rights were so important, the editor observed, that his passion had spurred Southerners to ask if he were "a negro or mulatto." This "compliment," the editor replied, meant he was doing something right.[2] His magazine had once been an antislavery enterprise; it was not surprising that after the spectacular burning of Henry Smith in Paris, Texas, in 1893, *The Independent* had paid special attention to lynching in both South and North. Chaplain Steward was not the first black minister to appear in the periodical's columns. Henry H. Proctor, a graduate of Yale University Divinity School and pastor of the First Congregational Church in Atlanta, Georgia, was one of several who corresponded with the magazine.

In 1897, Proctor had discerned a "quickening of conscience" after his state had been plagued by an epidemic of violence "under the very shadow of the cross of Christ." Governor W. Y. Atkinson's forceful opposition to lynching had undoubtedly inspired him to believe that blacks and whites together could find ways to stop both rape and lynching.[3] In linking the crimes as Southern whites did, Proctor hoped to nudge them to work harder to prevent mob murder; but the "quickening" he had sensed was a flash in the pan. The Newnan atrocity occurred a few weeks after a lynching in nearby Palmetto of accused black arsonists.

This "barbarism," the *Independent*'s editor claimed, was a failure of religion. He was incensed at the "shame" lynching states brought on the nation. Even lives of the guilty in America, he insisted, "must be held sacred."[4]

A SOUTHERN WOMAN EXPLAINS

Corra Harris was offended by such "extreme Northern views." Living in Rockmart, Georgia, with her sister's family, this daughter of a slaveholding planter thought she knew something about the Southern way of life inaccessible to Yankees! She had to explain it to *The Independent*. Her missive launched her into a career as critic, novelist, and columnist, although for the moment she was the estranged wife of a disgraced former minister and college professor. The black chaplain who offended her had mentioned "facts!" "Facts" were clearer to Southern white women than black men or New York editors. "Facts" would not, to be sure, "mitigate the atrocious conduct of the Newnan mob," she admitted, "but they would explain its savage fury." Her "facts" were especially alarming as she portrayed a South engulfed in sexual danger so pervasive that "at no time, in no place, is the white woman safe from the insults and assaults" of the "negro [sic] brute." Harris announced that the South had for years "been a smoldering volcano, the dark of its quivering nights lighted here and there with the incendiary's torch or pierced through by the cry of some outraged woman." Daily life, too, was "feverish with suppressed excitement, and concealed animosities." Briefly, she explained, "It is the fact of lambs and wolves in one sheepfold."[5]

Black women were to blame, Harris huffed. They had birthed the "brute" who was invariably a "bastard and probably the offspring of a bastard mother." In this case, "probably" meant "always." She imagined a deep-seated licentiousness in black people passed on from generation to generation. Had she been writing a century later, she might have sited the taint in black women's DNA, although she also conceded white men's participation in begetting it. These men, she explained, had bequeathed to their mulatto sons a "Caucasian audacity" that compelled the latter to rape white women. Mothers of rapists had seduced white men and trained their own families in unrestrained sexuality, which had produced a vast "cesspool of vice."

The accusation was folkloric among Southern white women. Before Emancipation they had held enslaved women, and not their masters, responsible for interracial sexual relations and the presence of mixed-race children on their neighbors' plantations, if not their own. Harris found no way to drain the disgusting sinkhole or save such wretched people from it. Christian piety could not do so, she scoffed, because even "the most prominent women in their religious enthusiasms are oftenest public prostitutes." Only yesterday, she had watched a black woman street preacher proclaiming the Gospel in a "lewd and blasphemous" manner. A man raised by such women would naturally become a "menace to every home in the South." The menace had provoked the "savage fury." You Northerners, Harris charged, look on our tormentors "through stained-glass windows of poetic sentimentality"; you sympathize with them while ignoring their crimes. She had never before commented on this matter, she confessed, but now had to do so because of her intense "anxiety."[6]

Harris' anxiety did not diminish for the next few weeks. She could surrender neither her fury nor her contempt as *The Independent* allowed her to continue exploring what she thought was the pathology of African American life. The editor made clear that he did not agree with Harris, but he admired her "vigor and crispness of style." He did not, he explained to her, care to publish only articles that reflected his magazine's view; he also knew that despite his editorial policy he had many Southern readers. Therefore he invited her to submit more essays, an offer that helped heal the recently impoverished woman's badly damaged self-confidence, even as other reactions to her writing profoundly distressed her. One letter, for example, charged her with "gross immorality with Negro men" and promised, she shuddered, "in the most threatening language" to investigate "my character." She thought the author could be a black man offended by her invective.

If Harris denounced the "debased motherhood of the negro [sic] race," she conceded that it was possible to think of a woman from within that milieu as a victim "hardened by crimes and poverty." Such a woman could be "prey to the first [white] wretch who approaches her with deceitful kindness." Harris seemed to concede white men's abuse of young black women; the former's presence hovered over everything she wrote, but she ignored its implications. Conceding white men's sexual predations, she could write about the "scar of the lash" inflicted by masters but never think about the power of white rapists and torturers. The editor pointed out that her essay implied an indictment of white men she herself was unable to issue.[7]

A few weeks later, Harris returned to the unrelenting danger that black women nourished in their families. Black women had taught their sons to hate whites. African Americans were not, she insisted, managing their shame at having been enslaved in a very positive way. The lash, poverty, dishonor, and humiliation had led black men to perfect their "savage capacity to hate." They wanted to avenge the wrongs done them; they pretended to be civilized and struggled to get an education, to be sure, but not in order to improve their lot. Rather, they meant merely to avoid manual labor and invent clever ways to "outwit the hateful white man." Their education, she had written earlier, made the black man "a more formidable factor for evil."

She linked "negroes," "vice," learning, "lust," "license," and voting in a free association of ideas that continued to sweep through her mind like a whirlwind. The linkage suggested a full range of aspirations that would lead black men, Harris wrote, to "the same fireside with white women." That goal was one of her "facts." The hatred she attributed to black men in her final essay on lynching had claimed her as well; but at last her rage was spent. Eventually, *The Independent* would embrace her for a while as one of its most important writers and she would surrender her denunciation of Yankees and African Americans.[8] She would even come to respect the positive contributions of blacks to American culture.

The "facts" of which Harris complained had in the previous fifteen years been established as dogma. Not to understand this would have the same disastrous consequences, it was assumed, as ignoring the law of gravity. When Ida B. Wells of Memphis challenged such facts and denied black men were rapists, she could not safely return home.[9] A similar challenge by Alex Manly in Wilmington, North Carolina, had been used to justify the "Revolution of 1898." The political campaign that prepared whites for "Revolution" had posed white women in parades under banners pleading "Protect Us!"[10] Wells was wrong when she claimed no one believed "Negro men rape white women." The claim was actually an article of white faith! Everyone who talked about lynching agreed that sex, rape, and race dominated conversation. Black people did not necessarily deny, as Wells did, that "Negro men rape white women," but they knew the bromide was essential to white supremacist ideology. They knew with greater certainty that "white men rape black women." Harris, one woman observed in *The Richmond Planet*, had ignored this basic fact and the "great wrong and sin [white men] have placed on this people." Later, a woman told *The Independent* that white men on the trail of Sam Hose had raped at least one young black woman.[11]

CORRA'S GENDERED CONTEXT: RACE AND RAPE WITH
REBECCA FELTON

Not every Georgia white woman was as oblivious as Harris to white men's abuse of black women. In fact, one of the women she most admired had tried in the 1880s to get the Georgia legislature to prevent white guards from raping black women convicts. Rebecca Latimer Felton had been her husband's campaign manager when he ran for Congress as an Independent. After three elections, William H. Felton was eventually defeated, but continued his efforts for reform as a Georgia state legislator. In 1885, his wife urged him to introduce a bill to house black female prisoners in reformatories apart from men in the convict lease system to protect them from being raped by white guards. When the bill lost amid contemptuous denunciations of black female convicts as the "vilest of the vile," she turned to the newly organized Georgia Women's Christian Temperance Union for help.

The WCTU recruited Christian women to lobby for quashing the sale of beverage alcohol and protecting women's chastity by raising the age of consent. It is not surprising therefore that Mrs. Felton got the newly organized Georgia Union to endorse her husband's bill in the 1886 session of the legislature through a petition campaign. Once again the bill failed. White men did not want to be held to account for raping women, especially if they were black. Legislators did not like "women in politics"; the female invasion of male precincts was degrading. In the fall of 1886, an editorial in The [Atlanta] *Constitution* attacked the national WCTU for petitioning Congress to establish the age of legal consent at eighteen years. The editor's delicate sensibilities had been assailed. Proper women did not discuss such things in public, he chirped; such publicity "lowers the tone of public morals."[12]

Rebecca Felton must have thought the "tone of public morals" could not fall much lower when men refused to protect women. Such comments from men did not deter her from challenging the white men of Georgia to do what they claimed was their duty: to protect women and children. She continued to speak in public to such gatherings as the state agricultural society, legislative committees, and women's groups. She lobbied on behalf of education for white girls and women and emphasized the terrible toll that drunken violence took on the domestic life of innocents both black and white. At this point, race, sex, lynching, and danger intersected. She believed that white women owed it to "the colored people of Georgia" to remove the "poison which makes demons of human beings" and "destroys womanhood and our young maidens on the public highway." She went on to say, "We owe it to our white men, young and old, to keep their minds and hearts clear, that law may rule on dealing with crime and thus keep the nation from anarchy and bloodshed."[13]

Whiskey, rape, and lynching were fused in Felton's mind. For a while, her focus continued to be whiskey as a poison that enflamed emotion and ignited violence, but "whiskey" was less potent as a symbol than a drunken black man. And that evocative symbol was one that would eventually dominate Felton's perception of threat. She was, of course, not alone. The national WCTU made the same connections. Ida B. Wells' "threadbare lie" was the stark fact of Corra Harris' imagination and that of thousands of Southern white women who were frightened of "black fiends." The women knew that white men took advantage of black women and they wanted it stopped for their own sake, but they were more easily moved by the alarm at "fiends" who could assault them in a drunken fantasy of equal rights.

For Rebecca Felton, the issue remained the responsibility of white men. When she addressed the Georgia Agricultural Society on Tybee Island, Georgia, in August 1897, she once again emphasized that theme. She insisted that the white men of Georgia had endangered white women. The churches (ministers) were culpable, she declared; they were "incapable of handling the subject of lynching." They could not prevent it. They spent millions of dollars on foreign missions but "ignore[d] the [black] heathen at our door." The courts (judges and juries) were culpable, too. They could not protect the innocent or guarantee justice. White men could not enforce the law because they themselves refused to respect it. They broke it when they bribed the black voter and "made him think he [was] a 'man and a brother'."

Such exploitation dashed the hopes of respectable African Americans, Felton insisted; it promised privileges never conceded and thus justified the black rapist in his own mind. When he acted, white men reacted by lynching. She went on to say that when "there is not enough religion in the pulpit to organize a crusade against sin, nor justice in the courthouse to promptly punish crime, nor manhood in the nation to put a sheltering arm about innocence and virtue, IF IT NEEDS LYNCHING to protect women's dearest possession from the ravening human beasts, then I say, lynch a thousand a week if necessary." Her reference to lynching was *conditional*, she later insisted. *IF* the churches, courts, and politicians were incapable of protecting "women and girls" and "law abiding people were helpless," our only resort would be "lynch law." She was angry with people who did not see that she had simply demanded white men punish crime. If they wouldn't, they encouraged a "cyclone of violence and lynch law." She feared for the future.[14]

Felton's speech became famous throughout the South but not, she at first claimed, in the way she had intended. As a sister Georgian and Methodist, and as an avid reader of *The Constitution*, Corra Harris had undoubtedly read excerpts of Felton's speech. References in Harris' essays reflected the activist's assumptions and rhetoric, especially that concerning danger to white women along the rural highway. When her speech had a brief resurrection in North Carolina a year later, Alexander Manly, the black Wilmington editor, had embraced Ida Wells' view of such a hateful screed. In response, Felton called for Manly to be lynched, charging that "the black race will be destroyed by the whites in self-defense unless law and order prevail in regard to the crime of rape and lynching that follows."[15] The statement is a far cry from Felton's original defense of the speech as softened by her conditional "Ifs." Something had changed. Northerners had attacked her and her homeland. She had become the victim, she wrote, of a "savage editorial" in the *Boston Evening Transcript*. The editor, she observed in *The Constitution*, is "eager to fling reproaches at the women of the South and denounces my address and the applause it received as 'almost fiendish sentiment.' I favor shooting mad dogs," she wrote, and she favored dispatching any "human beast" that destroyed a child. Blame for lynching rests, she contended, on white politicians in both sections who made "the Negro and his political influence so important."[16]

This last point was another article of faith among white Southerners who defended lynching. It had issued from another Georgian in *The Independent* the week before Corra Harris' commentary on the "facts" that "explained" the murder of Sam Hose. The Reverend William P. Lovejoy had written to denounce the lynching, and he may very well have discussed the matter with Harris before she sent her essay to *The Independent*. He had presided over her "conversion" as a young preacher and had helped her navigate a traumatic familial crisis.[17] In his essay, he had provided the broader political framework, as he understood it, to the passionate commentary she provided a week later. Lovejoy pointed out that a "mob of masked men" had lynched African Americans suspected of arson several weeks before Hose's murder. He then recounted the approved narrative of homicide and rape, which he refused to defend. He denounced the lynching of an African American preacher whom he probably knew. Such a "record of blood" was, he wrote, profoundly unsettling and he tried to explain the facts that had led to violence.

First of all, Lovejoy insisted, Southerners faced a generation of young black men filled with "an exalted notion" of their own "importance and rights." They had been taught by Northerners to believe they were better than "Southern 'white trash'." Worse, politicians had enfranchised black men, inflating their sense of worth still further. As a result, young blacks believed they could mingle with white people in public facilities. To rein in such dangerous aspirations, whites should restrict the suffrage of African Americans to the educated few and place the coming generation of black children under the tutelage of white Christians. He wanted black people to behave: They should become more responsible, respectful, deferential, abstemious, and pious. Lovejoy did not say so, but his expectations for black folk were the very same as those recently celebrated by a historian of Southern Methodist missions to the enslaved.[18]

ENTERING EDEN

When Corra Harris ventured into the national discussion of lynching, she had known men like Lovejoy for a long time. Only a few years after his preaching had launched her into the faith, she had married a Methodist preacher. When she first wrote to *The Independent*, she had lived for almost a decade in a hothouse of Methodist piety: the tiny village of Oxford, Georgia, where Emory College and the Methodist Episcopal Church, South dominated daily life. Lundy Harris had brought her there a little over a year after they wed in February 1887. They had met while teaching in a local academy and were married soon after he received his license to preach. He had experienced a profound personal transformation preceded by a long period of shame, remorse, and prayer. He was now ready, he announced, to meet "God's demands on the soul," which meant accepting the pastoral care of five churches in rural Georgia.[19]

Lundy seemed destined to assume this role; his father and grandfathers had been Methodist ministers: neither he nor his brothers, Henry and William, could escape the family business. When Corra first met him, he had been an enchanting, well-read, and delightful conversationalist. It was Lundy's charm, wit, and eloquence that had drawn her to him, not his piety. In addition, he was well acquainted with important people; his mentor after graduating from Emory College was one of the most influential churchmen in the South. Atticus Greene Haygood, former president of Emory College, had married them on that cold wintry day, and soon, to Corra's great relief, one of Lundy's close friends was named the new president of the same college.[20]

Brides once learned early in their married lives that courtship does not prepare them for reality. This theme carried many of Corra's novels, and much later she "remembered" her mother's countenance at her own wedding as having conveyed a wretched foreboding. A few months after the ceremony, Corra was once again living with her parents; the penurious life of a country preacher's wife was too harsh for a young pregnant woman who had not yet celebrated her nineteenth birthday. She had nevertheless gathered experiences, disappointments, surprises, and insights she could later use to write her most famous book. After giving birth to her first child, Faith, Corra joined Lundy in Oxford where his friend, President Warren Akin Candler, had summoned him to preside over the pre-collegiate courses preparing boys to enter Emory College.

Lundy had been there before. She surely knew that, but she may not have understood exactly why he had so abruptly left Oxford in shame four years before they met. In the spring of 1882, Lundy had broken the calm of Sunday morning worship in the Oxford Methodist Church by publicly confessing to an embarrassed congregation that he deserved to be stricken from the rolls of the church. He had enjoyed a drunken debauch – possibly in a nearby brothel – during which he had behaved quite "indecently." He resigned from the faculty and fled to his mother's farm where he expected physical labor to cleanse him. The next six years allowed Lundy time to grow in grace. Consequently, when Candler began to think of reforming Emory's faculty, Atticus Haygood insisted their repentant friend be appointed. Lundy "is absolutely competent," the former president wrote, and "he will be absolutely loyal to us." The Emory College student paper welcomed Harris, absent evidence, as a "thorough scholar, a deep thinker, an excellent teacher and a Christian gentlemen." Thus introduced, Lundy and his Eve entered the village she would remember as her Garden of Eden. Oxford was, she would write much later, "where the mind I have now was created."[21]

God planted Eden; Methodists planted Oxford. The village was a mile away from a railway station near the county seat of Covington to which it was connected by a mule-powered trolley car. Oxford was named for the English University town where Methodism had emerged under the aegis of John and Charles Wesley in the 1740s. Emory was founded in 1836 and named for a dead Methodist bishop; it produced the Methodist aristocracy of Georgia. The college's most famous alumnus was Lucius Quintus Cincinnatus Lamar, who was an elected public official in both Georgia and Mississippi. He was also a Confederate officer and diplomat, a US Senator, and an Associate Justice of the United States Supreme

Court. In 1875, the college began a long recovery from the agony resulting from the Civil War; it benefitted from Haygood's presidency as he persuaded Northern and Southern philanthropists to invest in its future. When his protégé, Warren Candler, was elected president in 1888, both men knew the institution still needed extensive aid, as all small colleges did, but they were more optimistic than they had been for a long time. Lundy Harris was supposed to be a partner in renovating the College.

How Edenic Oxford was depended of course on one's perspective. Looking back from the early twenty-first century, the village appears to have fostered a priggish, conformist, and excruciatingly *petit bourgeois* environment where everyone knew everyone and no one could escape the curiosity or censure of her neighbors. "The whole town," Corra later remembered, "steamed with religious fervor" and some denizens simmered in an "outraged piety" that could have profited from a dash of humor. From the perspective of people committed to the late nineteenth-century Methodist version of Christianity and to the training of young men for professions and businesses in the New South, Oxford could be a welcome haven from the poverty, violence, uncertainty, and disappointments of agricultural depression, urban conflict, and political warfare. Sanctuary did not necessarily prevent disagreement, of course: Lundy once came home fuming after "words" with the President, because, "When you touch one of his puritanical prejudices Candler has got a mind like a bone felon."

Other words, which might have been exchanged in possible disputes between the races, were probably repressed by African Americans in a reluctant and sometimes testy silence; at least they are absent from available written records. For white people, the labor pool of black cooks, gardeners, washer-women, handy-men, and day laborers provided a matrix of "help" to sustain a way of life that could be very pleasant indeed for whites. There was very little crime; the high jinx of adolescent college boys were usually rather tame, and the institutions of lascivious worldliness such as sporting houses and bars were over a mile away in Covington.[22] The lay of the land did not allow a moat. For Corra, the improved income and housing in Oxford were certainly better than the bleakness surrounding a country church. For Lundy, the prestige, salary, and professional camaraderie provided by his appointment initially made Oxford as Edenic for him as it was for Corra.

Unlike most small towns, Oxford had been the home to actors in a national drama. The event was triggered by Yankee fanaticism that broke the largest American Protestant denomination. At least this was the way Southern Methodists remembered the story. In 1844 at the national quadrennial General Conference of the Methodist Episcopal Church in New York City, moderate antislavery ministers, prodded by testy abolitionists, forced most Southern Methodists into schism. Bishop James Osgood Andrew, who lived in Oxford, was discovered to have become a slaveholder. The man came from a slaveholding family and had, not surprisingly, married women who owned slaves, but he denied that he was legally a slaveholder, thus honoring rhetorically at least, the antislavery innocence of the Wesleyan past.

But then he had to reconsider: maybe he was a master, he admitted, but only accidentally and reluctantly. He still felt compelled to admit that being a slaveholder was a burden rather than the stewardship proslavery theorists claimed. He had, he explained, been bequeathed a young mixed race girl whom he intended to send to Liberia when she became of age, if she so desired. Or, she could remain with Andrew's family and live as if she were in fact "free." The bishop had acted responsibly, he claimed, and the young girl was enslaved only in law, not reality. Andrew neglected to tell the conference that he was also actually if not legally the master of fourteen other slaves. In response to what was known at the time, the Yankee-dominated General Conference asked the bishop to "suspend his labours" until he had rid himself of his "impediment," that is, his slave(s). Abolitionist extremists had created a martyr. Kitty became a petted servant who cared for Andrew's wife and lived in "freedom" in a little house on the bishop's property until she died victorious in the faith.

When Corra and Lundy settled in Oxford the story had been told, retold, improved, and polished by villagers into a morality play of Yankee hypocrisy and Southern duty. White Methodist sentimentalism remembered Andrew as a Christ figure: "Noble man! He suffered himself accursed for the sake of his brethren and his kinsmen. He was never heard to utter a word of complaint." The story was inspiring, but African Americans may have had a different version. Since the tight little community knew of many erotic crossings of the color line in and around Oxford, shouldn't we be suspicious of Andrew's special care for Kitty? This is a question that a recent student has asked because it flows from the conventional wisdom of black folk based on the experience of generations.

The enslaved and the freed knew that whites' understanding of their relations with blacks flowed from positive interpretations of the master-slave relationship salved by evangelical piety. African Americans knew that the innocence claimed by most whites was degraded by the realities of power and sex; thus many if not most of them believed that Kitty could have been Andrew's daughter. Others thought she could have been related in another capacity. Knowing the ways of white men, ministerial or not, African Americans in Oxford to this day believe Andrew's relations with Kitty were indeed personal, and possibly more sexual than benevolent.[23] Corra would not have credited this version when she entered Eden, but her husband might have. Much later, she, too, would have reason to believe it.

Corra's sense of well-being in Oxford was not the fount from which streamed her angry essays. Neither did the ideology of Christian service and missionary outreach associated with the College stoke her fury. Personal prejudices learned within her family of origin may of course have made her more susceptible to warnings of peril from black men but there is no evidence to suggest that she was ever in any personal danger or even believed that she was. She never mentioned learning danger signals from her parents, and they certainly never came from the climate of opinion that settled on the College. African Americans may have been invisible to her, or seen as merely part of her environment or furnishings. To be sure, Corra could remember her parents having employed domestics and field hands but even the black woman who cared for her as a child was a mere shadow in her memory. Her fiction included no black people save for one dark mistress of a wayward husband, and in her memory of Oxford they seemed not to have existed – except in one traumatic case.[24]

When Harris recalled Emory and its village as sources of "the mind" she possessed in 1924, she thought of the religious obsessions of her husband, the nitpicking sermons of tedious ministers, and the suffocating piety of "a few cloven-hoofed saints."[25] Oxford had its flaws, but it was still Edenic. Her quiet nights in Oxford had never been "pierced through," as she imagined in her essays for *The Independent*, "by the cry of some outraged [white] woman."[26] Rather, she had slept in safety within a world that, superficially at least, reminded her of the garden from which mankind had once been dispatched.

DISTURBANCES IN EDEN

Oxford was founded to exemplify the evangelical Protestant emphasis on personal salvation through faith in Christ Jesus. If that emphasis was complex enough to have many different denominational expressions, it was, nonetheless, a mood and regimen that provided believers with a firm conviction of their righteousness, confirmed by a subjective experience of God's Grace. That experience was authenticated by reference to select verses and chapters of the Protestant Bible and acceptance into the community of believers. New converts were supposed to believe the same things that their elders believed. Consensus was highly prized; but what if all believers did not repent of the same sins? What if knowledge of the Bible birthed unexpected interpretations or the familiar language of faith was spoken or written in new ways with suspicious nuances? The plasticity of Southern Evangelical Protestantism had allowed change in emphasis and insight before, when it benefited those in power. The mood that had encouraged preachers to "proclaim liberty to the captives" and elevated outcasts, women, and slaves through faith into a redeemed people at the end of the eighteenth century had been tamed long before the Civil War. Slavery and Christian masters had changed that mood and allowed the splintering of Christianity into adaptations dictated by race, gender, and class.

The evangelical ethos affected both black and white, which meant that the two peoples might share certain moods and styles at times and on certain things. Both appreciated evocative public oratory and a catharsis of emotion that converted the individual from unbelief and carelessness to faith. Both shared a commitment to self-discipline in Christ, and the supreme authority of the Bible – in as much as it was accessible to and believable by blacks.

As Dixie was being transformed into the New South, change confronted the religious once again. The new towns, schools, and cities dramatically enlarged the middle classes. Their wealth helped build new kinds of Methodist, Baptist, Presbyterian, Episcopalian, and Disciples churches. These included not only country churches and simple piety, but also urban ostentation, ecclesiastical complexity, educational reform, and conflict about the meaning and authenticity of religious faith. Christian denominations were publishing new periodicals, recruiting new ministers, and strengthening their institutional presence in colleges and schools.[27]

In the wake of Reconstruction, these changes required ministerial leaders to develop marketing and negotiating skills. They had to finance new enterprises, cooperate with churchmen across denominational lines, and persuade the new men of the New South to help build new urban ministries, hospitals, training schools, and colleges. Building institutions carried the logic of contracting and bargaining that seemed far from the expressiveness of revivals in which charismatic preachers elicited the spontaneous shout of "Glory!" Middle class women in towns and cities expanded domestic and auxiliary roles into public responsibility. They became Sunday school teachers in new educational programs; they became missionaries to the Orient or the city. Lottie Moon, for example, became a symbol of Baptist mission and the personification of Baptist women. Activist Methodist women became urban missionaries or deaconesses who in some cases took on "pastoral" functions.[28]

As the Harrises settled in Oxford, their coreligionists were struggling with how to celebrate the Divine within the logic of this New South. The results of their grappling reflected progress and anticipation for some, and loss, regret, anxiety, and anger for others. With so much human activity, divine action seemed to disappear and religious intensity to diminish. "The roar of commerce, the click of the telegraph, and the whistle of the engine have well-nigh drowned out the voice of God," complained one evangelist.[29] Daily life was becoming more "worldly" and the "world" was becoming even more attractive, and worse, more accessible. This worldliness had stoked what Lundy Harris called Warren Candler's "puritanical prejudices" as he fought the forces of darkness by emphasizing traditional Methodist asceticism. He attacked dancing, drinking, and drama. While a pastor, he had expelled members of his church for attending the theatre because it yielded to the "vain pomp and glory of the world."

The fact that those expelled defended themselves eloquently and without any trace of guilt suggested the depth of the danger Candler faced. He castigated staged productions for enflaming the passions, encouraging wit, and portraying farce and tragedy as if normal people experienced them. Remember, he admonished his flock, Abraham Lincoln had been shot in a theatre. It was bad enough for recalcitrant church members to defy him, but when an actress actually challenged Candler's condemnation of the theatre in the middle of Sunday service the enemy was becoming far too impertinent. Who knew but that church members might even be dancing? That distraction was even more dangerous than the theatre because it excited much more than the imagination, and this insight, too, made Candler's pastorate a tempestuous one for a few of his (former) church members.[30] Drinking alcoholic beverages also elicited Candler's wrath. As the chief Southern Methodist partisan of traditional propriety, Candler fought for temperance legislation but not in league with the Women's Christian Temperance Union. Those women had actually demanded the right to vote![31]

Other traditionalists were as disturbed as Candler at changes that suggested a loss of religious fervor and Christian discipline. Although they agreed with Candler's diagnosis, they thought he was not radical enough. Labeled as censorious and bigoted "Holy Ghost people" by their enemies, not a few ministers and lay people began sensibly to suspect that the evangelical preoccupation with the new birth had become more form than substance. They therefore insisted that the conversion experience be followed by a "second blessing," an indwelling of the Holy Spirit, which they claimed had once been essential to Methodist piety. To be sure, in the eighteenth century, John Wesley had expected his people to go on to "Christian perfection" after conversion, a process he called "entire sanctification," which meant "Holiness." Wesley's critics among strict Calvinists and latitudinarian Anglicans had condemned the idea of "perfection" and later Methodists reinterpreted it.

During the nineteenth century, the trajectory of most American Wesleyan theology was to consider perfection less a "blessing" and more an ideal. But during the 1840s and 1850s there had been a revival of holiness among Northern Methodists, and after the war, this revival invaded the South. Candler was suspicious of this Yankee invasion and he was never comfortable with holiness partisans for damaging Methodist unity. A few had even had the gall to condemn Coca Cola, the new drink popularized by Candler's wealthy brother, Asa. In 1882, when holiness ministers began to publish *The Tongue of Fire*, bishops feared the worst. As perfectionists began to discipline church members for insufficient seriousness, schism loomed. The asceticism of the reformers could also spark domestic as well as denominational disquiet. The Reverend J. O. A. Clark discovered to his great dismay that his earnest young daughter had embraced a "second blessing" while he was under attack. These "crazed" people, he wrote her, "sentence your father to the pains of hell because he smokes cigars. His life of devotion to Christ and the Church for forty years goes for nothing." Condemning Clark's habit suggested the nature of the conflict; a cigar was not always a cigar.[32]

Most Methodist clergy followed the lead of Lundy Harris' mentor, Atticus Haygood, who condemned what he feared was censorious and schismatic fanaticism. He and his like-minded colleagues insisted that Wesley's emphasis on holiness meant seeking spiritual maturity through a lifelong agenda of learning, meditation, and practice. This commitment was acceptable to "holiness" folk, but they wanted to be sure that people gathered into the flock under the Good Shepherd were sheep. They saw a few wolves. They feared the flexibility of those who invited Christians to "be brought into sympathetic communion with opinions that are living truths to other men." Holiness folk did not want "sympathetic communion" with such thinkers as the Yankee Transcendentalist Ralph Waldo Emerson or the Scottish philosopher Thomas Carlyle. Equally dangerous were the English cultural critic Matthew Arnold, the English novelist George Eliot (Mary Ann Evans), and the French philosopher Victor Cousin.

They were suspicious of a temperament that could embrace "Evolution as a Method of Creation," and which encouraged a theologian to rewrite doctrinal standards in modern language. They could not agree that "higher criticism" of the Bible could explain scripture. Engaging the Bible as a compendium of texts to be understood within their historical and cultural contexts, not as the unchanging word of God, was anathema. Conservatives were profoundly disturbed by such treacherous flexibility and found it difficult to engage innovators in civil conversation. The latter hoped discussion could be conducted according to the aphorism: "In essentials unity, in non-essentials liberty, in all things charity." If the faith were in danger, however, charity was no virtue. The debate, of course, was over what was essential. [33]

Corra Harris personified believers who disturbed holiness people. As a young wife teaching Sunday school in the Vatican of Georgia Methodism, she had revealed an "outlaw streak." She denounced the misogyny of St. Paul and dismissed Biblical passages that reflected poorly on the divine. She once claimed to have early embraced God as creator in an evolutionary process inferred from Genesis after being "compelled to take off [her] shoes before the mighty progress of science." But never, she insisted, "has my faith in this first chapter of the Scriptures been shaken." She confessed to having received inspiration from the Bible when the Holy Ghost unleashed her imagination, but she pointed out that she was no literalist. "I prefer to spell out my own scriptures," she confessed, "and interpret them according to my own case, and in this way I have been able to preserve what may be regarded as an archaic and astounding faith in the Word as a mirror of the Mind of the Almighty."

She detested the wielding of scripture as a weapon by angry preachers; it was impossible to defer to a "man who has literal-minded damnation ideas." Living among earnest Methodists much of her life, Harris concluded that the "satisfaction of saints in their piety has always seemed to me despicable." She thought it "a form of deceit never justified by the facts. And the gratified air they give themselves is not to be confounded with simple honest human happiness." It was easier to forgive sinners than saints and she could never forgive "perfectionists" for demanding a piety that was "worse than damnable." Religion was supposed to enable women to become self-reliant, secure, and happy. Everyone, Harris believed, was "entitled to his [meaning "her"] own God, which is the same God no [one] can escape."[34] This was not orthodox theology, she knew, but it was satisfying and sensible to her.

ATTICUS HAYGOOD'S GOSPEL: BROTHERHOOD IN BLACK AND WHITE

When Corra and Lundy entered Eden with the blessings of Atticus Haygood and Warren Candler, the College was touted as the training ground for a Christian elite. The College, Emory students were told, was founded to improve "the human race" by teaching students how to think. The platitude was belied, however, by an emphasis on discovering one's appropriate place by deferring to authority, obeying rules, cultivating politeness, and avoiding drink and dance.[35] Not all students professed faith in Christ, of course, and after becoming president, Warren Candler tried to reach the reluctant minority in nightly protracted meetings in late October 1888, but failed. Some students still played cards, and some undoubtedly went to Covington, where dangerous distractions awaited adventurous students. Indeed, some realists thought Emory students to be just as rowdy, mischievous, and undisciplined as those at the University of Georgia (even if they didn't dance),[36] but the favored fiction was that they were the future Christian leaders of the South.

The aspiration to Christian manliness valued by Haygood demanded courage, honesty, self-discipline, sobriety, knowledge, faith, and wisdom. These qualities were to be achieved through "free but reverent inquiry" that brought, proclaimed Corra Harris' husband, "Jesus Christ to the front; where the great blazing issues, moral, political, and social are enlisting for their decision the energies of all the most holy, the most stainless and the most devoted spirits of our time." In rhetoric all too familiar to students in Southern Christian colleges, Lundy Harris announced, "Never before in the history of the world was cowardice by educated men in the face of evil and wrong so black a treachery against God and humanity, or apathy so dark a crime."[37] Harris' language was grandiose; it was deficient in specifics, and it was delivered from a conviction that the young men who heard it could actually recognize the "face of evil."

Some Americans thought that face should be evident to such men when they looked into a mirror. Many beyond the reach of Harris' voice could have made a damning case for the cowardice and apathy of young educated white Christian men. Rebecca Felton had made it on behalf of raped black girls and women. She and the WCTU had made it on behalf of women who were denied citizenship rights and safe haven from male predators. The Reverend Henry Hugh Proctor of Atlanta, Chaplain Theophilus Steward, and the editors of *The Independent* had made it on behalf of lynched African Americans. Ida B. Wells had done so as well. Thousands of African Americans throughout the United States could very easily have made it in their own behalf. Harris, however, could not see what he called the "face of evil" so obvious to women activists, Northern critics, and African Americans. Harris wanted, he said, to release the creative energy of his students; he was a dedicated teacher and he wanted them to do their best to succeed. But the inflated language of manliness, courage, and honor lost its grandeur when it lapsed all too easily into propriety, work, success, and Christian chauvinism.[38]

Lundy Harris' heroic ideal was shared by all contesting parties within the Church–traditionalists like Candler, rigorists like holiness reformers, and latitudinarians. Religious individualism was as obvious among refugees from literalism and sectarian discourse as it was to Corra Harris, when she insisted that everyone was entitled to his/her "own God."[39] The individualism that all parties sustained was not a system of values that encouraged dissent from conventional wisdom or entrenched prejudices, or respect for unpopular conclusions. The focus on individual salvation through a "new birth" or a "second blessing" or her "own God" was evangelical in emphasizing personal transformation through self-discipline, inner conviction, and emotional satisfaction. Such devotees might not be able to cite specific Bible chapters or verses as justification for their beliefs, but they were sure their values and insights were consistent with a "Biblical" understanding.

The best example of a heroic Christian life, Lundy Harris believed, was that of Atticus Haygood.[40] Haygood had been a chaplain to Confederate soldiers and, after the Civil war, had joined the renewed Methodist bureaucracy in Nashville. He was elected president of Emory College in 1875 and three years later began to edit, with Lundy Harris' assistance, the Methodists' *Wesleyan Christian Advocate*. He resigned the editorship after three years but continued as President before serving as agent for the Connecticut-based John L. Slater Fund that dispensed money to Southern black schools and colleges. In 1882 he was elected a bishop of the Methodist Episcopal Church, South [MECS], which office he refused until elected once again in 1890 after having left both Emory College and the Fund. By 1893 he was once again ensconced in Oxford, from which seat he continued to exercise his episcopal duties until his death.[41]

When Lundy brought his wife and child to Oxford in 1888, Haygood lived in Decatur, Georgia, but his influence still suffused the campus. Both Lundy and President Candler were bonded to him if in different ways.

Haygood pushed colleagues to include black people in their plans for higher education. Emory became an early source of support for joint efforts by the MECS and the Colored Methodist Episcopal Church to establish Paine Institute in Augusta, Georgia, for the education of black men and women. He encouraged Morgan Calloway, chair of Emory's Department of English, to accept the presidency of Paine. Later, as agent for the Slater Fund, Haygood channeled money into Paine and encouraged his protégé, Warren Candler, to work for the Institute, which became a source of personal pride to Candler until his dying day.[42] African Americans' energy, eloquence, and progress could sometimes move Haygood to extravagant emotional outbursts in private when with intimate friends such as Lundy Harris. At an 1881 ecumenical Methodist meeting, to which he took Lundy, he heard African American eloquence surpassing that of whites and was mesmerized. This was, he insisted, a "marvelous age" and he had felt this way before when he had written *Our Brother in Black*. He thought the future would be much brighter if white Christians engaged blacks within the familiar solidarity of Christian fraternity and sorority.

The book was published in 1880 and scolded Southerners for not trying to solve "race problems" they had created. He hoped his church could cease its "fearful tendency to live in history for its sentiment." The reference was probably to Methodists' boasting of missions to the enslaved, but may also have referred to their feted role in helping launch the Colored Methodist Episcopal Church. These labors were history; they had been "temporary expedients." Haygood wanted longlasting improvement. We should now, he insisted, remove all hindrances that whites have thrown in the way of African Americans. Haygood knew Southerners were angered by entreaties to renounce racial prejudices, which they denied embracing. He nonetheless plunged into a discussion that he knew most whites believed was "contamination" itself. He had broken a regional taboo by writing like a meddling Yankee and inviting other Southerners to do the same.

Once confessing their sins, Haygood believed, Southern whites would be freed to support black people aggressively by improving their educational institutions and funding them more generously. Haygood broke taboo further by praising the work of Northern teachers and missionaries as well as that of the federally supported Freedmen's Bureau during

Reconstruction. He admitted he had once dismissed Northerners' support of blacks as harmful but was now shamed by Southerners' ignoring the good these selfless Yankees had done. As the foundations had been laid, he insisted, white Southerners could improve on the missionaries' accomplishments, but that would require radical change. Respect black people as you respect yourself, he pleaded; respect their family relations; respect their autonomy; respect the honest labor that they do. Respect would yield more equitable contracts with black workers and better pay; it required increased ownership of land by African Americans and improved farming methods. Respect also meant refining the religious life of African Americans and supporting their churches. Unlike most whites, Haygood believed blacks should continue to vote.

The respect on which Lundy Harris' mentor insisted called for an empathic understanding of blacks. Such emotional maturity was beyond the capacity of most white Southerners. Haygood employed Biblical metaphors, which Christians could not fail to concede as appropriate guides to daily life; he did this to shame them. The Negro, he wrote, is our *Neighbor* – as in loving the neighbor as oneself. He is our *Brother*, implying in the argot of the day that she is also our *Sister*! By appealing to whites in familiar evangelical language, he hoped to entice white co-religionists into "mutually helpful and affectionate" relations between the races. Aware of the stranglehold of fantasized illicit sex on the Southern white imagination, he faced a momentous task. He nonetheless challenged whites' contempt for blacks, which was based on assumptions of African American licentiousness. He demanded whites respect the sanctity of blacks' family life and the chastity of their women.

Slavery had damaged the virtue of both races, Haygood wrote, but we can heal injuries of the past if we whites teach "Negroes" to respect our rights by respecting theirs. In thus appealing to the familiar moral theology of reforming others by personal example, he had been unable to slough off the missionary fallacy of accepting those who are different as they become more like the missionary. As for the universal white Southern accusation that such ideas as his favored "social equality" and intermarriage, he dismissed the "hysterical" notion as "lunacy." He hoped there was a "new south forming freed from the prejudices of the past."

In calling attention to Southern whites' racial prejudices, Haygood had condemned himself. In praising the work done by Northern teachers and the Freedman's Bureau he had committed treason. In dismissing any dangers from "social equality," he had committed heresy. In pleading for whites to respect black people he had challenged reality. His enemies let loose a "torrent of mendacity and abuse," but his appeal won the support of other progressives – few though they were.

The phrase, but not the sentiments of "Our Brother in Black," became famous in the late nineteenth-century South among African Americans and whites who loved or hated it. An African American minister remembered the phrase in 1898 when condemning the white insurrection in Wilmington, North Carolina; he hoped for a better future with "our brother in white." What Lundy Harris thought of the phrase is to be inferred from his silence. He was well aware of Haygood's enthusiastic appraisal of African American leaders' capacity for excellence, but Harris did not celebrate his mentor's ideas on race in memoriam. As for Warren Candler, in a rare act of Oedipal rebellion, he attacked his mentor's book in the Nashville *Christian Advocate* when it first appeared. The South, he whined, "does not need a baptism of tears over crimes that she never committed in order that she may be christened 'New South.'"[43]

When Corra and Lundy Harris settled in Oxford, they knew that the man who had married them the previous year was committed to improving African American life. The Harrises also were aware that after resigning the presidency of Emory College, Haygood had become the agent of the Slater Fund. They probably did not realize how "full of hope & joy" Haygood was "in the full assurance that the cause of Negro education is taking fast hold of the minds & consciences of opinion-makers in the South."[44] If neither shared the intensity of Haygood's commitment to improving blacks' lives, both would nonetheless have known that he continued to be a public voice on behalf of his "Brother in Black."

As the Harris family entered Oxford in the fall of 1888, Lundy's mentor was engaged in a public exchange with a man who hated the philosophy of Haygood's most famous book. Senator John B. Eustis of Louisiana started the discussion with an article for the October 1888 edition of the *Forum*. In it, he denounced New Englanders for preventing African Americans from working in their chosen professions; he celebrated Southern race relations that made African Americans "happy, contented and satisfied" with a life absent "the terrible distresses of poverty." Anyone who wanted to "equalize the condition" of black and white in the United States, he wrote, possessed "a false estimate of the moral attributes or mental capacity of the Negro."[45]

In reply through the columns of *The Independent*, Haygood confessed he had had to read Eustis' article twice in order to make sense of it because it was so confused and confusing. Eustis, Haygood wrote, had satirized Massachusetts but ignored the topic the Senator had been asked to address by *Forum* editors: that is, Race Relations in the United States. Haygood could have asked the Senator how "happy, contented, and satisfied" were his black constituents when recently driven from their homes by white mobs in the Louisiana parishes of Vermillion, Lafayette, and Iberia, or forced to bury family members massacred in the village of Freetown,[46] but he didn't.

Eustis had insisted that race relations in the South were not the concern of anyone but Southerners. Haygood thought this comment foolish because a discussion of race was national in scope and Southerners of both races needed all the help they could get. African Americans had made "marvelous" progress, Haygood argued, but they needed further aid and if we take into account the providence of God they will receive it. We cannot solve the problems of race by ignoring the "saving influences of the Christian religion," which he believed Eustis had done. What the Methodist sage meant is easily teased out of his approach to *Our Brother in Black* and the final sentences of his reply to the Senator. Those "saving influences" dictated that whites respect African Americans; they required putting into practice the values emphasized in the "Sermon on the Mount." The theme was inherent in most of what Haygood had written about African Americans since 1880. If he did not mention the white atrocities in Eustis' Louisiana, he knew they existed. He insisted that "no question involving the rights and wrongs of men, civilized or savage, white or black, was ever settled by any system of mere repression." In closing, he wrote: "If there be a Divine Providence, no man need be afraid to do right to-day; nay, he will fear only doing wrong."[47] He implied Eustis was fearless; it was not a compliment.

COMPLICATING BROTHERHOOD

Haygood's article in *The Independent* was supposed to launch a campaign organized by famed novelist and essayist George Washington Cable. Unlike many ministers,[48] the author of *Our Brother in Black* found in Cable a kindred spirit. The latter hoped to publish essays in national journals about matters of concern to Southerners. With the help of Professor William H. Baskervill of Vanderbilt University in Nashville, Tennessee, Cable recruited several renowned Southerners such as Haygood to join his Open Letter Club as a vanguard to encourage Southerners to help blacks better their lives. Cable was well-known not only for his fiction but also for his essays on the ways in which Southerners had oppressed African Americans, a thesis that most whites could not abide. The master class had made black people aliens, menials, and demons, Cable insisted. Whites had assigned "a disqualifying moral taint [to] every drop of negro [sic] blood." Cable was far more ferocious than Haygood in attacking whites for ignoring the manifestations of their oppression and lynching; "it is the fashion to ignore them. And yet," he wrote, "there they stand in all their naked, shameless, unpardonable savagery." Cable brought moral clarity and precision to Lundy Harris' flight of homiletic fancy as he lashed out at what Harris had called the "cowardice by educated men in the face of evil."[49] Harris and Cable lived in different worlds.

During the 1880s, Cable shared his insights in lectures throughout the South. He hoped to use the Open Letter Club to reach even more people. He was, however, naively optimistic and contemptuous of Southern manners, which made his task difficult. He soon committed one of the gravest sins possible in his native land when he accepted an invitation to dine with the family of J. C. Napier, a distinguished African American attorney in Nashville. The result was a furious public outcry from enraged whites who condemned Cable as an apostle of interracial sexual intercourse and, worse, marriage. Baskervill chided Cable that dining with a black family had allowed "the prejudices of thinking people [to be] joined to ignorance of the unthinking" and prevented a serious discussion of race.

Cable was furious at demands for caution: "I tell you, this soothing and pacifying and conciliating these people intoxicated with prejudice and political bigotry, is helping neither them nor any worthy interest."[50] This simple act and the subsequent demise of the Open Letter Club, suggests how difficult it was to achieve the goals suggested in *Our Brother in Black*. It is not clear what Haygood believed about Cable's breaking taboo. If the minister seems never to have commented on the squeamishness of whites who could not break bread or share the Eucharist with black people, he was clear in his dismissive contempt, rivalling Cable's, for those horrified by the phantasm of interracial marriage.[51]

By 1890, when he was elected to the episcopacy a second time, it was clear to informed Northerners and Southerners that Atticus Haygood was a champion of improved relations between whites and blacks. He believed that whites had to lead the drive toward that goal because they held the power. His article challenging Eustis was followed in *The Independent* with a symposium supporting his plea for advancing African American education. He then left the South for California to assume his episcopal duties. To his dismay, he found in the West a culture he experienced as alien, secular, and unpleasant; in 1893 he fled from exile back home to Georgia and settled in Oxford. He returned to his favorite task of writing. Apparently uninformed as to what was actually happening in the South, he celebrated a growing consciousness of "brotherhood" that would eventually "let the oppressed go free." But the oppressed were still being lynched and one hideous event seized his attention: the burning in February of Henry Smith before ten thousand people in Paris, Texas.

He thought about the spectacular murder for several months; it horrified him. In the October 1893 edition of *Forum* he attacked lynching as "a crime against God and man." He added: "The government that winks at lynching is vicious; the government that does not care is foolish and wicked; the government that cannot put it down is weak." Having thus returned to public discourse by condemning lynching, however, why would Haygood have his Christian commitment questioned by Ida B. Wells? Why did the woman who was fast becoming the best known anti-lynching activist in the nation not welcome Haygood's confessing his "horror" at the barbaric burning of a man in a supposedly civilized nation? Why did she not welcome him as an ally instead of a hypocritical enemy?[52]

The answers to these questions lay in Haygood's understanding of the crime for which Smith was burned. Few whites in Paris doubted that the "weak-minded" African American had killed four-year old Myrtle Vance, daughter of a police officer. A few Parisians thought Smith had killed Myrtle to avenge his having been "cruelly mistreated" while in custody; all thought he would be hanged legally.

Myrtle's father refused to wait. He claimed she had been "outraged with demoniacal cruelty and then taken by her heels and torn asunder in the mad wantonness of gorilla ferocity." Haygood believed Vance: Wells did not. She accused the bishop of being unable to assign responsibility for what he called a "crime against God." The bishop conceded it was "horrible to torture the guilty wretch"; he thought "the burning was an act of insanity." The word, "insanity," seemed to justify the lynching. If his own baby had been "dismembered," Haygood wrote, "I might also have gone into a [never-ending] insanity." Insanity erupted, he mused, when men found their loved ones violated. He slipped into a soliloquy on rape, claiming falsely that over 300 white women had been ravished by black men in the previous three months. Sexual violation, horrific violence, and false reports overwhelmed him. Hysteria trumped reality. Haygood had ditched his renowned hostility to conventional "Southern thought and deed," wrote a black author in *The Christian Recorder*; the bishop's words felt like "the sting of death."[53]

In pleading "insanity" for the mob, Haygood revealed none of the critical suspicion of popular opinion that characterized his earlier writings. In two books exposing the dangers of fanaticism he had condemned a dogmatic mentality that brooked no challenge to unverified notions. He had cautioned against capitulating to panic; "fixed ideas," he had written, could spawn "a dangerous sort of lunacy." But "lunacy" in Texas trumped moral accountability. In picturing the crime of which Smith was accused and imagining his own "insanity" at so horrendous an act, the bishop confessed that he'd have lost his capacity to act rationally. Vance and the people of Paris, he thought, must have been Christians; they must have been decent people who lost their minds to a rage that relieved them of blame and guilt.

Haygood insisted that Southerners "were never cruel-hearted people." Never! They were kind. They had been kind masters. They were kind to animals. They were kind to peaceable blacks, but "kind-hearted people could not tolerate the rape of their women." He then plunged into the swamp of Southern cliché. When blacks stop raping, he wrote, whites will stop lynching. If critics condemned rape as much as they condemned lynching, he huffed, both black and white Southerners would behave differently. He sank further into cliché as he excused the horrific moral catastrophe in Paris, Texas. Unless "the negro [sic] race" realized "the enormity of assaulting white women," he concluded, "the worst for both races is yet to come."[54]

The worst, however, according to Wells, had already been on display in Texas. Smith's torturers revealed a savage capacity for cruelty and a commitment to inflicting pain that was nauseating. Before an estimated crowd of ten thousand, men erected a platform on which to enact their sacrificial drama. In Myrtle Vance's little body innocence and purity had been destroyed. The result was a void in the communal imagination. To fill that void, the murderer had to be punished, but not according to the rules of due process. Those rules could not restore communal solidarity and peace. The violent killing of a child demanded that destruction of a monstrous evil be witnessed by the entire community so that all of them could participate in a ritual of purification achieved through unimaginable pain.[55] The drama was a human sacrifice that punished not just one man but all the evil imagined to be personified in him. Thus the sacrificers repeatedly rolled red hot irons down the length of Smith's body as his screams filled the firmament; they blinded him with the same irons and thrust a flaming rod down his throat after his shrieks had registered the awful pain that engulfed his universe. Then they burned him, hoping he was still alive, and "a hush spread over the people."[56]

Wells was not alone in her response to Haygood's explanation that "provocation" made men mad and rendered their actions guiltless. Provocation, wrote Chief Justice Logan Edwin Bleckley of the Georgia Supreme Court, "has nothing to do with the right or wrong of lynching negroes [sic]." The renowned Georgia jurist insisted that "No kind or degree of provocation will justify or even mitigate it." Lynching is evil in itself. Provocation did not cause lynching; lynching was caused by ethical failure and moral blindness in people who believed their "intense feelings" licensed them to punish wrong with wrong. The idea was absurd even if it was widely embraced. Setting aside the rule of law in the name of a so-called higher justice was beyond absurd; it was dangerous to a well-ordered society.

E. L. Godkin of *The Nation* agreed and a profoundly disturbed Roman Catholic priest did so as well. Father John Richard Slattery, rector of St. Joseph's Seminary for Negro Missions in Baltimore, argued that defense by provocation eviscerated Haygood's "whole argument." The Methodist's comments on black rapists had no basis in fact, Father Slattery wrote, as statistics demonstrated. The bishop's tortured reliance on insanity to explain Southern savagery relieved lynchers of guilt, the priest charged; it "exonerates [their] shocking crimes," and robs the goddess of Justice of her scales. In addition, Slattery observed, rumors of black rapists hid the damning acts of white rapists. Haygood had ignored relevant data and attempted to cover his fallacious assumptions with gross exaggeration. He had, Slattery conceded, justly condemned lynching – that was good. And maybe his hyperbole could "toughen" African Americans in their continuing battle to excel. "They are rising," the priest exclaimed; "and that is the root of all Southern complaints."[57]

Father Slattery was undoubtedly correct in his assessment of Southern complaints. Haygood's sympathy for Texas lynchers had rendered his own support of African American progress irrelevant in so far as Bleckley, Godkin, Slattery, and Wells were concerned. His rhetorical plea for whites' assistance in creating an independent African American yeomanry and honoring black women, workers, and families was lost before it could become a plan. He thought the joint enterprise with the Colored Methodist Episcopal Church at Paine Institute in Augusta was a sign of racial progress, but the school was never well funded. Blacks did not have the resources and whites did not have the will. Paine was a monument to good intentions rather than a vanguard institution of racial conciliation. Haygood believed that accepting the agency of the John L. Slater Fund was a Christian duty,[58] but that effort, he knew, could never deliver the support black colleges needed. His actions could not match his words; and he was good at words. Haygood was a preacher and an exhorter. Like Cable, he thought words could open minds and change biases. Then a Roman Catholic priest dismissed his hatred of lynching as mere "words, words, words." Wells called Haygood a hypocrite. He had tried to explain the "insanity" of a people in peril; but he was accused of justifying what he thought he had condemned. He still hoped the "oppressed" could be freed.[59]

Yet Haygood was changing in the way he understood race, current events, and lynching. The transformation occurred between his exchange with Senator Eustis and the burning of Henry Smith. From 1888 to 1893 he became more expressive about his identity as a "Southerner" and more sensitive to "attacks" on his region. In California, he had become desperately uncomfortable in what he experienced as a hostile environment. As a result, he felt his Southern origins most acutely as he returned home to Oxford. He was getting older, suffering strokes, and declining in health despite his relatively young age. He was in debt; he was terribly depressed; and he fled his demons with the help of whiskey. He did not answer those who criticized him on the Paris holocaust, but he did denounce Northern labor violence as "lynching by wholesale."[60]

Haygood ended his public life hoping that Americans could solve their "negro problem," as he called it, at least in one hundred years. Once insisting that whites change, he now repaired to the missionary model of progress. The Mission to Slaves had been dedicated to changing the enslaved, not the masters. The Mission was supposed to "recreate" Africans who resisted as best they could by recreating themselves according to their own religious knowledge. The drive to educate blacks after Emancipation was fueled by a desire to make them over. College professors can recognize this effort because they, too, want to change their students. Haygood shared the missionary ethos with associates who denounced lynching while insisting that things would not change until African Americans changed. White Christians believed black Christians should be more like their white mentors. The ways in which whites understood lynching by 1899 were shaped by this missionary mentality.[61] Few white Americans believed they should receive anything from Christian blacks except gratitude and deference. When they thought about lynching, well-meaning whites thought about what the victims had done and what black people generally were not doing. The evil of lynching lay not in whites' actions but in those they burned.

As Lundy Harris visited his mentor during the bishop's last days, he would have been keenly aware that Haygood had changed. He would have watched in dismay the depleted energy of the man who had given him his first job and supported him when he was disgraced. In commending Haygood to the Emory College student body, Lundy did not mention *Our Brother in Black*. He might have remembered the author's early optimism about race relations, but eulogies are not about failure as much as triumph in the face of death.[62] Lundy would have known that public discourse within which Haygood had once discussed race relations had been radically transformed since the publication of *Our Brother in Black*. Corra, who thought of her life in Oxford as having prepared her to become a writer, was a voracious reader. Haygood was one of her favorite authors, especially for his disgust at the pretensions of religious perfectionism. The bishop had married Corra to Lundy; he had encouraged Candler to bring Lundy back to Emory. He was a great man. He had thought about race for a long time. Corra would have learned from him, at last, that *Our Brother in Black* had become a rapist.

DISCOVERING THE BLACK MENACE IN THE WHITE FAMILY

In 1894, Lundy Harris was named Seney Professor Greek to replace Henry A. Scomp, whom Haygood had recruited in 1876. Scomp had studied in Germany and Greece for about ten years. He was steeped in classical and biblical Greek. At Emory he was known as a demanding teacher but one wholly engaged in college life. He hosted the junior class for Thanksgiving dinner and gave special tutorials in his home. No one believed he was a poor scholar or teacher. When Warren Candler became president he retained Scomp but by 1892 the two men were engaged in a heated dispute. They both supported the temperance cause, but Scomp was too radical for Candler because the professor supported women's suffrage. When suffragist Rebecca Latimer Felton praised Scomp and condemned Candler in public, the president believed that suffragists' "malice, and fanaticism" had harmed the college. He got rid of Scomp and persuaded the faculty to elect Lundy to the chair thus vacated. Lundy was safe; he disdained fanaticism. It was not clear, however, just how much Greek he knew.[63]

Lundy was a popular professor. One of his former charges remembered him as someone who had shaped his life for the better. Lundy had been an excellent mentor; he had strengthened the student's self-confidence and prepared him to be a popular minister in service to the Social Gospel and in opposition to segregation. Lundy's commitment to his students was shared with Corra; together they held symposia in their home for both colleagues and students. If a forlorn youth should happen to drop by on a late afternoon, he could find them ready to engage him in conversation that was both serious and playful. When they asked him to dine with them, the experience had been thrilling. Lundy's personal influence was complemented by his reputation as one of the most "eloquent preachers ever heard from the Oxford pulpit." In chapel, Lundy could challenge students to feel the "fatherhood of God – the perfect love and the perfect power." This desire for perfection, Corra complained, had all too often plunged him into a fearful depression. If she sometimes wondered if he would take his own life, in the spring of 1898 he seemed to be buoyant as he helped her prepare a wildly successful party after Emory's graduation exercises.

Lundy's shadow was gone for the moment, but two weeks later, in early June, it fell on her again. Lundy disappeared. Corra came home from shopping to find a note: He had gone to Texas. A man there had "the Spirit."[64] The news was devastating; it made no sense. But Corra realized that none of his religious torment over the past twelve years had made sense. He had far too often been torn by guilt and shame that afflicted her and paralyzed him. Lundy's older brother, Al, was convinced he was "crazy," she told Warren Candler, but she added: "I do not think he is any more insane than he has been ever since I married him." But why had his "madness" sent him to Texas to "consult two of the greatest cranks this country has ever produced!?" She was referring to Lundy's younger brother, Henry, and Nath Thompson, both recent Emory graduates and Methodist ministers in east Texas, but they had not beckoned him to Texas.

Rather, he had been pushed; the impetus came from a new colleague. Andrew Sledd had joined the faculty in January to teach Latin, which he had studied along with a major in Greek at Harvard University. Sledd's experience at Harvard had been invaluable. He learned he was not as intelligent as he thought he was and had to apply himself to achieve excellence. At Emory, Sledd learned less positive things: how low scholarly standards were and how high the rate of cheating. He also learned that the Seney Professor of Greek knew little Greek. Incompetence and hypocrisy seemed to be personified in Lundy Harris. Sledd discovered Corra's husband knew nothing of Pindar or Sappho and relied on an English translation for his study of Plato. Sledd's contempt must have stung;

whatever the two men talked about at the Harrises' party on May 24, it was certainly not Greek literature.[65]

If Lundy had been humiliated in private, Corra felt humiliated in public. She fled to her sister's home in Rockmart, Georgia. People, she feared, might think she had driven Lundy away; they might think anything and none of it good. She was at first in a panic – how could she pay the bills? How could she support her family? The answer came from Warren Candler, who became her confessor and guide. "Lean on me hard, Corrie," he told her; and she did so as the summer of 1898 became an emotional roller coaster. Her outpouring to Nettie and Warren Candler was therapeutic as she confessed how painful her marriage had been. I have, she sighed, suffered a "terrible expectation of disaster" in silence for so very long that when disaster finally struck "it made me garrulous." She "had to talk or go mad." But she found it profoundly difficult to talk herself out of the emotional trench into which she had been cast. She had lost all the comfortable artifacts of daily life and everything that sustained a positive sense of self. Something in her that "laughs and plans and sings" was dying. The same death hovered over her little daughter; she didn't know that a child could stay sad for so long. Corra poured out her heart to the newly consecrated Bishop Candler until she was spent.[66]

Lundy eventually returned home in disgrace. His Southwestern adventure became all too well-known as his "Austin debauch" among friends, students, relatives, colleagues, strangers, and the Emory Board of Trustees. Because his "debauch" in 1882 had mixed whiskey and sex in a brothel, it would not be a stretch of the imagination, given entries in a secret diary, to infer that he had awakened from a drunken night of sexual congress in an Austin, Texas, sporting house. Guilt-ridden and "in mental distress and moral confusion," he decided as penance to walk the twenty-five miles from Austin to his brother's home. Henry sent him back to Corra escorted by the Reverend William Lovejoy. In the meantime, Lundy was determined to confess his sins to as many people as possible. He was so enthusiastic in this penance that a minister suggested Lovejoy hide him in a mountain cabin until he stopped talking. Lundy, however, was relentless in confessing he had been "intimate with certain Negro women, married and unmarried in Oxford," as well as "others loose in their morals." He provided names, dates, and places "to set the record straight." Corra told him to stop! His "details" caused her "needless pain." He obeyed.[67]

Corra did not yet know what to do with what she had learned. Her first lesson was in the fragility of life. She learned danger could lie repressed until erupting in disaster, but she could not face the source of that danger. "Lundy's weakness," she had told Warren Candler when she first heard what had happened in Austin, was "not unchastity," but "madness!" "He is not," she insisted, a "deliberately unchaste man." His "madness" she had experienced for a long time, but she was numbed by his visiting prostitutes. She was also oblivious to his torment about sex, love, companionship, and marriage. In secret musings jotted down in a small notebook, he had wondered why Corra was so offended by sexuality. Did the offense cloud the meaning of love and marriage?[68] What he had hidden in his diary, he enacted in Austin. Then Corra realized that he had done something worse. He had bedded "Negro women, married and unmarried in Oxford." Those women may have been in her home as her cook, her washerwoman, or the daughter of the gardener who had strung the Chinese lanterns at her party in May. Someone she knew! They were the enemy.

Corra did not immediately record her thoughts about the details she didn't want to know. But the "details," as she imagined them, did appear in some of her novels when she wrote about weak and adulterous husbands. One is killed by his wife, whose female attorney wins acquittal for justifiable homicide. Others survive, but their inventive, strong, and assertive wives eventually surpass their wayward husbands in every possible way.[69] She did not, however, wait to become a novelist in order to vent her wrath; it erupted after the lynching of Sam Hose in the articles she wrote for *The Independent* to explain what she thought was the moral squalor of African American life. She had undoubtedly been thinking about the matter from the moment she began to reflect on the black women whom Lundy had detailed to so many men.

The couple separated to find gainful employment teaching; distance allowed her to avoid the censorship his presence would have imposed. Adultery and black women dominated her imagination more than the adulterer. To be sure, she conceded a black woman could be seduced by "the first wretch who approaches her with deceitful kindness." Corra may have recalled ways in which her husband had relaxed among black women servants. Lundy may have been all too willing to offer a "deceitful kindness" that allowed them to accept greater intimacy than Christian decorum permitted. It was *their* fault! Lundy did not agree. "My conduct," he raged to Candler, "was as criminal before God as if a white woman" had been involved. He was ashamed of what he had done to "poor wronged Negroes";[70] Corra was shamed by what *they* had done to *her*.

She displaced her anger with her husband and at their expulsion from Eden onto the women he had wronged. She broadcast her rage through

The Independent. She did not know the man listed as a boy in the US census as Thomas Wilkes. Sam Hose had never harmed her; no one like him had ever harmed her. Harris knew that the mob had been savage; she knew her friend, Reverend Lovejoy, had condemned the killing. She also knew the minister had assigned final responsibility for violence not to white people but a generation of aggressive black men. Corra sifted Lovejoy's insights through the sieve of her personal experience of black women's wickedness. She did not know any white woman who had been outraged; she never heard any guttural screams. She did not know Wilkes' mother, but she believed that the woman should have raised a better son.

Corra's self-consciousness had taken a terrible beating; she had had no way to strike back at the source of her trauma. She had not been able to call her husband to account even in private. She knew he was weak; she thought his religious torment signified that weakness; she feared for his sanity; and she protected him, as she believed good wives should. Her fury may not have matched that of Euripides' *Medea*, who slaughtered her own children in displaced rage, but more than a few Southern white women would have understood it.

Harris' way of dealing with her husband's sexual adventures was a strategy shared with white women throughout the region. The most famous diarist of the Civil War South, Mary Boykin Chesnut, had observed the habit in the context of slavery: Denial of what their husbands were doing with or to black women had sustained a carefully negotiated domestic peace. White women denied their men's adulterous sexual predations to protect themselves from the knowledge they feared could destroy their families. Denial was probably the least favorite but most pervasive pastime of white women in the South for over three centuries.[71] Corra's denial was not that Lundy misbehaved, he had! But he was not to blame. When the spectacular killing of Tom Wilkes became a symbol of white Southern savagery among Yankee critics, she needed to set them straight about the ultimate source of such evil. White men were not to blame; those who had birthed such a "hideous monster" as Hose were to blame. The pathology of Southern life lay not in the violence of white men but the licentiousness of black women.

THE GOSPEL ACCORDING TO CORRA

Corra's religious sensibility during this crisis can be inferred from her confessional letters to Warren Candler. Between June 7, 1898 and the end of October 1899 the distraught woman healed her trauma through writing those letters and sharing in the normalizing Christian practices

available to her in the home of her sister and brother-in-law. Corra's
words flowed out of the religion she had inherited and improved on as she
wrestled with her husband's threatening perfectionism and her neighbors'
self-satisfying piety. She could recall as a young girl having rushed to the
altar and returning to sister, mother, and father with an "air of augmented excellence."[72] The feeling was normal in the rituals of the Protestant South but Corra's submersion in the overwhelmingly religious
community surrounding Emory College was rare. She was underwhelmed
by her neighbors' self-righteousness; she thought their religion resulted
not so much in Christian charity as in tut-tutting scrutiny. She taught
Sunday school but never justified herself by citing scripture or mouthing
the conventional aphorisms of sin and salvation.

Within the intimacy of her family she was furious with her husband's
agonistic inner life, shadowed no doubt by episodes of shame erupting
from memories of his first expulsion from Oxford. As she unburdened
herself to the Candlers in the summer of 1898, she could not distinguish
between Lundy's depression and his religion. They seemed to collapse
into utter confusion. When, much later, Corra recalled for her admiring
readers the trajectory of her own spiritual pilgrimage, she dismissed
Lundy's religious obsessions as self-destructive. They demanded a certainty impossible to attain. Lundy's inner musings at the time, however,
may actually have been driven not by the desire for perfection, but by the
divided mind of his private and public selves as revealed in his private
notebook. Whatever the source, Corra thought his inner life was a mess
and hers more sensible. Her spiritual life lay in building a "nest for my
young ones."[73]

As Corra put her life in order, she believed that God had sustained her
and borne her pain long enough to allow her to transcend it. The terror
was gone, she wrote in relief; then it came back, making Lovejoy fear for
her life. But she was tough, and began to prepare for a new life beyond the
village. When she reported to Candler that her daughter, Faith, had been
"converted," the proud mother confessed her child's experience had
deeply affected her. Faith claimed to model her life on three biblical
axioms: First, "to 'cast the beam out of my own eye,' second, "the pure
in heart shall see God." Third, "that in as much as you do it unto the least
of these ye do it unto me!"[74] Faith's mother, however, ignored the
passages' implication of service and embraced instead self-discipline.
God was in the power that flowed into her when hers was gone. Maybe
that strength came from her Christian faith, even if at times she felt bereft
of it; maybe it surged from hope, but it was to her a gift from God. Faith's

"conversion" reminded Corra that life could be better through the familiar rituals of Southern culture.

Although Corra thought of herself and the South as Christian, the publisher of *The Independent* sometime later asked her how she could square that profession with her attitude to African Americans? William Hayes Ward had explained his own views of racial difference and elicited responses from Corra that were far more thoughtful than any of her essays on the subject. She was awed, she confessed, at Ward's "attitude to the negro [sic]," and suspected that he thought her illogical when she could forgive everyone who had wronged her except black women. "My conscience never requires me to be logical," she wrote. She later conceded Ward's position on racial justice was "the only ethical one," but insisted that "your northern power, ethics, and principles" made it impossible for Southerners ever to "do everlasting right." Corra doubted that "God will punish us any more for this that he will those who forced us into this position."[75]

To her editor, Paul Elmore More, she insisted that "equity [and] justice dwell only in the mind of God." Injustice to blacks was "not right, but it is the way of the world."[76] To Ward, she explained that only recently had she begun "to think"; she was admittedly confused. She was trying to keep her "relation to God simplified, [and] sincere through a faith which my reason does not always justify." To be sure, she conceded, I need converting, "for I think we often need that, the best of us, but I began a religious experience September 17, 1886, and I know that from that day till this, I have been sorry for my sins, my current sins, I mean, that I have done what good I could even to my own hurt and to the negroes [sic] no less than to the whites." She claimed never to have "lost that erectness of mind toward God in my most secret heart."[77] Time, reflection, and pain helped her relax the feelings she expressed to Ward. Thirty years later, Harris changed her mind about lynching and had become more conscious of African Americans' positive contributions to American culture. She confessed that the white man still did not know that he was "not God" and he did not know that he actually owed the black man "back wages for all those years he and his forefathers served as slaves."[78]

In the last years of the nineteenth century, however, Harris was still reeling from the trauma of faithlessness, betrayal, and loss. She could find the source of such wickedness only in black people, whom Southern white partisans had condemned as the enemy of purity, honor, and civilization. As she disclosed that, for her, race trumped the mind of God, she still insisted the authenticity of her Christian commitment had been proved by her experience of "September 17, 1886." If mentioned with enough intensity, the response could prevent further inquiry as to the authenticity of her faith. That her fusion of Christianity and culture would not have allowed a tired black washerwoman to sit down next to her was normal. Her views of African Americans were normal; white women knew the reach of erotic danger even if they were confused as to its source. Much later, after engaging men and women whose views were radically different from hers, distance and time freed her to change her mind. But in 1899, betrayal and loss triggered a response endemic to white supremacy: blame black people – especially black women.

EPILOGUE

The chasm that such suspicion and distrust created between Southern white women and their African American counterparts was almost unbridgeable. Well into the twentieth century, a few black and white women were willing tentatively to try to reach across that abyss. When a few met together in Tuskegee, Alabama, and Memphis, Tennessee, in 1920 the tension was as oppressive as 90 per cent humidity and 90 degrees in the shade. Lugenia Hope, an Atlanta-based activist committed to helping African American girls and women, had invited two white women to meet with the National Association of Negro Women at Tuskegee Institute in Alabama. Sara Estelle Haskins and Carrie Parks Johnson represented a commission appointed by the [Southern] Methodist Woman's Missionary Council to find ways to cooperate with black women in improving "race relations."

Black delegates were at first hostile to the white women and the latter were unable, Jacquelyn Dowd Hall writes, to understand why. By attentive listening and painful reflection, however, Parks Johnson began to discover a new world. She and Haskins convinced Will Alexander of the Commission on Interracial Cooperation (CIC) in Atlanta to sponsor a women's conference in Memphis. There, African American women explained to white women the realities of racial oppression. They were especially clear about the extensive abuse to which white men subjected black women and "the oppressiveness of the myth of the promiscuous black woman." This myth had launched Corra Harris on her career as a writer.

The conference called on the CIC to sponsor a committee on woman's work. The men obliged and Parks Johnson was named director of the Interracial Woman's Committee. That committee eventually became the

Association of Southern Women for the Prevention of Lynching. Birthing the Committee was merely a beginning and not an easy one. Black women discovered how broad the racial abyss remained and how rickety was the bridge spanning it. White women frequently revealed an unfortunate but abiding arrogance, abysmal ignorance, and criminal failure to accept black women as equals. The white bourgeoisie could not confront segregation, but a few white women were beginning to understand the danger white men posed to black women. In remarks to the CIC, Carrie Parks Johnson insisted that "The race problem can never be solved as long as the white man goes unpunished [for crimes against black people], and loses no social standing, while the Negro is burned at the stake."[79] Parks Johnson knew what she was talking about; she had been deeply mortified by Lundy Harris' behavior. He was her cousin.

3

Kindling for the Fire

"Lay up for yourselves treasures in heaven, whether neither moth nor rust doth corrupt; and where thieves do not break through nor steal: For where your treasure is will be your heart also."

Christian Bible KJV, Matthew 6: 20–21

"Lord, when saw we thee an hungered, or athirst, or a stranger, or naked, or sick, or in prison, and did not minister unto thee? Then shall he answer them saying, Verily I say unto you, Inasmuch as ye did it not to one of the least of these, ye did it not to me."

Christian Bible KJV, Matthew 25: 44–45

"Make a chain,/ For the land is filled with crimes of blood,/And the city is full of violence. . . ./ Destruction comes;/ They will seek peace, but there shall be none./ Disaster will come upon disaster/ And rumor will be upon rumor./ Then they will seek a vision from a prophet;/ But the law will perish from the priest,/ And counsel from the elders."

Christian Bible KJV, Ezekiel : 23, 25–26

* * *

On the third Sunday after Easter in 1899 about forty miles southwest of Atlanta in Newnan, Georgia, a white crowd burned to death a fugitive black laborer known as Sam Hose. This atrocity blended anger, hatred, arrogance, festivity, brutality and satisfaction into a mood just beyond comprehension. "Glory!" shouted an excited man enraptured by the intensity of the moment, "Glory be to God!!"

Corra Harris understood her trauma within the confusion of race, religion, gender, and sex that fashioned Southern culture for her generation. Her construction of reality suggested how the conventional understanding among whites of a threatening black presence and its rampant sexuality could affect white people as they responded to personal crises and public events. Her response to Lundy's sexual meanderings took no account of how his status conferred on him the power to use intercourse with black women to resolve his own confusion about sex, marriage, and God. She believed his weakness and mental chaos had made him vulnerable to licentious black women who through him had assaulted her. Even if they had been exploited by the "deceitful kindness" of a white "wretch," they had birthed criminal rapists that avenged their people's enslavement by ravishing white women in a mad desire for "equality." Her roiled imagination reflected themes from white supremacist ideology and social science that shaped American whites' conventional thinking about those whom they considered to be a perilous black criminal class at the end of the nineteenth century.

Christian stalwarts such as Bishop Atticus Haygood who had once told religious whites to confess their sin of racial contempt, had learned from distorted and alarmist news reports to be on guard against the black menace. Harris could never imagine a "Brother" in black, much less, a "Sister." The trauma of betrayal, separation, and impoverishment triggered by Lundy's collapse simmered in her mind and heart for almost a year until confronted with her religious mentor's alarm at the burning of Sam Hose. She would never have shouted "Glory to God" at a lynching, but she may have understood why one man did it. Her own "shout" in *The Independent* had simply been longer.

Corra Harris' personal trauma is not a perfect analogy for the alarm that incited the burning of Tom Wilkes, but it is close to it. The lynching was *not* a spontaneous outburst of fury at singular acts of violence by a black laborer known as Sam Hose. To be sure, before they tortured and killed their captive, lynchers claimed their acts avenged a rape, but they also acted as if Hose and they were participants in something far more complex and meaningful than an execution. Afterward, they justified their savagery as necessary to punish blacks for conspiracy, impudence, criminality, and aspirations to "equality." These explanations were crafted by partisans who gathered the kindling to set the fire that consumed Wilkes.

The kindling was not merely the "light-wood" gathered to ignite a blaze. The kindling was also the distress created by the presence of black soldiers stationed in Georgia during the Spanish-American War; the kindling was the pride that that presence elicited from black Georgians. Kindling was provided by armed white men who triggered incidents designed to intimidate blacks under the guise of law and order. The kindling was stacked higher by the lynching of blacks in nearby Palmetto and the fictional conspiracy whites imagined to be flowing from it. Kindling was piled higher during the feckless hunt for Wilkes. The kindling was topped off by news stories that fanned the fury of whites into a self-justifying transgression of civility, civilization, and law. The newly elected administration in Atlanta added to the pile when it dispatched militia to quell Palmetto blacks but failed to damp the flames ignited near Newnan. Whites' frustration with blacks in Griffin, Palmetto, and Newnan plus the homicide of Alfred Cranford helped gather the kindling into one place.

CHRISTIAN CELEBRATION, SOBRIETY, AND RESTRAINT IN THE CULTURE OF WHITE SUPREMACY

The ecstatic shout of "Glory" as the fire crowned was unexpected by the newsman who recorded it, but it was natural to the religious tradition of the "Shout." The expression mingled memories of collective expressiveness in African culture with the dynamics of periodic Methodist revivals in Virginia and the Delmarva Peninsula that wafted throughout the South before the Civil War. In meetings that drew both white and black into week-long camps, worshippers moved in processions, singing and shouting in celebration of the Divine. To those who knew their Bible, the cries called to mind the shout of Hebrews before attacking their Philistine enemies: they signified God's presence. Southern camp meetings and revivals continued the tradition after the Civil War. Cries of "Glory" and "Glory be to God" suggested joy in a Presence that evoked awe and hope. In the late nineteenth century, such excitement birthed images of fire and sacrifice among worshippers in so-called fire and blood revivals.[1] The collective solidarity of a crowd becoming a congregation through movement, sound, and emotion created a sense of belonging and dominion that signified the sacred.

Any dramatic act in gatherings within the culture of the Shout could ignite guttural celebration! The man who cried "Glory" as Hose burned probably did not know he was going to do so and he may not have known why he did it but he had sensed something ineffable. His was one of those "exaggerated" encounters on which the Harvard psychologist,

William James, would rely in probing what his 1902 book styled *The Varieties of Religious Experience*. Such an encounter would also be explained by the great Emile Durkheim, in his classic *Elementary Forms of Religious Life*. Assemblies that elevated the individual produced a "sort of electricity" that could launch one with others into an "extraordinary height of exaltation."[2]

The sacrament of punishment and solidarity near Newnan was reminiscent of crowds that had engulfed the man who shouted "Glory" ever since he had attended childhood festivals of Christian renewal. Then, the center of attention was not Jesus of Nazareth, who had preached the Sermon on the Mount, but Christ the sacrifice who had given His life in expiation for the sins of the world. His crucifixion had "enabled our God to instruct and melt and allure us by the example of Calvary without dishonoring his eternal justice." Old Testament texts warranted belief that approaches to God in "penitence must be accompanied with the streaming blood of a victim and the [a]venging fire of the altar."[3] As the sacrificial drama "allured" penitents to receive salvation, the incineration of Sam Hose seized the attention of hundreds bonded in punitive intensity. The assembly made Hose sacred in two ways. His emulation fulfilled the crowd's desire for solidarity, and this victory over Evil restored moral balance to the universe.[4] The rite transcended sect, yet was "familiar" enough to flow easily from the fury of those reared under the penumbra of the Cross.

The shout of "Glory," despite its familiarity, confused Christian ministers at the time. To them Sam Hose's last moments seemed void of religious meaning. Southern clergy might have understood the crowd's fury with Hose for allegedly raping a white woman, but with few exceptions, the savagery of the event stunned them. Its ferocity revealed a capacity for cruelty that was profoundly disturbing, but no one attempted to understand its source. Previous spectacular burnings in Texas and Oklahoma had also been heinous carnivals of nauseating brutality. Even if Christians sympathized with the "maddened" mentality that justified such events, many prominent Southern ministers, to the disgust of indignant newspaper editors, believed for the moment that lynching was un-Christian.

This view was shared by laity and clergy alike as they gathered in Atlanta for the ninth biennial meeting of the International Sunday School Convention a day after the Newnan holocaust. Southern attendees called attention to the pervasive influence in their region of an authentic Christianity nurtured by years of Evangelical activism. Their piety had led them, they insisted, to respect African Americans, but they refused to sit near them in the convention. This fear of pollution flowed naturally from a system of "exclusion and collective coercion" that justified the lynching even if Southern delegates could not make the connection. Lynching embarrassed them, but they hoped that it would not prevent fair-minded people from appreciating their piety.[5]

By the end of the twentieth century, that piety would lead novelists, publicists, critics, and preachers to think of the South as a "Christ-haunted" culture. And, to be sure, some of the best Southern writers have displayed the human condition within the context of a profound Christian understanding. Their achievements have inspired some critics even to imagine that America's redemption would come from a South guided by the Bible and graced by a crucified and resurrected Christ – a region imagined as the Church. The idea is not new; it had possessed antebellum Southern Christians, too, as they elevated the Bible as the ultimate text for defending slavery. Rather than the moral evil assailed by Northern fanatics, slaveholding was, according to most antebellum white Christian Southerners, merely the context within which Christian blacks and whites could live together peacefully.[6]

After warfare and defeat ravaged the region, Southern Christians renewed plans for creating a Christian country. The Bible still commanded respect, and such was the power of traditional religious discourse that even reformers continued publicly to affirm the creeds that explained their baptism. A resurgent religious trend, celebrated in denominational publications and punctuated by revivals, was transforming clergymen into public figures respected for their contributions to social order. Church membership and attendance were becoming more popular among political elites, and some officials even came from the ranks of the religious. General Clement Evans, ordained as a Methodist minister after the Civil War, campaigned for governor of Georgia in 1896. The equally pious Alfred Colquitt had even won that prize and a seat in the US Senate while he was a Methodist local preacher.[7] With such evidence, apologists could not avoid clothing the South in innocence and good intentions.

Christian service was less characteristic of politicians than it was of women. They continued to be praised, as they had been before the Civil War, for their consecration and moral example, but this combination afterward could be innovative. A few activist women began to magnify their role within Church and culture. They hoped to establish Christian discipline as the measure of public as well as domestic life in order to deal with the pathological effects of Confederate defeat. Losing the war and wealth had driven white men to drink. The women's solution was to prevent the sale of alcoholic beverages. The effort was part of the drive by middle classes throughout the north Atlantic world for restraint, control, discipline, and, as Sigmund Freud would later point out, repression.

Since the 1830s, Southern Protestants had censured the loss of self-control unleashed by whiskey. The "sin" had been drunkenness, not drinking, although some of the pious objected to that behavior as well. Their discomfort suggests that the religious mood of the pre-Civil War South was not as "other-worldly" as historians have insisted. To be sure, Christians believed life was a pilgrimage to a "better" world, especially at funerals. But evangelical Protestants were also determined to discipline themselves and fellow pilgrims before death. Church trials called the faithful to account for drunkenness, fighting, gossiping, dancing, adultery, and breaking the Sabbath. There was nothing "other-worldly" about trying to make churches, meetings, classes, and societies havens in which disciplined behavior confirmed Christian identity. If a few activists could encourage legislators to distance taverns from churches and schools,[8] the effort stepped over an important boundary between sacred and profane.

When Yankee radicals began to attack slaveholding after 1830, Southern clerics realized that the Church was a spiritual body. It was not, James Henley Thornwell of South Carolina declared in 1852, "a moral institute of universal good, whose business it is to wage war upon every form of human ill." It is *not*, he proclaimed, the "province of the Church" to change the "penal code" or organize "for arresting the progress of intemperance, gambling or lust." Neither could the Church condemn slavery. Thornwell and his Presbyterian colleagues were the best known Southern publicists of "the spirituality of the Church," but by secession most white Southerners agreed with them. Then came war, defeat, shame, and intoxication. Because of the immensity of a problem impervious to mere persuasion and beyond the disciplinary reach of the churches, Evangelical reformers began to see relations between the Church and politics in new ways. With slavery no longer cramping moral outrage, white Southern Christians decided that Thornwell might have been wrong, at least in some ways.

They discovered by the late 1880s that they could transform the Christian model of respectable behavior, which had been nourished in churches and homes for over a century, into a legal prescription for the "world" as well. Conservative churchmen and politicians resisted this invasion of electoral politics by the Women's Christian Temperance

Union and their male allies, but by the 1890s they were losing out one
locale after another. When Coweta County voted to outlaw the sale of
alcoholic beverages three and a half months before some of its citizens
lynched Sam Hose, voters had for years been subjected to Evangelical
campaigns to make public life sober. This had not been an easy battle,
Ted Ownby points out, because it was not only a function of modernizing
society but also a female attack on traditional masculine recreation.
Worse, according to Conservative politicians, opposition to drink sub-
verted white supremacy by dividing the "white" vote.[9]

When prohibitionists first breached the wall betwixt Church and politics, they had reached out to African American church leaders as natural
allies who shared a commitment to restraint and self-discipline. White
supremacist movements had yet to disfranchise all African Americans in
the 1890s. Georgia's Democratic and Republican activists still tried to
win black voters and prohibitionists hoped to do so as well because
whiskey damaged every man's ability to reason clearly, shun violence,
work effectively, respect women, save money, and plan ahead. As indus-
trialists, entrepreneurs, newsmen, and politicians tried to make a New
South, prohibitionists insisted that sobriety was the key to economic
progress; and for a while, at least, partisans believed that the "best
people" of both races could cooperate in this process. African Americans
spoke to white crowds extolling teetotalism; they organized black men to
vote "responsibly"; they prayed with whites at local option elections.[10]

But whites were wary of a people who on the whole, they believed,
were not ready for citizenship. Even whites willing to brave racist epithets
to work with blacks believed the latter were *different* and responsible for
almost ruining the region during Reconstruction. Then Southern white
prohibitionists began to understand – with the help of alarmist politicians – that the Republican Party's victory in the national elections of
1888 could mean Negro Domination. The resulting anti-black rhetoric,
which justified disfranchisement and segregation, enticed white Christian
prohibitionists to conclude that any set-back in their campaigns was
actually the fault of African Americans who voted "wet." "Wet" meant
drunken black men as the savage enemies of civilization.[11]

This way of thinking, especially after the Panic of 1893, made the
theme of *separation–and–purity* more compelling, at least, for teetotalers.
The fusion of Southern white Protestantism with prohibition, repressed
sexuality, and the veneration of white womanhood combined to blur
distinctions between sacred and secular in the politics of race. Elevating
the female body to sacred status helped white elites secure their mastery.

The local option election fifteen weeks before the burning of Sam Hose suggested the majority of men in Coweta County and Newnan were comfortable with this understanding, if by only 101 votes.[12] Georgia Democrats, after all, had recently elected a governor whose partisans pointed out that as a Christian he had never ever quaffed a drop of whiskey.[13] What Allen D. Candler might have done in Cana of Galilee when his Lord turned water into wine is of course beyond speculation (Christian Bible, John 2:10). Justifying a politician's ambition by identifying him as an abstemious church member was a public relations victory for Christians. They had woven sacred and profane so expertly on the loom of public life that they cloaked the region in resplendent piety.

CHRISTIAN FAITH: THE HALLOWED PAST IN THE CULTURE OF WHITE SUPREMACY

Piety had originally been written into the Confederate Constitution, which – unlike the US Constitution – acknowledged God. One clergyman praised statesmen who had penned a "religious unction into every clause and line" as true Christians. During the war, publicists could feel the ecstasy of ultimate victory as Southern leaders did "God's work on earth." Southern soldiers, they insisted, fought not only for honor, freedom, wives, and mothers, but also for Christianity. When consecrated warriors lost to "heretics" after a profoundly sacrificial effort, the theme of a distinct destiny remained. That destiny reflexively bestowed on the antebellum South an aura of benign tranquility and domestic well-being that made it a model of civilization. In antebellum times, white Southerners recalled, both races had lived together in perfect harmony. Slavery had created the wealth of the nation, guaranteed the equality of all (white) men, and provided Africans with an apprenticeship in Christianity.

The Christian stewardship of the master class had been remarkable and the drama of Christian salvation had helped Southerners understand the meaning of their destiny after Emancipation. Suffering, martyrdom, and defeat meant not providential punishment for sin but the eventual victory of God's Chosen. The drama of Christ's passion from Gethsemane to Calvary became a foreshadowing of the South's passion from Gettysburg to Appomattox. Southerners, Charles Reagan Wilson has written, had been "baptized in blood."[14] Crucifixion confirmed the South as a chosen people if they could reclaim the promise of antebellum times.

Those times stirred a sense of pride among white Newnanites but lingered less positively in their opinion of blacks. In 1887, for example, when two black clergymen were killed at a railway crossing, each widow sued the Atlanta and West Point railroad for twenty thousand dollars. Such action by whites would have accepted as proper, but a columnist for Newnan's *Herald and Advertiser* could not agree. These cases revealed that times were changing, and not for the better. "I can't see," the writer complained, that black men should be "more valuable now than they were before the war; and in *ante-bellum* times you could buy a very likely negro [sic] man for $1000."

This comment reflected an ordinary bias and what passed for ordinary humor. A generation earlier African Americans had been property and commodity. Profit not paternalism had thrown them into the magical venue of free market capitalist exchange. They'd been identified not by relationships but the shouts and nods of the auctioneer and the gaze of sellers and buyers. The idea that "negroes" who had once been commodities should now be conceded a civic identity equal to that of former masters and auctioneers was preposterous to a man who spent his summers attending revivals and hymn-singing conventions. That women who had lost their husbands should try to hold a railroad responsible for the deaths of men whose fathers had been chattel property was ridiculous. Black women who inflated the worth of their husbands should be laughed out of court.

In such dismissive derision, the mist of "*ante-bellum* times" hovered over Newnan. The "humor" signified the discourse flowing naturally from the reservoir of Confederate memory and spilling into whites' collective consciousness. As the columnist prepared for publication, veterans of the war had been meeting in the city. The soaring rhetoric of Confederate celebration had glorified the South as the "most prosperous country on Earth" in "*ante-bellum* times." The planter's home was recalled as the "ideal abode of refinement, culture, and contentment" where "existence was a delight." Refinement and delight were of course relative, even in "*ante-bellum* times," as more than a few veterans would have known. But a flawed memory could be forgiven an orator who praised the Newnan Guards for their valiant defense of principles "as strongly implanted" at the end of the War for Southern Independence as at the beginning. Those principles still guided white Southerners, if not widowed black women.

The words and images of *ante-bellum times* helped white Newnanites meld pride, sacrifice, race, innocence, and meaning into myth, that is, stories people tell to celebrate their heroic origins. Myths give meaning to the present and guidance for the future. They may be told as if they were history but they are not, for they have not been subjected to the criticism of scholars who read every account against credible evidence that may belie it. The truth of myth rests not in the ambiguity and confusion of reality but in a false clarity that inspires commitment to the society within which myths are imagined. The prevalent myth embraced in varying degrees by Southern whites after the Civil war was that of the *Lost Cause*, "a public memory," David Bright explains, that rested on "a cult of the fallen soldier, a righteous political cause defeated only by superior industrial might, a heritage community awaiting its exodus, and a people forming a collective identity as victims and survivors."[15]

This particular public memory, however, was misnamed. The "Cause" had not been lost. Since Appomattox, Southern whites had successfully sabotaged Federal attempts to protect blacks' civil rights and liberties. They had done so, Newnanites were told, in the name of "human liberty and not human slavery," motivated by the same principles as those of Southern patriots in 1861 when "despotism" had threatened "every stronghold of freedom." All those strongholds, orators insisted, had been in the South where every [white] man was a king. Only crazed despisers of a highly refined people would see slaveholding as evil, for when it was abolished, Republicans had "loosed" four million slaves on "a land of desolation and mourning." They had subjected an "imperial race" to rule by a "barbaric enslaved race," the Christian apprenticeship of the enslaved notwithstanding. In response, white patriots restored freedom with remarkably little if any violence. "Negro rule" was so terrifying that one should have expected thousands to have been slaughtered, partisans observed, but white elites had been motivated by nothing less than Christian charity. "Brotherly love" had guided them.[16]

African Americans remembered rule by the "imperial race" somewhat differently. They had not noticed much "brotherly love" after Reconstruction; peace had been enforced by torture, rape, and murder. Immediately after Emancipation, Georgia's elites acted with a fury unsurpassed in any other state to put down what they believed was a servile insurrection. In 1868, when a convention of African Americans and Republicans wrote a new constitution and submitted it to the voters for ratification, Conservatives threatened supporters with death. When the constitution was approved anyway they moved beyond threats. During the next election for the legislature in that same year, Democrats murdered a Republican leader and attacked African Americans meeting in Camilla, leaving thirty men wounded and at least seven dead. When the polls finally opened, armed white men in contested precincts prevented blacks from voting. The result spawned a legislature dominated by illegally

seated Democrats, who expelled twenty-nine duly elected black representatives and three senators. In the election of 1870, armed white men
prevented blacks from voting once again and in 1871 the new legislature
forced the Republican Governor to flee the state. To be sure, the legislature ratified the Thirteenth, Fourteenth, and Fifteenth Amendments
so Georgia could be received back into the Union, but Democratic
leaders refused to defer to the letter much less the spirit of constitutional
change.[17]

Having wrecked the state's brief and tepid Reconstruction,[18] whites
continued to rely on violence. By 1871 the Georgia Ku Klux Klan was
strong enough to beat and rape hundreds of African Americans and
murder a select few well-known men without fear of arrest. Klansmen
knew that literacy and successful enterprise among black people were as
perilous as voting. By weakening the chains of ignorance and illiteracy,
blacks claimed the right to participate fully in the negotiations of everyday life. They could interpret contracts, keep track of public events,
develop informed opinions, and communicate with kith and kin beyond
their neighborhoods. In short, they could develop the skills and facilities
to assert themselves effectively. That was why blacks' churches and
schools, preachers and teachers could become targets of white
vengeance. African American offences were not limited to education,
protest, or voting, which some black men still managed to do. Possessing
a "bad" attitude, fine clothing, desirable land, or a substantial home
could also justify bullying, assault, rape, or murder. Pervasive violence
or the fear of it, not "brotherly love," shaped day-to-day relations
between the two races.[19]

There were notable exceptions of course – men like Atticus Haygood
personified them. Years before the lynching of Sam Hose, however, black
people knew their relations with white people were shaped by the etiquette of white supremacy, not Christian solidarity. The etiquette came
more naturally to former slaves than to black youth whose attitude
evoked widespread complaints by chronically offended whites who
yearned for the obeisance of *"ante-bellum times."* Tension between the
races could be dangerous for black men in dependent positions when they
negotiated the return that tenants and share-croppers should be allowed
by landlords in distributing funds paid out for the sale of a staple crop
produced by black labor. White planters and farmers kept the books on
economic transactions. Black tenants and share-croppers were at a disadvantage not only because of the accounting mechanisms of the white
planter, but also because it could be worth a man's life if he were to

challenge what he thought was an unjust reckoning.[20] Danger cloaked any transaction in which African Americans were assertive.

Conflict about the reality of antebellum times would have been remembered briefly in Newnan two weeks before whites killed Tom Wilkes. Citizens would probably not have recalled the former slaveholder who was excommunicated after confessing to the Newnan Baptist Church that he had always thought slavery was wrong. But if they read the *Herald and Advertiser* with any interest at all in the past, they would have learned of the death of the Reverend John H. Caldwell who had once served the town's Methodist church. Thinking of him would not have called up treasured memories, for in June of 1865 Caldwell had explained to a shocked congregation that Confederate defeat had been Providential and just. Our offense against God, he insisted, lay in our un-Christian treatment of slaves. The next Sunday he preached the same Gospel to the few angry communicants who may have returned to be sure that they had heard what they thought they had heard. They had. Thus, at his death, Caldwell was remembered in Newnan as an able man who had "forfeited the respect of old friends and brethren by his radical politics in reconstruction times."

Caldwell's white congregation, smarting from the loss of kin, neighbors, wealth, and privilege, simply could not repent of the way they had lived. The "imperial race" had sent seven companies of soldiers to fight the US government and these men had a greater claim on white elites than did their former slaves.[21] Rather than guilt, the emotion felt by most white church members was the anguish of undeserved suffering. The leaders who marched Georgians into secession and defeat may have endured a soul-wrenching shame, but that emotion reflected a feeling of trampled innocence. Shame may also have evoked the violence of Georgian elites after 1865 when they attempted to atone for defeat. Remembering the traitorous Caldwell's death would have helped confirm the justice of the Lost Cause.[22]

A more memorable death than Caldwell's imparted a religious aura to the memories of Newnanites. Before the minister died, Varina Anne Davis "passed" on September 18, 1898. "Winnie" Davis had been born into the Confederate President's family during the war and had been christened in effect, "Daughter of the Confederacy." She came to personify the women of the South who had inspired their men to set the South aright after the depredations of Reconstruction. In sermons, public addresses, and popular fiction, the [white] women of the South had been praised as the spiritual center of their people. They personified Southern purity and morality and secured their personae through memorial societies shortly after the war. They later formed the United Daughters of the Confederacy and sponsored campaigns to write the myths of the Lost Cause. Winnie became their model.

To the delight of Georgia's Confederate heroes, she had attended the annual reunion of United Confederate Veterans in July of 1898 in Atlanta. An excited reporter imagined her presence as the visitation of an angel. "The extravagant and universal praise" of Davis would have been "bewildering" to Yankees, he wrote; they could not appreciate how much she "typified the lost cause." Nonbelievers could not imagine why an old veteran should have pleaded to "see Miss Winnie just once again before I die." Skeptics could not feel the magic that made her beloved of little children. The reporter succumbed to her "charm and sweetness"; he especially recalled her eyes "shining as though full of tears." It was an epiphany of Our Lady of Perpetual Sorrow,[23] and indeed, a holy visitation could easily be imagined within the sacred history of the eternal South.

When Winnie's father died nine years earlier, the language of piety had also elevated him above the ravages of mortality. He was praised as a "Christian gentleman" whose name would "go down to posterity luminous with the magnificence of his Christly life." Lost Cause mythmakers had proclaimed Jefferson Davis a man of sorrows bleeding from "a crown of thorns for his people." It was to be expected, therefore, that Winnie's death would also release the religious effusiveness of Southern whites when they learned of it. The entire region seemed to slip into mourning. She was transfigured as the feminine ethos of a resurrected South that fused the pieties of religion, politics, and collective consciousness into one evocative figure.

As Newnan gathered in Reese's Opera House to honor her, politicians and preachers found that in celebrating Miss Winnie they were celebrating the South and themselves. Exaggerated sentimentality was essential to both evangelical Protestantism and the Lost Cause, especially when women were acclaimed. Miss Winnie symbolized a people without the baggage of defeat carried by her father. She possessed qualities that demanded a religious commitment. How may we best "perpetuate the memory of this lamented heroine?" asked one of the women speakers. We should, she answered, think of ourselves as "worthy descendants" of a "chivalric ancestry" and act accordingly.[24] The words bespoke masculine honor and feminine virtue; they promised serenity under the canopy of white supremacy. The words reflected a moral posture, a set of assumptions, an obsession with purity and danger, and a glossary developed throughout the South to define "the imperial race."

CHRISTIAN FAITH: BELIEF, BEHAVIOR, BONDING, AND BENEVOLENCE

The mood that birthed a temperance crusade and sanctified regional identity did not dominate Southern culture in the 1890s, but church people hoped that it soon would. They were on the way, they believed, to perfecting institutions that could achieve cultural hegemony. They hoped to modify manners, limit masculine excess, shape education, and convert the masses to the true religion. Historians have been accustomed to think of that religion as "evangelical"; and when in 1879 the Protestant ministers of Atlanta created a council through which they could speak in an authoritative voice, they called themselves the Evangelical Ministerial Association. "Evangelical" could sometimes be linked with "liberal" and sometimes with "conservative."

The adjective was supposed to be broadly inclusive rather than exclusive, yet some ordained men were left out. The association included Episcopal rectors but not Roman Catholic priests. A Methodist would try one day to include a Jewish rabbi and fail, and Unitarians were specifically not welcome although a few thought they should be. The laity, however, probably settled for one of two options. Some thought of themselves as members of a specific faith community: as Episcopalians, Baptists, Methodists, Presbyterians, Disciples of Christ, Lutherans, or one of the new denominations fashioned from revivals in the 1890s. Others simply considered themselves Christians.

In the section on religion in *The* [Atlanta] *Constitution*, white Newnanites who paused to think about the religious life of their fellow Georgians could find a variety of views. One preacher imagined the church as a "hospital into which the disabled and diseased can enter and be healed," promising forgiveness to those in need of it in a mood of hope and reconciliation. Another condemned the "masses" for their stupidity, blindness, and deafness, and then ordered his congregation to "find your duty and do it." He imagined a better society through the conversion of individual bankers, judges, legislators, governors, mayors, and chiefs of police. He also hoped for fewer "loose women." The clarity of this list matched that of the Baptist evangelist and pastor, Leonard Broughton, who scandalized Atlanta's city fathers with specific references to specific places where specific officials failed to

punish specific sins at specific times. Broughton believed Atlanta was
sinking in vice, drink, and dancing.[25]

Newnan was in danger, too. When the local dancing master
announced that his recently concluded class had been especially successful, the Presbyterians' Reverend James Stacy arranged to preach against
"Dancing" in the Methodist church. Suspicious monitors of community
morals could still assume that a few so-called Christians were drinking
and dancing, or worse: some were probably attending the theatre.
Evangelist Sam Jones and Warren Candler preached scathing attacks on
such worldliness, but the successful manager of Reece's Opera House did
his best to assure potential patrons that his productions were "pure,"
"clean," and devoid of any word "that could possibly offend the most
fastidious." Purity, modesty, and restraint were essential to good
Christian discipline: African American ministers might even receive
whites' approval if they scolded young black women for loitering in front
of the post office.[26]

More serious matters also claimed preachers' attentions, of course.
Immediately after a lynching, a number of ministers regretted the
"tendency to mobocracy and lynch law" but avoided substantial discussion of the causes and consequences of such crimes. The most that the
average man of the cloth would admit was that the code of civilized
behavior had been broken. A few went further to argue that the code
demanded – in addition to lawful behavior – charity and empathy. They
frequently addressed the terrible conditions in which some of their neighbors lived. They scored the belief that as "special favorites of heaven"
Christians could solve grave physical distress simply by converting the
poor to a self-disciplined piety. Reformers insisted that the church had a
mission to people's bodies as well as their souls. Poverty, class conflict,
disease, and ignorance demanded Christian action, they insisted, but
suggesting specific solutions could be hazardous. Detailed plans to
achieve the ideal risked objection, resistance, and complaint that one
had stopped "preachin'" and stooped to "meddlin'."

References to "justice, liberty, and brotherhood" suggested that one
preacher had been exposed to a social gospel marching under the banner
of the "Fatherhood of God and the Brotherhood of Man." The phrase
had erupted in religious publications during the 1880s and 1890s in the
North and was drifting further south. After the turn of the century the
words would inspire Methodist authors of Sunday school lessons and
Bible study guides.[27] The gendered shading of the phrase may seem
insulting to contemporary feminists but critics at that time were outraged

for different reasons. The "Brotherhood of Man" is a "poor substitute for the Christian," sniffed one finicky cleric, who warned that Satan comes clothed as an angel of light. This led to his defining the correct understanding of the "vicarious and substitutionary work of Christ." Christians needed "brothers" only among those who believed the creed,[28] and the creed demanded a "blood sacrifice" to escape, as W. J. Cash later recalled, the just wrath of God.[29] Humanitarianism was a false god. The Beatitudes (Christian Bible, Matthew, 5:3–10) and sacrificial love were not what Cash remembered from his Christian past.

The man who attacked "Brotherhood" was angry with Christians who did not embrace orthodoxy as furiously as he. He would have approved a Baptist's dismissal of Methodists' "easy ways and shiftless doctrines"; he would have condemned the laxity of a future bishop. John C. Kilgo had all too generously suggested that rationalists could see the truth even if they didn't use traditional language to express it. Kilgo admitted that Ernst Renan had rejected the divinity of Christ in his famous *Life of Jesus*, but note, the president of Trinity College (the future Duke University) insisted, Renan did concede Jesus was "unique." Bishop O. P. Fitzgerald also signified offensive Methodist laxity when he praised the piety of a Swedenborgian physician whose practice commended him even if he did "dilute in some degree the aggregated orthodoxy of the congregation" when he worshipped. A famous Darwinian biologist, Joseph LeConte of Georgia and the University of California, might do the same, Fitzgerald observed, but the scientist, he believed, personified an admirable faith.[30]

The Bishop believed that religious life had many positive expressions beyond a restricted asceticism and the disapproval of congenitally offended heresy-hunters. Corra Harris, a professedly born-again Methodist (as of September 17, 1886), agreed. She recalled with approval the commitment of a poverty stricken woman who, during an epidemic, had nursed the sick and dying when church members refused to do so. The woman had embraced a God who "makes flowers ... bloom for sech as me," the God "that makes the rain fall in my garden" as well as anyone else's. He could, Harris recalled the woman saying, "change a heart like mine" and "make it so I can think good thoughts and be kind and enjoy His hills and hear the birds sing again," as they did when she was young.[31] Kilgo, Fitzgerald, Harris, and "Sal Prouty" were anathema to Holiness folk, partisan Calvinists, and "Hard-Shell" Baptists. The ecumenical generosity of such people, however, suggests a range of belief broader than the unforgiving orthodoxy of insistent traditionalists and distressed purists.

The culturally approved means of identifying "Christians" was church membership and attendance. Those who participated in worship and attended revivals may not have become Christians *yet*, to be sure, but if sober, respectable, and generous to the church they might convert. In the meantime they lived under a religious canopy that framed public events between prayers of invocation and benediction. Public hangings required prayers from the clergy, who attended as essential participants in the institutional and moral validation of such events. Some ministers became what a later generation would call "celebrities," especially if they were bishops, successful revivalists, exceptional preachers, or active spokesmen for their people. Distinguished clerics, whether black or white, were conceded some kind of public role, and newspapers carried stories about ministerial appointments, ordinations, visitations, and other activities (including sexual misconduct). Sermons on topics of general interest could draw audiences; revivals could attract far more people than were listed on church rolls.

If religion entertained, it also betokened cultural power as reflected in the building of a great many substantial new churches in Georgia during the 1890s. A monument to this power in Newnan was the magnificent Central Baptist Church, dedicated in July 1898 when eleven hundred white people attended. The building was, one proud Baptist claimed, the largest marble structure in Georgia – twenty-five rail cars carried the stone to Newnan; the chandeliers, organ, and furnace had cost three thousand dollars. The entire project had cost twenty thousand dollars; it had been supervised by the R. D. Cole Manufacturing Company – its owners were on the building committee. No one could deny that the architecture was awesome; a picture of the new edifice dominated the *Herald*'s front page. The "cathedral glass" windows were framed for the dedication by a "luxuriance of Palm and Fern and flowers." One worshipper praised the "beauty and grandeur" of such a testament to the congregation's "Christian character and self-sacrifice." After the dedication, members and guests dined at the "most extensive spread ever seen in Newnan."[32]

The Christian ethos of Newnan was expressed not only in monumental buildings but also in doing well by doing good. The *Mission* to which Coweta's Christians committed themselves was good. It was so good that in 1897, *The Herald and Advertiser* began to publish a regular column from the Methodist Woman's Missionary Society. Baptist as well as Methodist women supported the *Mission* as an ideal and practice. The ideal was essential to the mythic understanding of slavery because Christian heroines had carried the Gospel into the quarters of the enslaved.

After Emancipation, women formed societies to support missions to foreign countries and Southern cities and by the end of the 1890s such efforts were becoming institutionalized. The women, however, were still scrambling for funds. They told Christian businessmen that missions served commerce as well as Christ and provided a salve for consciences by doing "great things for others." Those "great things," enthusiasts believed, would "elevate" women everywhere. This was not a feminist dictum, but it did indicate a gendered solidarity attractive to many women. They supported churches, missions, hospitals, shelters, dispensaries, and schools for ill, ignorant, and destitute girls and women.[33]

References to the commercial advantage of missions, however, reflected the culture in which they were embedded. Partisans submerged the Christian story in American and Protestant stories. They hoped to save Asian, African, and Latin women from practices that brutalized them, but also from Catholic priests, the Pope, and the Virgin Mary. Women appreciated beauty in other cultures but could not hide the conviction that missions offered something to people who were not quite civilized. As American forces were about to defeat the Spanish in the Philippines, one woman celebrated the fact that the world was "coming under the domination of intelligent Christian nations."[34] Such language transformed the South and the United States into "Christian" lands on the basis of no credible evidence and helped reinforce the emotional hegemony of white supremacy.

The proud "maternalism" of foreign missions frequently compelled women to develop home missions as well. And this innovation allowed a few to engage the baleful effects of white supremacy. By focusing on missions to cities and among African Americans, a few independent women were beginning to think about the flaws in Southern society for which they believed whites responsible. These reformers seemed to be taking seriously the confession that Christians' sins included more than drinking, dancing, and drama. A few writers acted from a sense of guilt and shame at whites' poisonous relations with African Americans, although how far this feeling settled on Newnan's white women is unknown. Methodists in Coweta County had been exposed to thinking about the "race problem" since the early 1880s. They knew about or perhaps had even read Bishop Haygood's plea for *Our Brother in Black*. They knew about the formal commitment of their church to help support Paine Institute in Augusta, Georgia, and some probably did so.

Encouraging white women to improve "race relations," however, was difficult within the ethos of the Lost Cause. Reformers had to work within a culture in which African Americans were imagined as licentious, reckless, and irrational, the very traits that justified white mastery. Long-standing Northern condemnation of Southern whites' relations with blacks as tainted by bigotry, exploitation, deceit, and violence seriously impeded Southern reformers' criticism of whites' relations with blacks. Anything even remotely resembling what "Yankees" might say had to be avoided in order for Southern progressives to have a chance of accomplishing anything at all. The best way to proceed, women activists agreed, was not to demand repentance but to offer Christian service to people wounded by society.[35]

The tactic would eventually allow whites to face their own complicity in delivering those wounds and to attempt an empathic approach to black people (especially women) where awareness of difference had once reigned. To achieve this goal, activists had to create a social base. In 1892, the Methodist Episcopal Church, South dedicated the Scarritt Bible and Training School for Christian workers in order to prepare women as missionaries in foreign lands and then as nurses or deaconesses in the cities and mountains of the South. By 1897 white Southern Methodist women were helping to build schools, missions, dispensaries, and settlement houses – Wesley Community Houses for whites and Bethel Houses for blacks "worthy of respect and consideration." Belle Harris Bennett of Kentucky campaigned tirelessly for Scarritt, Southern women, and service; she created a female constituency that honored her as if she were a bishop.

By 1899, the editor of *Our Homes*, sponsored by the Women's Home Missionary Society, was urging white women to learn from the "social" gospel how white society had ravaged workers, blacks, women, and the poor.[36] Progressives were not free of racial arrogance, to be sure; they shared many of the assumptions that they fought, but they were a van-guard that could respond sympathetically to Edwin Markham's famous poem, "The Man with the Hoe." By the spring of 1899 Markham's poem had become well-known from New England to California! The piece was Markham's meditation on Jean-Francois Millet's painting "The Man with the Hoe." The poet described "The Man" as "bowed by the weight of centuries" who carried "on his back the burden of the World." He had become "monstrous" and "soul-quenched," Markham insisted; he had been shaped "to the thing he is" by the hideous acts of "masters, lords, and rulers." How would "kingdoms" and "kings" respond if "this dumb Terror shall rise to judge the world/ After the silence of the centuries?"

The poem and its popularity infuriated the chronically offended American upper classes, one of whose spokesmen sponsored a hefty prize for the best poetic defense of "masters, lords, and rulers." Markham insisted the poem represented a long history in which the oppressed performed "their drudgery" not in "gladness," but simply to prevent starvation. "Their work is not done in the large and noble spirit of the freeman," he insisted.[37]

Kentuckian Mary Helm, an editor of *Our Homes*, agreed. She printed the poem in the July 1899 issue on the front page together with a rendition of Millet's painting. She also wrote an essay to explain why she believed no informed person could fail to agree with Markham. She confessed her own "personal responsibility to this Man, who stands for a great host." Chastened by her own understanding of the Cross as the signifier of God's love, she insisted that the Christian Gospel promised "the Man" redemption through the "law of love in Christ." She concluded that "if we refuse to be led by this higher law of love, then let us be driven by the lower one of fear." Redemption or Revolution! She pleaded the former. We must share with this man, she wrote, "whatever God-given powers and advantages we have inherited through no merit of our own, or have gained through [his] toil and suffering."[38]

Helm knew Markham's "Man" was black as well as white. So did the African American Bishop, Henry McNeal Turner, who applauded Markham's sentiments, an act that revealed, one critic hissed, Turner's "incendiary wildness." Clark Howell of *The Constitution* scorned the poem as a parody of Millet's painting, but printed an argument that "the catalogue of damnable wrongs inflicted upon the weak [by 'rulers'] is absolutely appalling." A pro-lynching newsman in Hancock County, Georgia, printed the poem on his front page. He saw no application to the South; he liked the poem because it was about Russian peasants.[39]

The cadre trying to move the Southern Methodist Women's Home Missionary Society toward the goal of racial justice was quite small in 1899. The Society would eventually channel some of its members into the Association of Southern Women for the Prevention of Lynching a generation later. In 1899, women like Helm were themselves still in the gestation stage of reform. If Helm's response to Markham's poem suggests how the missionary ideal could become self-critical, the white women of Newnan most arrested by the "Man with the Hoe" were probably more comfortable with the views of clueless editors than those of Helm and Turner. Newnan's women supporters of *Mission* were certainly well-intentioned and the missionaries they supported did meet needs of women whose lives they touched. The women hoped to include in the Christian narrative people whom they had never seen and would never meet.

Yet their stories as Protestants, Americans, whites, and Southerners
tainted that narrative. While a few reforming women tried to bridge the
chasm of racial distancing, white Christians in Newnan – culture-bound
and culture-proud – were fashioning a Southern cult of innocence within
a syncretic American religion.

BLACK COUNTERPOINT

African Americans' religious lives, self-consciousness, and bonding were
imagined and experienced in a way much different from that of their
white neighbors. Bishop Turner, who presided over the ministry of the
AMEC in the area including Atlanta and Newnan personified African
American difference and experience when he offended conservatives by
insisting the Man with the Hoe was black. Recently he had also been
insisting that God was black: "God is a Negro," he announced; "God is
not white." The phrases were scandalous.

Turner's less confrontational colleague, Bishop Wesley John Gaines,
who also lived in Atlanta, did not say such things, but he nonetheless
believed they were true. His people, he wrote before the lynching of Sam
Hose, had a "spiritual and divine energy and power" quite superior to the
dead formality of worship among unnamed others. Gaines praised the
welcoming sympathy, innate hospitality, emotional bonding, and
religious solidarity of his people, insisting they would eventually become
a model for true Christianity. They would do so against great odds. They
faced "contempt," "prejudice," "distancing," "ostracism," and the
disgust of whites who treated black people as if they were not human.
The stigma of slavery, Gaines believed, had been branded on African
Americans by whites; their ignorance had been fashioned by whites; their
poverty had been guaranteed by whites. Against all odds, however, black
people were nonetheless advancing. Given their Christian faith, the
bishop contended, surely "our white brothers," could "accord to give
us simple justice" as we ascend the "steep pathway of progress."

The Protestant ethos of both black and white encouraged renunciation
of and protection from the dangerous world. The menace Christian
blacks faced daily was to a certain extent composed of the same sins
whites condemned; but African Americans experienced far greater
danger from the "world" of white power: injustice, persecution, exploitation, murder, rape, contempt. Those were the realities behind sermons
that insisted it would be easier for an elephant to pass through a
"cambric needle" than for the "rich" to enter the kingdom of heaven.

Black ministers preached the "Christianity of the lowly Jesus, who was no respecter of persons, but went about doing good, ministering to the poor and unfortunate and to every class and condition of mankind." Their congregations knew who were the "lowly," the "poor," the "unfortunate," and those oppressed by their condition. Jesus belonged to them as they fought "force, fraud, and violence."

The theology of a suffering and resurrected Christ blended well with the realities of black lives. African Americans had no difficulty in imagining Christ as "suffering and betrayed." They knew the "trial in which [he] stood arraigned before an unjust judge and bitter enemies" was corrupt. It was also familiar. When black Christians envisioned Christ's being "condemned amid the acclamations of the incensed mob" that demanded crucifixion, they could feel Christ's agony as their own and their agony as His. They knew that suffering was rarely redemptive; they sometimes felt, as did their crucified Lord, that God had forsaken them. (*Eli, Eli, lama sabachthani?* [Christian Bible, Matthew KJV, 27:46]). But they hoped that suffering was a prelude to victory, however it happened. Contemplating the faith of whites, black Christians sometimes wondered why there was such a pervasive and damning silence from them on lynching, "persecutions," and "inhumanities" when they could be so furious with dancing and drink. The mood, tone, and theology of African American Christianity were simply different from the triumphal Christianity of imperialism, mission, orthodoxy, and penalty.[40]

Black Christians, like their white neighbors, belonged not only to local churches but also to associations, presbyteries, or conferences with others sufficiently like themselves. Local black Methodists were visited by their bishops and local Baptist ministers attended associational meetings and read *The Georgia Baptist*. The gifted and eloquent editor, William Jefferson White, kept Baptists informed on black institutions and political issues, as well as the daily injustices afflicting African Americans. All black Methodists did not agree with Bishop Turner's plea for emigration to Africa as a solution to their problems, but they could agree with him that they should be protected as citizens from white atrocities. They may have winced at the Bishop's outspoken if accurate criticism of white arrogance and black accommodation, but they came to hear him preach to and for them when he visited. He always said something memorable.

He was, like White, a celebrated leader of the race, representing them as a public man and saying things that they could not say with the same fervor in their daily conversation. He was clever, intelligent, eloquent, and insistent; he projected a toughness that served him and his people well.

Editor White had a similar aura. If White feared that God sometimes slept while his people suffered, the editor nevertheless printed Silas X. Floyd's promise of eventual progress. "I remember," Floyd insisted (contra White), "that the God of Israel slumbers not nor sleeps and that if we trust him, the God who brought us safely through the Red Sea of slavery will also deliver us from the hands of wicked and unjust men." Hope sometimes made reality bearable.

White and Floyd, like other black preachers, preached deliverance. In April 1899, White reported that the Reverend H. L. Bennett's new Zion Hill Baptist church in Newnan had been dedicated with a sermon from the Epistle to Ephesians: "There shall be," the scripture promised, "showers of blessing." Three days later, whites burned Sam Hose to death.[41]

NEWNAN, GEORGIA: NEW SOUTH CITY

In April 1899, Newnan was a prospering little city of four thousand souls. By scanning its weekly newspaper, the *Herald and Advertiser*, over the previous twelve years, a twenty-first century reader would never have guessed that over forty per cent of Newnan's citizens were African Americans. The *Herald* was a white man's paper. If black people wanted to read stories consistently sensitive to their condition they would have had to subscribe to the *Voice of Missions*, the *Georgia Baptist*, the *Atlanta Independent*, or *The Christian Recorder*. The *Herald* did report some news of African Americans, especially if they had been arrested, hurt in accidents, or successful in activities whites considered important. White citizens wanted to learn about the death of a respected black person whom they or their kin knew, and they could even respect the accomplishments to be inferred from special events in black churches and schools. When a black Democrat died, he was noted as a sterling example of his race, and a black man's handsome estate could be noticed as an admirable if surprising achievement. African Americans' personal tragedies could elicit genuine sympathy and those in the black community who were well known as retainers of a select few could be praised at their deaths for their "faithful" and "obedient" relations with whites.[42]

Despite approving well-schooled black children, the editor disapproved of a new generation of African Americans "impertinent" enough to think themselves equal to whites. This new cohort did not appreciate the "friendly relations of master and man" that had existed during those antebellum "days of immunity from care." How many whites believed the fantasy is difficult to say but the phrase does suggest how the community was supposed to imagine ideal race relations.[43] This younger generation was not the only threat to white Georgians, of course. Just as dangerous was the Federal Government. True, it did not try to restrict Southern representation in Congress for disfranchising blacks, but white Newnanites knew that Radicals wanted to do so. The US government did not demand equality of education for both races in the South, but Radicals had hoped to do so and they might try again. The Supreme Court had approved segregation and Congress had refused to defend African Americans' voting rights, but Yankees still hated the South, and Republican administrations still refused to respect Southern culture.

The evidence was clear to any right-thinking white who witnessed Republicans' patronage appointments of black postmasters to Southern communities. Whites condemned such tyranny, and none more vehemently than the editor of Newnan's weekly newspaper. Those postmasters represented "NEGRO DOMINATION" and were an insult to white women who had to accept mail from a black hand. When someone tried to murder an appointee in Hogansville, Georgia, in 1897, for example, this "OUTRAGE" was explained as merely the counter-balance to the original "OUTRAGE" inflicted on Hogansville when the McKinley administration appointed him. Attempted murder was merely an appropriate response to the government's forcing a black man into a position for which his race disqualified him. A contrived alarm over the matter entertained readers off and on for over five months as if the "OUTRAGE" in Hogansville could happen in Newnan, but it didn't. The warnings seemed to have no immediate effect! Citizens did not want "Negro Domination," to be sure, but they appeared to have been too busy to worry about it. Democrats had, after all, beaten back a flawed but threatening interracial coalition.[44]

The census of 1900 provides data that suggests what Newnan's citizens were doing before April 1899, when Sam Hose was burned. Black and white people lived in different sections of the city but in some areas the boundaries were porous and permeable. Portions of the fifth census district, for example, reported scattered white households within a black area. A few white families were headed by "managers" or "engineers," who lived close to black ministers. The small white population of the district was literate, but a majority of black men were not, although many of their wives were at least able to read. Throughout the city, most black men were laborers, but there were also clergymen, blacksmiths, shoemakers, barbers, masons, carpenters, roofers, teamsters, and at least two assistant engineers (working on a stationary engine in a mill).

In addition, Dr. John Henry Jordan had just brought his practice to Newnan and was preparing to establish a small hospital for African Americans. Most black women in Newnan worked when they could as seamstresses, washer-women, nurses, midwives, teachers, cooks, or maids.[45]

White women worked as milliners, dressmakers, shopkeepers, or teachers; a woman managed the Western Union telegraph office. A German-born actress added a cosmopolitan tinge. White men worked at a broad range of occupations. Many were mill or foundry workers; some were cotton-choppers, contractors, salesmen, insurance brokers, accountants, draftsmen, grocers, boiler makers, or pharmacists. One man was an electrician. The city had a healthy band of white professionals: lawyers, physicians, dentists, clergymen, and two editors. Most merchants in Newnan seemed to be white, as were the bankers. A well-known restaurateur, James Reid, who catered to whites, was black. Several white families had black live-in servants – butlers, maids, and cooks. Black Newnanites for the most part served the white middle class, and a white working class serviced the mills, foundries, machine-shops, a lumber yard, and construction companies. A few white men were serving in the Philippine war and James Reid's stepson fought in the Battle of Santiago with the black twenty-fifth regiment of infantry. Over twenty white men from the county had manned garrisons in Cuba under the command of the former mayor, Captain J. S. Powell of the Third Georgia Regiment of militia.[46]

By the spring of 1899, despite the lingering effects of the Panic of 1893, Newnan's boosters believed the city to be the very model of middle class success. In 1898 a visiting newsman had thought it one of the richest cities per capita in the South. The year before that, the *Herald*'s editor had gushed that the city "is famous for everything that is worthy and commendable – religiously, socially, educationally, politically, industrially and commercially – and no town in Georgia [possesses] a fairer reputation."[47] The well-informed and highly professional superintendent of schools would probably not have agreed either then or in 1899, for he knew the town and county could do much better by his students. The Reverend H. L. Bennett of Zion Hill Baptist church pointed out that high matriculation fees put public education beyond the reach of poor black students. But even in the face of the depressed cotton economy, most public statements celebrated a bustling and affluent manufacturing town. There was a real estate boom in East Newnan, new dry goods were arriving daily from New York City, and the Ladies Memorial Association was thriving.

If prosperity had not enriched every citizen, there seemed to be nonetheless a solid basis for confidence in the future. R. D. Cole's imposing manufacturing company was complemented by the Coweta Fertilizer Company, the Newnan Cotton Mills, the Newnan [Cotton] Oil Company, the Newnan Ice Company, the Wahoo Manufacturing Company, the W. S. Askew [Lumber] Company, the Moreland Manufacturing Company, and three banks. One company produced the "Newnan Girl" cigar, and businessmen had established a telephone exchange. A new waterworks was functioning beautifully as was the revolutionary Newnan Light and Power Company. The sewage system may have needed repair, but that was a minor glitch. Literary clubs, a historical society, a public library, ten churches (four black), and the Women's Missionary Society betokened piety and refinement.[48] The month after Sam Hose's lynching, *The Savannah Press* complimented the town as "one of the wealthiest and most cultured communities in Georgia," one "eminently religious" and famous for its "elegant sanctuaries."[49]

The town was also famous for its "favorite son," former Governor Atkinson. In his early thirties, the energetic and ambitious lawyer had been elected to the Georgia General Assembly from Coweta County. During his second term he had pushed legislation to create a college for white women at Milledgeville. In 1892, as state Democratic chair, he organized the campaign to re-elect Governor William J. Northen and defend the Democratic legislature from the rebellious People's Party. When he ran for governor in 1894, Atkinson had a partisan network ready to help him win the nomination against an ineffectual, elderly Methodist minister whose primary qualifications seemed to have been three wounds suffered during the Civil War. The Reverend General was no match for the eloquent Atkinson in public debate and his partisans were relatively unimaginative in everything but slander and libel. Atkinson won the general election, and when he ran two years later, he won once again, this time with the overwhelming support of African Americans.[50] If Atkinson played the politics of white supremacy successfully, black voters knew he was a supremacist with a difference.

After his inauguration in October of 1894, he learned how to use the militia and work with local elites to check violence. In his first address to the Georgia General Assembly in January 1895, he asked for laws to thwart the likelihood of lynching just as his predecessor, William Northen, had done. The response was tepid. In December 1895, refusing to give up, Atkinson once more called the General Assembly to pass laws to stem the violent "contagion" that threatened civilization. He spoke and wrote in opposition to lynching throughout his two administrations. He even got the General Assembly to pass legislation that on its face punished by fines, payment to victims, and short jail terms those who "took the law into their own hands." Nevertheless, by the end of his second term in 1898, he had to admit that twenty-two (actually more than thirty) lynchings had occurred while he was in office. He was discouraged; he knew the results of his opposition to lynching were negligible.

The new "anti-lynching" law required juries to punish illegal collective violence. But juries included men who had either joined the mobs or approved their actions. A Georgia legislator would have been especially clueless not to have understood the proceedings in local courts. Atkinson was no less aware than members of the General Assembly but dispatching the militia, offering rewards, and pushing the General Assembly did set him apart from most politicians. Faith in the law led him to hope legislation would eventually be effective, but it would take time. He knew how perverse white fantasy could be. While writing his address to the General Assembly in December 1895, the governor was hiding a black fugitive from a mob seeking to kill him for attempted rape. The evidence against the man was clear. He had failed to address a white woman christened "Mary" as "*Miss* Mary."

Through a public statement urging anti-lynching legislation in October of 1898 Atkinson cited several instances in which he knew mobs had killed black men innocent of any crime. He also knew of cases in which whites falsely accused black men of a crime for personal reasons so that they could be killed by white mobs. There were simply too many ways in which a crowd had deprived accused blacks of the protection provided by due process; he believed he was speaking for those who, as victims of white criminality, could not speak for themselves. The impact of lynch law on the South, Atkinson insisted, was damaging in many ways: Talented people with capital who might invest in the state were wary of its lawlessness; unchallenged mob rule would lead to ever greater violence. Men who had once "stained their hands with blood" would do it again, he warned. Whites had to stop the "odious and dangerous" practice. That was what he wanted; he hoped the legislature would act. If the governor could not quash the mentality that immersed mobs in legitimacy, he thought that doing *something* was better than doing nothing. Whether this was true or not, African Americans agreed with him.[51]

What Atkinson's neighbors in Newnan thought, however, is something else. They knew what he said and where he stood; they claimed him as their own but it is not clear that they agreed with him. They could dismiss his opposition to lynching as a role demanded by his office. In the summer of 1897, for example, the *Herald*'s editor defended the Governor for trying to raise a public outcry against lynching. On July 19, a small band of thugs in Talbotton hanged a white mentally disturbed physician, W. L. Ryder, who had had his conviction for murdering a young white woman overturned on appeal. Spokesmen for the gang claimed they had been justified by a "paralysis of justice." The same "paralysis" justified another troupe of white men who lynched an accused black rapist in nearby Griffin.

In response to these incidents, the *Herald* printed a statement by a furious Atkinson, accompanied by an old article by Georgia's Chief Justice, E. L. Bleckley. In *The Forum* in 1893, Beckley had scolded those who claimed the "provocation" of rape justified mob violence. In his column, the governor argued that mobs were a "virus," which he hoped "all the forces of 'higher civilization'" would destroy. The Talbot County grand jury was not, however, such a force; it refused to indict anyone. "In Georgia," taunted one of Atkinson's enemies, "Judge Lynch is still on the bench." The *Herald*'s publisher apparently agreed, although he defended Newnan's native son from the inane accusation that he sympathized with rapists. Remember, the publisher pleaded, the governor "in his official capacity . . . must repress his sympathies however deeply moved he might be." The newsman implied that citizens were free of the restraint imposed by holding public office; tradition trumped law. Lynching, the editor had recently written, was actually a "time-honored Southern custom."[52]

NEWNAN'S DRAMAS OF PUNISHMENT AND DANGER

That custom was not "time-honored" in Newnan. There were frequent shootings in the countryside, often by accident, but most violence lay just beneath the surface of social interaction and in discourse that sustained the powerful. That is, violence was implicit when publicists spoke the language and followed the logic of admonition and threat. A collective attempt to kill a black man for addressing a white woman by her Christian name was violence. Defining attempted murder as equivalent to appointing a black postmaster was violence. Accusing Atkinson of encouraging rape by condemning lynching was violence. Justifying collective murder by "provocation" was violence. Such discourse was more than roguish hyperbole common to community conflict, heated preaching, and trumped up political campaigns. Supremacist rhetoric rested on the fact that coercive and punitive power, whether exercised legally or illegally, was in the hands of white men. This was never more obvious than when exchanges between black tenants and propertied whites resulted in death instead of negotiation.

This commonsense observation does not mean that latent violence was always about to become manifest but that it could. The possibility did not indicate that all whites were pleased when their fellow citizens engaged in dramatic threats or acts of carnage but that some whites could be. Authorities throughout Georgia in 1893 and 1894 condemned acts of destruction, exile, and death by white night riders attacking black farmers in counties northwest of Coweta.[53] But white people never admitted that the manners, discourse, and politics that demanded deference and segregation were sources of such acts. To the complacent, the naïve, the clever, or the clueless such acts seemed to be cloaked in mystery.

There was nothing mysterious, of course, when jurisdictions near Coweta County legally hanged convicted murderers. Two well-publicized executions were dramatic enough to show Newnan's citizens how such matters could be conducted. In March 1895, a young black, Joe Dean, was hanged for the murder of A. B. Leigh, 55, on the night of December 1, 1894. Leigh had lived in Campbell County on the Coweta County line, but as a member of the Newnan militia he was part of that city's civic culture. Dean, a former employee, had appeared at Leigh's door one night ostensibly to fetch aid for one of the white man's tenants. Dean desperately needed money and believed that if Leigh and his family could be enticed from their house, Dean could slip back and steal enough to solve his problem. Nothing went as planned. The family stayed put, and a frustrated Dean killed Leigh as they walked to the tenant's cabin. Dean found no cash on the body. He returned to the house with gun in hand, but was chased away by a furious teenaged girl with a shotgun. When arrested, he pleaded not to be lynched but executed "like a white man." He was spirited away to Atlanta on the governor's orders and held for trial. News reports described the black man as a "fiend," a rapist, or a victim of his own stupidity. A reporter found Dean's speech, dignity, and remorse to be impressive. A white jury found him guilty of murder.

Public executions had been illegal in Georgia since 1893, but five thousand witnesses arrived at the scaffold to watch Dean's hanging. At 9:30 on the morning of March 1, 1895, Dean arrived in Fairburn, the seat of Campbell County, Georgia, about twenty miles northeast of Newnan. He was escorted by an Atlanta policeman and the Reverend A. A. Mathis of Atlanta's Mount Zion church together with two of his women communicants. To obey a court order to guarantee the privacy of execution, the sheriff sheltered the gallows with an exceptionally tall fence; twice the crowd demolished it. Soon Dean appeared on the court house steps; all eyes were on him. For ten minutes he spoke on themes appropriate to the day: "I am here to pay my last debt and it was all caused by my craze for money: ... nothing else." (Not for sex or hatred of the white man!) "It was money, ignorance, and the devil," he insisted, "made me do it. For God's sake, don't be misled by me." The statement was classic, similar to many such speeches in eighteenth-century America. The devil, Dean warned, "will take your soul if you don't repent!" Then he posed for the photographer.

Because there was plenty of time remaining before the execution, he, his family, and his friends followed the Reverend Mr. Mathis into the courthouse for worship. An hour later, Dean was escorted to the gallows, "cool" and "resigned." Ministers intoned their final prayers and the sheriff then killed Dean in a horrible way. When the trap door was sprung, he fell to the ground; the rope had broken. With a stronger rope Dean was once again hurled into space but because the noose had not been fixed correctly his neck did not break. He slowly strangled. It took fourteen minutes for him to die.[54]

Two years later, another crowd gathered fifty miles south of Coweta County to witness the dramatic spectacle of yet another public killing. Even if not in attendance, Newnanites could learn about the event in a series of articles in the *Herald and Advertiser*. On June 18, 1897 thousands of people flooded into Zebulon, the small seat of Pike County, to witness the hanging of twenty-four-year-old Tom Delk, a notorious white outlaw who had murdered Pike's sheriff. Petitions to Governor Atkinson had failed to persuade him to commute Delk's sentence to imprisonment for life. The new sheriff did not try to hide the execution, possibly recalling the failed attempts to do so when Dean was hanged. Reporters believed the event to be one of the most "picturesque executions that ever took place in Georgia."

In interviews, Delk boasted of a criminal career that had taken him from Zebulon to Chicago, St. Louis, Atlanta, and back home. He boasted of his sexual prowess and told the guard to protect him from reporters but not any young women who wished to visit him. On the day of execution, Delk's sisters pinned a yellow rose to his lapel and deputies led him to the gallows as he greeted friends and flirted with young women. A manic Delk tried to find humor in the event only to be scolded by the Reverend J. T. Wright to behave. Spectators tried to tear down the bagging hung to hide the body as it dropped through the trap door but the sheriff prevented them. Officials moved the ceremonies at a faster pace because people were beginning to faint from the heat.

Authorities introduced Delk to the crowd; they cheered. Dressed in black and shaded by umbrellas held by a minister on each side, he spoke: "I have made my peace with God and I am prepared to go." I have "done wrong," he admitted, but added: "we all have. I believe that God has forgiven me." The cliché was followed by another. Beware of "bad company and whiskey," he warned, but he did not mention women. His comments reflected a ritual flowing from Anglo-American culture. A minister failed to preach an "execution sermon," to be sure, but he did offer a prayer. Delk also prayed. He appealed to God to grant mercy to his friends and his father. Then guards bound Delk with ropes and the sheriff fixed the noose. The condemned man twice shouted, "Good bye, people," and hundreds twice replied, "Good bye, Tom." Then the sheriff shrouded Tom's head with a hood – prepared by the widow of the man he had killed – and tripped the trap door. Tom's body dropped, but his neck did not break. Like Joe Dean before him, Delk slowly strangled to death hidden from the gaze of the crowd.[55]

Reporters did not describe the event as "sacred" because there was too much cheering, but they were mistaken. The cheering transgressed the solemnity valued by ministers, officers, and reporters, to be sure, but this betokened a moment of "excess" when wonder at death and oblivion ignites sound beyond content. Cheering seemed out of place save for those who cheered: They felt welling up from within themselves a plethora of passion that saved them from the clichéd trivia of solemnity and restraint, just as Durkheim would later explain in *Elementary Forms*. Delk's execution became a "vicarious sacrifice" that freed the crowd from the normativity of everyday life as the prisoner declared, "We have all done wrong." Tom was for a moment their substitute! In the acts of officers and ministers the state tried to take charge of death but failed. Officials surrendered their authority when cheers exploded in a carnivalesque moment through which the sacred flowed beyond the confines of traditional rubrics.[56] Exchanging farewells with the man at center stage, the people had become actors in a drama no longer directed by officers of the law. By forcing authority to make the execution public, the people had violated the law they had come to see enacted. Democracy, *not* the state, reigned.

Transgression and the sacred had been even more obvious in the killing of Joe Dean. The white crowd drawn to Dean's hanging was different from the black public in the same place. The latter had come to celebrate the life of a confessed sinner who, in acknowledging his guilt, had placed his hope for salvation in the sacrifice of his Lord. Dean and Reverend Mathis enacted a morality play that revealed a redemptive meaning to Dean's repentance. As he paid the legal penalty he admitted was just, he was saved from an even greater one. Mathis led his people into a moment of openness to Divine grace and the realization that through Christ who suffered with them, their brother, Joe, had been redeemed. The power and the glory in Mathis' preaching would have been affirmed by song and shout as Dean faced his earthly fate in the hope he shared with all Christians. Dean and Mathis made the execution into something other than punishment; this offended whites who wanted Punishment not Redemption.

Michael Trotti, in a compelling study, certainly makes a convincing case for this interpretation. As Dean's religious public of kith and kin followed him and his minister to worship, the white public destroyed the hastily rebuilt fence. They celebrated when Dean was hanged twice; they watched his terrible agony as he strangled to death. Both publics acted according to a logic independent of *legality*; but the black congregation had honored life instead of death.[57]

Michel Foucault is probably correct in observing that in Europe, at least, "punishment as a spectacle" was disappearing at the end of the eighteenth century.[58] At the end of the nineteenth century, however, the citizens of Campbell, Pike, and Coweta counties in Georgia were still resisting the trend. Most knew that community leaders wanted the spectacles gone, but the people were not cooperating. A few Georgia newspapers might call public executions "demoralizing and hurtful" for gratifying the "worst passions" of the "lowest class." Yet newspapers printed detailed descriptions and crowds came, one scholar believes, because they wanted to see justice done in "spectacles of white power and black culpability" that could spawn "a visceral identification between white spectators and the power of the state."[59] But something else was going on. Transgression of the law in both Dean's and Delk's executions reveals the power *not* of the state, but of a rampant democracy. The People *transcended* the State.

The crowd's desire was something beyond "morbid curiosity" or entertainment, or tasteless satisfaction; it was an openness to a sacred reality that transcended the restrained sobriety of self-discipline and good manners. "Morbid curiosity" or the "morbid appetite" of the "morbidity-minded" crowd had offended reformers for years. They wanted executions restricted to what Annulla Linders has pointed out should have been a "professionalized" audience. Privatizing executions was supposed to avoid a contest between authority and those who wanted to participate in dramas of pain and death. Critics condemned the irreverent emotionalism of a cheering, laughing, and drinking crowd. These censors shared a contempt for the "lower classes" who did not appreciate what was really going on.[60] Such critics never considered that maybe the "lower classes" were precisely the people who did know what was going on. Execution day was a special day; it displayed the reality of mortality, transience, finality, and death that made the execution more compelling than any other public event.

One of Newnan's public voices may have suggested as much in an aside. He noticed that despite the fact that 1897 was devoid of special events as an "off" year in politics, "it has certainly been an 'on' year for barbecues, reunions, conventions, lynching, hangings, and other diversions."[61] That "lynching and hangings" could be considered "diversions" may invite derision for its implication of mere entertainment, but each of these "diversions" was a celebration that *extracted people from the ordinary* and placed them in a special time or timelessness. Each event had its own rules and aura; two of these "diversions" had the capacity not only to divert "attention," but also to plunge subjects into a confrontation, in varying degrees of intensity, with their sense of self and humanity through an experience of "being" that transcended cognition and speech. "Lynching and hangings," besides the punishment they inflicted, were distinctive because they ended in death. These were not the natural deaths to which most people are heir, but unnatural ones that were punitive and "deserved" in the eyes of executioners and witnesses. Among the latter would have been those who found in such deaths the dramatic confirmation of how valuable were their own lives.

Punitive death was the magnetic power that drew white witnesses to the gallows. Death, if spectators were Christians, had secured their salvation. Death for believers and nonbelievers alike was the ultimate just punishment for ultimate crime. Sacrifice and blood, white Southerners had been told repeatedly, were not only bedrocks of their faith, but essential to the Lost Cause, and necessary for the preservation of law, order, and white supremacy. The culture of twenty-first century America, drenched as it is in the blood of school children and collateral damage, and entertained as it is by vampires, zombies, and serial killers, suggests that "morbid curiosity" or even a "morbid appetite" is not so strange or abnormal as bourgeois reformers claimed to believe over a century ago. Indeed, such mental states were probably too "normal" for the taste of offended elites. People in the vicinity of Coweta County in the 1890s were drawn to executions because those events were punitive and could be cruel as well as final. Their fascination demands investigation rather than dismissal.

Maggie Nelson has taken on the task with regard to modern America by studying *The Art of Cruelty*. She fears that "meditating on cruelties and violent spectacles" may "sow seeds of aggression" and confirm a belief she abjures in the "inevitability" of evil. She confesses that compassion is still her hope within a world of suffering but reminds contemporaries that the "art of cruelty" in its many forms exists because cruelty and pleasure at the suffering of others (*Schadenfreude*) saturates our culture. Americans, she writes, have "ample and wily reserves of malice, power-mongering, self-centeredness, fear, sadism, or simple meanness of spirit that we ourselves, our loved ones, our enemies, skillful preachers, politicians, and rhetoricians of all stripes can whip into a hysterical, destructive froth at any given moment, if we allow for it."

Theatre, painting, and especially the cinema depict a cruelty and callousness that indicates Americans do indeed "allow for it." There is also well-known scientific evidence to suggest as much. In famous psychological experiments, empathy yielded to authority, and more recently the pain of others has been justified as cathartic release. The ways in which so many Americans assimilated the "horrific images" of torture at Abu Ghraib during the war in Iraq reveal a disposition that would draw thousands of witnesses to public executions if such events were reinstated. When radio commentators justified the torture of prisoners in Iraq by US soldiers as nothing more than the plausible "need to blow some steam off," we have relegated callousness to nothing more serious than a juvenile prank. From the perspective of contemporary culture it is easy to see that the desire to watch Joe Dean and Tom Delk die in agony was not unique, but compelling, distinctly human, and contemporary.[62]

A much more confessional and "light-footed" commentary assumes that Carl Jung would encourage us to believe that the act of contemplating "morbid phenomena is necessary for mental health." Eric Wilson, like Nelson, writes about contemporary America and defends the artistic representation of brutality, torture, pain, and cruelty, but *not* the acts that inspire it. These acts, however, do compel him to think about the millions who watched the actual beheading of actual Americans by actual terrorists on the actual Internet. One witness justified his watching as the "thrill of quasi-participation." He had felt "titillation" because the beheading was "happening to a real person. The fear is real, the brutality is real, the blood is real; it is all real." The agony of Joe Dean was real, too, but what kind of reality is assumed in watching a real beheading and a real strangulation? Wilson attempts to explain. He admits that "morbid eruptions" invite the "dehumanizing" of victims if the imagination cannot find meaning in them as early Christians found meaning in the torture and death of their Lord. From others' experiences of a dark night of the soul, as well as from his own, Wilson concludes that the "compulsion toward grim happenings" helps "one to manage dangerous fears and desires, to learn what is essential and what is not."

"Morbid curiosity is," he continues, "yet another plane, a spiritual yearning, a hunger to penetrate the most profound mysteries of existence." In his travail, Wilson wrestles with the mingling of sexuality and death – not the most surprising turn in a post-Freudian world. "Sexual arousal," he writes, "and fascination with death have much in common; both are extremely stimulating, often uncontrollable, primitive, taboo, and ecstatic, pushing us outside our habits into the intractable mysteries of creation and destruction, and their inextricable connection." Georges Bataille has helped us become aware of the connection of death and sensuality in which both are brought to climax in consequence of "superabundance," an explosion of "being-into-nonbeing" in one overwhelming experience. Wilson points out that famed British novelist, Thomas Hardy, was also well aware of this sensation.[63]

Even if Wilson's musing and confession do not bring others to the same conclusion, Hardy, Wilson, Bataille, and Nelson help us realize that public executions were more complex manifestations of culture than mere entertainment. Such events mixed transgression, sacrifice, punishment, death, and popular democracy in ways that can remain mystifying and only partially explained despite a disinterestedness sanctioned by distance and the passage of time. Originally, these events dramatized punishment, power, and justice to some, and *white* punishment, power, and justice to others. Some citizens from Newnan and Coweta County probably attended Dean's execution, and a few may have traveled to watch a celebrity outlaw such as Tom Delk die – after all, thousands did so. Most, however, would have had to read about both incidents from detailed reports in *The Constitution* and the *Herald and Advertiser*. Reading these stories helped citizens translate public events they had not seen into exemplary dramas of right and wrong, crime and punishment.

Reading stories of democratic and transgressive justice in lynching helped buttress further the conventional wisdom of a culture of rectitude and judgment. Although prominent lawyers, former governors, sitting judges, men of the cloth, and not a few other leading citizens emphatically disagreed, a frequently enraged white Georgia democracy believed that lynching was a quickened form of justice superior to that dramatized in legal executions. Between February 27, 1890 and April 22, 1899 at least seventy-three black and six white men are known to have been murdered by Georgia mobs.[64] Excess, transgression, and democracy trumped reason and justice.

No mobs gathered in Newnan until April 23, 1899. In Coweta County, a white man might kill a black man in "self-defense" and avoid a trial. Blacks might try to kill a white man in a case of mistaken identity without igniting mob violence. Individual animosities and tension between tenants and landlords could be assumed as part of normal social relations but the dramatic violence of the early post-war years was over. This was so even though citizens of the city and county knew that white vigilantes had tried to rid counties to the northwest of blacks. The people of Coweta County chose not to emulate such action. If they read *The Constitution*, they knew of violent incidents throughout Georgia and the South that attracted the editors' interest. They learned of the lynching of a white Yale graduate for rape, or the beating to death of an old black woman and young boy for trivial crimes they had not committed. Newnan's citizens knew that the county's favorite son as governor wanted lynchers indicted but grand juries never agreed. When black children were reported to have hanged one of their playmates "all in fun" no one seems to have thought much about what this revealed about Southern culture.

Newnan's informed citizenry knew lynching was always "out there" somewhere. Lynching seemed normal to black children; it seemed barbaric to many frustrated ministers; it seemed just to leading citizens of Columbus. To Atkinson, who had in vain offered thousands of dollars in rewards for the conviction of elite murderers, lynching was failure.[65] The *Herald*'s editor did not write at great length about such matters, although he did seem to believe that men and boys in nearby Griffin were too prone to criminal violence. As a partisan of Governor Atkinson, he would never have written, as did the editor of *The* [Sparta Georgia] *Ishmaelite* in 1901, that lynch law "is part of the religion of our people."[66]

By the summer of 1898, Newnan's white citizens betrayed little evidence of a smoldering anger. No one in Newnan reported widespread uneasiness among the rural population; no outrageous murders yet alerted whites to a pervasive threat from young black men. No screams of violated white women were reported to have pierced the night. For the first six months of 1898, public life was entangled in the Democratic gubernatorial primary, which led to the nomination of one of

Governor Atkinson's severest critics, the Old Guard's Allen D. Candler. He was a former Congressman and distant kinsman of the newly elected Bishop Warren A. Candler. That October, in his final address to the legislature, Atkinson pleaded for more effective legislation to suppress lynching.

Hours later, in his first address to the same legislature, the victorious Candler avoided specific recommendations and encouraged the body to exercise "virtue and intelligence" lest evil befall the state.[67] Candler's campaign had been lubricated by attacks on Newnan's favorite son for his deference to African Americans and his attempt to entice younger men into positions of power. The upstart from Newnan, Candler claimed, had "raped" the party; and the younger man had certainly shaken it up for the moment, but the moment was gone. Populism had threatened Democratic rule, but its moment was gone, too. No one expected any serious reforms within the foreseeable future. But the future was less foreseeable in the fall and early winter of 1898 than it had been for some time. Political partisanship may have subsided; domestic tranquility may have blessed Newnan, but beyond Coweta County, things were changing. Georgians were about to be affected by events over which they had no control.

KINDLING THE PUNITIVE PYRE: BLACK SOLDIERS

Those events began on February 15, 1898 when an explosion sank the *USS Maine* in the harbor at Havana, Cuba. Spanish authorities claimed the blast originated from within the ship and one US naval officer agreed, but investigators who insisted it came from outside won the argument. President William McKinley had sent the vessel to Havana to protect Americans presumably endangered by the Cuban revolution against Spanish rule. Erupting in 1895, insurrection had theoretically damaged United States business interests on the island. McKinley had acted after Northeastern newspapers and hawkish Congressmen aroused public opinion by accusing Spanish forces of unspeakable atrocities in crushing "democracy" and "freedom." These hallowed words saturated the language of American interventionists who accused Spain of sinking the American warship. When McKinley asked Congress for authority to invade Cuba on April 11, therefore, a majority approved; the US navy blockaded the island and Spain declared war on the United States on April 23 – precisely a year before the burning of Sam Hose.

Patriotic publicists told young American men to "Remember the Maine," but the Newnan *Herald*'s editor thought they should forget it.

He believed the war was a Yankee-inspired fraud. The spirited call to liberate Cuba from Spanish control in the name of freedom and democracy was merely a sentimental cover for the self-interested exploitation of Cubans by greedy businessmen. There was absolutely no reason, the editor wrote, to spill American blood to "make citizens" of "half-breeds and niggers."[68] Newnan's citizens who hungered for news of the war, therefore, had to rely primarily on *The Constitution* rather than their local weekly. The themes of Spanish tyranny, Cuban freedom, and American democracy dominated the rhetoric that justified the subsequent invasions of Cuba, Puerto Rico, and the Philippine Islands. American imperialists exposed Spanish General Valeriano Weyler as a "Butcher" who had drenched the Cuban people in "blood, blood, blood."

Historian Stuart Miller believes almost "every segment of American Society clamored for intervention" in the spring of 1898. The sinking of the Maine and Weyler's atrocities, however, were merely dramatized details to be exploited from within the discourse of exultant imperialism that had infected the American body-politic for some time. Although, as Kristin Hoganson points out, many prominent Americans advocated an approach in both national and international politics based on "intelligence, morality and self-restraint," there were also champions who trumped up a "more robust style." These jingoists maintained that assertiveness, confrontation, and uncompromising honor in international affairs served the nation far better than disciplined diplomacy. Those who insisted on arbitration of international disputes, for example, were not "true men," and far too many of them were actually women.

War, imperialists believed, would strengthen the United States by building "manly character in the nation's male citizens." Cuba could offer a stage on which American men could restore a manhood depleted by industrialization, urbanization, immigration, feminism, and African Americans. The Cuban War for Independence seized the imagination of Americans who claimed their government should intervene in order to win the laurels of a "chivalric ideal." Journalists praised the valor and daring of revolutionaries whom American writers and cartoonists imagined as champions of that fair maiden, Cuba. If a Mississippi congressman declared "the age of chivalry" dead, his colleagues found it resurrected among Cuban revolutionaries.

Americans thought Spaniards had long since degenerated from the ideal of the Man from La Mancha. Unlike Don Quixote, they had ravished those they should have protected. Spaniards' atrocities damned them; chivalry and honor now belonged to the Cuban knight who inspired his North American neighbors. "Which cause is morally right," a partisan asked; "Which is American?"[69] The heroic imagination fancied US soldiers fighting alongside valiant defenders of democracy, freedom, and women. The fancy bestowed a penumbra of nobility to the more practical concerns of markets, military bases, and international prestige. The celebration of honor marked the ethos of manliness similar to that which feted Southern lynching.

The discourse of manhood applied to African Americans, as well, although citizenship rather than empire motivated them. The question asked by African Americans, even before the Maine sank, was: Why should the "Negro" fight for a government that "denies his manhood," "moral character," and rights? The answer was that he should fight to stake his "claim" to "every privilege ... growing out of citizenship in this great country." Black soldiers should fight for Cuban freedom to gain their own. The valor and ability, which African American soldiers had demonstrated during the Civil War, would in future battles win the respect of white authorities and citizens. This respect, it was to be hoped, would secure the rights as well as the responsibilities of citizenship. The promise of white empathy and respect seemed to some blacks a wistful fancy instead of a realistic appraisal of white culture, but the assertion was about black action not white prejudice.

The patriotism of black soldiers would demonstrate what African Americans believed their country *should* be. The martial ethos of citizenship was thoroughly embedded in young black men's commitment to the principles of the Declaration and the Fourteenth Amendment to the Constitution.[70] Black troops were more "patriotic" than whites because the latter fought to display their manhood whereas blacks fought to make America truly exceptional. They fought for their race, to be sure, but they also fought to transcend race. In doing so, they had to face not only Cubans but also white officers, white governors, white lies, and white arrogance. Their war had many fronts.

The editor of Newnan's *Herald and Advertiser* never wrote of manhood and principle to justify the "splendid little war" of three and a half months. As the conflict gathered momentum, the editor did carry news of deaths, victories, and General Joseph Wheeler. As commander of the volunteer army, the former Confederate general and was one of the few Georgians who actually engaged the enemy. The volunteers called up in Georgia by the Federal government and Governor Atkinson remained in the state until hostilities ended. Georgians sent to Cuba in December of 1898 were assigned garrison duty. The state had, however, supported the war effort for eight months by hosting twenty-five training camps that prepared soldiers for the invasion and occupation of the island. The first camp to be opened, and the one closest to Newnan, was near Griffin, about thirty-five miles to the southeast. The largest staging area in the state was Camp Thomas at Chickamauga, the site of one of the Civil War's bloodiest battles. Seven thousand regular army soldiers and sixty regiments of states' troops were stationed there, but that did not impress the *Herald*'s editor as anything "splendid." Historians could never justify the war, he predicted; the military achievements were not worth mentioning, so he didn't. Spain deserved the sympathy of the civilized world.[71]

The Spanish American War was memorable in Georgia, but not as a foreign adventure that launched the nation into a new era of international affairs. Neither was the war necessarily memorable in 1899 for reuniting the country as Clark Howell, editor of *The Constitution*, claimed. The experience of fighting a common foe, Howell insisted, had drawn "heroes" and "martyrs" from all parts of the country to blend them in "equality, love, and peace." Once divided by war, we are now, he declared, united "by the same agency."[72] If many white Americans in both the North and South shared this view, they ignored racial tensions in the South. The "equality, love, and peace" that Howell celebrated were reserved for white people trying to heal sectional wounds, not for blacks, who were still being wounded.

Many of Howell's fellow Georgians felt as if the state had been invaded once again by armed forces of the United States. Among them were thousands of African American, battle-hardened regular army troops who had fought Native Americans in the West. Black volunteers also trained in Georgia; they had much to learn about military discipline, perhaps, but they had enlisted to prove their citizenship. The learning process was painful. Camp life was difficult enough for black and white soldiers to negotiate because of the stereotypes, suspicions, and hurts spawned by the society that sent them to Georgia. When black soldiers went to town on leave things got worse. The men were challenged by white civilians who believed them to be insolent "niggers" who didn't know their place. The soldiers, for their part, believed they had been cast beyond the jurisdiction of the US Constitution into a never-never land that mocked the premises of the Declaration of Independence. The tension erupted in violence so often that whites throughout the state, as in other Southern venues, claimed to be endangered once again by US troops.

Governor Allen Candler certainly believed as much. In March of 1899, when asked about a lynching in Palmetto, a few miles north of Newnan,

Candler answered that it had been triggered by whites' reaction to the antics of black soldiers who had stirred dangerous desires among Georgia blacks. As a seasoned politician, the governor knew how to stoke whites' racial fantasies. Candler was as clever an observer as one could have found. The governor believed that one of his predecessor's worst traits had been his willingness to help African Americans.[73] *The Constitution* had helped Candler see the menace posed by black soldiers in news reports of exchanges with white civilians across the whole region, but especially in Georgia.

In May 1898, for example, the paper reported that the African American Twenty-Fifth Infantry Regiment in northern Georgia had "terrorized" nearby Chattanooga, Tennessee. The men had forced the railroad serving Chattanooga from Lytle, Georgia, to discontinue service via the Jim Crow car; resorts near Camp Thomas closed as soon as black soldiers requested service. The soldiers were invading white space in Macon, Atlanta, Waycross, and Augusta. If the men carried pistols, the word "terror" might very well have honestly come to mind for people schooled in the manners of white supremacy. If taunted by whites, young black soldiers might very well reply, as did one sergeant, that they'd whip the Spanish just as they had the rebels in the Civil War. To emphasize the point, black soldiers sang "Hang Jeff Davis from a Sour Apple Tree."[74]

Macon became contested territory. In November and December of 1898, trains brought troops from Ohio, Virginia, and North Carolina into Fort Haskell, about one-and-a-half-miles from the city. Macon lay about ninety-five miles southeast of Coweta County in central Georgia on a rail line running between it and Atlanta via Griffin and Newnan. Black soldiers knew their enlistment had been controversial but they were prepared to defend their right to participate in a war begun, wrote one, "for Justice to Humanity." "The stars and stripes," he explained in his home-town newspaper, were "the eternal emblem of Liberty, equality, fraternity, [and] justice to everybody." The flag "must not, shall not, touch the dust, if the black arms of ten million negro [sic] Americans are given a full and fair chance to help hold it aloft."[75]

Holding the flag aloft, however, became especially difficult for volunteers. Regular army black regiments saw action in Cuba and fought valiantly at Santiago, where black soldiers earned medals for bravery.[76] Most volunteers, however, remained in American camps such as the one near Macon, where white civilians frequently treated them as the enemy. White Georgia volunteers had fired on black troops in another venue before the latter were sent to Fort Haskell in December of 1898. When the troops returned fire they had been placed under the protection of Northern white troops and sent to Macon. They were joined by the Sixth Virginia Regiment of African American volunteers who were smarting from having had their black officers replaced by whites. The newly arrived troops shared their experiences with their new comrades, and the knowledge in turn raised the level of resentment and frustration. The anger festered as Virginians refused to drill under white officers. The men were disarmed, placed under arrest, and guarded by other black troops. White newsmen claimed mutiny, but when black officers explained the men's complaints to superiors, the regiment was released and allowed leave to Macon as a Christmas present.

The gift was a mixed blessing. As they left camp, black soldiers knew they were entering the territory of hostile whites and admiring blacks. Macon's white citizens noticed how well black citizens received black men in the uniform of the US army. Black soldiers basked in the esteem and smiles of young black women, as well as their elders. Some soldiers thought that some white civilians even approached them in a less arrogant way than they did black civilians and some even concluded that their presence helped improve the behavior of Macon's white citizens. But these were minority reports. Far too many interactions between black troops and white civilians were remembered as laced with fury that sometimes resulted in the killing of soldiers for sitting in the wrong seats on trolley cars. Their comrades were not surprised when the court ruled such incidents as justifiable homicide, but they were shocked by the intense animosity during trials. Prosecutors called black soldiers and officers "ni____s" and "black s___ of B_____s." The same expressions applied to Northern white soldiers who defended black volunteers or rescued them from custody; then, of course, "damn" and "Yankee" were added to the curse.

One incident, remembered in different ways, captured the tensions between Fort Haskell and Macon. Trudging to town, black soldiers had come upon a park surrounded by trees tagged with the sign, "No Dogs or Negroes allowed in this Park." (Or maybe: "Dogs & niggers not allowed.") The soldiers found a tree on which a "colored man named Singleton was lynched." (Or: On which six or seven "Afro-Americans had been lynched...") The soldiers felled the tree. One report claimed the "owner" had cooperated but another indicated that an angry park keeper was "given a good thrashing." Someone recalled that none of the men "were ever found out," but it was more than likely they went to town to celebrate, were arrested, and restricted to camp. Black men had acted in contempt of white Southerners. Some white US Army officers defended their men's actions and a few protected troops from Macon police. Worse, officers marched the black men, four thousand strong, together with 3500 white comrades, through Macon in review.[77] Some were probably humming, "Marching through Georgia"; whites certainly would not have put it past them.

From news reports it is difficult to know what actually happened in each incident between black and white because reporters were as hostile to black soldiers as any easily offended white policeman or civilian. Seeking service and entering certain spaces could be interpreted as political or illegal acts and sometimes they were. Laughing, jeering, cheering, or condemning calculated slights could also become political or "illegal" depending on the whim of white policemen or merchants. Groups of young black men walking down the street bonded by their uniforms and military discipline were much more formidable than a few nondescript poorly dressed day laborers such as Maconites usually expected to meet.

Local whites had no economic hold on soldiers; the latter couldn't lose their jobs because they misbehaved. Local authorities couldn't arrest soldiers for vagrancy or lacking visible means of support as they did local blacks. Police could arrest soldiers for drunkenness even if they weren't guilty, but they couldn't make white Army officers believe them rather than their soldiers, which was especially galling. Delaying tactics by army officers to protect men arrested for no justifiable cause also angered white authorities. Yankee commanders were no less outraged. Captain Amos Brandt told reporters in Des Moines, Iowa, immediately after arriving from Macon that Georgia was the most "hellish" place imaginable. Authorities there "arrested our men without cause and gave them heavy fines," he reported; "They lied about our men, perjured themselves to get our money and threatened our second lieutenant with a year on the chain gang for an offense he was not responsible for." *The Constitution*'s editor complained that the captain should have made his statement before he left Macon, but Brandt was neither masochistic nor stupid.[78]

Newspaper editors helped Georgians understand how dangerous African American troops were when the time came for sending them home. In Macon, white civilians were relieved that a white regiment would remain to police Fort Haskell until all black troops were gone. From daily reports, a reader could easily infer that whites were besieged by black troops seething for revenge, but their reason for doing so was never explained. Stories circulated about incidents that *might have happened* if whites had not threatened violence. Headlines announced,

"Macon Worried about Negroes," and "Afraid Negroes will be Riotous." Those "most anxious," however, "that the [black] regiments be mustered out," a newsman observed, were frequently the most disappointed when it became clear that local merchants would not be allowed to sell their wares to departing soldiers flush with severance pay. Capitalism trumped race when sales raised the spirits of black Tar Heels as they boarded the train.

The volunteers became so boisterous that a few discharged pistols in celebration. These antics encouraged Macon authorities to warn Atlanta police by telegraph that they would have trouble with the soldiers when they stopped *en route*. In response, Atlanta authorities refused to allow black troops to leave their train because they had, reported *The Constitution*, threatened to "Tear up Atlanta" and kill policemen. There was no evidence to support such claims; but one man was arrested for a misdemeanor. Whites could never be too careful when young black men tried to behave like whites. That this offense sparked whites' reactions is suggested by *The Constitution*'s postscript that some black soldiers had "high notions" about travelling by train; they had actually hired sleeping cars.[79]

After a few North Carolina companies departed Macon, other Tar Heels left without incident. The *Macon Telegraph* reported that the remaining black Tenth Immune regiment was what a later generation would call "a credit to their race." The men were reported to be from the South; thus they knew how to behave at least until March 8, 1899. Then, a train carrying black volunteers left Fort Haskell for Macon. Elation at leaving Georgia got the better of some men, who shot into the air. A white youth was wounded in the arm, but no one was arrested. The *Macon Telegraph* dismissed the matter as an unfortunate accident. To prevent another incident, the Macon police asked Colonel Thad Jones to restrain his men until they left the city because "rash spirits" planned to use the incident as provocation to shoot at the train. The Colonel agreed and the first section of the Tenth Immune Regiment left for Atlanta without incident.

The train stopped briefly in Griffin. Just before entering the city, a few men shot in the air but at the depot were quiet. To local officials, however, a few enthusiastic black men were "half-drunken fiends" threatening "desperate circumstances" that required "desperate means" in the future. The "fiends," who left Griffin without harming or insulting anyone, became, in white newsmen's fancy, guilty of riotous acts they did not commit. Fictional acts and the fancied motivations behind them became the excuse for "desperate means" when the second section of Immunes chugged into Griffin. The city was especially devoted to keeping the racial peace. Lynching was reported to be fairly normal there. This aura had encouraged white men to organize the Griffin Rifles, a quasi-military group attached to the county militia. They did not meet the train that carried the first section of the Tenth Immunes to Atlanta, but they did meet the second.

Passengers were astonished when about 200 white men surrounded the train with guns raised. A policemen claimed to see a black man holding a pistol, and proceeded, according to a reporter, somehow to avert a major riot. The menacing crowd alarmed Lieutenant-Colonel C. H. Withrow, who asked Governor Candler by telegraph to send state militia to protect his men. White reporters contemptuously scoffed. The colonel's request, they insisted, was "a fabrication of lies" to hide the fact that the Immunes were "shooting down innocent men and endangering the lives of women and children [while] Withrow was quietly in his car surrounded by his negro [sic] officers and their wives." This childish fantasy, if true, would have brought a bloody response by many more white Georgians than Griffin could have mustered. The soldiers knew better than to leave the safety of railway cars when surrounded by self-styled "desperate" whites.

The latter were actually creating an incident to justify their claims of a widespread threat, and, true to this fantasy, the governor refused Withnow's request. Candler could not honor the word of a white officer who associated with "negroes" and "their wives." The colonel had cause to fear for the safety of his men. The white militia were prepared to fire their weapons; most soldiers were unarmed; all wanted to get out of Georgia as fast as possible. As the train cleared the depot, a volunteer couldn't resist shooting into the air from the front of the train. In reply, whites fired a volley into the sleeping car where officers and their wives were sitting. They killed a white trainman. The single casualty of the Immunes' "riotous" presence was a white man slain by incendiary white alarmists. Withrow charged Griffin's leaders with stupidity and cowardice.[80]

Georgia's political elite transformed the "episode in Griffin" into a social drama that proved a widespread dangerous restlessness among African Americans. Armed whites had, according to the script, prevented a major riot by undisciplined black men who had been terrorizing the countryside. The soldiers' incompetent white officers, Georgians claimed, made no effort to prevent the (nonexistent) rampage. It was stopped in its tracks only by the quick thinking of Griffin's valiant white establishment. There had been no racial friction in Georgia, Governor Candler explained on March 17, until "regiments of insolent, drunken negro soldiers, the scum of the dives of the cities north and south were quartered here and there in this State and in [those further to] the South." He insisted that for months "lawless vagabonds wearing the uniform of United States soldiers terrorized [towns] ... in north Georgia to say nothing of the Griffin episode and other similar circumstances."

Candler made his statement to explain why a group of masked white men had earlier lined nine black men against the wall of a warehouse in Palmetto, Georgia, and shot them in cold blood. Those black soldiers, long since gone from Georgia, were also blamed for inciting three African American men to rape a white woman in Leesburg. The subsequent lynching of those three, as well as the murders in Palmetto, were, Candler believed, in "retaliation" for acts by black soldiers. The editor of Griffin's newspaper attacked Candler for placing the lynchings within the context of anger at black soldiers. The publisher of the Newnan *Herald*, however, agreed with Candler and offered as verifying evidence the rumor that black soldiers had somehow *almost* caused a riot in Birmingham.[81] Whatever black US troops were *almost* ready to do – except leave Georgia as swiftly as possible – justified whites' inventive paranoia. Alarmists had fabricated a nonexistent threat to warrant white violence.

Palmetto and Griffin were towns that Newnan's citizens knew well. The former was just over the county line a few miles to the north and was thought of as Newnan's sister town. Griffin was a rival to the southeast. The Palmetto lynching for Newnan's citizens was a local event and the crimes that preceded it were local affairs, especially when fires "ravaged" parts of Palmetto's business district in February and March of 1899. An African American was arrested for arson, but there was not enough evidence to convict him. When fires flared once again and white people were afflicted by disturbing pranks, authorities became unhinged. Police arrested nine men, based on the confession of a black "vagrant." The men were locked in the warehouse where the masked white men shot them. Details were confusing but editors found to their great dismay that the Northern press had transformed the lynching into a national event.

Yankees seemed to "froth at the mouth" with regard to the "tragedy" that local authorities at first agreed "was most unfortunate." The Governor immediately offered a five hundred dollar reward for the arrest of each criminal in the mob but no one was apprehended. After the lynching, Palmetto's "leading citizens" were reported to be furious that outsiders had invaded their town to murder men who would certainly have been found guilty at trial. On reflection, however, officials began to fear Palmetto blacks would "retaliate" for the murders and asked for protection. Governor Candler sent the militia. Reflecting on the "Palmetto Affair," the Newnan *Herald*'s editor observed that in other communities the "lawless element" had often made "demons of peaceable men," who had had to act in a way "beneficial to the community." Whites transformed an "unfortunate" tragedy into a necessity.[82]

The Palmetto arsons and lynching erupted into a public consciousness set on edge by alarmist rumor, official posturing, and sensational reporting. To be sure, the aura of public discourse and the climate of opinion did not necessarily prepare all white men to kill black men. Anxiety among whites intensified as they heard reports of acts by insolent black soldiers, but the anxiety did not necessarily compel most whites to prepare for a black revolution. Such fretfulness did allow self-appointed guardians of white supremacy, however, to justify killing unruly black men when "necessity" demanded it. White Georgia volunteers who fired on black North Carolinians in an army camp during drills in September 1898 had many sympathizers in the general population long before the Tenth Immune regiment boarded the train in Macon to return home. The presence of black soldiers that filled black Georgians with pride could be terribly unsettling, as Governor Candler pointed out. The cultural milieu of black-and-white from Griffin to Palmetto, however, seemed peaceful enough under white surveillance, but kindling for a fiery incident had been gathered and piled high.

Griffin whites had gathered together more than once unnecessarily to threaten black troops with violence; the Governor was furious with the troubles US soldiers had brought into his state. Palmetto whites feared retaliation for the lynching, which many came to believe had been justified. Corra Harris may have been more accurate than she knew when she wrote that "The days are feverish with suppressed excitement, and concealed animosities," because "animosities" that may not have even existed before were becoming an excuse for white vigilance and violence. Incidents crafted by whites in Palmetto and Griffin and the fury that linked them in white men's minds left white imaginations to smolder in combustibility. A match was all that was needed to ignite the flames of racial vengeance.

Within this context, an African American day laborer listed long before in the Federal census as Thomas Wilkes asked his employer, Alfred Cranford, for back wages owed him. He also appealed for time off to visit his ailing mother. From the perspective of a much later time the request seems innocent enough, but in the spring of 1899 near Palmetto, Georgia, it was not. It was a match.

4

Burning Sam Hose

"Let your light so shine before men, that they may see your good works and glorify your Father which is in heaven."

Christian Bible KJV, Matthew 5:16

"And the tongue is a fire, a world of iniquity: so is the tongue among our members, that it defileth the whole body, and setteth on fire the course of nature; and it is set on fire of hell.... But the tongue can no man tame; it is an unruly evil, full of deadly poison."

Christian Bible KJV, James 3: 6, 8

"Nevertheless we, according to His promise, look for new heavens and a new earth in which righteousness dwells."

Christian Bible KJV, Peter 3:13

* * *

On the third Sunday after Easter in 1899 about forty miles southwest of Atlanta in Newnan, Georgia, a white crowd burned to death a fugitive black laborer known as Sam Hose. This atrocity blended anger, hatred, arrogance, festivity, brutality and satisfaction into a mood just beyond comprehension. "Glory!" shouted an excited man enraptured by the intensity of the moment, "Glory be to God!!"

When Tom Wilkes asked his boss for time and money to visit his mother he broke the strictest rules of white supremacy. He had assumed that Alfred Cranford owed him wages and respect. For a young black man to think that a white man *owed* him anything at all, especially respect, was dangerous in April 1899 when whites were especially wary. Georgia militia patrolled Palmetto's streets just a few miles north of Cranford's farm and monitored African American churches. Authorities claimed to fear retaliation for the murder of accused black arsonists by a white mob. Whites in the little mill town and all along the railroad south to Newnan and Griffin were reportedly on edge. The lynching in Palmetto had stoked the embers of a smoldering disquiet that settled a toxic mist on the land. The "Griffin Incident" suggested what whites would do if anxiety erupted into alarm. *The Constitution*'s editors thought vigilance was justified by a hostile Yankee-instigated unrest that had been, they claimed, escalating for eleven months among blacks. Editorials scolded African Americans. If they were to be accepted as "law abiding" citizens they would have to break "the fitful fever of the past few years."[1] That fever, fantasists claimed, had arisen from blacks' craving equality. The effrontery seemed to fill the air so that even the most innocent request could be taken as an unwarranted challenge.

When Wilkes approached Cranford, he enraged a man notorious for his bad temper when dealing with blacks. Cranford did not simply refuse the request for time and money, but transformed it into an issue of power and rebellion. He was, after all, the son of a prominent farmer who lived nearby, and in no mood to be challenged by a worthless black who presumed too much for his own good. Cranford turned to his father for advice and a gun. The weapon was scarcely called for. Tom Wilkes usually found it difficult to look a white man directly in the eye when addressing him, so he was understandably nervous when he approached his employer. Cranford possessed a surfeit of power, if not decency, but needed for some reason to transform Wilkes' request for time and money into defiant insolence. The pistol was supposed to solve any problem he might have with the black laborer. At least this is how African Americans began the story of Sam Hose.[2]

What happened next was told in various ways by white reporters, but none mentioned back-wages or a sick mother. The standard white story reported that Cranford had cautioned Hose for "slighting his work," which implied sloth and negligence. The accusation applied to any black man who "caused trouble," whether virtual or actual. In response, "Hose became sullen," the usual complaint of whites who admonished blacks: "sullen" meant "dangerous!" To prove it, Cranford's family told reporters that Hose had been "heard by other negroes on the place to make threats against Mr. Cranford." Since whites chronically complained blacks would never ever share such information with them, the story is suspect.

Both black and white stories, however, reported that Cranford possessed a weapon and that Wilkes had killed his employer with an axe. There was agreement on little else. The white story – amplified and polished over the course of a few days – imagined Mattie McLeroy Cranford seated at dinner with her family after a hard day's labor. Peace and prayer reigned until she saw a barefooted Hose silently appear behind her husband; for some unexplained reason she did not scream in warning. Hose then cleaved Cranford's skull to the bridge of his nose. He kicked the body aside and forced Mrs. Cranford to collect the family's valuables. Afterwards, he dashed her baby (who miraculously survived) to the floor and ravished Mattie Cranford in her husband's brains and blood. Thus spent, he gathered his plunder, histrionically taunted Mrs. Cranford with a melodramatic flourish best suited to the Victorian theatre, and disappeared into the night.[3] The story flowed from the predispositions of white men who had inherited them from supremacists who imagined every act by black men against whites to be ultimately gendered and tantamount to rape.

The story told by black informants was shorter and less complex. While dutifully chopping wood for his employer's stove, Wilkes was said to have asked about his earlier request. Cranford raised his gun to shoot the black man. Frightened, the latter threw the axe in self-defense and fatally struck Cranford in the head. In a panic, Wilkes fled the yard. He tried but failed to find help from a suspicious black minister and headed for his mother's home near Marshallville in Macon County 100 miles to the southeast.[4]

PURSUIT AND FRUSTRATION

The authorized version of the Sam Hose story eventually focused on his having raped Mattie Cranford. A recent commentary on Hose's actions explains that there is an argument to be made "for some kind of sexual assault" because the Cranford and McLeroy families were well-known in Coweta County. The Cranford spokesmen would not have stigmatized Mrs. Cranford, it is claimed, unless she had in fact been violated. No reporter, however, was allowed to interview her; she was unable to gather enough poise and strength to talk with anyone about what had happened. A man known to the family spoke with her briefly but revealed nothing about the conversation. He did not confirm the rumor that there had been a rape. Stories ground through the sifters of rumor, fantasy, and innuendo explained that the experience had driven Mattie

Cranford to the edge of sanity, allowing readers to accept the supremacists' narrative based on rape.

If the testosterone-driven ideology of white supremacy dramatized
white men's fury in response to black men's ravishing white women, it
was scarcely forgiving of the women it presumed to "protect" or avenge.
The pain white hunters wished to inflict on Sam Hose was foreshadowed
by the pain those same hunters and the reporters who spoke for them
carelessly but insistently inflicted on Mattie Cranford. She steadfastly
resisted their assaults on her privacy. White men seeking the rapist,
however, were encouraged to imagine the ravishing over and over again
in a way that could damage any woman's sense of self and bruise her
soul.[5] The stigma attached to a lie about her having been raped would
have cowed Mattie Cranford into a despondent and reclusive silence as
much as the shame and horror at actually having been "ravished." There
is no doubt that she was shattered and that what had happened had a
devastating effect on her for the rest of her life.

When the crowd brought Wilkes to Pitt McLeroy's door in Newnan on
the way to execution, Mrs. McLeroy appeared in her daughter's stead.
She did not ask Wilkes, "Why did you hurt my daughter?" Rather,
she demanded, "Why did you kill Mr. Cranford?" A mother furious at
the man who savaged her daughter would not have focused on Alfred.
Mattie was her little girl (even if the mother of four) and in great pain
because of her husband's death and the ugly speculations associated with
it. Mrs. McLeroy mentioned death not rape (hurt). G. E. Cranford was
much more prominent than Pitt McLeroy, and a member of the extended
family was in charge of explaining on its behalf what had happened. For
the Cranfords, the killing of a son would have demanded a story designed
to ensure draconian punishment. According to the mythology of lynching,
a white woman's being raped in her husband's blood, whether it was
literally true or not, *ought* to have been true. The moral imperative of
such a narrative elevated the enormity of the crime to stunning propor-
tions that demanded a spectacular punishment.[6]

Almost as important as a requisite rape was the myth of a black
community plotting rebellion. When white publicists transformed the
Palmetto lynching of March 16 from a tragedy into a public service, the
small but respectable black middle class of Palmetto vanished in a panic,
at least for the moment. The governor sent troops to Palmetto not to
protect black people who were the targets of violence but nervous whites
who feared "reprisals" during an imminent black reign of terror. Fantasists "knew" the terror was coming because black community leaders

refused to deliver the villains white alarmists believed had set fire to the business district. Many of the latter claimed that all of Palmetto's African Americans were suppressing the truth and hiding criminals.

Indeed, the highly regarded black Methodist minister J. W. Tharpe was falsely accused of being "at the bottom" of unrest among the African American community after the lynching. He had addressed his congregation in what alarmist whites claimed had been an inflammatory and threatening manner. None of his enemies ever reported what he said, and whites who knew him and knew what he had said defended him, but he feared for his life. Tharpe escaped Palmetto for Fayetteville, Georgia, with the aid of Bishop Henry McNeal Turner of the African Methodist Episcopal Church who appointed him to the AMEC pulpit there. Had he remained in Palmetto or been discovered in Griffin, reporters explained, Tharpe would have been properly lynched.

This hostility shocked a renowned white minister who knew the African American population of Palmetto and its clerical leaders very well. Wilbur P. Thirkield, president of Atlanta's Gammon Theological Seminary for black Methodists, had been dramatically impressed with "the cordial relations between the white and colored people" of Palmetto when visiting in December 1898. As a result, he persuaded a religious convocation to praise the village as a model "of tolerance and good will" for "this commonwealth and . . . the [entire] southland." When in February 1899 the first fires were set, the president pointed out in a letter to *The Constitution*, black citizens helped douse them only to be falsely accused of looting. When the second plague of arsons broke out, maligned African Americans were less inclined to help, and this reasonable reticence became proof to panicky whites that black men had started both sets of fires. This accusation further alienated African Americans, Thirkield explained, but the rift could be repaired by enlightened white leadership. If the murderers who gunned down black prisoners were brought to justice by "the best people of Palmetto," he wrote, "the peace and welfare of both races" would be well served.

Expecting white leaders to care for the welfare of "both races," however, was to expect too much. In reply, Dr. Hal L. Johnston, a dentist who was one of Palmetto's best people, attacked Gammon's president for ignoring facts. Ninety percent of the white population of Campbell County knows, the dentist wrote, that "prejudice created by the Methodist clergy among the negroes [sic] against the whites" had caused the arson and subsequent lynching. The dentist knew that three-fourths of the African Americans in the county could identify the arsonists:

He claimed to have absolute proof. Johnston insisted that the whites knew blacks would not bear "witness" against other blacks. He failed to mention that arrests linked to the arsons had relied on blacks' testimony alone. Johnston concluded that ninety per cent "of negroes [in Palmetto] are responsible for the mob and their blood is on their hands and those [like Thirkield] who teach them."[7]

Hal Johnston was one of those public men who have a firm grasp of what is going on even without evidence. There are some things men know because of their position, experience, intuition, arrogance, and the unerring ability to convince themselves as well as others that they know what they are talking about even when they don't. The Palmetto dentist knew that black men in Palmetto were conspiring to avenge fictitious wrongs by innocent whites. As he tried to make sense of what he thought he knew, Johnston began to realize that Wilkes was part of that conspiracy. The dentist had had time to think about this connection when he joined in the fruitless pursuit of the "will 'o' the wisp" who had "chopped" Cranford to pieces. When he returned from exercising his civic duty – scruffy, exhausted, famished, and empty-handed Johnston found a note, he claimed. It warned him to "Prepare for Death, for you are a marked man." Others had been warned, too.[8] Martyrdom was imminent.

Anger and frustration simmered in Johnston's narcissistic reflections as he projected onto the black community his own feelings of contempt and fury at a people who would simply not behave. He attributed to them his own aggressiveness. The notes that sparked his zealous inventiveness proved the existence of an extensive threat no one could ever find. His explanation of what was happening, or possibly about to happen, helped transform the hunt for Sam Hose into a crusade against a rebellious community. The imagined rape of Cranford's wife revealed what lay ahead for all white women unless the "fiend" were captured and punished in a way that would prevent further desecrations. The punishment planned was justified by rape; but it was supposed to terrorize a seditious people.

The editors of *The Constitution*, Clark Howell and William Hemphill, helped their readers keep track of what Dr. Johnston and men like him said had been happening in Palmetto ever since the lynching in March. After the killing of Alfred Cranford, Howell and Hemphill became part of the stories their reporters told when they offered a reward of five hundred dollars for the arrest and delivery of Sam Hose to Atlanta. The governor had been able to offer only two-hundred fifty dollars but he soon doubled it to match *The Constitution*'s generosity. Eventually over 1300 dollars in reward money was offered.

In addition to defining reality, *The Constitution* defined morality for the "thousands" who sought the killer and rapist. Howell and Hemphill believed justice demanded speed beyond the sluggishness of the legal system and pain beyond human endurance. They relied on the smoldering violence that lay beneath the surface of the segregated social order to justify a powerful eruption of fury at the actions of a monstrous 140 pound fiend with a nervous tic. After burying Alfred Cranford next to his Uncle Zack (also killed by a black man years earlier), the family announced that Mattie "wants to see the negro [sic] lynched." He was not, however, to be hanged or shot. Justice demanded death by fire. Thus from the very beginning of what was to become a long and frustrating hunt, trackers, searchers, posses, and "lone wolves" carried with them the images of rape and murder, torture and fire.

The hunters began in Palmetto the morning following the homicide when they forced suspect black men to quit the town after brutal and fruitless questioning. They probably burned a black church near the Cranford's farm, too; but no one admitted it. When searchers reached the plantation of Major W. W. Thomas, they questioned one of his tenants, the Reverend Elijah Strickland, who was more than willing to help. He reported that Hose had contacted him last evening with a strange request; he wanted Strickland to exchange clothing with him. Strickland had refused and sent him on his way not realizing what his visitor had done. Strickland told the white men that he thought Hose was going to Marshallville to visit relatives, but the party never reported this information. They certainly did not act on it. Mobs are not necessarily competent or easily convinced by facts that do not fit their treasured preconceptions.

Other stalkers learned from another black man that he had fed Hose and lent him a pistol. The possession of a weapon confirmed in the huntsmen's minds Hose's commitment to killing even more whites and was consistent with the alarm sounded by *The Constitution*'s editors. A fictional gun was more important to the mob than a fact-based narrative. Now that Hose was armed it was not surprising that he exchanged shots with his pursuers in Turin just to the east of Newnan. Alas, the shooter (if there had in fact been one) was definitely not Hose. The fugitive was nowhere near Turin, or Palmetto, or Fairburn, or Newnan, or Griffin, or Woodbury – all places in which hunters were about to capture him. The stories kept flowing from the imaginations of "excited" men who had apparently sloughed off their "cool" as they continued to corner a man they could not find. He was everywhere and nowhere. The frustration at repeated failure stoked the trackers' fervor for a violent outcome to their hunt.

The search area extended from Fairburn, slightly to the north of Palmetto, to the outskirts of the small village of Woodbury about seventy miles to the south. The swamps, thickets, and woods between Griffin, thirty-five miles east-southeast of Newnan, and La Grange, about thirty miles to the southwest, were also part of the targeted area. Sightings, however, were also reported from Auburn, Alabama, and Columbus, Georgia, both well outside the range within which Hose was "known" to be hiding. The hunters were looking for a young, slim, and "coppery colored" man who was about five feet eight inches tall and weighed probably 140 pounds. His hair was cut close to the sides of his head but it was longer on the top; he had a small, pencil-thin moustache, or at least had had one when he killed Cranford. In conversation with whites he held his head to the left and suffered intermittent small involuntary spasms.

If posses had paid attention to the description published at least three times by *The Constitution*, a dark (not coppery) African American man from South Carolina would not have been arrested six times or lodged in the College Park jail near Atlanta. Miles to the south, a black woman admitted talking with Dan Hose, who freely confessed, she said, his crimes against the Cranfords. The news sent the posse after the man who was "skulking" along the road. Hose was seized and taken to the Cranford home for identification; but he wasn't Tom Wilkes and he wasn't Sam Hose. He wasn't even Dan Hose; he was Dan Holt. He later confessed he was now afraid to leave the Fairburn jail. It was not safe for an unknown African American man to be walking along the public right of way.

A mob of whites in faraway Columbus chased a terrified man out of town who then emerged in Auburn, Alabama, where he was the target of an excited town marshal who emptied his gun at him without result. Finally, one Charley Hargett, a loner apparently from West Point near La Grange, tracked Hose to Cusetta, Alabama, and captured him. No doubt relishing the reward money he was about to receive, Hargett headed to Palmetto, but he, too, had the wrong man. Sam Hose could be anyone whites wanted a black man to be until he became visible from evidence previously ignored.

Griffin's huntsmen were especially active. *The Constitution* reported that since April 15 groups of men "almost daily" had fanned out from the town in different directions only to return without their prize. Griffinites were becoming especially frustrated according to Abe Rogowski, who was later identified as one of the primary actors among Griffin's many posses. (The man's surname was either Polish or Russian and may have been Jewish. An Abraham Rogowski had arrived in the United States from Russia on the ship *Gellert* in 1881 at the age of 22.) Rogowski was absent to the city census of 1900 but a frequent, eager, and "reliable" source for reporters in April of 1899. On April 16, which was the fourth day of the hunt, he claimed that men from Griffin would have taken Hose, but for a bungling idiot who falsely reported the prey had been captured and removed to Palmetto for burning.

The volunteer posse had, Rogowski complained, tracked the real Sam Hose to Concord, a mere eighteen miles south-southwest of Griffin. They did so reportedly by following a trail of Confederate money, which the fugitive had presumably attempted to pass. Finally, the traveler stopped at the plantation of J. P. Crawford, who hired him and informed authorities. When the posse found Hose's bloodstained clothing, they knew they almost had him but then came news of the arrest. Rogowski asked if the informant was sure; the reply was "Yes!" When he learned the truth, Rogowski was indignant because he was "confident his party would have caught Hose but for the unfortunate dispatch." The man with the "foreign" name was as well informed as Hal Johnston. Tom Wilkes was nowhere near Concord; he was not working for Crawford; he was hiding in his mother's home near faraway Marshallville. Elijah Strickland was right.

Griffin's hunters followed all the leads they could muster, imagine, or fabricate. Constant failure was wearying; it could explode into brutal punishment of African Americans who failed to cooperate. On April 20 it became clear just how frustrated Griffin volunteers had become. Trackers seized Henry Harris in his home because they had heard he knew where Sam Hose was hiding. To encourage Harris to reveal the fugitive's hiding place, they offered him ten dollars – a small fortune. Harris claimed he had no idea where Hose was but unfortunately added that even if he had such information, he wouldn't admit it. He announced he was absolutely fed up with how whites treated black people. In response to this effrontery, the searchers bound Harris to a tree where generations of black men were said to have been lynched and beat him so badly he was not expected to survive. Harris had served as a visible surrogate for an invisible man.

To avoid Harris' fate, most African Americans knew better than to express themselves as freely as he. They knew that self-preservation dictated they appear cooperative. If challenged, they had to appease whites and deflect attention from themselves. They could not be too careful when confronted by angry, armed, frustrated, and ignorant white men. Black people had had centuries of practice in telling "white folks" what they wanted to hear or believe – Henry Harris to the contrary notwithstanding. The emotions stirred by a white public outcry decreed caution. Many African Americans undoubtedly wanted Hose caught. They believed he had committed a serious crime or, worse, they feared white vengeance on black communities if he were not found. They also knew that white men would not allow "due process" to play out in court once Hose was captured. They were caught in a double bind.

Defenders of lynching often excused themselves by claiming they had to deal brutally with a community that would never help white men capture criminal blacks. Hal Johnston had relied on this supremacist fantasy when he claimed that African American community leaders in Palmetto had lied when they denied knowing who set the fires there; he knew that it was in their very nature to lie! Later, Georgia whites and their governor would justify the burning of Sam Hose on the same ground; African Americans would not cooperate in sustaining law and order. The claim was false and searchers knew it was false because they had invaded swamp and forest together with black men who were also armed and ready to capture a fugitive who, they believed, had disgraced their race. Near Milner, just south of Griffin, many black men had fanned out into the wasteland to find the fugitive; Bob Baker was mentioned as being especially helpful.

So was Monroe Mitchell – in fact, he was too helpful. *The Constitution* reported that he "was a negro [sic] holding the friendship of all residents here, [who] was shot by mistake owing to his zeal." At twilight, Mitchell confronted a white man who was dark enough to be suspect. Mitchell ordered him to identify himself; when there was no reply the black man fired twice. In response, Oscar Harden, a white citizen from Pike County, shot Mitchell in the left shoulder. Whites who recognized Mitchell then rushed him to a surgeon and began raising money to support him until he could return to work.

Anyone reading news accounts of the hunt for Sam Hose would conclude that after ten days, "determined men" were frustrated and less "cool" than they had been. The surfeit of false leads, fanciful stories, and "imminent" captures seemed to stoke a "fever heat" that claimed ever more actors in a carnival of fury and fantasy. Entire villages, it was reported, had been shuttered to allow their men to mount horses and bicycles, hitch buggies and wagons, or strike out on foot in the multiple county manhunt. The widespread participation by white men in a collective enterprise helped augment the narrative of danger, threat, and alarm.

The storyline improved on the implications fabricated by the "Griffin incident" and the Palmetto arsons that fed the fanciful but deadly imaginations of men like Hal Johnston. Incidents of possible threat from probable exchanges between black and white suggested to some people that they could claim that the entire countryside, and especially white women, lived in a state of absolute terror. On the twentieth of April, Hose, now christened Holt, was reported still to be "near the scene of his terrible crime" where he once again threatened a white woman. "Wild-eyed" and obviously "hunted," the menacing Holt had approached a Mrs. Sewell while her husband was absent. Holt reportedly demanded money. Later, editors, politicians, and reporters realized – through inventive rumination worthy of Hal Johnston – that she had actually been in danger of being raped. The furious and capable Mrs. Sewell, however, had driven Holt away by brandishing a pistol that she was fully prepared to use. She then alerted the police in Palmetto.[9]

A COUNTRYSIDE TERRORIZED?

This dramatic encounter acted as a minor prelude to an extensive article published in *The Constitution* on April 23 and entitled "How Shall the Women and Girls in the Country Districts Be Protected?" The authors did not mention Hal Johnston's theory of a vast African American plot, but they did insist that there was a widespread threat that was even more perilous than conspiracy. Every white woman in the countryside was in danger. It was the kind of mythic fabrication that had triggered Ida Well's condemnation of the "thread bare lie" in her last Memphis editorial of 1892. In 1899, the "lie" seemed to have even more credibility than seven years earlier. Constant repetition had turned it into a "reality" that forced even opponents of lynching to affirm its credibility. The article was inspired by Mrs. Loulie Gordon, the widow of Captain Walter S. Gordon, CSA. She had written a letter to prominent Georgians asking them how to lift "the cloud of fear" hovering over white women in the countryside.

Gordon was a wealthy planter from Dougherty County in southwest Georgia, where the previous year one black man had been accused of attempted rape. Only seventeen crimes had been serious enough to send blacks to the chain gang; none targeted white women. If there was a "cloud of fear" cloaking the county it hung primarily over black people, one man reported, and made the county a "Hell" for them. The chain gang was, sensible blacks believed, a reliable source of forced labor for local plantations. Workers had dropped dead in the fields under the white man's command. Debt not rape bore down on black and white alike until it settled most fiercely on black laborers, bent "beneath the burden of it all." The county was also a place where police could shoot a black youth simply "for loud talking on the sidewalk." To some people, the area had been known as the "Egypt of the Confederacy."

Gordon did not mention the crushing poverty of black people of course, but neither did she report any terrorized white women in Dougherty County. She focused on the rape of Mattie Cranford. Mattie's cry of "pain at the outrage on her womanhood" had become a "wail of prayer for the protection of our women and girls" throughout the state. Gordon was not a feminist, but she supported charities to protect working and aging white women. She was active in the American Red Cross and had presided over its Southern auxiliary. She was always ready to serve, as were most of the women she invited to write, on special committees that required a white woman's insight. The planter had also lobbied effectively for the Georgia woman's college in Milledgeville and now she asked ten friends with whom she had worked in various capacities to express their views on how to protect country women. She also recruited eight men.[10]

Gordon launched the essays with "A Word to the Negroes." Praising the "faithful slave" who had protected white females during the War, she went on to exalt the "mammies" who had nurtured white culture. Their children, Gordon pleaded, should now train a new generation of African Americans to be as deferential as their enslaved grandparents. The assumption behind Gordon's mythic narrative was that current black leaders had failed to teach their young right from wrong.

Gordon's reprimand introduced an essay by a former governor, William Northen, who was well-known for opposing (most) lynching. Like other essayists, including Gordon, he suggested creating a well-trained county constabulary. He also suggested instructing white women in the use of firearms. He thought that "an occasional negro [sic] lying dead in the hay yard shot by a brave woman in defense of her honor, will do more to stop this awful crime [of rape] than all the lynching that may occur in a year." Guns would bring peace! Other essays suggested fanciful and impossible social engineering. The nation could colonize black people beyond the United States at public expense or establish black states in the West. Southerners could hire only white servants and laborers from Sweden, Germany, or France to supplant the exiled black populace. Perhaps whites could live closer together in what could be imagined as fortified hamlets. Each proposal rested on the assumption that a black menace had to be controlled, punished, or removed; all were so expensive and coercive they were simply unrealistic.

If the question that linked them was how to protect women, the essayists knew that one of the answers was *lynching*. And that was the answer all but one rejected. They thought they could prevent lynching by making the courts more efficient and lawyers less sleazy; mob violence flowed from flaws in the criminal justice system. Two of Northen's colleagues, W. B. Lowe and Porter King, agreed with him that the primary flaw was the axiom that the accused were innocent until proved guilty. Because the phrase was so thoroughly engraved in the folklore of Anglo-American law, however, reformers did not attack it candidly or precisely. Rather, they attacked defense attorneys who acted on the axiom by winning acquittal for black men, who, white men knew without supporting evidence, were actually guilty. Such disreputable lawyers were frequently deceitful enough to appeal verdicts to higher courts based on error by judges, misconduct by jurors, or other "technicalities." Due process, guaranteed by the US constitution, was offensive nonsense to men who knew, as did Hal Johnston, that the accused were always guilty.

Due process was too erratic, slow, and undemocratic. Trial lawyers who requested continuances or delays should be disbarred; at least Governor Northen (a former slaveholder) thought so. Lowe and Northen believed that the appeal process should be accelerated at the very least; in fact, there was almost universal agreement among both opponents and defenders of lynching that the judicial process should move more swiftly than it did. Maybe special courts could be established to deal with accused rapists; certainly executions should follow almost immediately after a guilty verdict. Porter King, former mayor of Atlanta and a renowned attorney, also hoped that a streamlined criminal justice system could count on law-abiding citizens to bring murderous white mobs to justice.

Most women essayists also wanted to stop lynching. Sarah Harper Mims' solution to a dangerous countryside was a revival of religion. As a well-known and assertive Christian Science lecturer, she knew the perils of being different in a culture that privileged orthodoxy. An eloquent public speaker, she modeled her belief that women were equal to men "in talents [and] genius"; she scoffed at the disgraceful image of helpless women. She believed in punishing crimes, to be sure, but she wanted newspapers to spend less space on crime and more on establishing relationships reflecting the all-abiding presence of God. She meant in effect, "Let us act out of Love not Hate." Although mired in a theology that

denied the reality of evil, Mims hoped for change: She had no truck with
militias or killing, and she was not alone. Sallie Chase Patillo was much
more orthodox than Mims, but she, too, believed education and religion
were the long-term means to a peaceful countryside. She conceded
"savages" lurked from within black communities but they originated in
white communities as well. She wanted to change whites as well as blacks.

If Mims and Patillo did not offer detailed solutions, they did refuse to
declare war on African Americans. They were segregationists, of course,
and represented a sensibility rather than a clear position, but they agreed
with another essayist, Mary E. Bryan. The well-known novelist and
famed editor insisted that the supremacist axiom of "terrorizing the negro
as a means of preventing barbarous deeds on his part" was neither
efficacious nor moral. Torture brutalized the torturer, she insisted, and
cruelty incited cruelty; neither solved anything![11]

Rebecca Latimore Felton disagreed; she wanted *Blood and Fire*. Earlier
in the year, *The Constitution* had identified her as a woman who had
never "made a statement that she has had to retract." At sixty-four years
of age, she was still the public figure she had been for thirty years and was
more than ever happy to clarify her position on any public issue in a
highly quotable way. Her 1897 speech at Tybee Island calling for the
lynching of thousands of black rapists was well-known in both North and
South. A Baptist clergyman had condemned her torrent of words as
delivered in "the incoherence and fury of madness." Felton did "fury"
better than most men.

She did not disappoint partisans of lynching now. The criminal justice
system, she proclaimed, was a farce. If you don't think so, just remember
that the governor can commute the sentence of black rapists and the
courts can refuse to allow just punishment of double murderers. She
had evidence. "When I think of the Allen home," she wrote, "and Flanagan eating three meals a day," she was furious. She imagined that if Sam
Hose were to be jailed, he would be the petted guest of the state. He
would be free to eat breakfast, lunch, and dinner in "fiendish unconcern."
Such an outcome was unconscionable. Lynching Hose, she went on,
meant that "No reprieve – no executive clemency" would be available
to lend hope to a monster who should know only terror and pain.

Felton's readers knew what "executive clemency" and "Flanagan"
meant even if the references are now meaningless. "Executive clemency"
referred to Governor Atkinson's having freed Adolphus Duncan after the
young man had been wrongly convicted twice of attempted rape. The
entire legal establishment of Atlanta knew the accused was innocent, but

Felton claimed that the juries who convicted him had been correct! She also knew that many white voters were still rankled by the former governor's "executive clemency" in the case and that her words could play on the emotions of men ready to accept any story that justified lynching. Clemency, Atkinson's opponents had decreed, was rape.

Felton's reference to clemency rested on her contempt for "due process," and so did her reference to "Flanagan." The name conjured another "flaw" in the legal system. Edward G. Flanagan was a white man who boarded with the family of Dixon E. Allen in Decatur, Georgia, adjacent to Atlanta. Flanagan became obsessed with eleven-year-old Lela Allen and asked for her hand in marriage. Allen's father angrily refused and in response the mentally challenged Flanagan shot wildly at the family killing Mrs. Allen and a younger woman. Flanagan's attorneys claimed he was insane but he was convicted three times. Three times, the Georgia Supreme Court ordered a new trial based on obvious errors by an incompetent judge and feckless jury. While hunters were stalking Sam Hose, Felton pointed out, Flanagan was living "in leisure" at taxpayers' expense. "Clemency" and "Flanagan" proved the criminal justice system failed women. Protection and satisfaction could be gained only through ruthless and swift executions.[12] There should be no "clemency" or free breakfasts for Hose: only pain.

Felton could make others feel as she did. Few public figures wove words into a fabric of accusation, contempt, and fury as skillfully as she. She artfully imagined enemies, knaves, idiots, and fools in ways to delight the most demanding apologist for merciless vengeance. Her homiletic fancy transformed the act that women like Mary Bryan believed to be a crime into a moral imperative. What did Bryan know? She had lived and worked in New York City! Felton's narrative began of course with the rape of Mattie Cranford and continued by imagining its cause, the "beast" who did it, and the only appropriate penalty available: excruciating torture and death by fire. Ravening beasts such as Hose had been unleashed by Yankees who "gloated over the poverty and suffering of the southern people and used depravity and ignorance to foment discord and wreak revenge under the guise of sympathy and maudlin philanthropy."

Yankees had trained "misguided negroes" in "hellish hate and fiendish cruelty to the white women and girls of the south." Hose's violation of innocence on a bloody floor slippery from gore was no longer merely a crime, however horrendous, but sacrilege. It transcended the profane world and approached the demonic, that is, the sacred. Hose had already been found guilty and "a thousand men, are qualified to execute the

sentence without delay." To "rescue other victims from the beasts
of prey," whites had to inflict unbearable pain in a dramatic
display designed to strike fear into the soul of African America. Such
displays would also send a crucial message to Yankees. Felton's answer to
Mrs. Gordon's question was, "Terror!"[13] Her evocative style fit
W. J. Cash's portrayal of religion as "primitive frenzy and a blood
sacrifice."

DISCOVERY AND CAPTURE: STRICKLAND'S TRUTH

The "symposium" of eighteen essays appeared the morning after John
B. Jones captured Tom Wilkes. The fugitive had leapt on board a freight
train after fleeing the Cranford farm and eventually alighted near
Marshallville, sixty miles to the south of Macon. Elijah Strickland had
accurately reported what Wilkes told him. The latter knew the area well;
he had been born in adjacent Houston County in 1875. After his father
died, his mother, Harriett, eventually found herself on the Jones plantation near Marshallville where Tom grew to manhood. He cared for his
ailing mother and a mentally disabled younger brother; an elder brother,
Jones claimed, was the farmer's foreman. When Wilkes' mother regained
her health in 1897 or 1898, he left Macon County. Why he adopted the
alias, "Sam Hose," is unknown. Houston County reported over forty
"Hoses" in 1880 but only three in 1900: Sam Hose, his wife, Minnie, and
their baby. The family lived in a black section of Perry and Sam cared for
guests' horses at a nearby inn.

Wilkes could have known Hose, although Perry was about fifteen miles
east of Marshallville. He more probably simply knew of the family name
and adopted it to reinvent himself. His captor and former employer
reported in one story that he had originally left the farm because he had
sexually assaulted an old black woman. Later Jones recalled, instead, that
Wilkes had raped a woman on the Jones plantation while he was actually
over 100 miles away in Palmetto. If any of the stories were true, Wilkes
may have become Hose to escape the law, but every negative story about
him was shaped by the claim he had raped Mattie Cranford and is
therefore suspect. Jones had originally thought Wilkes had left Macon
County simply to get a better job. Jones' flexible memory allowed for a
variety of accounts.

The planter recalled he had eagerly awaited the desperate man and
planned precisely what he would do. Another source reported Jones'
surprise at finding the "quiet" young man living in his mother's cabin.

Wilkes had lived on the plantation for most of his life. Seeing him once again, and recalling the description in the newspapers, Jones realized that Wilkes was Hose. The tell-tale clue was not that Hose's complexion was "coppery"; thousands of Georgians shared this trait. But the depiction of Hose's manner of addressing white people (looking off to the side) and his involuntary "tic" would certainly have been clear to someone who had known him since childhood. However he came to seize Wilkes on Saturday evening April 22, Jones had the assistance of his brother and a black laborer to whom he promised fifty dollars. A distracted and trusting Wilkes was an easy catch.

Almost at once, ran one narrative, Wilkes admitted he was Hose and that he had killed Alfred Cranford and assaulted his wife. Most credible stories about the capture, however, had Wilkes admitting only to killing Cranford. One inane version imagined Wilkes dismissively "laughing" and insisting he had committed no crime, but whatever the fugitive said or did, he knew he was in trouble. The Jones brothers applied lamp-black to his face and the top of his hands to prevent identification by onlookers as they spirited him to Atlanta. The next morning, Sunday the twenty-third, they hustled their prize into a buggy to meet a rail connection to Macon. From there they took passage to Griffin, where they expected to transfer to Georgia's capital city in order to deliver Wilkes to Fulton County authorities, avoid his lynching, and claim their reward.

Escaping detection, however, was impossible. Passengers in Macon and on the train discovered that the brothers were escorting a slender African American man clothed in a slicker as if he were special. The most curious observers concluded that the man was Sam Hose. The Jones brothers hid Wilkes in a closet on the train to Griffin where vigilantes tried to seize him. They wanted to enhance their city's reputation by burning Hose immediately and tried to prevent his captors from continuing on to Atlanta. After heated debate, the mob's leaders agreed to allow delivery to the Coweta County sheriff, one of two peace officers the governor had authorized to receive Hose. The fact that the sheriff of Fulton County (Atlanta) had more fire power to prevent a lynching dictated the decision. Coweta's sheriff could sign a receipt to certify the Jones' claim to the rewards, but he could not protect Wilkes from a crowd intent on murder. Mattie Cranford, someone pointed out, was staying in Newnan with her mother and her late husband's farm was closer to Newnan than Atlanta. Newnan made sense to the mob but they had to find a way to get there.

For those unable to find seats on the train from Macon, an agent at the Griffin depot, R. J. Williams, arranged for a special engine and coach to take passengers to Newnan. Because Williams sold more tickets than he had seats, men and boys scrambled onto the locomotive and into the cab as the train moved slowly to Coweta County. On the regularly scheduled train, Griffin police officers forced Wilkes' head outside the window so he could be seen. The *Atlanta Journal* reported crowds of men and women cheering as the train chugged to Newnan. Telegraphers had alerted stations along the way to allow as many as possible to get a glimpse of the fiend. The passengers, cooed the *Journal* reporter, were so orderly that they appeared to be going to a Sunday school picnic.[14]

CARNIVAL

Tom Wilkes' hunters did not find him. Their widespread and feckless pursuit never reached Marshallville, where Elijah Strickland had reported that the man he knew as Sam Hose had fled. The Jones brothers discovered Wilkes by simply paying attention to detail. They knew there was a reward and they were pleased to receive it, but they had not been beating the bushes, wading through swamps, or shooting at imaginary fugitives. The men who were doing those things had found, however, something as valuable as Hose, a feeling of masculine solidarity. They were emotionally bonded into a short-lived but intensely committed moral community based on the presumed rape of Mattie Cranford. The crime, they were told, had to be understood within the context of rising aspirations to equality triggered by the presence of black US troops and sustained by Yankees' mischievous hostility. Public figures such as Governor Candler and Dr. Hal Johnston had, after all, called attention to widespread white vulnerability and black conspiracy after the "Griffin Incident." But it was the rape of a high status white woman by an unknown outsider who, men like the Palmetto dentist, Johnston, claimed, was associated with the arsonists that sent hunters scurrying across the countryside.

Mrs. Cranford's reputed rape allowed alarmists to imagine a widespread and imminent threat to innocent white country women. This paranoid style had justified Rebecca Felton in calling for terror, and terror meant burning. As soon as it was announced that Sam Hose had committed the most hideous of crimes, public opinion reflected and molded by newspaper editors knew that burning was the goal of the hunt. Burning was in the minds of Clark Howell and William Hemphill, who published stories about the hunt. Burning seized the minds of reporters who imagined imminent captures during the hunt. Burning was the goal of Griffin vigilantes who accosted the Jones brothers and Tom Wilkes after the hunt. Burning was the end.[15]

To justify death by fire *The Constitution* printed a simple, emotive and disturbing story, which was reprinted in newspapers throughout the state:[16]

An unassuming, industrious and hard-working farmer, after a day's toil, sat at his evening meal ... Noiselessly the murderer, with uplifted ax, advanced in the rear and sank it to the helve in the brain of the unsuspecting victim. Tearing the child from the mother's breast, he flung it into the pool of blood oozing from its father's wound ... The wife was seized, choked, thrown upon the floor, where her clothing lay in the blood of her husband, and ravished. Remember the facts! ... And above all remember the shocking degradation that was inflicted by the black beast, his victim swimming in her husband's warm blood, as the brute held her to the floor! ... When the picture is painted of the ravisher in flames go back and view the darker picture of Mrs. Cranford outraged in the blood of her murdered husband!

"Blood," "degradation," "outrage," "beast," "ravished," "ravisher" – the words streamed easily from imaginations schooled in the fantasies of sexuality, power, condemnation, and violence. Mattie Cranford was branded. She had been *ravished*. Her desire for privacy was vexing; her silence suggested insanity. Imagining her fate had led white men to "Remember the facts!" Remember the *ravished*! Remember the "beast' who held "her to the floor" and *ravished* her! "Beast," "ravisher," and "outrage" were conflated into one fact on Sunday April 23, when vigilantes found Tom Wilkes with his captors. Sam Hose was in custody and on the way to Newnan!

No one knows precisely what happened in the Coweta County seat after the Jones brothers, the Griffin mob, and Tom Wilkes arrived. The men there at the time probably didn't know either; reporters, peace officers, and lynchers were busily competing with each other to dominate the narrative. The most important version – that of Tom Wilkes' understanding and experience – is beyond retrieval, although it is possible to infer something of his horror, pain, and grit. The silence and blinding light that engulfs one who tries to imagine the unimaginable is sobering, admonishing, and chilling. Yet it is possible to patch together a story that seems credible enough without the certainty theoretically allowed by interpreting "all the evidence."

The trains reached Newnan shortly after 1:00 p.m., moving slowly through the crowd that welcomed them.[17] No one was allowed on board until Sheriff Joseph Brown arrived to settle a logistical problem created by the differing goals of the Joneses, the sheriff, and Griffin's volunteer lay-constabulary. The three parties agreed that the fugitive had to be identified as Sam Hose; Mattie Cranford was unavailable but a man from Palmetto who knew Hose exchanged familiar words with him. Wilkes supposedly then confessed that he had killed Cranford. The next step was to move the man safely from the train to a cell in the small Coweta County jail. The crowd, however, was frustrated, angry, and menacing; Brown was apprehensive as a group from Newnan and another from Griffin each seemed ready to pounce on Wilkes as their prize.

The sheriff hailed a merchant from Griffin: "If you can control your crowd I can control my people!" The merchant replied that Griffin's citizens were "not hoodlums and we can give our word of honor we will not harm the negro *until he is delivered to . . . your jail.*" The sheriff then asked his people to do the same and a voice rang out: "Hose is safe until he is delivered and signed for." The reply may have satisfied the sheriff and the Jones brothers, but Wilkes must have heard it as a death sentence.

The Newnan *Herald*'s printer, Sam Murray, then explained to those who had not been privy to the negotiations that Wilkes would be settled peacefully in jail. Armed guards ushered him from the train and escorted him slowly west down Hancock Street to the jail on the corner with Perry Street. A reporter for the *Atlanta Journal* described the parade as a public event wholeheartedly approved by the entire community. "At every house," he wrote, "women and children stood on the verandas and waved their handkerchiefs and cheered the captors." Naturally, "men left their residences and fell into line." Newnan's citizenry had never seen anything like it. As "church people were leaving their churches," reporters observed, many "rushed headlong into the crowd, took their position at the end of the line, and marched in solemn order toward the jail." To insist that women, children, and church people approved and even participated in what was happening was to insist in a muddling way that the proceedings were baptized in the wellsprings of community virtue. The solemn procession that implied communal approval frequently erupted into a "mighty shout" of excitement and celebration.

The shout came from agitated men fed up with what seemed to be delaying tactics by the sheriff and his deputy. It was not the churchgoing and "solemn" party that rushed the jail and clamored into the hallways leading to the second story cell block. It was not the women and children whom the sheriff's men tried to hold back amid the chaos of pushing, tripping, and shoving. The contest between law and transgression was uneven and Brown finally had no choice but to sign a receipt. He acknowledged that the planter, J. B. Jones, a merchant from Griffin (R. A Gordon), a plant superintendent from Houston County (Wilson Matthews [sic]), a clerk from Griffin (Charles Thomas), and Abe Rogowski from Griffin had delivered Sam Hose (Thomas Wilkes) to the sheriff of Coweta County. The Jones brothers (and probably also Mathews) then left the scene to go home. Immediately, men from Griffin led by Rogowski rushed down the hall and threw Bailiff John Alsabrook aside before he could open the door to a cell for the prisoner. They seized Wilkes, and dragged him out of the building. Griffin vigilantes had finally caught Sam Hose.

The captors did not execute their prize at once. The vanguard seemed compelled to create something beyond themselves through unscripted actions that in process seemed to take on meaning immediately for the vanguard and gradually for the assembled crowd. They had to do what they intended to do in a way they could defend as "right." They took Wilkes outside, down Hancock, past butcher and bakery shops to the court house square where they were hailed by former Governor William Yates Atkinson and Judge Alvan D. Freeman. The Griffin party knew the former governor well. Douglas Glessner, the Ohio-born editor of the Griffin *News and Sun*, had contemptuously pilloried him for trying to get a small group tried in 1897 for lynching a white man in Talbotton.

Every citizen of Coweta County also knew where Atkinson stood on mob murder even if they couldn't stand with him. Judge Freeman was as well-known in Newnan as the former governor. Both men had probably come from worship services, Freeman from the Central Baptist church, and Atkinson from the Presbyterian. They faced an impossible situation in confronting a crowd that had already transgressed law and due process by seizing Wilkes from the jail. The abstractions, Law and Authority, were personified in the former governor and the judge; they were good Christian men, "civilized" men, men who believed in the "majesty of the law." The contest between Law and Transgression erupted once again as Atkinson ascended the court house steps to plead with the crowd not to disgrace their state. Let the courts, he insisted, decide the fate of Sam Hose.

For a moment there was silence; a reporter thought he saw a man point his cocked pistol at the speaker, who dismissed the danger. Then someone shouted, "Burn him!" and chaos erupted. The former governor realized he had no power to dam the emotional torrent flowing from the crowd, but he hoped at least to divert it from flooding the court house square. Take Hose to the Cranford farm for identification, he called out, but don't do what you intend to do "in the midst of our homes here in the city." Burning Hose on the court house square would terrorize women and children! If Wilkes' captors lynched Hose there, Atkinson warned, he'd testify in court to the acts of everyone he could identify. That was the best he could do as he conceded the crowd to Freeman, whose own pleadings evaporated into the heated atmosphere of the moment. The assembly refused to listen. The judge plunged into the impatient throng to engage individuals he knew and with whom he hoped to reason, but they would not listen. "We are your friends, judge," one man reportedly explained, "but this is the wrong time to talk to people who have been outraged by one of the most revolting crimes the mind can conceive of."

Then a great roar launched the vanguard into action. One of them was probably Rogowski, who had appeared in news reports during the hunt as one of the most dogged trackers of Sam Hose. He apparently led in storming the jail and was one of the men acknowledged in Sheriff Brown's receipt. Whether he was recently from Pennsylvania, as was reported, or originally from Russia, he was committed to fitting in and claiming the respect of men into whose company his travels had thrust him. The best way to gain acceptance and honor in Griffin, Georgia, at the time was to burn Sam Hose alive. Other men were later named with him as having led the mob but it is difficult to confirm their identify even though they boasted of their participation to Louis Le Vin. In June, Le Vin would interview several white men in Griffin, Palmetto, and Newnan, all of whom professed proudly to have had a leading part in killing Sam Hose. The private investigator from Chicago listed their names in his report to Ida B. Wells, but, like Rogowski, most were absent from the census of 1900.[18]

As for the crowd itself, Amy Wood points out that mobs such as the one that seized Wilkes "tended to be dominated by skilled laborers and white collar workers" who were members of an aspiring class not yet secure in its future. They placed a high value on male authority within the household as a base for respectability, self-confidence, and success. Many were young and single, and eager to demonstrate their manhood in a dramatic way. The excitement of joining a crowd, already sanctioned by provocation and journalistic exaggeration, promised emotional rewards enhanced by the widely recruited and touted hunt. The event became a contagion for those not inoculated by an ethical counterforce. The crowd acted as an intentional community set aside from the ordinary rules of the world, yet shaped in their culture of masculine privilege by conventional expectations of white mastery. They were expected to protect or, failing that, to avenge their desecrated women. They were rebelling against the law and expectations of obedience that had failed to protect Mattie Cranford. The crowd may also have been angry at new legal restrictions on drinking and hunting. Law and creeping prohibition, associated with women's acting like men, were not serving manhood well. Rebelling against the coercive powers of the state represented by an ex-governor who tried to stop them could have added an emotional thrust to their resentment and festive transgression.

Wood is right to point out that such a crowd was produced by the New South. Griffin and Newnan were both small industrial cities on the make. Newnan's center was flanked by large and booming cotton mills, prosperous manufacturing plants, and a variety of smaller but respectable enterprises that relied on public facilities that supported the city's substantial contribution to modernizing Georgia. Local capitalists had created a sizeable population of young white male workers that could supply a crowd intent on doing something memorable, especially on a Sunday when the only open venues were churches.[19]

Whoever they were, both the vanguard and body of the crowd knew that once released from the ordinary rules of the world they could do anything. But they wanted to do something spectacular. Reports of the hunt had promised as much. Many in the crowd would have known about the sensational public executions of Tom Delk and Joe Dean for crimes presumably less horrific than those assigned Hose, and they would have wanted to prevent a recurrence of those scenes. Both men had played remarkably prominent roles in their own executions; Dean had even testified to his redemption in Christ Jesus. Delk thought he was dying for everyone's sins. Hose, however, could be permitted neither performance nor redemption. By the time he was taken from the train, it was common knowledge that Hose's crimes demanded that responsible men transcend the normal, the formal, and the legal.

Extraordinary crimes required extraordinary penalties, and this was an extraordinary time. Such time demanded actions that were meaningful, shaped by the images, emotions, memories, and experiences of the crowd led by men who imagined rape, murder, judgment, and burning. The vanguard gradually led their fellows into a series of celebratory actions that would lead to a killing they could believe was meaningful, memorable, and just. In their freedom, the crowd was making a community through unscripted acts; their drive for Justice required they do the "right" things. Shared values and expectations guided them; with shouts and cheers, Wilkes' captors began a parade that flowed naturally from the restive assembly on the court house square. Through exciting interaction among its members, the crowd was forging a communal bond not only by their possession of Sam Hose and their collective transgression but also their movement, physical contact, and voice.

As they passed through the central business district of Newnan, they shouted out their collective pride in white supremacy. African Americans were depicted as fleeing before them; white women and children were described as waving in enthusiastic support – at least until a few realized what the procession would eventually do. The vanguard pushed and pulled Tom Wilkes, "choking from the binding of the chain about his throat and the anguish of soul and body," out of the square and onto Washington Street. The procession then moved east past Pinson's Virginia Hotel and then back again to the west and south until it reached the Central Baptist Church. It changed direction and eventually flowed east to Jefferson and turned north past the cemetery on the road to Palmetto. At each corner, the parade stopped to allow men to hoist Wilkes high above their heads so that everyone who wished to do so could gaze on the quiet, surprisingly stoic, and unresisting man.

These ritual acts transformed Hose into something other than a man who had broken the law. He was becoming an offering, a symbol that transcended the possession of a mere trophy: Thus displayed, he signified what he had done, where he had come from, who possessed him, and what his captors would do to him. Because of the "enormity" of his crime and the ways in which the crowd had "risen" above the ordinary, he signified transcendence. Wilkes, no matter how he actually felt, would not allow his captors the bounty of terror they had hoped to wreak. His silence and outward calm were his only defense; self-transcendence his only ally. As Sam Hose, Wilkes was the mob's prize; he was their effigy; he was their symbol of evil. A reporter celebrated the fact that Hose was at last "in the grasp of the people," the ultimate power in a democracy and thus beyond reproach. Against them, Wilkes struggled to be himself.

Such democratic action, Bertram Wyatt Brown has argued, had a long tradition in the American South. Shivarees (charivaries) had long taunted, shamed, humiliated, or punished persons who had offended the moral economy of the community. At least, they may have offended an "aroused" and effectively led *portion* of the community where objects of public humiliation had few defenders. Young women believed to have ignored the rubrics of virtue could be shamed by being paraded before a raucous crowd; newly married couples could sometimes become the sport of puerile ribaldry; suspected homosexuals might suffer from a range of indignities. Men who acted or talked in ways that violated the community's sense of decorum night be tarred, feathered, and banished from the neighborhood on a pole or rail. Shivarees were celebrations of values shared by the community (or at least by its hooligans), which meant that they were entertaining. Shivarees existed outside ordinary time; they promised satisfaction and pleasure. They were the very opposite of the Sabbath, the day of rest set aside to ponder discipleship and destiny. It is not surprising that a reporter thought the procession in Newnan was a "turbulent tide of human passion."[20] Festivity had erupted into carnival.

"Carnival" and "festivity" come easily to mind in thinking about the parade that wended its way through Newnan. An exceptional analysis of Southern lynching is entitled *A Festival of Violence*, a "festival" presumably celebrated in all the states covered by the study. The authors concede that most lynching was a "straightforward" murder with little "ceremony or celebration," but point out that the burning of Sam Hose possessed a "carnival-like aspect." "Festival," therefore, could be a metaphor suggesting widespread appeal and celebration and is appropriately applied to one kind of lynching. Other studies of lynching mention celebration or "revelry" similar to that of a "traveling carnival" with "dancing, laughing [and] cursing"; a festive air as women waved to the crowd; "the gamut of emotions" ranging "from jubilation to rage to something approaching sexual rapture." Lynching could ignite merriment with jeers, laughing, and taunting that for the moment at least had no truck with reverence![21]

"Carnival" suggests a way of understanding a lynching that attracted hundreds or possibly thousands to participate in a singular moment of collective violence and awe. Jeers, cheers, laughter, taunts, revelry, and curses flowed from the procession, suggesting a fixed determination, a clarity of purpose, a righteous wrath, and a furtive sense of moral rectitude. The crowd reveled in contradiction, ambiguity, paradox, and confusion to be resolved by a spectacular act. "Carnival" promises a climax that ends as well as justifies the disorder many observers fear as destructive. Celebration ends with a moment of calm. No wonder a witness could think "sexual rapture." For some, of course, climax could erupt in "Glory!!"

That observers and scholars could see carnival in lynching spectacles suggests the work of Mikhail Bakhtin. The Russian critic called attention to carnival in *Rabelais and His World*, and sent scholars to seek and learn the nature of carnival celebrated during the Middle Ages and Renaissance. Following Bakhtin, they teased out its meanings not as a *spectacle witnessed* but as a *transgressive world enacted.* In this world lived no observers, only participants who declared their freedom from traditional manners, institutions, and elites. The negativity implicit in this world is transcended by the unity created in festive movement through exchanges and responses among celebrants who find an extravagant freedom from law and everyday normality in dynamic concert with others. Those exchanges generated popular rule (sovereignty) beyond structure and freed celebrants from the law just as would the crowd that displayed Sam Hose. They began to enact an *ad hoc* ritual no one had written or planned. The idea spawning their performances may have sprung from the quotidian experience of displaying trophies after a hunt, but it was also inspired by the almost complete power of the white assembly over one black man and his signifying to them – as they would demonstrate – all African American men.

Each time the vanguard elevated Wilkes above their heads, he became not just a trophy but a symbol and an offering to gaze on. It was a simple ritual that stripped away his humanity and individuality. If Bakhtin could argue that carnival "transformed old truth and authority into a 'comic monster'" that the "crowd rends to pieces in the market place," Wilkes could be understood as having become such a "comic monster." The monstrous signified not only Hose's presumed crimes, but also "truth and authority."[22] The ritual did not enact the "stations of the cross"; this was, after all, a community hugely suspicious of liturgy, but it was nonetheless evocative of the passage of sorrow to Golgotha. The hoisting of Wilkes and the invitation to gaze on him before the holocaust suggest a feint toward a religious sensibility, and privileging the transgressive in carnival encourages curiosity as to whether or not the "burning" of authority meant also contempt for religion.

Carnivalesque Renaissance crowds were beyond the hegemony of the Church; processions were devoid of prayer, piety, and reverence. This absence was clear during a lynching near Statesboro, Georgia, in 1904 as educated Presbyterian and Methodist ministers tried to stop the mob from burning their captives. They were answered with a scream: "We don't want religion, we want blood!" "Religion" meant propriety and rules; "blood" meant sovereignty, death, and transcendence! Laity were more legitimate than clergy. Amy Wood points out that when whites lynched a man behind the Methodist Church in Oxford, Mississippi, in July 1885 the proceedings represented "evangelical church discipline." (The "trial" resembled a Baptist disciplinary meeting more than a Methodist conference.) The murderers argued that they were justified in protecting the "sanctity" of "white womanhood." The performance and its alibi legitimized collective action within what *The Constitution* labeled the Realm of Religion. In Newnan, the procession included church people, or at least one reporter insisted as much, in order to demonstrate that the "best people" supported the cascade of events leading to fire.

Church trials were, however, not the model of religion when the ecstasy of death and judgment welled up among celebrants at the lynching of Sam Hose. Rather, the carnivalesque celebration of camp meetings and revivals in the South that released emotions and promised salvation throughout the nineteenth century had taught worshippers to express their rapture in the shout – realizing "Glory!!" These incidents, plus the prayers that launched spectacle lynchings elsewhere suggest that a friendly critic of Bakhtin was correct when she wrote that carnival did not necessarily target religion.[23] In these cases, to be sure, institutions and elites were renounced: church (clergy), courts (judges), legislatures (elected officials). But religious feeling could not be contained: it *was wrested from the clergy and claimed by the crowd.* The Statesboro burning was eventually blessed by a part-time Baptist preacher and not elite ministers. God could be present in carnival by joining the mob and revealing sublimity through an ecstatic expressiveness erupting from within the thrill of collective solidarity and punishment that ignited death.

After parading Sam Hose through the city as trophy and effigy, the vanguard needed to create a liturgy of recognition and confession in an exchange between Mattie Cranford and her ravisher. They headed for Pitt McLeroy's house where Mrs. Cranford was staying with her mother and children.[24] There they expected to prevail on the raped widow to identify the man known as Sam Hose and demand a confession. Such a confrontation was, partisans of lynching insisted, a better exchange than that in a court room, because it spared the female victim the gross indignity of being subjected to cross examination by disreputable defense attorneys. Why acknowledging rape before a raucous mob was less damaging to a woman than doing so in a closed courtroom is unclear, and Mrs. Cranford adamantly refused to appear. She was not about to expose herself either to the crowd that stigmatized her or the man who had killed her husband and destroyed her world.

Mattie's mother, Mrs. McLeroy, however, did come to the front door. Fatuous reports represented her in a hysterical state when confronting Wilkes, but credible accounts described her in a state of controlled fury as she asked "Sam" why he had killed "Mr. Cranford." Wilkes did not answer that he had done so in self-defense, although he had earlier insisted as much to a reporter. One observer claimed he answered that "Elijah Strickland paid me to do it." Wilkes may have thought the preacher had sent hunters to Marshallville, and was therefore responsible for his capture. In his last hour of life, Wilkes may have been seeking what little vengeance he could inflict on those who harmed him. Or he may have mentioned the minister in an innocent way that could be exploited to warrant another lynching. Or he may not have mentioned Strickland at all. On April 23, 1899 all black men in Coweta, Campbell, and Spalding Counties were legitimate prey to white men driven by the testosterone of racial contempt.

BUTCHERY, FIRE, RAPE, SACRIFICE: TRUTH

After the exchange between Wilkes and Mrs. McLeroy, one of his captors suggested burning him then and there, but the angry woman ordered the crowd to leave! They did so, wondering where better to stage their final act. The vanguard believed symbolic as well as draconian action demanded executing Wilkes near the site of his crimes. They proposed going to the Cranford farm or beyond it into Palmetto, but then someone from Newnan arrived to warn that a train had been dispatched from Atlanta. It possibly carried a company of militia tasked with preventing the lynching; the captors had to move quickly. (No one at the time knew that Governor Candler had called out the Fifth Regiment of the state militia, not to keep order in Newnan, but to prevent the lynching of a white Sunday school teacher who had murdered a young woman.) A few men ran to a nearby country store to pilfer kerosene and confiscate a cord or so of dry split pine from the yard of Joe Featherstone, a local cotton buyer. The crowd then claimed a clearing in nearby woods with a sapling at its edge about fifty feet from the highway. They chained their victim to the sapling and stacked the wood about him. Those with knives then fell on their victim; they cut away his humanity as they forced a bloodied Tom Wilkes to enter American history as Sam Hose. They consecrated the space and carved their "whiteness" on him by mutilation. They broke him into bits, sliced him into portions, grasped parts of him as souvenirs, or sold him off at ten to twenty-five cents apiece.

Within a vortex transcending law and the ordinary rules of the world, the crowd claimed sovereignty as they governed through brutality and pain.[25] Reporters later attempted to explain what happened, or at least what they believed should have been happening. They did not realize the meaning of the unequal contest being waged before their eyes between the sacrifiers and their victim. In referring to a similar situation in the eighteenth century, Michel Foucault famously observed that spectacular punishment in France during the *ancient regime* was designed to show that the power to take a life had not only to be seen by the king's subjects but also to be acknowledged through confession by the accused. Just as important, the event was not merely to be observed but also to be remembered. The best way of doing so was to inflict "unbearable sensations" of pain through torture, which could be slow and dramatic by using horses, for example, to pull the criminal's body to pieces. The executioner could then cut up the remains and burn them in full view of the crowd. In such a spectacle, sovereignty, pain, and power would certainly be remembered.

Absent confession, the killing was violence without meaning. Violence wanting confession meant that the victim felt no guilt and possibly embraced death on his own terms, which could have implied *martyrdom*. Or if the victim simply believed s/he had been selected for no good reason the indignities of pain and torture could have elicited a feeling of unqualified innocence in the victim's mind.[26] Wilkes already believed he was justified in killing the murderous Cranford. He never confessed (contrary to misinformation) the act for which the crowd punished him. He held on desperately to his innocence and in his silence challenged the contempt of his killers.

The short narrative describing whites' transforming Wilkes from a human being into purchasable souvenirs is one way of remembering those events. The narrative is clear and horrible, but it is bloodless and painless; it signifies little but cruelty and murder. Yet it is clear from the actions of the crowd after seizing Wilkes that white men were determined to enact a social drama rich in meaning and sanctified by blood. Claiming sovereignty over life and death, the vanguard assumed power superior to that of the state and aspired to the prerogatives of God. When they held Wilkes aloft, presented him to Mrs. McLeroy, and started for the Cranford farm, they were behaving in ways they thought significant within the world they were creating. As they unsheathed their knives and ignited the fire, they were enacting the meaning of all the rules, written, and unwritten, of white domination in the American South. They were enacting the meaning of segregation, disfranchisement, and what it meant to be a white man in any contest (imagined or real) with black men. The "rape" of Mattie Cranford had signified the African American desire for equality – as politicians would claim. The torture of Tom Wilkes suggested what that desire meant to white men.

Jacquelyn Hall indicates as much in her study of lynching when referring to an essay by Clifford Geertz. In "Deep Play: Notes on a Balinese
Cockfight," Geertz recounted his settling into Balinese culture through
reading that cockfight as a "cultural text." He demonstrated how this
popular sporting event could evoke a dramatic playing out symbolically
of action in which "esteem, honor, dignity [and] respect" were at stake.
A cock-fight could remove observers "from the ordinary course of life,"
and launch them into "social or social-psychological" concerns derived
from themes of the "ideal," the "narcissistic," and the masculine. These
were associated with power, prestige, savagery, and blood sacrifice.
A contest between cocks could become a "status bloodbath." Thinking
of the cockfight in this way allows the scholar, Geertz wrote, to understand "cultural forms" in much the same way as did such men as Spinoza,
Marx, and Freud. In such a case, participants could say "not merely that
risk is exciting, loss depressing, or triumph gratifying..., but that it is of
these emotions, thus exampled [in the fight], that society is built and
individuals put together." Geertz points out that "every people ... loves
its own form of violence."

Taking this cue, one can see the lynching moment, not only as the
masculine narcissism of violent men playing out the meaning of being
male, as Hall points out, but beyond that also a moment of creation and
transcendence. In the immolation of Sam Hose, sacrifiers were enacting
masculinity, to be sure. But they were also creating a moment in which
some among their congregation of blood-and-punishment could imagine
the ineffable. They were awed by their realization and experience of a
world that was just beyond their understanding. That world was transcendent to the one they had left and to which they would eventually
return but it was also fulfilling and for some at least, "wonderful." It was
a religious moment.[27] "Glory!"

As white men cut Tom Wilkes, his blood oozed, flowed, and splattered.
It stained the clothing and soiled the hands of his executioners with what
had once been life but was now death. Blood is tacky and indelible; when
it is one's own it is disheartening. But in the case of torture and the pain of
others, it can be exciting even as the abattoir becomes an altar. Blood in
this sacrifice compensated for the blood in which Mattie had supposedly
been raped; sex and violence and blood merged in the vanguard's
imagination and consequently in its actions. Men seized parts of Wilkes'
body – his ears, his fingers, his penis, and his testicles. One can imagine, as
William Faulkner once did, that at least one of his torturers could think in
a flash, "Now you'll let white women alone, even in hell." Wilkes'

tormentors cut or hacked other parts as well: They may have eviscerated him. They could have twisted corkscrews into his flesh or blinded him with acid as other mobs had done before or would do in the future. They could have rolled red hot irons across his body or plunged them into his eyes, mouth, throat, and anus as other whites would do at other times, but they didn't. Like other white men in similar rites they tortured not to gain knowledge useful for self-defense but to "know" Tom Wilkes' body as *rampaging rapists* and to "know" what it felt like to inflict pain in a perfect freedom gauged by blood. They *ravished* him in blood and fire to signify the meaning of crossing sacred boundaries and polluting sacred space. Blood and fire purified them.

By cutting him they did not transform him into a woman; they took his "maleness" to signify black men as eunuchs before white men. The cutting was *destruction* not *transformation*. The liturgy of blood-letting and rape inscribed on this body white rage, desire, contempt, and transcendence in one horrific moment. The torturers were more obsessed with what they could do to Wilkes' body and therefore his soul (self-consciousness) than with justice even by their own lax standards. They, like the SS torturers of the Nazi-inspired Holocaust, were intent on proving that there were "things considerably worse than death."[28] They were sending a message to African Americans that Rebecca Felton, for one, wanted sent. Horror and terror awaited those blacks who break our [white] law, which only we can break with impunity because we have created it to enforce our dominion. Lynchers called it Justice, but it was really Power, Contempt, and Transcendence. This drama, such as those of executions past, surely would be memorable. Truth came as blood, pain, and glory.

How could anyone do what this crowd did to Tom Wilkes? The question seems natural to people who believe they could never have done "it," but asking it also invites us to continue the search for meaning. If Felton's essay of April 23 was the rhetorical embellishment of political and homiletic oratory, it was also a prescription to be taken seriously by people who seemed to ask "How could we *not* have done it?" What Wilkes had done to Mattie Cranford was so terrible, Felton insisted, that if he were "burnt with slow fire, his fate would be elysian [compared] to the torture" endured by his victim. In this way of thinking, the Christian feminist reflected the popular assumption not only that Sam Hose would be burned alive but that he should be. Southerners had burned only a few black men before Emancipation; between 1845 and 1862, possibly thirteen black men had been burned to death in the South. Henry Smith, as we have seen, suffered such a fate before ten thousand witnesses at Paris, Texas, in February of 1893 when "red-hot pincers" were thrust down his throat before being burned alive. In Oklahoma five years later the two teenage Seminoles were burned alive because a visiting Texan wanted the lynching done right.[29] By 1899 burning was reserved for those whom whites considered to be the worst non-white offenders. Burning was the ultimate punishment.

This had certainly been the case in 1741, when New Yorkers burned thirteen Africans to death for planning an insurrection. Authorities did not allow the absence of credible evidence to prevent their executing perhaps a total of thirty-six people for conspiracy. A plot made sense because the British and Spanish empires were at war and military leaders feared the Iroquois confederacy might attack from the north. The African population of Manhattan had grown exponentially in the previous few years and strangers sharing the Catholic faith of the Spanish could be especially dangerous if they happened to steal into New York undetected. When petty crimes alerted alarmists that the "negroes are rising," authorities discovered, writes Jill Lepore, "a phantom black political party – of real slaves … lurking in the shadows."

Similarity to the phantom threat in 1899 Georgia is clear. The danger of conspiracy by marginal people such as slaves or free blacks justified executions by fire in 1741. The slow pace of burning could create the pain appropriate for the worst offenders either in eighteenth-century Manhattan or nineteenth-century Newnan. Burning in Europe had once been reserved for witches who consorted with demons and defiant heretics who refused to confess. Perhaps burning signified a rite of purification or represented the fires of hell in sermons warning of the Last Judgment. Burning was certainly part of the *auto da fe* under the Spanish Inquisition, and Jean Calvin's Protestant Geneva burned Michael Servetus alive for denying the Trinity. The remarkable story of Joan of Arc ended with her being consumed by fire because she had broken almost every taboo possible for a woman possessed of extraordinary spiritual insight, clothed in male apparel, and blessed or cursed with charisma.[30]

Burning is associated with *sacrifice* in myth, legend, and scripture, Mark Fearnow points out. He relies on insights and theory associated with Rene Girard and Mary Douglas to argue that the executions in Manhattan were also sacrifices. Fearnow calls them "sacrificial cleansing rituals" because they purified society by both symbolically and literally removing polluting Africans, "Papists," and outcasts, but that is not all the rituals did. Girard begins his classic essay on *Violence and the Sacred* by pointing out that "the sacrificial act assumes two opposing aspects, appearing at times as a sacred obligation" and at "other times as a sort of criminal activity." Sacrifice is a complex, often mysterious ritual enacted by those who often do not understand its sacred (sacrificial) quality even as they claim benefits that flow from that very property. Robert Lifton and Greg Mitchell clarify this phenomenon when they write about the sacrificial nature of legal executions. In 1741, Manhattanites were punishing as well as cleansing; they ritualized violence against victims found guilty of crimes they did not commit to resolve social tensions (potential violence) by laying on their victims responsibility for "all crime – and beyond that, for the overall violence in society."[31] Victims became sacred as their deaths were freighted with the power to punish all evil, not one profane crime.

Burning was Tom Wilkes' fate as soon as he killed Alfred Cranford. It was, however, not only punishment reserved for one man but also a warning to all black men, whom whites transformed through him into a monstrous threat. Wilkes was never alone in the imagination of whites who hunted and destroyed him, or of those who justified what the sacrifiers had done. As soon as he vanished in ashes and smoke, Georgia's public men and women began to condemn the black community throughout the area from Palmetto to Macon as the source of widespread danger. By doing so they transformed a wanted criminal into the symbol of African American community and all African Americans into accomplices to rape and murder. If they knew their Christian Bibles, some men in the crowd may well have believed their quarry was like the "beast" envisioned in the *Revelation of St. John*, which a wrathful God casts "into a lake of fire burning with brimstone." Burning the "beast" alive became necessary because of the ways in which the magical thinking of whites such as Hal Johnston and Rebecca Felton imagined the man they believed to be a fiend. He, like the beast of Revelation, personified Evil.

Burning became an *auto da fe* that public men such as Clark Howell and Hal Johnston expected to be performed when Hose was captured. They imagined burning because it was a spectacle to be wondered at far beyond the precincts of Newnan and Palmetto. Burning was supposed to taunt Yankees as well as terrorize black people; it demonstrated the ultimate meaning of white supremacy. Burning enacted white men's will to transcend all imaginable limits, to inflict any pain, to embrace the plenitude of excess against any black person who contested white power. It warned black men, as if they didn't already know, what they could expect from an enraged white community. Burning had been the fantasy and goal that moved the festive crowd through Newnan to a site where "sacred obligation" and "criminal activity" fused in one spectacular moment. If burning was offensive to all but one of the essayists in the April 23 edition of *The Constitution*, all of the men and some of the women agreed with the lynch mob that extant law could not protect endangered white people from African Americans. Burning told squeamish "sentimentalists" what was really at stake when black men broke law and taboo. Burning was reality and, like blood, pain, and glory – truth.

Conceding the symbolic power of burning in history and Newnan, the question of how the mob could have acted in that way remains only partially answered. The "morbid curiosity" that had enticed crowds to watch the legal executions of Joe Dean and Tom Delk had undoubtedly drawn many men to the clearing near the road to Palmetto. They may not have been able to torture or burn by their own hands but they could applaud the men who did so. In witnessing such acts they could see something dramatically different from the banality and uneventfulness of their disgustingly normal lives. The newspaper stories of the prolonged hunt had promised an exciting end to the drama begun in blood and horror, and if most of the crowd could not participate in the search, they could certainly witness one of the greatest events ever to be staged in Campbell or Coweta counties. Afterwards, they could talk about how this very different death held them in its power. Some could even display bones, cooked flesh, or ashes.

The mob's sadism is, of course, not unknown to generations sobered by tortures of the twentieth and twenty-first centuries. "Anyone disillusioned (even incredulous) when confronted with ... evidence of what humans are capable of," writes Susan Sontag, "has not reached moral or psychological adulthood."[32] Wilkes' tormentors inflicted as much pain as their utterly human fantasies could conceive because there was nothing, certainly not conscience, to restrain them. Cruelty made sense to white men ready to assume responsibility for enforcing white hegemony under extreme conditions. "Extreme" came to mean "justifiable" when referring to white men's acts in retaliation for extreme, that is, criminal, behavior by black men. Clark Howell, Hal Johnston, Abe Rogowski, and Governor Atkinson's neighbors believed conditions justified extreme action as Atkinson and Judge Freeman learned at the court house square.

Such action existed on a continuum of whites' understanding of blacks pervasive throughout American society. The difference between enslaving, segregating, and disfranchising African Americans and torturing them to death is a difference of degree, not a difference of kind. Sadism in this continuum is made possible, Kathleen Taylor points out in her study of *Cruelty*, by a process of objectification, or condemning those who are "other," i.e., who are an "essentially evil force." The mental gymnastics of "objectification" fluttered about whites' conceptions of innocence, guilt, gender, race, and sexuality as they sought Hose. When they caught him, the same gymnastics created a space both literally in a wooded clearing and metaphorically in the minds of Wilkes' killers. Whites cast Wilkes as Hose beyond culture, society, and the rules that allow humanity to live at peace. The transformation allowed him to be burned alive and mutilated in a way that would disturb anyone thinking about it even at a distance.

The cumulative effect of hunt, carnival, confrontation, and igniting the fire created a space and time in which none of the ordinary rules of the world applied. The actors had complete freedom: Few human beings are ever as free as they! They were becoming godlike, answerable to no one in a soul-destroying act. Within that ecstasy, acting in concert with others in sadistic destruction of sex and sexuality could trigger chemical reactions in brain and body that brought sensual gratification. Like the Marquis de Sade a century earlier, Wilkes' tormentors discovered how utterly pleasurable it could be to hurt one weaker than they.[33] It is one of the wonders of the human condition.

EMBERS, COURAGE, AND CONTAGION

The torturers were a relatively small group acting on behalf of probably five hundred men, according to the *Herald*. Possibly twenty men were close enough to claim to have started the fire; a few others thought their fellows certainly deserved to know what was happening. They therefore loudly described to their widely dispersed comrades what was going on step by step and slash by slash. Everyone could follow the proceedings and participate in some small way. The voices of the interlocutors, when combined with the taunts directed at Wilkes, must have created enough distraction and noise to belie reports of an orderly and serious execution by "calm and determined" men. One of Newnan's "most prominent citizens" boldly announced his approval of what was happening as someone cried out "Let him die by inches."

The mythic narratives of spectacular lynching, of course, demanded order, dignity, and seriousness as befitted a crowd of the best people, but witnesses to the punishment of Sam Hose also had to convey the enormity of the victim's crime. Thus, according to one reporter, "citizens who had prided themselves on their peaceful community went almost wild while venting their righteous wrath." What "wild" meant is unclear when applied to the "best people," although one man remembered that "terror thrilled the hearts of the vast majority." The old man shouted, "Glory" but Wilkes was silent. He was supposed to whimper and beg for mercy. He was supposed to scream in anguish; he was supposed to shout and cry out in the sounds of desperation, isolation, and pain. To be sure, some witnesses reported that when white men cut off his ears, fingers, and genitalia, he did shout, "O, My God! Oh, Jesus!"[34] *But that was all*!

That shout was his only sound, and he refused to cry out further. It may seem to be a small victory in the midst of world-consuming conflagration, but silence was the last possession available to him. Those closest to the fire saw him writhe in agony, strain against the chains, struggle against the flame. They knew he was in pain; they could smell it; they saw his blood vessels burst from the heat; but they could not claim his voice. Imagining pain inflicted by torture in a highly regarded study, Elaine Scarry observes that in state-sponsored torture the torturer attempts to "induce sounds so that they can be broken off from their speaker" and "made the property of the regime." Voice becomes the property of the powerful.[35] In the contest between Wilkes and his executioners, the latter wanted him to scream in order to claim his Voice, but they failed. They wanted him to confess he had raped Mattie Cranford but he refused, and this defiance and the pain inflicted on him in blood and fire made him innocent in his own mind. Wilkes denied the sovereignty of his torment- ors. Newnan's "most prominent citizens" wanted Hose to cry out in terror: that is what "niggers" did. Wilkes refused; he kept his voice as his own.

As the fire began to die, trains from Atlanta arrived and possibly two thousand more men and boys, according to press reports, scavenged through the ashes for baked flesh and charred bone. They seized links of the chain that had bound Wilkes; they found pieces of the sapling; they folded ashes into their handkerchiefs. For some, however, "the sound of frying, sizzling human flesh, and the smell of the charred and slowly baking body [had been] nauseating and revolting beyond all description." Finally, the *Journal*'s reporter admitted he had become "sick and faint" along with "everybody who was within reach of the odor of frying flesh." Then Tom Wilkes was gone. He was consumed by fire and borne aloft by smoke.

A few white men began to talk about Sam Hose's silence. A few were amazed at his having endured "the ordeal of fire with [such] surprising fortitude." One man thought Wilkes "went to the stake with as much courage as anyone could possibly have possessed."[36] The young man who found it so difficult to speak with whites that he couldn't look them directly in the eye had brandished remarkable pluck and self-discipline. The black man who had been afflicted with a nervous "tic" when addressing whites had found a resolve that would later inspire blacks who heard of it. They would think, "Martyrdom." In the end, Tom Wilkes was true to himself and to his people. In the torrent of words that flowed from the nation's press like lava from a volcanic eruption only a few mentioned his courage; none captured his silence as Voice. Yet silence, grit, and transcendence were *his* truth.

The fleeting recognition of Wilkes' humanity sobered perhaps a few white men at the site but it swiftly wafted away and disappeared. Elsewhere to the north in Campbell County, white men were furious that they had been unable to participate in the carnival of blood and fire. They needed another sacrifice to satisfy their lust. They chose the Reverend Elijah Strickland possibly on a whim but probably because they had heard an unverifiable claim that Wilkes had mentioned him during torture. In frustration at being denied the pleasure of burning Hose, Palmetto's avenging angels pounced on the black man who had tried to help hunters find Hose the day after Cranford's death. They seized Strickland late the night of April 23 from the plantation of Major W. W. Thomas, a Confederate veteran.

When Thomas was alerted by Strickland's wife that her husband had been abducted, the planter and his son rode swiftly after the night riders. When they found the crowd, the Thomases tried to persuade them to release the preacher, or, failing that, to jail him pending trial. The Major relied on his public stature and personal dignity to plead for Strickland's life. He, like Atkinson and Freeman, was one of Georgia's "best men"; he had served in the legislature; his word meant something. He scoffed at the accusation that Strickland had wanted Cranford dead: No sensible person would believe Hose, Thomas insisted. No one should be condemned on the word of an adversary. A man such as Strickland who had the respect of a great many white people should receive a fair hearing, the Major argued. Most of the crowd finally agreed and voted to move their prize to the county jail. The Major then left the scene but a new mob soon transformed it. As the original crowd headed to Fairborn, the county seat, late arrivals seized Strickland. When the Major heard what had happened he and his son sought help because they knew the second gang would not abide by the compromise to which he and the original captors had agreed, but he failed.

The reconstituted mob tortured Strickland to force a confession for something he had not done. They hoisted him by the neck into the branches of a tree and then released him three times but he had nothing to confess. Thugs then cut off his ears and part of a finger and lifted him just a few inches off the ground by his neck so that he could die slowly by strangulation. Later the morning of April 24 the preacher was found hanging from the limb of the small persimmon tree. Murderers had attached two messages to his chest: "N.Y. Journal, We must protect our Ladies. 23 – 99." The other was: "Beware all darkies. You will be treated in the same way." The killers had tried to warrant their action within the mythology of rape-and-honor by appending it to the grander narrative of sex-violence-justice that vindicated the burning of Sam Hose. They wanted to be part of the twisted morality play that elevated them in their own minds into the democratic regions of Southern imagination in defiance of the mythic North. Thus they combined "New York," "ladies," and "darkies" in a puerile boast that revealed the savage but deadly nonsense of their collective mindlessness.

Prompted by Major Thomas, the acting coroner of Campbell County, Justice of the Peace Cummings, immediately empaneled a jury. They found, according to the scripted folk wisdom of Southern convention, that "an unknown mob" with "malice aforethought" had killed Elijah Strickland. The gang had acted "contrary to the laws of the state and the good order, peace and dignity thereof." The jury, however, lied; the mob was not unknown. Major Thomas announced that he had the names of the first crowd that abducted Strickland. He insisted that the original kidnappers who were escorting Strickland to jail could give the names of all the men who had taken the preacher from them. Justice demanded authorities act at once, the Major argued, but the coroner and his jury refused. They did not want to know as much as Thomas knew; they did not want to waste time attempting to track down a group of their neighbors or friends.

The authorities did not want the unknown to be known, so they issued the kind of public statement officials reserve for saying something without saying anything significant. The killing was bad, they explained, but in a muddled way they implied that the killers were not. Campbell County officials refused to seek the murderers because they already knew who they were; some undoubtedly sat on the coroner's jury. In conversing with reporters, officials appeared to be smarting from the results of the lynching in March. They had not sought the murderers then so there was no reason to seek these others now. No wonder black people once again left Campbell County in droves; possibly 1300 African Americans disappeared. Thomas himself confessed that many of his own tenants were leaving. People who had nowhere else to go were understandably wary of all whites. If a respectable and law abiding man such as Elijah Strickland could not receive justice despite the support of a man such as Major W. W. Thomas, blacks knew they were all in great peril.[37]

The white men who tortured Strickland to death had taken advantage of a brief suspension of the ordinary rules of the world that had begun with the hunt for Sam Hose. The suspension allowed the parade, the offering, and the fire. Public discourse, collective action, and the abdication or powerlessness of elected authorities had created space and time within which men could slough off the moral irrelevance of the law to punish, purify, and sacrifice. The report of murder had been trumped by the cry of rape that allowed editors to demand ecstatic punishment by fire that transgressed the ordinary world of law and order and celebrated sacrifice. The excitement of transgression that animated the crowd that paraded Sam Hose through the streets of Newnan had been nourished for over ten days. The long search for the accused and the many false leads and mistaken arrests created a moral community justified by its continuing action and the horror that white editors, authorities, and columnists tolled in the "tin-tintabulation" of Rape, rape: rape-rape-rape.

To be sure, many of those who justified the burning of Sam Hose condemned the strangulation of Strickland because it did not fit the narrative of rape and punishment. But that flaw did not diminish the moral force behind the destruction of Sam Hose. For a moment the lynching was justice within the magical white ethos emanating from Atlanta to Macon to Marshallville, but it was also profit. A day after the Newnan holocaust, *The Constitution* reported that its editor and publisher had handed a check for five hundred dollars to J. B. Jones. The money rewarded Jones for capturing Tom Wilkes and delivering him safely to the authorities for trial. Jones also accepted compensation from an Atlanta banker, the state of Georgia, and the people of Coweta County. Jones was $1350.00 richer before he shared some of the money with members of the mob and returned home. The newspaper on that day was devoted to articles and interviews justifying the lynching and warning readers of the dangers posed by young black men. Wilkes, who had wanted nothing more than wages and time to visit his sick mother, was, as Sam Hose, becoming a symbol not of white lawlessness, racial contempt, or savage brutality but of the black menace.

5

After the Fury

Rape and History

"With what judgment ye judge, ye shall be judged: and with what measure ye mete, it shall be measured to you again. And why beholdest thou the mote that is in thy brother's eye, but considerest not the beam that is in thine own eye?"

The Christian Bible KJV, Matthew 7:1–3

"Recompense to no man evil for evil. Provide things honest in the sight of all men. If it be possible, as much as lieth in you, live peaceably with all men. Dearly beloved, avenge not yourselves, but rather give place unto wrath: for it is written, Vengeance is mine; I will repay, saith the Lord ... Be not overcome of evil, but overcome evil with good."

The Christian Bible KJV, Romans, 12:17–19, 21

"But the fruit of the Spirit is love, joy, peace, longsuffering, gentleness, goodness, faith ... If we live in the Spirit, let us walk in the Spirit. Let us not be desirous of vainglory, provoking one another, envying one another."

The Christian Bible KJV, Galatians, 5:22, 24–25

***

On the third Sunday after Easter in 1899 about forty miles southwest of Atlanta in Newnan, Georgia, a white crowd burned to death a fugitive black laborer known as Sam Hose. This atrocity blended anger, hatred, arrogance, festivity, brutality and satisfaction into a mood just beyond comprehension. "Glory!" shouted an excited man enraptured by the intensity of the moment, "Glory be to God!!"

The lynching of Sam Hose had just begun. Tom Wilkes' body had been carved into souvenirs, hacked into trophies, and reduced to ashes; it was gone. The person he had been was gone. His brothers, sister, and mother must have faced an unimaginable chasm, an overwhelming emptiness. Terror rooted in a devastating sense of vulnerability would have naturally mixed with fury, but we do not know. We cannot. The younger brother and son who had tended his mother and little brother for so long had been transmuted into a monster and slain in a manner too terrible to imagine. He had undoubtedly told his family he had not hurt Mrs. Cranford and had acted only to defend himself against her husband, but that was enough to condemn him to world-destroying pain. They knew what would happen as soon as the Jones brothers took him. Tom's brother who worked for Jones left the plantation with his mother and little brother almost immediately, perhaps to join a sister and her family to the west of Marshallville. False stories about the family circulated for a while after the burning. Some claimed Tom's elder brother was planning revenge, but the narratives misplaced the family and misnamed its head. The impact of Tom's horrendous fate would linger for years and affect his family in ways they would never be able to resolve.

The trauma of knowing how Wilkes had died was different from that experienced by Mattie Cranford, whose world was also destroyed by homicide, rumor, innuendo, and masculine fantasy. Whatever Tom Wilkes may have done, he had certainly devastated her. Her emotional collapse and reclusive withdrawal into the womb of her mother's home resulted from trauma that might as well have been the result of rape even if it were not. When an "overwhelming violent event" happens it may not be "fully grasped" in detail immediately; it may later afflict the victim in dreams or other "repetitive phenomena." This was certainly true of John Mathews' second son. As Cathy Caruth points out, "traumatic experience ... suggests a certain paradox: the most direct seeing of a violent event may occur as an absolute inability to know it." Immediacy, "paradoxically, may take the form of belatedness." The family legend has it that Mattie "never smiled again."[1] She may not have. Her trauma was different from that shared within her husband's family, which had lost another man to black violence over a decade earlier. As wrenching as these traumas were, they were private and not public, although exploited to make a political point.

Alfred Cranford was almost forgotten in public discourse; Rebecca Felton dismissed his death as secondary to his wife's rape. Mattie was remembered as a victim of Sam Hose's lust and an uncaring Yankee public who scorned her pain. Tom Wilkes wasn't forgotten because he had never been "known" beyond his family. If Sam Hose was "remembered" at all it was as the personification of all dangers luridly imagined by a white South. Publicists, politicians, and patriots chanted a mantra of *innocence-rape-beast-justice-blood* in various turns of phrase. Imaginative cantors of wrath reminded faint-hearted preachers, prissy lawyers, elitist judges, self-righteous Yankees, and insolent blacks that what Hose had done justified everything done to him. Punishing Hose, however, became, in the aftermath, a political act by besieged Southern whites who had to defend themselves against the seditious acts of young blacks inspired by reckless Yankees to resist white supremacy. By June 1899, the lynching had become submerged into the mythic narrative of the Lost Cause.

BURNING: YANKEES CAUSED IT, "NEGROES" FORCED IT, HONOR DEMANDED IT

At first, of course, the issue was Rape. Clark Howell of *The Constitution* had insisted that Georgians "Remember the Ravishing!" Rebecca Felton's rhetorical genius permeated the language of righteous vengeance. Horror justified horror; terror justified terror; rape demanded mutilation; desecration commanded fire. Partisans claimed that the horror of burning men alive was necessary to cow potential killers and rapists into good behavior. The theme was one of those commonplace insights that, when repeated often enough, is supposed to confirm a position, even when belied by circumstances as well as several millennia of human history. As if to dramatize how utterly vacuous the claim was, three months after the crowd left Wilkes in ashes two black men viciously raped a white woman and forced her husband to watch.[2] They ignored the message Tom Wilkes' murderers had sent and delivered their own. The white men who captured them a short time later slowly flayed and cut the rapists to death inch by inch amid screams at excruciating pain that did nothing to prevent either more rape or more lynching.

Anyone who could think knew that lynching did not prevent rape, insolence, impertinence, pride, anger, theft, arson, or murder, no matter what publicists promised. Punishment not prevention was, after all, the immediate goal of collective violence, but so was participation in a *rite* of transcendent meaning. Whites possessed many ways to punish blacks: fines, peonage, chain-gangs, rape, or assault – all different degrees of violence. Lynching was the next level of penalty: and a fiery *auto da fe* such as that enacted on Sam Hose was the most dramatic of such punishments. Within this punitive ethos, it is clear that for vengeful whites at the stake, the rituals of transgression, torture, and killing were far more important than the profane functions it was supposed to serve. Afterward, however, as it became necessary to justify what happened, defensive whites revealed the history, myth, reasons, and assumptions that helped them clarify the meaning of what was done, and vindicate it.

Burning Tom Wilkes was made sacred by the ways in which ten days of public discourse had transformed the presumed rape of Mattie Cranford into an act that transcended the ordinary rules of crime and punishment. The *mentalité* exposed in *The Constitution*'s symposium on the demonic threat to white country women transformed Wilkes from a criminal who had committed a specific crime into the personification of widespread terror. When the crowd paraded him through Newnan, its vanguard presented him as a monstrance to their savage god at the altar of each intersection. They made him sacred by ritualizing their acts as a prelude to sacrifice. Sacrifice was supposed to do what other deaths could not do: prevent crime, terrorize blacks, avenge Reconstruction, and protect white women. Partisans said so.

If magic could not deliver such results, it nevertheless made the shedding of blood and purifying by fire *sacred* because these acts signified a reality beyond their performance. The "sacred," writes Paul Kahn, "always shows itself as the *infinite in the finite*." French scholars Henri Hubert and Marcel Mause had, the year before the killing of Tom Wilkes, demonstrated "that expulsion of a sacred spirit, whether pure or impure, is a primordial component of sacrifice," and sacrifice is an intense drama that transforms a specific offender's death into the symbol of a community's destruction of Evil.[3] Sacrifice made Hose's tormentors blameless and also holy. A local "poet" made the case in familiar words that claimed Sam Hose's killers did "no wrong/ To burn this monster at the stake."

The "poet" continued:

> 'Twas but right he should die
> With lurid fire to light the same.
> 'Twill teach these brutal beasts to know
> That vengeance dire will quickly come;
> God's righteous wrath is never slow
> To avenge the Christian home.

In brief, "God ordains it just and right/ To avenge this hellish crime." Faith justified vengeance as any believer could claim by reference to the twenty-fifth chapter of the Bible's Book of Numbers. Although "vengeance came from God on high," a Christian could expect unbelievers to be critical of "God's righteous wrath." When Newnan's *Herald and Advertiser* reported that the popular atheist Robert Ingersoll had denounced the lynching, the *Herald*'s editor thought Christians should rejoice. The free-thinker's condemnation confirmed the ultimate justice of what white men did in Newnan; Ingersoll would undoubtedly meet Hose in Hell! This comment reflected a fatuous attempt at dismissive humor to avoid thinking seriously about what whites from Newnan, Palmetto, and Griffin had done. Some people used the word, "barbecue," in the same way. Two restaurateurs announced, "Newnan's reputation as a barbecue town is not intended to include such functions as that which occurred on Sunday afternoon last. That affair was a rank departure from the orthodox variety made famous in the past by Harry Fisher and Jack Driskill."[4]

The doggerel, exegesis, and "humor" of a few men suggest the privileged feelings among Newnan's citizens immediately after the lynching. Most people, of course, did not express themselves publicly. Some undoubtedly did not want to think about what had happened. The Methodist women's missionary society continued to focus more on saving China than Coweta County. Governor Atkinson and Judge Freeman were probably sobered and emotionally spent by the savagery of an impassioned democracy. If they had tried to stop the lynching, they nonetheless had to live in Newnan. Their neighbors, whom they knew by name and in many instances respected, had participated in the carnivalesque procession and burning.

Atkinson understood how and what these people thought. As a politician who hoped to continue as a player in the Democratic Party, he did not want to alienate future voters any more than he already had. The day after the lynching he issued a statement to the *Atlanta Journal* that disclosed his take on popular opinion in Newnan. Most significantly, Atkinson did what apologists for the lynching did. He ignored the mutilation and burning, and focused instead on Hose's "crimes" against a high quality family; he also conceded the dominion of his neighbors' wrath. No one, he confessed, could have restrained the crowd on the court house square. He did not apologize for what he had tried to do; but he did concede the power of "an *outraged* people" who had (strangely enough) displayed a "marvel of *coolness*."[5] Newnan's favorite son knew his neighbors did not want to think about cutting, gutting, and burning; they wanted to think about their principled wrath and virtue. They believed their rage at the horror of rape exempted them from the law, but they also insisted that they were rational. Horror, passion, and reason justified them.

Conversations among twenty-five leading white citizens of the city confirmed that inference. Less than a month after the burning, these men sat down with a Northern journalist who seemed to sympathize with them. George Hepworth was a columnist for the *New York Herald* with a reputation for fairness, at least among authorities, after having investigated the Turkish government's actions against Armenian "revolutionists." A liberal Christian, Hepworth had once been a popular preacher in New York City. Editors of *The Constitution* and *Atlanta Journal* ardently welcomed him because for some reason they believed he could give Northerners the best possible explanation of the culture within which Sam Hose was lynched. They did not know that he had once, in youthful bombast, demanded Confederate President Jefferson Davis be hanged for treason. Georgia elites apparently believed Hepworth would vindicate them as he had the Turks.

In early May, the journalist spent twenty-four hours in Newnan, where he met with Mattie Cranford who remained in a wretched, "pitiful and pathetic" state. Without reference to Mrs. Cranford, Hepworth seemed to accept as factual the authorized version of Tom Wilkes' crimes, which had, he observed, "projected an epidemic of insanity into the community." That lunacy, he insisted, did not in any way justify breaking the law; lynching had to cease in the name of progress, civilization, and Christianity!

To men who believed that Newnan already modeled progress, civilization, and Christianity, the statement would have been offensive save for Hepworth's incessant reminder that he sympathized with them. He knew that the Newnan elite's collective sensibility had to be deftly massaged to encourage frank and revealing conversation. Besides, he was charming; he personified empathy and compassion. His hosts faced problems, he conceded to their relief, which Northerners did not, but law, the columnist insisted, cannot be broken to maintain the law. He was challenged. How would he feel if a beloved woman were raped? He would have been furious and vengeful, he swore, but such feelings were private and not reliable as a source of public policy. They did not justify taking the law into his own hands. What he personally would have wanted to do and what he as a citizen ought to do were two different things. He was clear. Citizens had "no right to lose their heads!"

The distinction between feeling and act was lost on the audience. In reply, someone spat out that Northerners were no more moral than

Southerners. Hepworth agreed: lynching was as evil in the North as in the South. Although he refused to scold them, his hosts became defensive as he graciously deflected their attacks on the "North" by admitting the obvious. A perfect society, he observed, did not exist. Some of the men in the room confessed regret at illegal violence but, when corrected by their more insightful fellows, remembered actually that they regretted the *necessity* of resorting to violence! The New Yorker pointed out that half of them believed violence was necessary and all of them agreed that "violence is harmful." It was an injury, however, that his audience was willing to suffer, they claimed, for the sake of innocent women and children. Rape, honor, order, and women became the themes that elevated defensiveness into a moral posture. One man spoke for many when he objected to Northerners' believing that lynching was a Southern "pastime"; rather, it was an "inexorable duty."

"Negroes are human!" the liberal Christian blurted out. They are not as "much impressed as exasperated" by lawless violence. The comment hit a nerve. Despite the pervasive belief that African Americans were a hostile and dangerous segment of Southern society, his audience hoped Hepworth would "understand the motives which led to our action and not credit us with a hostility to the negro because he is a negro [sic], for that is not true." They were innocents! The columnist conceded, as best he could, the moral posture of his audience but pointed out that no one was made better by burning even "the worst and most vicious criminal." Torturers did "moral injury to themselves," he declared, but his audience was not convinced.

Trying to end on a positive note, Hepworth repeated a conventional, meaningless bromide in euphemistic language that he knew would please his hosts. A "necessary swiftness" in court cases would help avoid incidents that "would cause regret." The reform would not be sufficient, he admitted, but it would be a step in the right direction. The suggestion reflected the emotion and defensiveness that cloaked the room; Hepworth had ended discussion with a polished banality. He then praised the men for listening in an admirable "temper" to his criticism. He thanked them for their hospitality and left for New York. There he reflected on his hosts' obsession with sexual possession, masculine duty, and rape, which had created a perverse moral ethos extremely dangerous to black men. He then wrote a comment that Southern editors understood as the most "deliberate and cold-blooded libel" ever to have "indicted" the "women of any time and place." If a Southern white woman held a grudge against an African American man, he observed, all she had to do to punish him was to cry, "Rape." Newnan's elite must have been furious at what they no doubt believed was a betrayal.[6]

TRUTH AND CANON: BLACK/WHITE

Hepworth listened to African Americans as well as whites, but he had little to say about that meeting. He did discover that no one there believed Hose had raped Mattie Cranford and he also learned how wary black people were of saying anything to offend hypersensitive Southern whites. Blacks knew what they were supposed to believe even though they didn't. They knew that whites were alert to any criticism from black people that could be inferred from comments about lynching. Sometimes, of course, African Americans forgot how closely they were monitored. When James Reid ignored the script, he had to explain himself. After scavengers had picked the burning-site clean, the black restaurateur innocently observed that it was strange for a black man to have possessed relics from Sam Hose's body as rumored. James Reid's outrage had ignited his outburst. As a prominent African American businessman who read the local newspaper's bad poetry and gross humor, he knew his white neighbors well. His surprise at a black man's mindless possession of a relic was natural.

Hostile white Newnanites were incensed, and – to defend himself from violence erupting from white rage – Reid confirmed in a long public statement that white people were justified in wanting to punish Hose. Any "respectable colored man," Reid wrote, would have "delivered [Wilkes] into the hands of the law." He emphasized "the law," setting it by implication against lawlessness. Reid learned that even a simple comment implying a divide in the moral perspectives of black and white could be dangerous. Southern racial etiquette demanded he join the Greek chorus incanting approval of Sam Hose's fate. Other African Americans from Coweta County did much the same thing as he. Only a few heedless or brave souls commented on the accusation of rape in a manner "too vile for publication," which justified Griffin's vigilantes' whipping them. "Any col[ored] man," wrote a black Methodist preacher in a confidential letter, "that says a thing contrary to the way they killed that man last Sunday will be killed at once." He feared for his life. He should have; whites had already killed at least two men for denouncing the "barbarism of the mob."[7]

In his novel, *The Autobiography of an Ex-Colored Man* (1912), James Weldon Johnson imagined how an African American would collapse into stunned humiliation after observing a spectacular burning. As a black man himself, Johnson knew his protagonist had to feel a "great wave" of "shame that I belonged to a race that could be so dealt with." As an American, he would be shamed that a nation that aspired to be a "great example of democracy" was "the only civilized state on earth, where a human being would be burned alive." He was dazed; his "heart turned bitter." A democracy should treasure the rule of law; citizens should therefore obey it. But Johnson "could understand why Negroes are led to sympathize with even their worst criminals, and to protect them when possible." Humanity and equity dictated "nothing less." Thinking of the many whites who littered the nation's press with professions of sympathy and good will, he doubted that a people who tolerated the burning of a human being to death could be "entrusted with the salvation of a race." Johnson imagined himself reeling from such a burning as consumed Sam Hose, "weak as a man who had lost blood."[8]

Nausea, shame, bitterness, anger, hollowness, grief – agony: all are words that come to mind as natural to the black people of Newnan in response to the lynching. Within families, African Americans had to clothe themselves in the normality of everyday life before venturing into white space on the street and at work. They had to protect themselves and their dependents from the agony of their private emotions and fears and from the scrutiny and surveillance of hostile white strangers as well as those they knew. They had to fight the "shame" Johnson believed was natural to such situations, which meant that they felt the weight of being unjustly condemned even when no one accused them specifically. The problem was that as African Americans, they were already accused, as James Reid discovered.

Even before the mob captured Wilkes, local black ministers knew the temper of their white neighbors and shaped their statements carefully. During the hunt, Baptists had dedicated a church in Newnan with a sermon that promised "showers of blessing" sometime in the future. A black Baptist editor, however, believed the message signified the prom-ise of freedom to an oppressed people even if whites ignored it. The latter were more interested in what African Americans said about black crim-inals, so the *Herald and Advertiser*, for example, approved comments by the Reverend John Harmon of the Newnan African Methodist Episcopal Church (AMEC). He reminded his congregation that they could not match the weapons, wealth, and power of the white race. They could, however, become a "terror to evil-doers" in order to "prove ourselves worthy citizens. Then, and not 'til then c[ould] we hope to be respected as a race." He was speaking about whites' power as well as his people's public personae; he knew they would be scrutinized once Hose was caught, which happened later that same day.

After the burning, African American ministers reaffirmed Harmon's admonitions to prove themselves "worthy citizens" as if they were not already doing so. Years of living among a suspicious people who monitored their public discourse helped blacks speak a language packed with many meanings. The *Herald*'s editors did not realize what Bishop Henry McNeal Turner of the AMEC meant when in Atlanta he condemned the rape of Mrs. Cranford, but explicitly ignored the lynching (at least for a while). "We can write no more," he confessed, "because we are at a loss for words to express our regret and horror." For a man who was rarely, if ever, at a "loss for words" and who was known to believe that American whites thought all blacks inferior and suffered their presence only in a servile capacity, the silence at what was done to Wilkes after his capture was damning if one paid attention. One white man did so: He thought Turner should be shot. The bishop was not surprised. He had long insisted that white America promised nothing but "Sackcloth and Ashes for the Negro."[9]

He, of course, was not alone. In Augusta, where white as well as black editors blasted the lynching, William Jefferson White of The [African American] *Georgia Baptist* dismissed excuses for "the latest example of Southern civilization." Justifying the lynching by accusing Hose of rape was the "veriest prattle" because everyone knew that whites excused their violence for any crime imaginable "from chicken stealing to murder" with that claim. We live under a government "founded on prejudice and nourished on the blood of the helpless," White wrote. We live in a culture that vindicates "civilization with butchery" and upholds its "dignity with a torch." The most savage of Roman emperors (Caligula and Nero) could stand by the killers in Newnan and "feel pure."

The editors of *The Savannah Tribune* were more detailed in their accounting of the torture and burning, suggesting Georgia was "drifting into a state of cannibalism." They cited a well-known white man who lamented the inability of the federal government to protect American citizens, and wondered if Southern whites were insane. The barbarity he denounced was perfected, the editors observed, when "an old white haired man exclaimed glory to God." How could God glorify "such an occasion?" Black commentators wondered if Governor Allen Candler would pursue the murderers. At the very least, they thought, he could offer a reward for the apprehension of the killers. The act would have been symbolic even if not substantial. The editors knew, of course, that

the governor was committed to doing less than the very least; they knew
that local authorities in Palmetto protected white killers. The editors
could only try to shame shameless men by printing comments from other
white men, such as the editors of the *Washington Post*, who condemned
"savages" acting "with such fiendish cruelty." African Americans further
south and west objected to whites' condemning them as a criminal class as
lawless white mobs reached the "limit of human savagery."[10]

White Georgians who wanted the approval of prominent blacks
awaited the reaction of Booker T. Washington. The man by this time
had become the darling of white paternalists, as W. E. B. DuBois later
observed, through a "program of industrial education, conciliation of the
South and silence as to civil and political rights." His program had
become a way of life that made him, at least for a while, Du Bois
explained, "the most distinguished Southerner since Jefferson Davis."[11]
Washington had launched his "way of life" soon after becoming head of
Alabama's Tuskegee Institute in 1881; it was clarified in an address he
delivered on the opening of the Cotton States and International Exposition in Atlanta on September 18, 1895.

Washington's fame and rhetoric bordering on the deferential had
brought him to the rostrum. Educated at Hampton Institute in Virginia
in "discipline, moral sobriety, self-control, and seriousness of purpose,"
Washington had used Tuskegee as the base from which to establish a
widespread political network among African Americans, build credibility
among white elites, and draw funds from the coffers of Northern paternalists. Washington's address on the opening day of the Exposition had
made national as well as southern headlines and came to be known as
"The Atlanta Compromise." His was a "Faustian bargain," David
Levering Lewis points out, but one that most Southern whites never
believed they had to honor. In Atlanta, Washington told whites what
they wanted to hear: "Negroes," he promised, shall "make friends with
the people around them," as if they had not already tried. They will
"learn to dignify and glorify common labor" and "make blossom the
waste lands of your fields" and "run your factories" to become the most
"faithful, law-abiding and unresentful people the world has seen." Then
he made one of the most notorious if ambiguous remarks in American
history: "In all things that are purely social we can be as separate as the
fingers, yet one as the hand in all things essential to mutual progress."

Most whites heard this comment as a concession to segregation, deference, and accommodation. Only a few whites would have heard "mutual
progress" and fewer still would have committed themselves to it. Most

ignored Washington's plea for securing African American citizenship but they may have felt uneasy when the educator insisted that "changeless justice bind oppressor and oppressed." Washington evaded the implications of this polarity, however, to deride demands for "social equality" in the struggle for rights. If he insisted that "all privileges of the law" should be "ours," he was quick to assure his white audience that this goal could be achieved without animosity from blacks. Somehow working together for "material prosperity" in "our beloved South," we shall bring "a new heaven and a new earth." Whites loved the speech. They ignored Bishop C. C. Petty's address to the Exposition appealing for justice and the same protection for blacks as that guaranteed to whites. Bishop Henry McNeal Turner was more confrontational. He later explained to a Congress of Africans and African Americans that the "colored man" who claims we do "not want social equality" and then predicts a great future for his oppressed people is either ignorant or committed to "perpetual servility."[12]

"The Atlanta Compromise" puts in perspective Washington's response to the lynching of Sam Hose. What he thought immediately is unknown. The apostle of good manners, practical education, and careful planning who avoided confrontation with whites was reported to have reacted in a fury. His friend, ally, and sometime critic, T. Thomas Fortune, told a conference of blacks that Washington had written a letter to Governor Allen Candler that Fortune had had to destroy. Washington tried again with the same result. Finally, he gave up. He explained that expressing his feelings on the lynching would jeopardize his school and the ability to attract support for his many projects on behalf of Southern black people. He later blandly confessed that he "opposed mob violence under all circumstances" but needed to avoid "controversy" in order to continue building an ethos to prevent "outrages" in the future.[13]

The comment reflected Washington's understanding of the white South: It was simply not safe for a black man to say what he truly thought. The violence inherent in that deformity prevented an authentic dialogue between black and white. The African American vanguard knew the rhetorical demands on them as a suspect people and Washington was more sensitive to these demands than opponents thought he should have been, but when confronted with "Newnan," words failed him at first. In the face of horror, silence may have been the only rational response, although banality was frequently its surrogate.

Some Southern black people signified their current predicament and hope as their predecessors had done in slavery. They spoke from a more sophisticated religious sensibility than that of their white watchers. They knew in times of crisis they had to please whites; they also knew that whites did not have to please them. The contempt implicit in this moral imbalance was clear. African Americans knew their history better than whites did and knew how to limn their destiny rhetorically in religious language. Bishop Wesley John Gaines of the African Methodist Episcopal Church was master of the style. In 1897 he had written *The Negro and the White Man*, disclaiming resentment or animosity to white people and denouncing anyone "white or colored" who encouraged "discontent, division and hatred." Relying on the historical consciousness of students, clerics, and popular black writers, he pointed out that "colored peoples," who were "as purely Nigritic" as African Americans, had established the great empires of the ancient world. Such people would rise once again!

As for the present condition of American blacks, Gaines relied on more recent history. He condemned the "evils of African slavery" that had left his people in ignorance, poverty, and helplessness. Those same evils had conferred on whites the "imperious haughtiness that destroys [the] brotherhood of men." He reminded whites that blacks had not hurt white women and children during the Civil War in contrast to whites' violence against black innocents during and after Reconstruction. The violence had continued. Surely in gratitude for African Americans' service and protection whites could now call a halt to "the heartless mobs that often take innocent negroes [sic] upon mere suspicion or for some fancied insult, and hang them from the nearest tree." In conclusion, he had appealed "to our white brothers to accord us simple justice."[14]

The third Sunday after the burning of Sam Hose, Bishop Gaines claimed the pulpit of an Atlanta AME church to address once again relations between "The Negro and the White Man." *The Constitution*'s account of his sermon on May 15 offers a lesson in the language of resistance and hope when addressed to two audiences but fully understood only by one. African Americans gathered as a people to praise God, hear salvation, and engage the future. They were bonded by race, condition, faith, and shed blood. They knew they had been widely condemned as the source of civil unrest by whites who considered them resident aliens: inferior, insufferable, and unwanted save as appendages to those who ruled by race and right. They gathered under an umbra of suspicion and a penumbra of ambivalence among whites who needed to know that black people would not "sympathize" with Sam Hose. Bishop Gaines, however, insisted that they gathered as a people in "crisis." The word reflected his anger and criticism of whites in *The Negro and the White Man* while he was at the same time trying to appease whites' suspicions and anger.

The second audience was not a people but a few visiting whites and reporters who wanted to be assured that African Americans were not angry at what white outlaws had done. White attendees wanted to hear "Rape!" not "Fire!" Some may have wanted either to be shriven of sin they could not confess or absolved of a crime they could not concede, but they were few indeed. The editors printed parts of Gaines' sermon in bold face to reveal the message their readers should receive. One reporter observed that the bishop would have been willing to turn a rapist over to a mob if he knew without doubt that he was guilty. He quoted Gaines as having said that anyone sympathizing with "the inhuman monster who commits this crime" is a "traitor to his race." The Bishop dismissed all talk of retaliatory violence: "The good men of both races" will cooperate in securing "peace and harmony." Black and white are not adversaries, he insisted, thus pleasing white witnesses, but his comments were embedded within an appeal for discipline in the face of crisis and the promise of salvation to be achieved (not received). This, white observers did not understand. Bishop Gaines, after all, was preaching to people who knew how to hear a sermon calling on them to "endure cheerfully the hardness which is incident to this life and especially to the life of the Christian [II Timothy 2:3 of the Christian Bible]."

Gaines' people were Christians, and as such they would have to fight. I am, the bishop announced, addressing "my race" as "soldiers of Jesus Christ" who will "endure the crisis *through which we are passing.*" He knew his people understood what crisis he meant. We are, he said, in the process of "becoming." Like the "rude stone" that must be hammered into a beauteous "marble statue," we must bear the "discipline of time and of our lot; we must endure the fire of the storm, and by and by, in the process of years, and the Providence of God, we will come forth, purified, perfected, and ready to stand abreast of the greatest people of the world." He must have thought of his own words celebrating the magnificent achievements of the pyramids. The theme of racial destiny was familiar among African Americans throughout the nation. His book of 1897 had been a brief on behalf of African American aspirations, ambitions, rights, and promises based on the highest ideals of the US Constitution. The keys to his sermon were: *endure, hardness, crisis,* and "*we will come forth,*" that is, we shall "overcome!"

Gaines mentioned the lynching that had "excited" the countryside: He condemned the rape and scored the accusation that African Americans did not hate crime. Ninety-five per cent, he noted, were obviously law-abiding. And then at considerable length he denounced mob law and explained how it all too often destroyed the innocent and demoralized the entire biracial community. How that emphasis could have been interpreted by white newspapermen as favoring lynching beggars reason, but it was. Like Saint Paul, Gaines knew his people wrestled "against principalities, against powers, against the rulers of darkness"; the current crisis demanded they don "the whole armour of God," in order to "be able to stand against the wiles of the devil." He told his people to enlist as "good soldiers of Jesus Christ." Your spirit, he told them, "is chained by the bounds of time and earth, but one day your Redeemer shall come." Perhaps he was trying to stir what W. E. B. Du Bois hoped was the "deep religious feeling of the real Negro heart" that would one day erupt into an "Awakening." Gaines imagined his people freed to ascend to "your eternal home on high" but it was not Heaven he anticipated so much as justice, as he had written in his book. To ascend to such a state, he insisted, you must fight!

The congregation then sang "Am I a soldier of the Cross?" Each singer knew, "I must fight if I would reign." They prayed, "Increase my courage, Lord," and promised to "bear the toil, endure the pain, Supported by Thy Word." Only someone insensitive to the instant impact of such words and the urgent cadence of call and response could have dismissed the sermon as "otherworldly."[15] Only someone who had never needed such a sermon would have ignored its existential source. The people were not to "wait" but to *volunteer* and fight. Soldiers do not "endure pain" or summon "courage" in order to lose.

RAPE! RAPE?

White newspapers in Atlanta and Louisville, Kentucky, claimed Gaines had approved lynching. Gaines and Booker T. Washington encoded their language with care because they believed what the *Herald*'s editors told the citizens of Newnan – that the lynchers enjoyed the support of white people throughout the region. With Newnan's elite and a generation of white men reared in the language of white supremacy, Southern editors cried, "*Rape!*" The cry made sense within the mental context and long-nourished predispositions of whites who had contributed to *The Constitution*'s symposium on the endangered countryside. To be sure, nine of the ten women essayists dismissed lynching as a solution to racial tensions, but that did not mean they could easily dismiss the fears that animated many of their sisters. They had all been involved in "good works" on behalf of white women; they knew that they were becoming more independent, better educated, and more likely to be thrust into new situations of sexual tension, if not danger, as they took jobs and interacted with (white) men they did not know.

These essayists knew that some of their colleagues were trying to change the age of consent, protect imprisoned females, and restrict the consumption of liquor. They had to think about sex, gender, and self in ways that were not always comfortable. They had undoubtedly read the same articles that had prepared Corra Harris to write about the sexual danger flowing from African American life in an imminent issue of *The Independent*. If they could not defend the lynching of black rapists as Rebecca Felton did, the women associated with her could not deny the power of "Rape" to sober them. The presumed violation of Mattie Cranford had, after all, brought them together to think about Southern [white] women and the dangers they faced. *Rape* was not just a word; it was a way of characterizing danger, justifying white power, and explaining race in one part of the United States.[16] White supremacists believed it was the only way.

According to many Southern editors, Hose's *rape* of Mrs. Cranford in her husband's gore was a crime that "transcend[ed] the bounds of human law." The penalty had to transcend law as well. Most defenses of that penalty, however, ignored the details in which "the devil" resided: the cutting, gutting, burning, and stench. The defensiveness among whites allowed them to concede in private that those little details were relevant to the killing but if well-deserved, best left unmentioned. The important thing partisans wanted remembered was that the criminal justice system could not cope with *rape*! Courts moved too slowly; they were criminally erratic because *rapists* could actually be acquitted. Moreover, in formal trials, *rape* victims could be abused in cross examination by disreputable lawyers. If found guilty, *rapists* could even appeal the verdict. *Rape* was too serious a crime, partisans claimed, to be trivialized by form, rules, reason, or procedure; thus immediate draconian punishment was well deserved.

None of these comments was new; all were part of the approved language for explaining lynching within the cults of white supremacy and masculine honor. Enthusiasts had to believe that Northerners did not care that Southern white women were *raped* by black *rapists*; Yankees had "no thought whatever of the appalling mental and physical torture" inflicted on the black *rapist*'s victim. If Northerners had as many *rapists* as we do, partisans proclaimed, Yankees would act in exactly the same way as we. They know it as well as we, and that fact imbedded in an outraged human nature demonstrates Yankee hypocrisy when criticizing the South! An incident in Pana, Illinois, long before the burning of Sam Hose helped Southern partisans dramatize hypocrisy beyond the hypothetical. Illinois whites had murdered blacks imported by coal-mine owners to break a strike. The ethical equation of the regions was out of balance: Southerners killed the guilty for committing atrocious crimes; Yankees killed the innocent for wanting to work.[17] Southerners needed no lessons in morality from such people!

As lynching enthusiasts cried "Rape," other Southerners, who were less inspired by the chivalric torture of dying black men, pled "Civilization" and "Law!" Federal Judge Emory Speer told students at Mercer College in Macon that it was time for whites to stop lying about black people in order to justify the formers' crimes. "The South," he was reported to have said, "owes it to the nation to purge itself of the villainies perpetrated in the name of 'home protection'." Speer, Governor Atkinson, and Judge Freeman were not the only white Georgians to hope Southerners could serve Law and Civilization. The city attorney for Savannah scored the "unspeakably horrible and shameful" debauch in Newnan. One of his fellow citizens noted that the brutes had hoped to teach a lesson: "If only they had eaten some of the cooked flesh, they would have completed the picture and made the lesson perfect." The editor of the *Savannah Morning News* thought the "lynching will send a thrill of horror throughout the entire country." The burning damaged efforts to prove Georgia a state in which "nature, art, and humanity are all united."

Such horror compelled the Reverend Edgar Gardner Murphy to write from Montgomery, Alabama, that "The mob spirit is a form of madness," but the comment was not a defense as it had once been for Bishop Haygood. The "mob spirit" was, Murphy went on, "a species of social hysteria... [and] disgusting animalism." The "excuseless orgy" challenged "the very life of the law." Orra Langhorne from Lynchburg, Virginia, agreed, and explained to *The Boston Evening Transcript* that she, a former slaveholder, was devastated at what had happened in Newnan. Those white savages "hardly deserve to be called human," she wrote. She revealed a sensitivity that was rare: The problem was not a "Negro" problem, but a human problem created by whites in both sections who refused to accord black people "full justice and the courtesy we [should] show people of all races." She appealed for equity. The color line must yield, she insisted, to attain "liberty for all." Langhorne had long supported African Americans' claims for equality; she was not a typical Southern lady.[18]

Denunciation of supremacist anarchy by Southerners encouraged editors of the *Outlook*, a New York magazine to which Murphy had written, to be foolishly optimistic. From Augusta and Savannah, Georgia, from Birmingham, Alabama, and from Charleston and Columbia, South Carolina, the editors found newsmen who believed the merciless punishment of Sam Hose was not only uncivilized, illegal, and un-Christian but also damaging to the society that partisans pretended to protect. *The* [Columbia, South Carolina] *State*'s editors thought the actions near Newnan to be a "hideous orgy of torture and mutilation." The brutal ferocity had betokened racial warfare based on hatred that Newnan's elite claimed was a lie. Such loathing allowed "scruples" to be "thrown away [and] all restraints broken." The editors wondered "at what cost to [white torturers], with what shame to civilization is this supremacy in the arts of hell established?" There were, contrary to the claim of partisans, no "gentlemen" present at the site of such horror.

The governor wasn't "present" either, commented the Augusta *Herald*. Allen Candler could have prevented the lynching had he wished, the editor insisted, because he knew that the hunt for Hose had prepared his trackers to plan a spectacular lynching. Candler could have had patrols policing areas where he suspected the crime would take place. More specifically, he could have sought help from the US government, but calling out "Federal troops to suppress a mob" would have been bad politics in a state where a partisan of the governor insisted that the "common law" of lynching was "graven on the hearts of those of her men who have any manhood in them." The governor had failed to do his duty as chief executive, the newsman pointed out, even though Candler had sworn to "enforce the laws of the State."[19] The implication was clear: The governor had joined the mob. He was not William Yates Atkinson, but then, *not* being Atkinson had been his proud claim as he campaigned for governor.

Two days after the burning of Sam Hose, editors at *The Constitution* ignored criticism from Southern papers as well as the tortures Wilkes endured to congratulate their readers. Almost "all papers" had expressed "a warm sympathy with the southern people on their peculiar predicament with regard to the negro [sic] problem in all its ramifications." Like their colleagues in Columbia, South Carolina, they believed there was a basic divide between black and white. But whereas *The State*'s editors looked into the abyss of racial warfare and saw hatred and contempt, *The Constitution*'s spokesmen saw a "problem" created by African Americans. To explain, they surveyed the historical and social contexts within which lynching and the "problem" should be understood. Remember, the editors wrote, *ideal* race relations had existed under slavery when the master class had converted Africans to Christianity.

With Emancipation, Yankee politicians and teachers created a "generation of self-sufficient, aggressive negroes," whose "proudest boast was that they held the sidewalk against the white man." This underclass, empowered by the insolence of youth and driven by aspirations to "equality," had invaded the countryside to assault white women. The simplicity of *The Constitution*'s reconstruction of the American past was awe-inspiring. If dangerous young men were only 5 per cent of the African American population, they were able to disappear into a sympathetic and thus seditious black community for protection. Hose had been hidden for ten days by his race, *The Constitution* claimed, ignoring the fact that if blundering whites had acted on Elijah Strickland's information they would have found Wilkes with his family a week before Jones did. Strickland was not alone. The black man shot by mistake in the search for Hose was not hunting possum.

The fiction of black obstruction helped supremacists criminalize an entire people and transform white vigilantes into vanguard sentries defending the citadel of white civilization. It was not surprising that about five weeks after the killing of Tom Wilkes, the state of Georgia partially solved the "negro problem" by segregating railroad cars by race. The ethos of purity-and-danger continued to inspire. Whites' frustration during their ham-fisted search for Wilkes had reinforced their determination to stigmatize African Americans even more than they already had. The new law was a "solution" that solved nothing; it was the kind of violence that made blacks wary of "law" that was designed to nullify Emancipation. Distancing black Georgians from whites in public space by law served to buttress the idea that black people were dangerous in proximity to whites save as servants. Distance supported the fantasy that African Americans assaulted "civilization" simply by existing. Boundaries defended by any white against any black may have eventually become permeable as the market expanded in the twentieth century, but during the 1890s, the walls were going up instead of coming down. The watchmen guarding them correctly perceived African Americans' reticence to cooperate with lawless white mobs and they criminalized that reticence.

James Reid, for one, would have been very much relieved had he been able to deliver Wilkes safely "into the hands of the law" *for protection*. The law may have been stacked against African Americans, but it did not castrate, flay, or burn them. Law, however, had to be enforced by officers facing a violent white democracy that through law had already cast African Americans beyond the legal security of citizenship. Reid and other black Newnanites would have been pleased if the "hands of the law" could have protected Tom Wilkes but those hands were feeble. Their grip was broken by a lawless crowd. When Reid mentioned "the hands of the law" he was actually referring to an ideal blacks knew few whites honored on April 23, 1899 in Newnan, Georgia. Blacks living in the area of the hunt for Sam Hose knew newspapers had prescribed his burning; they also knew that magical thinking would make them responsible for it.[20]

Imbedded in *The Constitution*'s history lesson lay the assumption of Northern hostility and, to be sure, Northern editors, ministers, and publicists did condemn what Georgia white men had done. Critics thought lynching and torture could not be justified by any provocation, no matter how partisans imagined it. A few writers doubted that there had been a rape; E. L. Godkin of *The Nation* agreed with Ida Wells Barnett on that score. Godkin and others did not believe that a furious desire for justice motivated lynch mobs; such an excuse was fanciful. Illegal executions were really the result of what Newnan's elite insisted to Heyworth did not exist: racial hatred. A rabbi who had lived in the South observed that "The average Southerner, chivalrous, kind-hearted, and hospitable enough to men of his own race[,] is utterly devoid of all regard and consideration for the negro [sic]." Despite the egalitarian implications of our constitution, Rabbi Joseph Silverman told Temple Emanu-El in Manhattan, we "have not yet succeeded in making all men fair, broad, and liberal." Some were savages, as a Boston paper explained.

Godkin likened professing Southern Christians – "full of gospel, and schools and church sociables" – to Iroquois warriors thought to have burned their captives in eighteenth-century warfare. Barbarians who had so "brutally outraged" Hose had reveled in a ghastly form of entertainment that seemed to confirm Silverman's accusation of race hatred. Godkin was so possessed by the need to revile Southern culture that he dismissed what he called ex-Governor Atkinson's "faint appeal" to the mob and ignored Southerners who were dismayed and shamed by the lynching.

Most censorious Northern editors, however, respected, even admired, the nerve and courage of both the former governor and Major Thomas. The *Boston Evening Transcript* – a paper that Southerners loved to hate because it was so fiercely critical of their region – praised the former governor for having "bravely" challenged "howling savages" before they cast him aside. Their burning of a human being had raised a "stench in the nostrils of the nation, a reproach to Christianity and civilization" that would, as the *Chicago Daily Tribune* pointed out, damage the international reputation of the United States. The *Transcript* had already been alerted to "Georgia's Lynching Carnival" by the Palmetto massacre. Now it seemed that "The passion of man-hunting and man-torture grows with what it feeds upon." The editors also condemned "degenerate" New York ministers for extenuating the atrocity because it was triggered by rape. The *Transcript* was astonished at the moral vacuity of such religious charlatans. The paper's publisher joined almost every critic in all sections of the country in believing only a cultural transformation of the South could stop the hateful violence, but specific solutions were beyond their grasp.

Appeal to the abstractions of Justice, Civilization, Law, Education, and Humanity was the only weapon with which critics had to fight. They focused primarily on the spectacular brutality and "frenzy" that marked the killing. Breaking the law under emotional distress was for most observers less shocking than the cutting, maiming, and burning; one Yankee thought the event had been too terrible to be called a lynching. The comment suggests that some Northerners were offended not by lynching but by savage torture and carnivalesque emotionalism. Many agreed with the *New York Times* that the mob had been "out for sport, and horrible as the fact is, it is the joy of killing that inspire[d] them." The ferocity among supposedly civilized people who killed for entertainment was alarming; claiming souvenirs was sickening; the entire affair was disgusting. Nausea – for some Northern observers – seemed to be thought the normal response to what had happened in Newnan.

Most Northern critics of Southern brutality, as Jacqueline Goldsby points out in *A Spectacular Secret*, usually paid only "spasmodic attention" to lynching.[21] (*The Independent* and Boston *Transcript* were exceptions.) When events such as the burning of Henry Smith and Sam Hose occurred, newsmen could seize on these spectacular acts to call attention in as creative a way as possible to the full range of human depravity in the South. Minor incidents could also suggest a value system badly in need of reform. In early August, for example, one B. Goldberg of Atlanta was reported to have taken a "strong dislike" to a neighbor's cat. He tied it to a tree and tortured it by repeatedly pouring scalding water over it. Feline howls of pain drew his outraged neighbors' attention. They called the Humane Society and the police arrested the man for cruelty to animals. Public reaction to this episode, explained the *Chicago Daily Tribune*, was quite unlike that of whites to the burning of Sam Hose. For that atrocity no one was arrested; it was obviously "much better to be a cat in Georgia than a negro [sic]."²² Cats' lives mattered; blacks' lives did not. The vignette and its attendant emotions suggested an attempt at macabre humor as well as criticism. Many Southern whites would have bowed their heads in grief at such a reality, but the *Tribune*'s exercise was more akin to invective than analysis – revealing though it was.

It was easy for critics to condemn the "hideous carnival of blood and fire" that could "brutalize society." It was easy to wonder if Newnan were a better city now. It was easy to imagine what Southern women thought after their menfolk came home with "pieces of a wretched negro's heart and liver in their pockets." A few were astonished that Georgians should have such contempt for their judges and courts that they acted as if none existed. Editors of the *Los Angeles Times* at first thought the "wretched" affair" was a "disgrace to the State of Georgia and ... the American name." Later, they noted that the "better people of the South" had, like civilized people everywhere, been "pained and grieved" at such acts.

As for the inane belief that speedy trials would prevent lynching, wrote editors at the *New York Times*, the plaint ignored the motivation and character of crowds basking in the glory and drama of transgression. The *Times* also pointed out somewhat later that the Federal Government was legally unable to protect life and property in states. The editor neglected to explain that that power, which the authors of the Fourteenth Amendment believed they had written into the Constitution, had been quashed by a reactionary US Supreme Court heedless of original intent. Northern critics were left with a range of emotional responses that, together with the abstractions of the liberal ethos, left them as helpless as Judge Freeman, Major Thomas, and Governor Atkinson. Editors of the *Chicago Daily Tribune* admitted the uselessness of impassioned protest against such savagery; they thought Georgia needed extensive "missionary work."²³ Few if any volunteered.

Other Northerners were more sympathetic to the plight of beleaguered white supremacists. They embraced the mythology of rape and provocation: Frances Willard certainly did. She was famous for speaking on behalf of women as the driving force behind the Women's Christian Temperance Union. In 1894 at the WCTU's national convention, she had, as president, opposed a resolution against lynching. She could, however, condemn "lawlessness" provoked by "unspeakable outrages" that nonetheless "explained" it. Ida B. Wells severely criticized Willard for failing to understand the "facts" of lynching's *Red Record*, but the white woman found myth more convincing than statistics, history, or reality. Willard seemed empathically to imagine herself suffering alongside her endangered white sisters in the South.

She had been profoundly affected by the high drama of little Myrtle Vance's murder at the hands of Henry Smith in 1893. That burning before "thousands" had been justified by the horrendous imagery of rape and mutilation in public discourse flowing from the imaginations and acts of white Texans. Such lynching reflexively "proved" to Northerners as well as Southerners the concrete, factual basis of the myth in a rhetorical legerdemain to be envied by the most eloquent of advocates tasked with defending sinners at the Last Judgment. Before the lynching of Sam Hose, Willard had been much more concerned about "nameless outrages on white women and little girls" than specified atrocities on black women and men. White female susceptibility and sexual danger shaped her ideas about lynching; she was profoundly offended that Wells should refer to scandalous liaisons between white women and black men as if they existed! Willard embodied a female public well-disposed to thinking about the vulnerability of Southern white women, and the fiends who assaulted them.

Willard's generation of Northerners and their offspring were taught by court decisions, political compromises, and literature to celebrate a new nation reunited and redeemed from sectional division. They were encouraged to forget the realities of slavery, secession, rebellion, and war, and imagine a New South by reimagining the old one. In the process, they deferred to white supremacy in the South because they themselves were threatened by "inferiors" – immigrants, socialists, workers, blacks. They were fed up with accusations and complaints. After 1880 most of them believed that Reconstruction had failed because of Carpetbagger corruption and African American incompetence, both of which, many concluded, had warranted Southern violence. These Northerners seemed to think of African Americans as inferior malcontents who ought to quit whining and learn to get along with their betters. Yankees were learning to celebrate the sincerity, honor, and bravery of Confederate as well as Union soldiers. They read writers who extolled the virtues of the plantation South, peopled by kindly masters, gracious ladies, nurturing mammies, and loyal slaves.

Sadly, those "loyal slaves" had been deprived of white guidance by Emancipation. They became comical figures at best and licentious criminals at worst. Northern literary magazines referred to blacks as "nigger," "darkey," "'coon," and "yaller hussy"; a writer could describe African Americans as a "race alien, animal, half-savage," who were best characterized as thieves, poseurs, liars, schemers, or buffoons. Editors printed stories and poems in a concocted "Negro dialect," exposing the simplicity, naivete, superstition, and stupidity of the "typical Negro." To be sure, editors could also publish articles by distinguished black scholars, lawyers, ministers, and authors, but during the 1890s those pieces were more than counterbalanced by discussions of "negro criminality," Anglo-Saxon superiority, the defects of a "degenerate race," and the civilizing effects of American imperialism.[24] African Americans knew that Northerners as well as Southerners believed them inferior to the "imperial race."

The Constitution's editors were therefore correct when they told Georgians that Yankees as well as Southerners sympathized with them. A white Indiana editor thought that such a monster as Sam Hose, who "deliberately" murdered a man in order to satisfy his lust for the wife deserved everything that happened to him. An editor from Albany, New York, agreed. We would, he wrote, feel and act the same way Georgians did if wife, mother, or sister were violated as was Mrs. Cranford. He echoed the folk-wisdom of Southern partisans by insisting, "There are crimes for whose adequate punishment the slow processes of the law seem inadequate." Like many others, the editor accepted white supremacists' mythology of a besieged white South that needed no lectures on legal due process.

"Preach that doctrine to a mob" every man of which knows that "tomorrow he may be foully murdered and his wife, or sister, or daughter, or mother foully dishonored" and you preach utter nonsense! Composure and due process seemed to be obscenities when men were faced with such provocation as that near Newnan! Another editor encouraged readers to imagine themselves as helpless women witnessing their husband's murder and then suffering the fate worse than death. Mrs. Cranford, he wrote sensibly enough, would never be free from being "horror-whipped of memory through every awful day of her existence."[25] He thought only of the "ravishing" that Clark Howell of *The Constitution* had told him and men like him to remember.

A Northern social scientist delved into what he believed was the disturbing reality behind such homilies. He contacted black and white Georgians, George Hepworth, and ex-Governor Atkinson among others. As a result, Walter F. Willcox, a Cornell University statistician and economist, told the American Social Science Association on September 6 that the violence in Palmetto and Newnan during the late winter and on April 23 revealed a distressing polarity. African Americans had created a "public opinion" that was "distinct from that of the whites." The white narrative of Georgia's violence differed from that told by blacks. Whites in Palmetto and Newnan, he told colleagues, focused on black arson, the need for punishment, and murder by a mob unknown to the surprised guards. Whites claimed to have sought the lynchers but to no avail. Willcox found, however, that blacks believed the flawed evidence against the accused arsonists to be inconclusive and the reported search for lynchers to be creative fiction. As for Hose, whites believed the man motivated by lust. Blacks claimed him to be motivated by fear and self-preservation.

The professor then created his own narrative shaped by his obsession with black "criminality." He confirmed that Hose had suffered great pain in "stoical silence," and that blacks in the area had taken great pride in his courage and silence. This response indicated to Willcox something more dangerous than "lust," for it enhanced blacks' false sense of moral superiority. He believed Hose's crime was political; it avenged the Palmetto lynching because Hose, Willcox inferred on the basis of no evidence, believed Cranford had led the lynch mob.

The economist told his story to expose the dangers inherent in a black public opinion obsessed with lynching. Mob action had "an inciting rather than deterring influence" on "potential [black] criminals"; it invited blacks to retaliate by raping white women. Hose's presumed rape of Mattie Cranford had been as political as the homicide. The cycle of violence-rape-violence would continue, Willcox concluded, to enflame "race hatred between the lower classes of the two races in the South." Lynching may have been deserving in the case of Sam Hose, he conceded, but it was dysfunctional. In addition to angering blacks, it made whites blind to what was actually happening in the South. Southerners had spurned an empirical approach to events that would establish truth by collecting evidence in a rigorously disinterested way. In this conclusion, his audience of social scientists – religious or not – should have thought, "Amen!" The more attentive would have hoped Willcox would apply an empirical approach to his own thesis.

The statistician ended his paper by encouraging Southern whites to collect data and complementary evidence in investigating crime, and take full responsibility for improving "relations" with African Americans. Progress would not result from disfranchisement, education, or federal legislation but from a new initiative he failed to describe. Northerners, he believed, should understand the burdens carried by Southern whites: blacks' criminality, ignorance, and disastrous family life. If Southerners considered the facts, they would see, for example, that "Negro soldiers" were not responsible for black criminality. They would see that alienation between the races had not been caused by Reconstruction but by whites' violent response to Emancipation. Northerners, he insisted, do not oppose lynching out of hatred for the South, but out of love for democracy. And democracy, the professor believed, could come only when both races cooperated in developing "a common public opinion."[26] Willcox's suggestions could be embraced rhetorically by moderate Southerners such as Edgar Gardner Murphy, but nonetheless be lost to the gravitational pull of white supremacy.

THE "THREADBARE LIE"

Walter Willcox's dismay on learning that the public discourse of black and white differed, suggested that he had much to learn. Discourse is shaped by history, experience, knowledge, class, gender, and power as well as the ways in which people are given the opportunity to discuss issues without fear or favor. And "favor" is a complicated condition affected by the contexts of mind, language, and value that allow ideas to be understood by the disinterested and the adversarial as well as the like-minded. A free, open, and frank response to the burning of Sam Hose was shaped for both blacks and whites by their distance from Newnan and Palmetto. African Americans living north of the Ohio and Potomac rivers were more free to express themselves than, say, those living in Newnan or Griffin, but their white neighbors were not necessarily any more sympathetic than Southerners. Blacks knew that Northerners were just as likely as Southerners to approve lynching. Northern mobs had killed enough blacks to establish that fact. But the public culture of the region allowed for a broader and clearer discussion of white power and violence than was possible in Georgia in 1899.

Northern blacks were, of course, angered, dismayed, and appalled at the butchery that signified the boundless contempt of white men, but they were not surprised. They had been tracking white violence for a long time. As Jaqueline Goldsby found in her exhaustive research, "For the African American press, lynching was a chronic crisis that required regular surveillance." Before the Georgia killings in March a committee of the National African-American Council had already called on every "Negro pastor" to preach his (or in one or two cases, "her") first sermon in June on "Lynching and its Baneful Effects." After "Palmetto" and "Newnan," the sermons had a specific text, but they would be heard within the context of violence that had spread and intensified over the past decade and a half.

The best informed clergy and laity knew that since 1892 over 1200 men had been lynched, most of them black and living in the South. They would have recalled the spectacular lynching of three black merchants on March 10, 1892 in Memphis. They would have known that the event triggered the flight of perhaps 1800 people to the West urged on by a furious Ida B. Wells. African Americans rallied throughout the North to make the Memphis lynching a national issue. They called for nationwide Indignation meetings for May 31, 1892 to encourage a silent President Benjamin Harrison to take some kind of action. When he refused, Chicago's Ferdinand L. Barnett, attorney and journalist, observed that the Stars and Stripes were nothing more than a "dirty dishonored rag." By 1899 his readers knew, too, that the lynching had launched Ida B. Wells, who later married Barnett, into British and American public life.

By that time, too, blacks had been well-informed about the "threadbare lie" of the black rapist. Wells' condemnation of the lie was a common theme in her writings. In her pamphlets, *Southern Horrors* and *A Red Record*, she posed "facts and figures" against the many lies. One of the most horrendous "facts" was the torture and burning of the mentally disabled Smith. Whites' fury and delight in the man's agony – depicted in a cartoon entitled "Free (?) America" – reflected a pathological mood that scarred an American culture that presumably celebrated equality on the Fourth of July. The other 364 days were different, Wells charged. During them, torture and pain in spectacular punishment seemed appropriate for those whom "American" values could not protect. Blacks remembered the cheers of ten thousand Texans as Smith died because they were not limited to one state; they never stopped; they reflected a "chronic crisis," as Goldsby says.

The crisis was getting worse, Wells wrote. There was the well-publicized murder of a black postmaster and his infant in Lake City, South Carolina, in February 1898 by a white crowd that had torched the man's house. Nine months later, white insurrectionists overthrew the elected government in North Carolina's port city of Wilmington. The Palmetto lynching in March 1899 was also national news. Well before fire consumed Sam Hose, black leaders were already pleading with their people to help the "terror-ridden sections of our land."[27]

African Americans in the North, like those in the South, wanted not only solidarity, support, and full citizenship, but also the truth. At a series of meetings in Chicago that featured Wells-Barnett and her husband, participants agreed that the accusation of rape against Sam Hose was "infamously false upon its face. No human being could commit a murder in one minute and a criminal assault the next. We protest against the cowardly slanders which Southern apologists utter when they say that lynchings occur only to protect womanhood."[28] By June 4, Wells-Barnett and her colleagues had in hand the report of Louis P. Le Vin, the private investigator whom they had dispatched to Georgia to discover the truth about Newnan and Palmetto. Black and white alike had been talkative.

The detective discovered that when confronted with blacks' belief no rape had actually occurred, white men said it didn't matter whether she was raped or not. Motivation was not the issue. The fact was that a "negro [sic] had killed a white man and that was enough" to justify lynching. A few of those interviewed thought the event had been caused by insolent young men who "didn't know their place." Others said blacks were becoming too highly educated; some complained of the influence of "Northern negroes." They were undoubtedly thinking of the "Griffin Incident." Prominent whites whom Le Vin interviewed proudly flaunted their part in killing Sam Hose, although they did believe that Elijah Strickland was innocent of any wrongdoing. Major Thomas' word was good enough for them. Summing up, Le Vin concluded, "A Negro's life is a very cheap thing in Georgia." Wells-Barnett pointed out that the Southern press had wanted us to "Consider the facts," so let us do so. Facts would reveal, she believed, the nature of the "thread bare lie."[29]

The lie was not simply about whether or not rape had occurred; it was also about who African Americans were and what they could expect within the constitutional order of the Republic. The greater lie was that Southern whites were besieged by an inferior, undisciplined, and lascivious people whose existence threatened civilization. Blacks, white Southerners claimed, wanted respect they did not deserve and power, which as a criminal class, they should not wield. The mantra of rape was based on political calculation and had come easily to whites in contests for power after Emancipation. But the mantra also carried psychological and personal credibility flowing from the cultural logic of white men's raping black women for almost three hundred years. White men knew – or were supposed to know from personal experience – what power meant in black-white relations and they rested that meaning in large part on carnal knowledge. This knowledge was superior to that supplied by statistics and empirical evidence on which Ida B. Wells based her denunciation of the lie. White men knew what power meant because they or men they knew had exercised it,[30] and every African American knew it.

That carnal knowledge was condemned by the popular black novelist, Pauline Hopkins, in *Contending Forces*. After Sam Hose was burned to death, she excoriated the "utter hypocrisy" of white complainants. "Irony of ironies," one of her protagonists says in some heat, "*The men who created the mulatto race, who [continue to] recruit its ranks year after year by the very means which they invoked lynch law to suppress*, [are now] bewailing the sorrows of violated womanhood!" The "Negro," she wrote, is not killed for raping, but for voting, owning property, or protecting his family. If, after Hose's burning, Northern blacks believed Le Vin's stories and shared Hopkins' anger, many were nonetheless wary of arguing from the facts. They knew whites would not concede these facts because the emotional power of rape-mythology fused white innocence and self-righteousness into that one word.

The myth was like quicksand, drawing every discussion of lynching into its suffocating darkness. African Americans found it difficult to extricate themselves from the myth because it forced them rhetorically to distance themselves from the crime of rape as soon as whites claimed blacks had committed it. Publicists knew that paternalistic whites needed to believe that the "best people" of both races agreed on basic issues, and rape was undeniably "basic" to whites. Linking lynching to a crime instead of the race helped some black people imagine that they were not the object of whites' contempt because that sentiment was reserved for criminals. The "best" black people, those who were educated, disciplined, prominent, and well-spoken, knew they were not criminals; it was merely the worthless class of young ne'er-do-wells from which rapists sprang. That 5 percent, Bishop Gaines had charged, committed all the crime with which misguided whites so vehemently assigned to black people in general.[31]

Public statements from many African Americans thus began with a ritualistic denunciation of rape and black rapists that unfortunately tempered the criminal character of white violence. Sometimes blacks included in their denunciation of rape the fact that white men raped black women with impunity, but black rape was more powerful than white rape in the imagery and imagination of lynching mythology. Many whites claimed black women could not be raped. By trying to avoid the charge of condoning rape, black spokesmen and women often seemed – at least to whites – to authenticate the "threadbare lie" and the lies behind the "lie"[32] even if blacks did not believe them.

Burning Wilkes and killing a black minister confirmed the terror that had become a Southern convention. If these actions were not surprising, they were nevertheless shocking. When he heard of these latest atrocities, Bishop Alexander Walters of the African Methodist Episcopal Zion (AMEZ) Church told a conference of ministers in New Jersey to arm themselves. The bishop had recently been named president of the National Afro-American Council, which was launched in late 1898 to resurrect a national organization designed to speak on behalf of African Americans. Ida Wells-Barnett was one of the founders. The Wilmington *coup d'etat* seemed to demand such an organization; so did the continuing cycle of Southern lynching. The hatred and contempt that drove white terror had long since revealed the need and inspired the ambition if not the power to forge an effective national association to speak on behalf of African Americans.

As a peripatetic bishop, Walters had railed against lynching in North and South, but the "blaze of hatred and persecution" in the North Carolina election of 1898 that preceded the Wilmington whites' insurrection had shaken him. North Carolina was supposed to have been different but wasn't; the violent overthrow of constituted authorities there was a warning sign about an ever more dangerous future. It was not surprising that the Council should have encouraged every black pastor in the United States to preach against violence at the same time. And then with the burning of Sam Hose, the bishop could not "keep cool."[33] He wanted a gun; that is, he wanted something he could not get: the power to meet Southern whites' violence with something they could understand and would make them hesitate.

Such bravado made sense emotionally, especially while African American soldiers were fighting an imperialist war for whites in the Philippines. Black regulars had distinguished themselves at El Caney and San Juan Hill in Cuba during the late war with Spain and received five medals of honor. But black men who had volunteered to fight for Cuban freedom had created a "stir" among both black and white when stationed in the South. The crimes in Wilmington committed during an insurrection there against constituted authority while armed black militiamen remained in Southern camps should have evoked a federal response – or so argued some black pundits. They were furious at the refusal of the McKinley administration to punish insurgent whites after the "Revolution of '98." Walters' call to arms expressed anger, defiance, and frustration as long as black soldiers, illegal violence, black bodies, and white savagery were burned into African American consciousness.

If the call made sense emotionally, it was ill advised tactically given the *mentalité* and fire power of Southern whites. The Georgia militia had patrolled the streets of Palmetto in March to prevent black retaliation for whites' crimes against them. African Americans may have imagined such vengeance, but could never seriously have planned it. They had fled white violence. Despite supremacists' control of courts, police, militia, and commerce, they whined that whites were besieged; they were always about to be victimized by a people who cleverly hid their mischievous designs behind masks of deference.

Supremacists' paranoid style would have been laughable had it not been so useful in justifying repression and violence against black people who were condemned as tools of Yankee subversion. Douglas Glessner of the Griffin, Georgia, daily paper observed that the problem with Southern blacks' reading comments by Northern blacks was that the former would begin to believe that they had actually been wronged. Given the reality of white power (and calculated hysteria), Thomas Fortune, Washington's advisor, told Walters to simmer down: We need a fight we can win. Blacks were outgunned, which the bishop of course knew! After reflecting on his outburst, Walters pointed out that he had called for no collective black retaliation. He did encourage African Americans to find some way effectively to fight the pervasive white chauvinism that made possible the savagery in Georgia.

Fortune's own "simmering," however, led him to attack President William McKinley as the man who had done "more to breed disquiet and create these outrageous acts than anyone else." A spineless McKinley, Fortune pointed out, hadn't done anything about the insurrection in Wilmington; so it was not surprising that he now ignored the lynching near Palmetto and Newnan. As if that were not bad enough, during a recent visit to Georgia, the Republican President had actually "spread violets on the graves of ex-Confederates." This travesty had "permitted the people who committed these outrages to think they had the liberty to do so."

McKinley's attorney general had, to be sure, prosecuted the men who had killed the postmaster in Lake City, South Carolina, because the man was a federal employee. But the jury deadlocked seven to five for acquittal a few days before the lynching near Newnan. The case was not tried again. The government, one columnist argued, should have changed venues and judges, but the administration was never fully committed to the prosecution. Black observers dismissed the trial as a cynical ploy to "make political capital for William McKinley in 1900 and to gull the

Negroes in the South with the idea that the Federal government was in dead earnest in that matter."[34] Those violets damned McKinley. Angry men such as Walters and moderates such as Fortune agreed that the Federal Government would continue to betray African Americans even in areas where it claimed jurisdiction. These men and women were incensed and dismayed as Americans, Christians, and "Negroes"; they were frustrated by and fed up with the hypocritical pretense that America was a Christian and democratic country.

That pretense had shaped public discourse favored by partisans of the war with Spain. "Freedom" for Cubans and Filipinos had been an excuse for invading the Spanish colonial empire. Because those black soldiers at Caney and in the Philippines signified black Americans' proven commitment to citizenship and the ideal of equality that most whites could not concede, the butchery near Newnan was a national as well as a local event. The homilies praising American exceptionalism were lies, Bishop Walters observed to his audience in New Jersey. "The Cubans and Filipinos whom we have spent so much money and shed so much blood to free from Spanish oppression," he declared, "were never treated so barbarously in time of peace by that government as some negroes [sic] have been in Arkansas, Texas, North Carolina, South Carolina and Georgia."

Bereft of guns and federal support, and suspicious of emigration – attractive though it may have seemed – Walters wanted a miracle. He wondered why "the intelligent and far seeing white people" in the North would not "call a halt to these injustices before it is too late?" Had they forgotten the Civil War? Could there not be another one? Could they stop condoning Southern outrages as their grandparents had when they finally refused to condone slavery? Would somehow "far seeing white people" not bring justice to all Americans? They would if they recalled Thomas Jefferson's prophetic words that he trembled for his "country when I remember that God is just." To help them remember, the bishop appealed once again for a day of fasting and meditation among white churches as well as black.[35] His call to arms had fizzled into a call to prayer.

Walters' anger, however, was unabated. The hypocrisy of the American claim of fighting for "freedom" abroad while refusing it at home was clear. The US government justified conquest as a civilizing process. If Protestant leaders were conflicted about the war, missionary enthusiasts imagined conquest as a way to save the Roman Catholic islands for true Christianity. Even more compelling for jingoists was the opportunity,

Kristin Hoganson has pointed out, to regenerate American manhood through the transforming experience of command, battle, and triumph. Honor, jingoists insisted, required them to free Cubans, Puerto Ricans, and Filipinos. The flagging honor of a new generation could be renewed by subduing the savage enemy and displaying the power of virtue.

The Filipino leader, Emilio Aguinaldo, knew full well that white soldiers had committed atrocities against his people throughout the islands. When he found himself facing regiments of African Americans, he scattered countless numbers of placards asking why blacks fought for a people who treated them so brutally. The "blood of your brother... Sam Hose," Aguinaldo wrote, "proclaims vengeance!" A few young men agreed and joined the fight against American imperialism. Some were hanged for it. Most African American soldiers smarting under the hostility of white soldiers and commanders, however, refused to desert the "American mission." Many tried to soften the impact of American occupation on Filipinos with whom they sympathized, but they also believed they could be true to the best of American ideals even if their white comrades were not. Burning Sam Hose was part of a pattern of white contempt that belied those ideals, to be sure, but black soldiers, like their spokesmen and women in the United States, continued to hold fast to those ideals, which they hoped would transform America someday.[36]

Commitment to this goal called delegates to Chicago in August for meetings of the Afro-American Council and the National Association of Colored Women (NACW). The two organizations, Paula Giddings observes, were formed to find ways to effect public policy, hold policy makers to account, and create a credible agenda for shaping the future. They met in a city where black activists had already vigorously condemned the dodges, excuses, and lies whites told about the killing of Sam Hose. Delegates to the Council, where Walters presided, and to the NACW, led by Mary Church Terrell, knew that President McKinley had taken no action on black Americans' behalf. He had ignored the Wilmington insurrection; he had honored the Confederate dead; he had bungled prosecution of the Lake City mob; he had failed to notice the burning in Newnan.

Militants such as Ida Wells-Barnett, Giddings points out, wanted the NACW and Council to condemn the Administration and its sycophants such as the Wizard of Tuskegee. But the NAWC, which met before the Council convened, was guided by Washington's emphasis on securing black citizenship "by education [rather] than legislation" as he had announced at the Cotton States Exposition. "Education" meant blacks should focus on things they could do for themselves – create kindergartens, schools, clubs, institutes, nursing schools, mothers' clubs, or "old age" homes. "Legislation" meant trying to get whites to behave with regard to lynching, disfranchisement, segregation, labor unions, and higher education. The NACW was so fearful of confronting white elites that Wells-Barnett was excluded from the NAWC program, even the session on lynching.

The energetic and forceful woman, however, co-chaired the Council's program committee, which favored the militants who passed resolutions scoring McKinley for failing to protect African Americans. President Walters was more cautious in August than he had been when he called black men to arms, for he prevented militants from criticizing Washington's excessively modest response to the violence in Wilmington and Newnan. He did appreciate the commitments and ability of Wells-Barnett enough to appoint her to head the new Anti-Lynching Bureau. Within weeks, she dispatched thousands of anti-lynching appeals. For seven years she had written, published, lectured, and agitated; she had offended enough prudes, conservatives, misogynists, and Southerners to establish her credentials. As head of the Anti-Lynching Bureau, she addressed the country in a manner quite unlike that preferred by the NACW and the Wizard of Tuskegee. In the Boston-based *Arena* she announced: "Our country's national crime is *lynching*."[37]

The offence, she insisted, was neither an anomaly nor an aberration; it erupted from the "cool, calculating deliberation of intelligent people." It was the "unwritten law" whites obeyed to govern blacks; it was the culturally approved way of "protecting" white women. If one should declare "herself insulted or assaulted, some life must pay the penalty, with all the horrors of the Spanish Inquisition and all the barbarism of the Middle Ages." A case in point, Wells-Barnett claimed, was what happened in Newnan when the mob failed to force its victim "to cry out and confess." Wilkes' silence as voice was becoming an African American sign; for a while he could, as Sam Hose, symbolize for the most insightful critics a testimony to defiance. The [Atlanta] *Constitution*, the activist reminded her readers, had "keyed the mob to the necessary burning and roasting pitch," thus belying the nation's watchwords of freedom and bravery. A few months ago, Wells-Barnett recalled, Americans objected to a French tribunal's scandalous condemnation of Captain Alfred Dreyfus. Yet in America hundreds are condemned "to death without trial before any tribunal on earth." The fact was humiliating.[38]

HISTORY JUSTIFIES US

While African Americans discussed white violence and lynching, white editors, publicists, poets, and Newnan's elite were guided by Governor Allen Candler's explanation of the Newnan Holocaust. He, like other white authorities, ignored what had happened to Wilkes. Hose had raped and killed: that was the fact to remember; that was the only "horror" to ponder; that was the crime committed. In a world where Jack the Ripper bloodied the streets of London with gutted women, the Governor explained Hose's action as "the most diabolical" in all the "annals of crime." He then, as the *New York Times* pointed out, proceeded to "... Blame the Negroes." This comment, wrote a *Times* editor, had made him "about the most contemptible figure" of anyone commenting on the lynching. Candler whined that African Americans should have brought Hose to justice. They should have told posses where Hose was, which, of course, one black man had done only to be murdered. Black people were "blinded by race prejudice," the governor complained. If they wanted to "receive protection of the [white] community," he sniffed, they should protect that "community against the lawless elements of their own race."

The governor imagined not one public to which he was responsible, but two distinct civil bodies. One was an innocent, well-meaning, orderly white citizenry condemned by a hostile and duplicitous North and endangered by a criminal class and its guardians. The white civic body was sovereign. The black public was a treacherous population unfit for the equality to which their licentious troublemakers wickedly aspired. Candler could not concede even rhetorically the authentic civic identity of African Americans because they had long been imagined as an adversarial criminal class spurred on by Yankee fanatics. Candler agreed with a country editor who accused Northerners of thrusting "the negro into undeserved prominence in the South." A minister observed much the same thing in *The Independent*. Northern teachers had inflated African Americans' sense of self-worth, he insisted, by teaching them to believe they were equal to most and superior to some whites.[39]

Yankees and blacks had created a serious problem for the South, ministers and politicians agreed. Candler's immediate response to what had happened in Newnan, therefore, implied that lynching solved that problem. Unfortunately, still beyond the reach of Southern justice were vicious Northern fanatics who, Rebecca Felton had screamed, taught blacks to hate their kindly white neighbors. Candler and Felton expressed the default position for Southern apologists, but more than a few observers found themselves perplexed at blaming black people and Northerners for the stench of torture, mutilation, and fire.

To explain things to the baffled and heedless critics nestled safely within the cradle of Yankee radicalism, a former governor of Georgia agreed to address the people of Boston. William Northen had been known as an opponent of lynching when he was governor between 1890 and 1894. He had presided over the Southern Baptist Convention and was active in trying to entice Northern capital to Georgia. Because of his reputation for Christian piety and the rule of law, Bostonians invited him to speak about Southern race relations within the month after the slaying of Tom Wilkes. As governor, he had condemned Britons who planned to investigate race relations in his state because outsiders could not understand the South; for citizens of New England, of course, sympathy was next to impossible.

Thus Northen knew he faced a momentous task when he claimed the lectern at the Congregational Club in venerable Tremont Church on the evening of May 22, 1899. The event was to last two and a half hours. Half the time would be Northen's and the other half was assigned to Bishop Benjamin W. Arnett of the African Methodist Episcopal Church. Ignoring the rules, the Georgian took two and a fifth hours to tell a story that his audience found strange indeed. To be sure, those familiar with Lost Cause theology may have heard the story before because Southerners had been telling it for more than thirty years. Hearing it told in Boston, however, made it all the more bizarre.

The bearded former slaveholder began by insisting that he had not come to apologize for the South but simply to explain it. His section faced a momentous "negro [sic] problem." After reproaching his audience for believing the worst of his besieged land, the former governor explained the assumptions on which his speech was based. Two races can live together, he said, only under two conditions: either through intermarriage as equals or through the subjection of one race by the other. Sex and Power, as usual, dominated the Southern imagination; white supremacy was the text from which he preached. Legal intermarriage, he proclaimed, would never be accepted in the South, and whites there would never again submit to "Negro" domination as they had been forced (by you all) to do during Reconstruction. Northen did not mention the familial origins of mixed-race thousands in the South, and he did not discuss the violence of insurrectionary Klansmen and their allies.

He did point out that the race problem in his world had been created by Northern greed. Once upon a time, he began, servitude had existed in every state of the Union thanks to the aggressiveness of Yankee merchants. Yankees had forced African slaves on an innocent and clueless South. He did not explain how Virginians had resisted this unwanted intrusion in 1619 or how Separatists had managed somehow to establish a merchant marine before landing on Cape Cod in 1620. Economic conditions, however, forced the North eventually to abolish the institution and dump its slaves on the South at a profit. Thus, twice non-Southerners had forced an unwanted labor system on his region. The South, Northen claimed, had never ever been "responsible for the presence of the negro within her territory." In making this argument, of course, he ignored the early development of sophisticated slave codes in Virginia and South Carolina.

Then, sometime later, Northen continued, Yankees compounded their crimes against Dixie when one of their most famous and incendiary writers, Harriet Beecher Stowe, lied about us. The woman had paid absolutely no attention to just how much the master class had loved their mammies. In *Uncle Tom's Cabin*, Stowe had grossly ignored the fact that masters and mistresses had taught their servants self-control, obedience, perseverance, and the joys of delayed gratification by adapting means to ends. The master class had converted its hugely contented servants to Christianity, which explained why blacks had protected white women and children during the Civil War. The fidelity of Africans then had been remarkable. So how, Northen asked, had devotion turned into the animosity that Southern blacks had exhibited toward their gentle white neighbors?

The answer was that after Emancipation, Northern school teachers, politicians, and black adventurers had taught freed people that "liberty meant license, and that the domination of the white man was the one thing to strive for and attain." Yankees had destroyed the Christian ethos of blacks so carefully nurtured by Christian masters by releasing them from the self-discipline learned in slavery and forcing them to oppose everything Southern whites wanted. He told detailed, personal, and self-serving anecdotes to prove his argument. He then pointed out that he, as governor, had tried to stop lynching, and cited a specific case in which he had once pursued justice for a black man. Probably prompted by his own religious commitment, he insisted that his region was blessed with a devotion to Christian duty. Then at last he came to the issue that had drawn the audience to the Tremont Temple. Why, he asked, would such a culture as his support so many incidents of lynching? He answered his question with one symbolic word: Rape!

Northerners and Southerners lynched for the very same reasons. There was an "unwritten" law in both sections that guided Southern whites. Yankees would have behaved in the same way as Mrs. Cranford's avengers if Hose's crime had been committed near Boston. He then dramatized the rape of Mattie Cranford. "Hear her piteous cries," he was reported to have said, "as she writhes for two long, long hours in the embrace of a villain, and then see her as she falls at her father's [sic] gate – your gate (can you imagine) – half-clad and in death swoon, to tell her horrible, sickening, disgusting, loathsome story (a story I cannot tell here, and which has not yet been told because of its loathsomeness)."

When narrated in this way – or in an approximate facsimile – rape justified lynching. Northen ignored the fact that the Reverend Elijah Strickland had never been accused of rape. The violence that had erupted after Sam Hose's crime was, Northen insisted, an understandable "human" reaction, but then he added as an afterthought, that it was a reaction that "I condemn." He also had to condemn "the course of the northern press upon lynching in the South with all the vehemence of an offended nature. It is incendiary, unfair, and cruel in the extreme." He continued: "This whole bad business of lynching will never be cured by the indiscriminate denunciation of the Southern people; it will never be cured till the crime [rape] ceases out of which it grows." You condemn Southern "savages" but have no sympathy for Mrs. Cranford, he whined: It was a familiar refrain. Such Yankee callousness, Northen observed, was natural to a people dominated, as Northerners were, by blacks. It was a strange thing to say to a mixed race audience, most of whom doubted blacks dominated anybody.

Northen condemned Northern black leaders for demanding "retaliation" against Southern mobs that avenged rape and for failing to condemn racism and lynching by Northerners. How Northen inferred African Americans' long and widespread struggle against Northern racism and violence as silent acquiescence is unclear. He could not comprehend how that struggle helped African Americans develop a solidarity that was leading to a sense of peoplehood long before he got to Boston; research was not his strong suit. In transition, Northen then forgot the menace of Southern blacks who harbored rapists because they were now, under the right kind of white supervision by Conservatives, happily helping to improve the South. His rhetorical ping-pong continued as he thundered once again that blacks shall not dominate a "white man's country!"

Then Northen's "rape" alibi completely vanished as he explained the cultural logic of lynching blacks who were sent as postmasters to the

South. Republican administrations had sent those officials to the South simply to humiliate us whites. At last, the Georgian concluded by blending Christian piety with white supremacy and ending with the evangelical promise that the "gospel of the living God is sufficient for all human ills and human woes." With this flourish the former governor left Bishop Benjamin W. Arnett twenty minutes.

The well-known clergyman spoke as one would have expected: with a stirring appeal rich in symbol. "The Jamestown idea of civilization is that all white men are born free," he observed, thus addressing slavery. But "the Plymouth Rock idea has triumphed," he remarked rather optimistically, "and the negro [sic] has his place at the table of the races. All we ask is that we receive the rights and privileges of American citizenship and that the opportunities of our civilization be given to all alike." He hoped that teaching the Declaration of Independence to white and black students could eventually help both races realize the superiority of the "Plymouth Rock" ideal. He thought the goal could be accomplished even within segregated school systems. But he thought it would be much more fulfilling for whites to learn something about race by teaching blacks and if black teachers took charge of whites. He, too, believed the gospel would prevail, although it was not Northen's gospel. The bishop promised equality with an eloquence that launched the audience into stunning celebration. Each man represented his people perfectly.[40]

According to *The Constitution*, Georgians outdid themselves in praising Northen's history lesson. They paid less attention to Arnett: he was, after all, not Booker T. Washington. Governor Candler repeated Northen's theme on July 28 and bewailed the crimes entailed on the South by Northern "fanatics and fools." He then claimed Yankees had flooded Georgia with thousands of letters in the past three months encouraging "turbulent negroes" to murder white men. If the danger had been real, the Governor should have seized mail sent to Georgians from the North, mobilized the militia, and declared martial law, but he didn't. His claims were false, and he knew it. By his trumped up lies, he was attempting to portray a South under such pressure from a hostile North and an insurrectionary black population that it justified white men's determination to defend themselves by any means necessary.

Lynching was – by implication as the subject under discussion – the correct response to such threats. Candler would stop Yankee intermeddling, black insurrection, black rape, and white lynching by disfranchising black men. The solution, which was not settled in Georgia before 1908, had long been the preferred panacea favored by Conservative politicians discussing the "negro problem [sic]."[41] The governor did not explain how depriving black men of political power would prevent white men from killing them. Linking voting to lynching, however, revealed that he and men like him really believed that mob action such as that near Newnan was about power not justice; it was about white supremacy not rape. These men placed responsibility for lynching on a North that had imposed African Americans' citizenship on an innocent South and taught blacks to use politics on their own behalf under the shibboleth of equality. Lynching was the default response to rape (equality); and Candler had already condemned the one white governor whom African Americans trusted. Rape was a political symbol he knew how to use.

A few days later Candler seemed strangely to have cooled down and sloughed off the defensiveness that saturated his earlier comments. He issued a long and detailed criticism of lynching. He contradicted himself by emphasizing for the first time that lynching stopped neither "arson nor murder nor robbery nor rape." He pointed out that the state had been widely condemned. Newspapers had "magnified the fearful vengeance inflicted upon the despoilers of female virtue" and Georgians had seen people "denounced as barbarians." Instead of condemning the black community for failing to bring rapists to justice, as he had in April, he now conceded that "the entire negro race" in some localities had "lived in a state of constant terror and alarm." This had to stop. The mob, he pointed out "never knows where to stop, but after punishing the guilty, drunk with the blood of one victim, it thirsts for the blood of another" and "sacrifices on the altar of vengeance those who are guiltless of any crime."

Candler appealed to peace officers to remember they were the "guardians of the peace and happiness of the people of the state." He wanted women and girls protected, to be sure; he wanted rapists convicted at trial. He wanted grand juries to indict lynchers, he claimed, and he wanted petit juries to find members of the mob guilty. He wanted lawyers to stop appealing to a higher court. He wanted silence from Yankees, and he wanted peace. But he made no plans to get what he wanted. Words, as the special contrivances of preachers and politicians, were enough; instead of igniting action they certified innocence!

As a good, theoretically teetotaling Baptist, Candler then appealed for a moral reformation of the state. For a culture called on to do the right thing every Sunday and in every revival, the call was scarcely remarkable. It had all the force of pedestrian piety void of existential meaning. It had the marks of evangelical preaching but it could not trigger a stirring conviction of sin among Georgia whites. The homiletic ideal of evangelicalism was to lead worshippers to confess their own sins and not someone else's; the hope was absolution through God's grace. But the goal and hope, as any realist knows, would always be eroded by delusion and self-interest and, in this case, by a paranoid political style impervious to criticism. It is simply easier to confess the sins of others than face failures safely hidden in the lockbox of one's own rectitude. The political theology of lynching and race could not allow most white Southerners to confess responsibility for the violence and racial contempt so obvious to a few whites and most blacks.

The Reverend H. H. Proctor of Atlanta's most influential black church, however, praised Candler's statement. The appeal, Proctor told his congregation, was "statesmanlike." He added, "What we most need is friends on the spot. One friend in Atlanta is worth ten in Boston." Editors for the *Chicago Tribune* and New York City's *Independent* agreed.[42] Candler had at last, according to some observers, said the right thing more or less. The task had not been easy. The Reverend Mr. Proctor was more generous than facts warranted, and he probably knew that. Blacks did indeed need "friends on the spot," and the governor's plea for justice and due process – even if he was not actually committed to either – was an improvement over earlier statements. Candler had now avoided the hysterical nonsense he had spat out immediately after the lynching. Maybe Georgia's white religious leaders could say something relevant as well; maybe not.

6

After the Fury

The Blind and the Sighted

"The Spirit of the Lord is upon me because he hath anointed me to preach the Gospel to the poor; he hath sent me to heal the broken hearted, to preach deliverance to the captives, and recovering of sight to the blind, to set at liberty them that are bruised."
Christian Bible, KJV, Gospel According to Luke, 4:17–18

"He that saith he is in the light, and hateth his brother, is in darkness even until now. He who loveth his brother abideth in the light and there is none occasion of stumbling in him. But he that hateth his brother is in darkness and walketh in darkness ... because that darkness hath blinded his eyes."
Christian Bible, KJV, First Epistle of John, 2:9–11.

"Strait is the gate and narrow is the way which leadeth unto life, and few there be that find it. Beware of false prophets that come to you in sheep's clothing but inwardly they are ravening wolves. Ye shall know them by their fruits."
Christian Bible, KJV, Gospel According to St. Matthew, 7:13–16.

**

On the third Sunday after Easter in 1899 about forty miles southwest of Atlanta in Newnan, Georgia, a white crowd burned to death a fugitive black laborer known as Sam Hose. This atrocity blended anger, hatred, arrogance, festivity, brutality and satisfaction into a mood just beyond comprehension. "Glory!" shouted an excited man enraptured by the intensity of the moment, "Glory be to God!!"

Corra Harris tried to explain the "savage fury" near Newnan several days after it happened. Ida Wells-Barnett sent a private detective to Georgia to report what had happened. George Hepworth tried to understand how Newnan's citizens thought about what had happened. Editors in both North and South knew that a great many people at least for a short while were aware that "something remarkable" had happened. The fact that black and white could not agree on what that "something" was disturbed the naïve empiricist, Walter Willcox. He believed facts should speak clearly for themselves. Former Governor William Northen tried to explain what had happened within the myths of the Lost Cause. The current Governor, Allen Candler, was confused as to what had happened; and so were all too many white Christian ministers, who eventually decided to say as little as possible. The event did not have a sobering effect on Georgians who still gathered to lynch suspects; some of them were still successful. Others were prevented by determined authorities and influential African Americans.

Black moderates could be shaken enough by the events near Newnan to believe whites would never change because their Christianity had failed. Whites' defensiveness at the "savage fury" near Newnan could still erupt in outrage when a white college professor criticized the "fury" and its source three years after it happened. The impact of the lynching could have long-term effects, too. It shocked W. E. B. Du Bois as few events would; he would remember it for over forty years.

BLESSED BE THE TIES THAT BLIND

Saying the right thing was difficult for politicians, but ministers found it no easier. While William Northen was polishing his history lecture and Allen Candler was contemplating the moral transformation of Georgia, Atlanta's Christian ministers were trying to find the right words to help the public think about lynching. The difficulty was clear to the Reverend W. W. Landrum of the First [white] Baptist Church as he addressed his congregation the night white thugs, unbeknownst to him, strangled "Lige" Strickland to death and dangled his body from a persimmon tree. Landrum tried to convince his congregation that even if the countryside were imperiled by black criminals, there was cause for hope. First, however, white people had to think realistically about what was going on. Most black people, he insisted, were law abiding and busily improving their lives in ways that benefited everyone. Since Emancipation, African Americans had acquired wealth, education, religion, and middle class values. They were improving every day. Referring to our "brother in black" as had Bishop Haygood, Landrum pointed out that he, "was never . . . our enemy; the race as a whole[,] on the contrary, has been loyal to the white man." This loyalty and association with white people, the clergyman argued, had aided African American progress.

The comment was scarcely gracious to black people, but the praise of whites, deserved or not, was supposed to entice his congregation to change the ways in which they thought of violence in their region. "Civil government" must prevent carnage so obviously "against the laws of God and man." Nothing justified mob violence – not even *rape*! "The negro [sic] as you and I have known him from our childhood . . . is simply a man, a black man with intellect, affections, and will, like those of any human being." Apostolic teaching exhorts us, he went on, to "yield the negro [sic] his legal and political rights." For white middle class Atlantans this was a radical message in April of 1899. We should not, Landrum insisted, become "panic stricken," "hysterical," "sensationalist," or "insane" when it comes to thinking about race. We should be "Christianlike."[1] Landrum was not Rebecca Felton's favorite minister.

The morning after Landrum's address the state and nation learned the fates of Sam Hose and the Reverend Elijah Strickland. Delegates to the International Sunday School Convention meeting in Atlanta were clearly dismayed at the "un-Christian" acts near Newnan. Southern ministers at the Convention condemned the lynching. That night they were joined by Dr. Leonard G. Broughton of Atlanta's Baptist Tabernacle. The physician was a well-known and outspoken evangelist who frequently attacked Atlanta officials for being soft on vice. He unkindly exposed names, dates, and places. The day after the Newnan lynching he condemned it clearly and forcefully after conceding that Sam Hose "deserved death," but his killers were guilty, too. Every man in that mob yesterday, Broughton thundered, whether "active in participation in the burning of that man or whether he was simply there as rooter or looker," was an accomplice "to that awful crime, and stands tonight before the bar of God's justice with a heart streaked in human blood, to answer the charge of murder."

Running trains from Atlanta to allow thousands to "witness such hellish barbarity" was disgusting, the reverend physician charged, but no one in authority interfered. This lawlessness, Broughton declared, had the sanction of "the governor of the state," "officers of the law," and ordinary citizens. Widespread malicious celebration made the evangelist "ashamed of Atlanta and our civilization." In response to this statement, hooligans posted notices demanding Broughton be whipped and vandals damaged his church. The following Sunday fifty people walked out of the sanctuary after he once again condemned "the foul deeds of a howling mob of assassins."[2] He was glad to be rid of them!

Words were the professional tools of clergymen; they represented a moral stance and judgment that should have framed public debate, but didn't. Although the clergy were handicapped by their culture, they still faced the question: How could they not, according to Christ's teaching and sacrifice, condemn a savage holocaust – even if they thought the victim deserved a punitive death? Few of Broughton's ministerial colleagues chose to make statements as clear and evocative as his; instead they shilly-shallied. When Methodist ministers met in Atlanta on Tuesday, April 25 to discuss the lynching, one man began by condemning Sam Hose's crime and the mean-spirited way hateful Yankees had pilloried the South simply for punishing a fiendish rapist. The Reverend Joel T. Davies, like the Governor, blamed African Americans for recent events.

Wilbur Thirkield, president of Gammon Theological Seminary, responded. Renowned for supporting African Americans and attacking racist theories, he answered his effusive colleague in a manner consistent with his lifelong commitment. He had already raised the hackles of Palmetto's "best men" by defending the black community there; he raised them now among his colleagues. The debate became so heated after he spoke that the ministers had to adjourn without comment. Some undoubtedly pointed out that Thirkield was unable to appreciate the sensitive feelings of white Southerners because his famous abolitionist father-in-law, Methodist Bishop Gilbert Haven, had endorsed interracial marriage. Had his enemies known that Thirkield admired the work of W. E. B. Du Bois they'd have pilloried him for that, too.

A few days after the Methodists met, the Atlanta Evangelical Ministerial Association in conference also failed to pass resolutions against lynching. Instead, members discussed sending all black people in the United States to tropical lands "with their own consent," but the proposal was tabled in favor of a discussion of foreign missions. On June 5 the group was still in a cautious mood. Broughton, of course, wanted his colleagues to condemn lynching and "the present reign of mob law." He suggested reforms: 1) swift arrest, conviction, and punishment of offenders; 2) constant vigilance by authorities; 3) religious training of blacks. The man's solutions were not as sharp as his words; they merely repeated hackneyed suggestions, already embraced by whites, whether advocates or critics of lynching. The Baptist, however, grievously offended some of his vexed colleagues. One vigorously denied the mob "reigned" in Georgia and opposed any increased vigilance by authorities to stop it.

An equal number of men approved and disapproved Broughton's comments, but all agreed that blacks should be better behaved. A few approved Governor Northen's address in Boston, but most did not. After a tie-vote on the resolutions, the chair tabled them. Broughton then demanded the minutes show he at least opposed the Association's neutered inaction. His colleagues could concede that much and ended the meeting in a bold declaration commanding the city council to "enforce the now existing laws governing Sunday sales." Before adjourning, the Association appointed a committee to think about lynching and by early August was ready to make an official statement.

Finally, the ministerial association conceded the "possible justice of the punishment inflicted" in lynching. They went on, however, to warn against the "tendency to extend" lynching to cover offenses other than rape. Such action, the men thought, created a false impression by transforming black men who were actually guilty into victims. What Broughton and Landrum thought of such a stance is unknown; Thirkield would not have been surprised, but he would have thought most of his colleagues needed prayer. Thirkield's father in-law would have gagged. The ministers then called for swifter justice in cases of all "infamous crimes," stricter penalties for these crimes, and private testimony to protect the "delicacy of unfortunate female witnesses." They encouraged African American leaders to tell their young men not to rape white women and children. The mood was like that of Northern Presbyterians who in a national meeting proposed to end mob violence in the South by redeeming "the negro from his sufferings and his sins," especially the latter. In this spirit, Atlanta's ministers in concert promised to help "create a public sentiment" favoring law and order. They held "Negroes" responsible for the events that had led to stench and ashes in Newnan. Their report, according to a delighted Clark Howell of *The Constitution*, was "wise and statesmanlike."[3]

The ministers apparently believed that since lynching could not be confined to punishing rape, it was dangerous. The punishment experienced by Tom Wilkes was "possibly" just, despite its illegality and horror. The ministers seemed as incapable of thinking about what actually happened on April 23 as Georgia's politicians and Newnan's elites. Some may have understood that rape was violence, but they seemed to think of it primarily as sex, lust, and license flowing from what Corra Harris understood as the putrid "cesspool" of African American domestic life. Obsessed with black criminality, these ministers ignored white terror. In professing to oppose lynching they actually defended it and resorted to scolding blacks in a "wise and statesmanlike" supremacist manifesto.

Sunday sales, drunkenness, prostitution, profanity, or dancing captured their enmity, but cutting, burning, and strangling human beings could not induce them to wonder why such things could happen. They could not ask, "What kind of people do such things in pride and self-justification?" These clergymen could not see the hatred, contempt, and malice oozing from their culture. They were simply unable to engage the mentality that kindled the burning of Tom Wilkes because they shared it with the mob. They discussed the fate of Sam Hose under the intellectual canopy of sexual violation, black criminality, masculine duty, and white innocence.

Len Broughton shared his colleagues' distrust and suspicion of blacks even if he hated lynching. He did not share Wilbur Thirkield's respect for African Americans. Broughton thought they should be returned "to the land of their fathers"; he meant Africa not Great Britain. He was not as welcoming to black people as the paternalistic Landrum, but the good doctor at least hated mobs and hypocrisy and one can imagine his disgust at the useless words of his colleagues. He was clear in his denunciation of evil, whether delivered in great acts of blood and pain or in minor episodes of private vice. "Tender hides," observed evangelist Sam Jones of Cartersville, disliked Broughton's capacity for boldly exposing the deceit and hypocrisy of public men.

Jones tried to do the same, or at least he pretended to do so. Unlike the Baptist, he refused to insist on the right doctrine, the right creed, the right theory of atonement.[4] Right theology, Jones insisted, was "right living." His style and focus led him to challenge his audiences: "Quit your meanness!" ("Meanness" included all the negatives imaginable.) He was abrupt and clear: Christians did right! Thus, it was not surprising that he, like Broughton, should have immediately condemned the lynching of Sam Hose. But then, like Atlanta's white ministers, Jones gradually slithered into the compelling mythology of Rape-and-Manhood. His torturous path from objection to deference to approval of Hose's immolation suggests how many ministers found it so difficult to denounce lynching, even the hideous murder of Tom Wilkes, when it was justified by sex, gender, and honor.

Sam Jones was a man's man. He knew how to entice men into a feminized church: at least that is how fans and historians have understood him. A dry alcoholic, a failed lawyer, and briefly a Methodist pastor, Jones knew how to command an audience and raise money. Assigned the agency of a debt-laden Methodist orphanage in the early 1880s, he soon made the institution solvent and perfected his style as a tough, engaging, and popular preacher. Surrendering his credentials as a Methodist minister under assignment by a bishop, he remained a "local preacher" but achieved fame as an evangelist. He was, wrote one admirer, funnier than "two comedians," wiser than "four universities," and more Christian than a "half-dozen theological seminarians." Jones would have agreed. Thousands did so and rushed to hear him. It is not clear how many converts he escorted into a Christian life, but it is clear that men liked to listen to him.

As Chad Gregory points out, he dismissed "the reserved, stately piety of the church and its lack of virility." Reporters loved his jabs at "jackass" politicians, "red-nosed whiskey devils," and "effeminate 'pitty-patty' preachers." Jones reportedly insisted, "Give us strong, sinewy, muscular religion! Not this effeminate, sentimental, sickly, singing and begging sort! Give us a religion with vim and muscle and backbone and power and bravery!" He told men to accept Jesus as "the true road to masculinity." He told them that "the one thing that can make a man of you, the one power that can make you noble and true and good" is religion. And religion, he explained, ushered men into battle: "You have got to fight!" He repeated the command over and over again. He meant: You have got to fight dancing, gambling, and lying; you have got to fight trivial entertainments and whiskey; you have got to fight the devil and if men revile you for doing so, so much the better! "Brethren of the Church, take a stand and hold it." Celebrate your courage!

With the rapid delivery of a Gatling gun, Jones told his confreres to defend the sacred precincts of the family and their women folk. You men, he commanded, have got to be pure! He remembered what young men talked about after a dance; he knew they were obsessed with sex. Dancing, whiskey, and theatres were all shaded by lust. "If necessary," he once insisted, "I'd build a mile high wall around the virtue of every girl in the country." Real men protected women. Jones exemplified, one scholar has observed, a "grotesque gender minstrelsy."[5]

As a celebrated public man, Jones could be witty and caustic. He once accused Georgia legislators of being unable to "pass anything . . . not even a cheap bar room." Most of his political punditry was limited to such commentary, but he frolicked in the 1898 gubernatorial campaign as a "candidate" who was not actually "running" for office. His platform was "unadulterated, unpurchasable, unbulldozable manhood." His musing on the politics of W. Y. Atkinson's administration the previous four years was actually an endorsement of Allen Candler whom Jones described as a man of the people. He complained that in 1894 the Reverend General

Clement Evans had clearly been the popular choice for governor. Evans, however, had known better; he was not going to win after Atkinson embarrassed him in debate. Evans may have known the Bible, but not politics.

Jones clearly disliked Atkinson and agreed with Candler that the man had "raped" the Democratic Party by defeating the Old Guard and the sanctimonious general who commanded the Confederate veterans of Georgia. Jones ignored Atkinson's reputation among African Americans as a just governor who used his office to fight lynching; the man was by implication, according to the evangelist, unmanly. The manhood Jones touted was white, conservative, entrenched, and opposed to spending public funds on high-falutin' luxuries such as public education. As a wealthy bank director and owner of a sawmill, an ice house, a 700 acre farm, half a mine, and a palatial twenty-one-room house, he believed "manhood" characterized the propertied elites then creating a New South (without somehow drinking, dancing, or attending the theatre). He blended religion, morality, and politics into masculine responsibility and white privilege even when he preached to African Americans.[6]

Jones' reputation for insisting that real men take clear if unpopular "stands" should have prepared the public to learn that he, like Broughton, denounced the lynching of Sam Hose. The act, Jones contended, had desecrated the Sabbath and broken the laws of God: it would force participants eventually to face "the blazing light of the final judgment." Transgressing human law made the mob no better than Hose, he proclaimed. The brutality of the lynching, which Governor Candler and many ministers ignored, dismayed Jones profoundly, and he wondered, at least for a while, how "humane men" could "divide up the charred remains of a victim." Yet he was perplexed. "Good people" appeared to be compelled to lynch offenders, he conceded, but sorting out "the cooked bones and flesh of the culprit" meant fury had pushed them beyond the capacity to make the right moral choices.[7]

These people were, however terrible their acts, nonetheless still *good*; maybe they saw something he couldn't. He wrestled with a confusing reality. As a man of the people who basked in their applause, he was susceptible to their letters on behalf of democratic vengeance. They helped him believe that good people could do hideous things for good reasons. Jones could not probe the ways in which good white people had transformed the word, equality, into an obscenity. He could not imagine how their paternalistic condescension (at best), prevented them from imagining African Americans as free as whites to enjoy the rule of law and a guarantee of rights. The missives focused on a brute who deserved death. Finally, so did Jones. The question was, "Who would inflict the appropriate penalty?" Jones' critics provided the answer. As a result, about seven weeks after the lynching, Grem and Katherine Minnix point out, Jones began to waver in his adamant, world-defying and manly stand. In August of 1899 he wrote, "I am in favor of the sheriff executing the criminal, *except in cases like Sam Hose*, then anybody, anything, anyway to get rid of such a brute."[8] Glory!

Grem argues plausibly enough that Jones' "Sam-Hose exception" to his denunciation of lynching was affected by his "theology" of the home. Since Jones was an impulsive critic of sin rather than a painstaking thinker, his theology, such as it was, was more sensibility than system. Jones' own family life was anything but a model of practical Christianity, although he thought it should have been. He delegated to his wife responsibility for whatever semblance of Christian normality the family possessed. Mothers, wives, and daughters were supposed to guarantee the holiness of home life and Christian men were supposed to protect its sacred precincts.

Jones' public attacks on drinking, gambling, cursing, dancing, and entertaining were in defense of the home, which was as much a house of God as the church. Violence against this citadel of virtue and sanctity was, like sinning against the Holy Spirit, unforgiveable. This view shaped the way in which many editors imagined Tom Wilkes' crime. He had unleashed chaos, lust, and violence in the Cranfords' peaceful haven and mercilessly ravished the person at the core of the ideal Christian existence. Sacrilege, blasphemy, and rape blended into one terrible act. The evangelist's admirers certainly thought this way![9] If women could not be protected they must at the very least be avenged. As letters poured in to remind Jones of the evil visited on an innocent white home, he began to see why good *people* could do what they did: anything in anyway. Any *man*, Jones finally concluded, would think so.

The focus on "any man" meant that "Home" was not the ruling metaphor either for Jones or his correspondents. The more important figure was "Manhood." By the third Sunday after Easter in 1899, white men throughout the South had long since perfected a defense of lynching grounded on a canon of *righteous provocation*. The rubric made guiltless any collective action that punished black men for ravishing white women. The violation of women was so great, a writer defending the murder of Sam Hose insisted, that white men "placed in view of the guilty wretch, become crazed and unaccountable for the particular form their vengeance takes." Like the emotions released in an experience of evangelical rebirth, a moment of truth realized in response to the desecration of innocent women forced men to assume duties fundamental to manhood. They had to displace human law to do the right thing. It was the argument for which Ida B. Wells had lacerated Bishop Haygood in 1893 when he tried to explain the murder of Henry Smith. It was the argument Georgia's chief justice had attacked at the same time, but however dangerous and absurd Justice Bleckley believed it was, it was popular.

Provocation elevated manhood above all other ideals, and it could make sacred an act that critics believed demonic. A perceptive observer could imagine a "nimbus of holiness" radiating from the ethos of Coweta County "as the celebrated purity of white women refracted onto [lynchers'] bodies the cleansing balm of religion, honor, segregation, and collective violence." Students of lynching point out that mobs were often described as cool and determined as befitted Victorian men. And these scholars are correct that such reports existed, but *provocation* was not cool. Like the emotional catharsis of religious conversion, *provocation* was a transformative experience. The catharsis first allowed and then, in the process of realization, *forced* men to act according to their manhood rather than the pallid guidance of the law. The emotions triggered by *provocation* strengthened men to do their duty. As for self-possession, the reports were mixed. The Newnan *Herald*'s reporter did observe that citizens exercised cool restraint just before they "went almost wild while venting their righteous wrath."[10]

The pressure Jones felt from his disappointed fans led him to think more about rape and manhood than cutting, blood, and fire. Finally, he could not surrender his masculinity to moralists who ignored the obligation to punish. "Grotesque gendered minstrelsy" celebrated honor. The obligation to punish had ruled the South since 1619. Jones had to be the man who told men to man-up for Christ; he had to be a man of the people who expected men to act forcefully. Surely *Christian* men could not abjure their commission to serve those who depended on them for protection. One accomplished scholar, Joel Williamson, thinks white men may have lynched because they felt guilty about deceitfully coupling with black women. In Jones' case and those of many like him, however, if lynchers were able to feel any guilt at all, it was more likely to have been triggered by their inability to protect white women. This failure was much more public and therefore vastly more shameful than the secret exploits of randy adulterers.

Reports of rapes by black men throughout the summer of 1899 may have compounded that shame for Jones. The crimes did suggest to him the inability of the law to protect women and reinforced his sense of masculine obligation. He was bombarded by his chronic obsessions with punishment, manhood, gender, and sex. He thought about Mattie Cranford and her suffering. He thought about his own wife. For defiling them, a rapist would have had to be put down. "All Bible-reading men believe in punishment," Jones once said, even if they may differ on its duration. Men also agreed that villains should be punished according to the severity of their crime. Jones had preached that Christian manhood demanded clarity, moral rigor, and duty. He was learning that respectable Georgians such as his columnist friend, Bill Arp, saw these qualities in the lynchers. They were "noble men," one man wrote, "who defend the virtue of women and uphold the sanctity of the home."[11] Such men acted blamelessly in response to a provocation no true man could resist. Home may have been a sanctuary, but manhood was morality and, like pain, truth.

When Jones said that "Bible-reading men believe in punishment," he was simply affirming a commonplace; he could have added that men who didn't read Bibles generally agreed. Women did so as well. A few may have imagined punishment as a way to reform miscreants rather than as an end in itself, but they would not have repudiated punishment altogether. A culture nourished in the rules, expectations, and discipline of forced labor, and perfected in the racial etiquette of purity, danger, and white supremacy, was well acquainted with the morality and necessity of punishment in daily life. The religion that hovered over the South, and which Jones and evangelists like him personified, imagined a God of Wrath whose word declared justice and punishment: It was a condition from which sinners were saved by an act of violence – crucifixion.

When Jones linked knowledge of the Bible with punishment he was emphasizing that bad acts have consequences not only in everyday life but in the apocalyptic final judgment beyond history. The Revelation of St. John, after all, imagines no reform for sinners, only a richly deserved obliteration. Guilt, punishment, and blood were essential to the evangelical Protestant ethos. As a child of pious Methodists, Lillian Smith had learned the lesson well, she recalled; her religious awakening had revealed punishment as the prelude to righteousness. W. J. Cash had shuddered at the "frenzied" proclamation of "blood sacrifice," the punishment that "paid" for the sins of the world. Wrath and judgment were privileged themes in traditional Protestant theology. Christian white Southerners could insist with merciless certainty that Christ, in submitting himself to a human tribunal, had confirmed the righteousness of punishment in general and his own suffering in particular. A minister announced in a famous essay that "THE PRIMARY AND CHIEF END OF PUNISHMENT IS TO VINDICATE THE RIGHT."[12]

Sin deserved punishment; crime deserved punishment; the unconverted deserved punishment! The cultural justification of punishment nourished by slavery, religion, honor, law, fathers, mothers, teachers, and preachers was impossible to escape. That is why many critics of the Newnan mob prefaced their remarks about the event by conceding that Hose *deserved* punishment. Ida Wells-Barnett and her husband, Ferdinand, did not; their colleagues in Chicago certainly did not, and the novelist Pauline Hopkins didn't either. Indeed, many black people who said anything publicly probably did not believe Hose *deserved* punishment because he had not been tried in a court of law. Many nevertheless felt compelled to emphasize what he deserved, at least theoretically, because they had to convince whites they shared their moral universe.

If black opponents of lynching felt pressured in this way, it is not surprising that Jones should be so susceptible to the moral certainty among people he wanted to please: Sam Hose *deserved* punishment. Over the weeks that distanced Jones from the horror he first felt, he gradually sloughed off his reverence for law in cases of rape because he began to think that the law did not have a penalty that fit the crime! That was the excuse, justification, and rationalization! Provocation, rape, punishment, and manhood dominated his thinking. Hose *deserved* a terrible punishment: "everyone" said so. True men had to inflict it.

Ministers who in concert found it so difficult to condemn lynching and torture shared Sam Jones' gendered moral universe. Like politicians and evangelists, clergymen were alert to popular moods, views, and values. Not only did they share the familiar elements of childhood and upbringing with their congregations but they also needed to sustain good relations with them to be effective. As a former preacher once pointed out, ministers and their people "mirror each other. It demands a very rare, intrepid, and genuinely free and loving shepherd to challenge the habits and fears and assumptions of his flock."[13] A few were free, perhaps, but most understood that they relied on their congregations' good will to be effective pastors and representatives of the Christian community in the public square. Thus tied to a New South, they knew the history they were supposed to remember, the destiny for which they were supposed to hope, the laws they were supposed to obey, and the enemies they were supposed to condemn. They were bound to their families of origin by filial duty and to the women in their family by love and conscience. They were bound to a gendered ideal of what it meant to be a man.

Sam Jones knew that religion and manhood had to be joined *not* by what it meant to be religious, but by what it meant to be a man. Many preachers may have felt burdened by what historians have called a feminized church; certainly the Religion and Men Forward Movement of the early twentieth century seemed dedicated to crafting a masculinized Christianity. Nevertheless, a feminine constituency and dismissive secular men were probably of less concern to the clerisy than assertive women who were organizing missions of their own. Many churchmen felt besieged – Broughton, Landrum, and Thirkield to the contrary notwithstanding. Gendered ambivalence did not cause ministers to waffle on lynching, lawlessness, and punishment, but it did make many of them vulnerable to the plea of provocation and duty. Their alliance with women in promoting prohibition and public decorum could be forgiven perhaps if they demonstrated a robust moral masculinity in response to rape! They were immersed in a culture of racial difference. Schooled in the rules of gender, punishment, and atonement, ministers were all too often transfixed by the image of violated white women and the claim of *deserved p*unishment to do much more than wish – in bewildered passivity – that the law could somehow be obeyed.

Clergymen thought and wrote about the Hose lynching like politicians and secular journalists. There were four stages of commentary: "Shock" at the rape and burning; "Censure" of those responsible; "Defense" of white Southerners; "Solutions" to a "problem" that others (Yankees, African Americans, and defense attorneys) had created. Clerical editors could confess "shame and pain" at the "repulsive savagery" that stained the South at Newnan. The more adventurous agreed with the editor of *The* [Columbia, South Carolina] *State* that the terrible "orgy of torture and mutilation" proved "supremacy in the arts of hell." But shocked though many were at such savagery, Christian conscience could not allow their audiences to believe that "swift vengeance upon negro" men was the result of "white human diabolism." That accusation was too vicious to be believed because Southern white men were supposedly justified in avenging crimes against women. A future bishop observed, "In thousands of cases, the *provocation* has been terrible beyond the power of words to describe." Although "the hideous devils' dance" around a smoldering Sam Hose was to be condemned, Christians should nonetheless appreciate "the feeling" that inspired the choreography.

That "feeling" issued from the culture of distance, exclusion, and boundary that allowed the clergy to see blacks as a criminal class when one person broke the law. That criminal class aspired to equality, many clerics and most politicians agreed on that, and they thought the new generation of blacks hated Southern whites for refusing to extend it. That criminal class motivated by hatred had created a "negro problem," which the innocent white South was now forced to solve. Following the lead of politicians, Southern churchmen such as Len Broughton and Sam Jones approved disfranchising black men to remove the structural basis for the latter's reckless aspirations. Most agreed that blacks not whites had to change; W. W. Landrum and Wilbur Thirkield represented a small minority who did not.

That drive for "Equality," a reflective cleric lectured his Northern colleagues, was dangerous in the extreme. "There is nothing in the South for the negro [sic] but death if he demands it." The Sermon on the Mount had no bearing on white supremacy. Clerical discussion of lynching easily slipped into a defense of a "besieged" white South rather than a conversation about the foundations of white violence. This bizarre twist in discourse frequently made lynching synonymous with "the South," a fusion ministers usually tried to avoid, but they were unable to extricate themselves from the ethos of the "Negro Problem." The danger of equality had been transformed into sex which had been transformed into rape. As a violation of innocence, rape was always available to justify lynching because of its emotional and mythic power.[14]

LIFE GOES ON

After the events of April 23, 1899, citizens of Newnan and Coweta County needed to move beyond mutilation, fire, and murder. On April 28, the *Herald* reported, as fully as possible, the activities, rumors, comments, and lies linked to the lynching of Sam Hose and Elijah Strickland. The immediate "fall-out" from the holocaust between Newnan and Palmetto lasted for about three weeks at the end of which the poem celebrating Wilkes' destruction was printed and traditional "barbecue" was advertised. Newnan's citizens needed to find haven from the memory of what some of their finest had done with the invaders from Griffin. They needed to turn to those familiar things that make life normal, manageable, and innocent – the everyday chores and habits of personal and family life. They celebrated the promises of graduations, commencements, and weddings. They enjoyed ice cream socials. The pious found reassurance in prayer meetings. Others found time to gather at Reese's Opera House for a concert.

A group of young white men busily organized a tennis club. Confederate veterans sponsored a reunion attended by a host of "pretty women," and were reminded of the valor and greatness of Virginia's General Thomas J. "Stonewall" Jackson. A well-known preacher died in Macon and Newnan's sewer system needed repairs. The Newnan *Herald*, like all good local newspapers, filled its pages with details that may seem trivial but were important to the various communities surrounding Newnan. The revival meeting at Mills Chapel saved fourteen sinners from the wrath of God; that was good news for the pious. Dan Sewell lost two cows and some harnesses when someone burned his barn; that was bad news for Sewell. Judge S. W. Harris had his decision in the Senoia Bond Election case overturned by the Georgia Supreme Court. Judge Alvan D. Freeman was conducting the quarterly term of City Court, during which several men were fined for carrying concealed weapons. Governor William Yates Atkinson, once again a practicing attorney, was in Carrollton pleading a case. In the midst of returning to daily life as counsellor and litigator, he became seriously ill and was rushed home to Newnan. He died on August 7.[15]

Atkinson's funeral was one of those public pageants in which politicians celebrate their public persona as eloquently as possible. Governor Candler, who had condemned his predecessor for raping the Democratic Party, lamented the death of Newnan's favorite son at such a young age. He observed that Atkinson had been ambitious and as governor had managed an unusually clean administration. The former governor, William Northen, who owed so much to Atkinson, joined Candler, as did two United States senators, two congressmen, and a host of judges, attorneys, and lesser officials who, a reporter observed, comprised the longest procession ever seen in Newnan. (He ignored the crowd that escorted Tom Wilkes to his death.) Ten black porters from the state capitol were also present. Hundreds of mourners stood outside the Methodist Church as the Presbyterian minister, James Stacy, presided over his communicant's funeral with the Prayer Book of the Episcopal Church. Local Baptist preachers prayed.

In reporting the event, the *Herald* printed tributes from newspapers throughout Georgia praising Atkinson for leading the fight for the Normal and Industrial School for [white] Girls. None seems to have mentioned his losing the fight to reform the state's penal system. A few emphasized his "plebian" roots and all agreed he was what a later

generation would call a workaholic. His allies pointed out he had saved
the state from the Populist Party, and his enemies conceded his "courage
and pluck." *The Constitution*'s editor, Clark Howell, who had vehemently opposed Atkinson, extended "to the family the sincerest sympathy
in this hour of their greatest affliction." Had he survived, Howell pointed
out, no doubt with a sigh of relief, Atkinson would have been a power in
Democratic Party politics.

Bishop Henry McNeal Turner was more effusive. Atkinson was a "just
and righteous man," the African Methodist leader proclaimed. He was a
white man with a difference; he "towered" above the ordinary "white
man as high as the Rocky Mountains." His death was a "sad calamity,
because he was a friend of the lowly, oppressed, and the despised as well
as the great and mighty." The bishop called on his clergy to hold memorial services in the late governor's honor because for him "justice was race
and equity was manhood, greatness, and nobility."[16]

Atkinson's funeral was merely one of the many chores Governor
Candler had to take on after the burning of Sam Hose. He had little time
to meditate on mobs and murder. He had to appear at political gatherings
throughout the largest state east of the Mississippi. He had to become
better acquainted with the everyday demands of his office and to massage
the egos of political allies. He had to appoint judges and prosecuting
attorneys and to attend Trustees' meetings at the University of Georgia.
He had to investigate the ways in which state taxes were collected and, as
a result, to change which banks would act as depositories of state funds.
In Atlanta, he had to welcome African American delegates to W. E. B. Du
Bois' Atlanta University conference on "The Negro in Business" and
white delegates to a meeting of the Southern Industrial League on The
White in Business. Later, Candler learned the League had been warned by
a New Yorker that Southern progress would be difficult as long as the
"lynching habit" endangered "life and property" in the South. Candler
and Clark Howell of *The Constitution* resented such simple-minded
preaching, but both men knew that illegal violence still radiated from
the depths of their world. Not surprisingly, a month after the murders
near Newnan and Palmetto, a reluctant and indecisive governor once
again faced another "Griffin episode."

The city, which had spawned senseless violence against homeward
bound black soldiers in March and sent its youth to Newnan in April to
kill Sam Hose, remained a site of illegal white violence. On the night of
May 24, Governor Candler was forced to call out the militia to "protect
the property of the Kincaid Manufacturing Company" and prevent

violence against black citizens whom night riders had ordered Kincaid to fire. A band of whites had whipped black employees of the mill and ordered them to leave town. The mill owner did not take kindly to thugs attempting to manage his work force and finally got the court and sheriff to call on the hesitant governor to act. Forced to do something his predecessor would have thought was his duty to do, Candler denounced the contagion of lynch law. "If it had stopped at the burning of Sam Hose," he told the press in a most revealing statement, "it would have been far enough, but now [innocent] negroes [sic] are whipped and the mobs are threatening the lives of white men."

This mob, unlike the one that killed Sam Hose, had crossed a line. The Associated Press reported that self-styled "regulators" were part of a larger statewide conspiracy by young white laborers to deny jobs to blacks in cotton mills. Authorities arrested possibly eleven men for several "lawless acts" and set a trial date. Candler was forced to mobilize the militia a second time in order to prevent a mob from rescuing the accused from the city jail. On June 12, prosecutors indicted the leader of the regulators, G. V. Barnett, and impaneled a jury with some difficulty. White men already knew what the verdict should be and said so. Sure enough, charged with two counts of assault and one count of attempted murder, Barnett was acquitted. Tried once again for similar crimes against another black man, he was saved by a hung jury. The judge declared a mistrial. No one was ever convicted of doing what everyone knew the accused had done. The people had spoken.[17]

The most recent "Griffin episode" was remarkable primarily because Candler was twice forced to dispatch the militia, a sheriff had arrested white men for hurting black men, and a grand jury had indicted them. The acquittal and mistrial were unremarkable; such actions were simply part of common life. The violence, however, seemed to have awakened the governor to the possibility that white Georgians were part of a social fact about which he had been reluctant to think. His concession to the normality of Sam Hose's torture and murder did not prepare him to accept the legitimacy of violence designed to intimidate *white* property owners. Annoyed at the whipping of African Americans who were innocent, Candler resented being forced to mobilize the militia against lawless whites. The necessity suggested that the contagion of lynch law could damage Georgia's reputation and commercial life as Northerners had recently claimed. He could scarcely blame Reconstruction and the Republican Party for the lawlessness that blanketed Griffin. Well, actually, he could have done so, but he didn't, at least not in his statement on July 31, when he said something that black preachers could praise.

During the weeks after the aborted trials, reports of rape and female terror proliferated. The incidents appear in retrospect delusional, if understandable, social "paranoia." But in late July the rape of Mrs. W. B. (or possibly J. E.) Ogletree in the presence of her husband at a railroad station in Southwest Georgia seemed to ignite a "primitive frenzy" culminating in a "blood sacrifice." The flaying alive of the two rapists was of course terrible enough but the entire white countryside seemed to be absent law: possibly seven men were hanged, mutilated, or shot. Candler dispatched the militia, which arrived too late to save those men but in time to protect others. The sheriff was actually able to prevent the lynching of a black man discovered in too close a proximity to a hysterical young white woman. Candler's comments on July 31, therefore, were triggered not by his thinking about Sam Hose's fiery death – which he obviously believed to be justified – but by his own encounter with viral white lawlessness in Griffin and Southwest Georgia when whites as well as blacks were victimized.[18]

Neither of the incidents should have surprised the governor; before Sam Hose was captured at least eight black men had already been killed in 1899 by white gangs of various sizes. *The Constitution*'s stories about lynching were not daily fare, of course, and the Newnan *Herald* as a local weekly did not keep a tally of all the rapes, murders, arsons, and rumors that came across the editor's desk. But there was a continual recounting of black crimes and white vengeance in Georgia's newspapers, especially those in Atlanta, that made rape-and-provocation part of American as well as Southern culture.

Reports of black on white assaults came from Gainesville, Georgia, and Wilkinson County, Tennessee, as well as Ohio, Indiana, and Wisconsin. None of the reports were believable but all were presented in such a way as to allow the reader without critical acumen to infer that African American crime and lynching were a natural part of American life in the spring and summer of 1899. The "details" of each incident seemed to establish their truth even if they were continuously amended in subsequent news stories.

Only an informed skeptic like Ida Wells-Barnett could have confirmed or belied these fevered reports through careful investigation. Such behavior was not, however, expected when the collective knowledge of the white crowd ruled according to the myths of black criminality and white innocence. The incidents often began with a white woman's scream that alerted men to danger; communities became excited; "determined" white men sought the monster or fiend or demon; sometimes they found him. A rhetorical or physical contest usually ensued; either the sheriff took the fiend or the crowd dispatched him (or sometimes both in sequence). Each report, true or not, confirmed white people in their belief that whites were being threatened nationally as well as locally by the black phantoms of their excited imaginations.

Framing such stories was a relentless anticipation of lynching as an act natural to the familiar script of black crime. In a few cases, reporters could even ferret out of collective action by African Americans an approval of lynching. *The Constitution*, for example, carried an August 12 story out of Newnan under the heading, "NEGROES OUT FOR LYNCHING." A black man had tried to rape a black woman in Coweta County; her husband and his friends sought the culprit working closely with Sheriff Joseph Brown and a town marshal. Lynching was not the goal, even though the reporter wanted readers to believe that it was.[19]

Blacks in Florida, too, were reported to be on the verge of lynching several black rapists, one of whom had attacked a ten-year-old girl. Their natural and very human response to craven acts of violence seemed somehow to legitimize any lynching anywhere by anyone. In this milieu of rumor, innuendo, and possibility, the casual murder of a black man seemed to be so normal that it was scarcely worth investigating. From Fayetteville, Georgia, came the news that an "inoffensive negro" had been shot to death for no credible reason and the reporter expected nothing would be done to arrest his murderers because they were the "best citizens" in town. Lynching was simply the default mode for many white people whenever they heard of an event in which a white woman and a black man were the primary parties. Lynching was also the default mode when a black man did nothing more sinister than offend a county's best citizens.[20]

LYNCHING AVERTED – BUT PREFERRED

Four episodes in which lynching was prevented, ironically, suggest as much. The first began when Leonie Smith of Paulding County near Atlanta told her father, John, that Harvey Minifree had raped her. The sheriff informed Governor Candler on June 5 that armed men were pursuing Minifree and authorities offered a five hundred dollar reward for the desperate black fugitive's capture, which was, as usual, imminent. Hunters possessed a detailed description of the "mad dog," thanks to

Miss Smith, who appeared to know him rather well. A headline announced: "A great Vengeance Has Taken Hold of the People of the Community." The "People" were proving Ida Wells Barnett correct when she observed that "no colored man, reputable or not, was safe from lynching, if a white woman, no matter what her standing or motive, cares to charge him with insult or assault." A group of fifty armed men broke up a black church picnic in pursuit of Minifree, who was known absolutely to be hiding there: he wasn't. Excited observers believed the man would be shot on sight. The mood of the people changed, however, when the sheriff learned that Minifree had actually been well over a hundred miles north of Paulding County, working on the railroad, when Leonie Smith claimed the crime was committed.[21]

Candler immediately withdrew the reward without comment. The rape that stoked the emotions of a father, inventive reporters, and a vengeful posse disappeared into the ether of white supremacy. There had been no rape, but the accusation represented truth. It exposed the way in which whites thought about young white women and the communal vengeance required to protect them from a black menace that did not exist. Why Leonie Smith accused Harvey Minifree is unknown, although it is possible to guess, for she knew what would have happened had he been captured. Her anger, lie, and miscalculation revealed what every sensible black man knew, and which George Hepworth had explained after interviewing Newnan's elite just a few days earlier. Leonie Smith's accusation of an absent Harvey Minifree was believable within the ethos of sexual danger created by newspapers, confirmed by the hunt for Sam Hose, and dramatized by his death. During the search and after the burning, many white women reported threatening encounters with black men but they were all strangers, save in Minifree's case. Most results of their alarm are lost to the public record.

Other incidents suggest it would be a mistake to assume that every misunderstanding or suspicious act would result in violence or even a guilty verdict, when the criminal justice system was allowed to pursue due process. Grant Bell's agonistic experience, which occurred while posses sought Harvey Minifree, complicates understanding the suspicion, capture, and fate of accused black men. The language reporters used to describe Bell's plight reveals the way in which whites explained a situation that could have ended much differently than it did. On June 4, *The Constitution* announced: "AGED WOMAN BRUTALLY HANDLED." The incident happened near Cedartown in Polk County not far to the Northwest of Newnan. Grant's reputed crime was said to have had *"few if any parallels in ... criminal history"* for he had "heartlessly" beaten a sixty-five–year-old white widow senseless. Leading citizens of Cedartown feared "a repetition of the Sam Hose affair" and tried to find Bell as soon as possible in order to prevent it.

Fortunately, peace officers found Bell and escorted him to the Polk County jail. By five o'clock, on a Saturday afternoon, a crowd of 300 white men and boys surrounded the jail and demanded the prisoner. They were confronted by the mayor, a judge, a physician, and the deputy sheriff who swore that the mob would seize Bell only over his dead body or theirs. In the meantime, physicians interviewed the injured woman, who was the daughter-in-law of a famous ex-governor, and she told a story significantly different from her original complaint. Although a reporter repeatedly emphasized that Mrs. J. C. Lumpkin was in command of her senses, the physicians were not convinced. They could not discover what, if anything, had happened, and Dr. L. S. Ledbetter told the crowd as much.

This news reassured no one as the mob grew in numbers and enmity. Judge Charles Janes announced he would arrange a swift trial to see justice done even though that was not what the crowd wanted. They did not know what had happened but an arrested black man whose actions could be associated with a white woman supplied them with a reason to kill. They wanted blood; they didn't get it. The sheriff recruited armed white men to protect Bell and deposited him in safe seclusion. Cedartown's "best men" congratulated themselves on not being "Newnan."

On Monday morning several hundred people invaded Cedartown to witness vengeance against a man guilty of "the blackest horror in the catalogue of crimes." Governor Allen Candler congratulated the town for avoiding illegal violence. Judge Janes told the crowd he intended to see that Grant Bell received a fair trial and ordered two prominent attorneys to defend him to the best of their ability – even though they may not have wanted to. The reporter added this comment to protect them if they were successful. Janes then cleared the courtroom to spare the primary witness embarrassment and had a terrified Bell escorted to his chair. The white jury was then impaneled: two ministers, a merchant, a county commissioner, an engineer, a traveling salesman, and seven farmers, one of whom was an alternate.

At 2 o'clock in the afternoon the trial began when Mrs. Lumpkin identified Bell as the man who had struck her. On cross examination, however, she became confused as to what exactly had happened, and the case began to unravel. Then, black witnesses who claimed Bell was the assailant were exposed as enemies bent on seeking private vengeance on him; they had lied. One man now denied what he said he had said when first questioned by authorities. Even before Bell testified, it became clear that the evidence against him was nonexistent. The next day, a Tuesday, the jury retired to deliberate. A reporter confidently told his readers that ten men were ready to convict, but if they were, the two supporting acquittal must have been extraordinarily eloquent in Bell's defense because they all soon agreed he was in fact not guilty.[22] Bell then disappeared.

Almost a month later, on the second of August, John Mullens found himself in a situation not unlike Bell's and he was just as fortunate. His ordeal began the afternoon of August 1 near Senoia, a few miles north of Newnan. Mrs. John Cook claimed she "was suddenly seized from behind by a burly black negro." (The 140-pound Wilkes had been "burly," too.) The man was frightened by a passing vehicle and ran off without having "accomplished his hellish purpose." At about the same time, John Mullens observed that there were a lot of white men with guns scouring the countryside and, being of sound mind, decided that he needed to avoid them. He fled to the home of Jut Hays and asked him to find out what was going on. Hays, whom a reporter described as a "peaceable negro with more than the ordinary intelligence of his race," did so; he told the men about Mullens, whom they assumed was the "burly" brute of Mrs. Cook's imagination. They found him in Tom Brooks' fodder loft and escorted him to Newnan for safe keeping. There was one major problem: Mrs. Cook did not recognize him.

That night about 200 men gathered at the Coweta County jail from which Tom Wilkes had been seized ten weeks earlier. The crowd was waiting for men from Senoia to lead an assault on the jail but they never arrived. Sheriff Joseph Brown and Jailor John Alsabrook planned several different tactics for protecting their prisoner. They learned that a gang of white men had already stopped a freight train looking for Mullens and, worse, that all other avenues of escape were covered by would-be lynchers. To Brown's relief, however, the Newnan Guards of the state militia soon surrounded the jail. The next day the captive was delivered to the sheriff of Fulton County (Atlanta) to prevent a lynching.

Despite all the efforts by Coweta authorities to prevent white gangs from seizing the accused man, editors denied that there was ever a danger of lynching. Rumors spread by hateful Yankees that a lynching had been prevented were false. No one ever believed that Mullens was actually endangered, the newsmen wrote. This view was distinctly at odds with that of Sheriff Brown, Jailor Alsabrook, and Captain Herring of the Newnan Guards. Newspaper headlines had, after all, announced: "MULLENS IN ... NARROW ESCAPE FROM A MOB; UGLY LOOKING CROWDS WERE ABOUT NEWNAN JAIL." The accused, however, was spared the ultimate headline and disappeared into the anonymity of the Atlanta prison system.

Mullens reappeared in September to face justice in the Superior Court of Coweta County. His attorneys pointed out that Mrs. Cook had failed to identify him; two witnesses stated he had been with them at the time of the attempted assault. The court also knew that another man had been arrested for criminal trespass on the Cook farm and that he had incriminated two other men neither of whom was Mullens. The jury was confused. Judge S. W. Harris declared a mistrial, and a second jury immediately acquitted the accused. The blaring headlines that had proclaimed him a rapist were forgotten by those who penned them; his acquittal was hidden in a list of current sessions of Coweta Superior Court in the *Herald*. *The Constitution*, however, announced his good fortune and added that Sheriff Brown had told the innocent man to quit the area immediately for his own good.[23]

After Mullens was arrested, a white woman's accusation of Henry Delegale in coastal McIntosh County triggered what whites later called an "insurrection." In late August, Matilda Ann Hope gave birth to a mixed race infant and realized that nine months previously Delegale had raped her. When he heard Mrs. Hope had formally accused him, he hastened to the county seat of Darien where Sheriff Thomas B. Blount jailed him. When the prosperous farmer's sons learned Blount intended to take his prisoner to Savannah, lest he be lynched, they feared that doing so would guarantee his being seized by a white mob in transit. Their father, they insisted, would be safer in a well-defended building; they mobilized local African Americans to do so. Soon, as Fitzhugh Brundage reports, they were joined by "black men and women from throughout the county."[24]

The strength of that crowd and the confidence of its leaders were based on the economic and political foundations of the black community in Darien and McIntosh County. Many rural blacks were independent land owners, Brundage points out, and the town harbored substantial numbers of black "merchants and craftsmen" as well as a cadre of influential ministers. Although the sheriff attempted several times to take Delegale to Savannah, the black leadership explained each time that they preferred to protect his prisoner rather than risk a train ride. Finally, a frustrated Sheriff Blount, who felt that he had lost control of his town, asked for outside help. Governor Candler should dispatch the state militia to restore order, he claimed. Arriving in Darien, the troops were met by a crowd of black people who, now assured of Delegale's safety, returned to their homes. A "guard of militia" then escorted Delegale to Savannah.

The crisis should have been over. Blount, however, refused to leave well enough alone. He had been embarrassed. African Americans had armed themselves to protect their own. They had not hurt anyone and they had not rioted. They were highly disciplined and determined. Their independence and solidarity had sobered the sheriff because blacks had broken the rubrics of white supremacy. They were not deferential. Blount demanded the "mob" be punished by "the strong arm they have defied" and he arrested thirty-five "rioters" without incident. He then sent two deputies to arrest Delegale's sons, who agreed to surrender. For some reason, one of the deputies raised his gun in a threatening manner and someone in the Delegale house fired, killing one and wounding the other. Blacks had shot white officers; this was a lynching offense: Insurrection!

The Delegale family could have been slaughtered in another Georgia venue, but that did not happen. Colonel Alexander Lawton, at Mrs. Delegale's request, commanded the militia to protect her family and disarmed a white posse bent on revenge. Then he conferred with the county's ten most influential blacks. After meeting with the colonel, the leadership was confident the militia would protect African Americans and wrote a circular to that effect, urging blacks to avoid any act to incite white violence. "Colored" women, they insisted, should not appear in public lest they trigger an incident; gendered racial contact could be dangerous.

Ensured of their safety, other "rioters" turned themselves in, bringing the total to fifty-eight men and five women. At trial, twenty-one men and two women were convicted; charges against the other forty were dropped. The penalties were draconian: stiff fines and/or twelve months at hard labor in Georgia's notorious camps; a few were sent to a saw mill. Delegale, his three sons, and a daughter were granted a change of venue to nearby Effingham County. Two sons were given life sentences for murder but their brother and sister were acquitted. As for Henry, the jury did not believe he had raped Mrs. Hope; apparently no one did; probably no one ever had.

Brundage points out that the "insurrection" ended with white authorities firmly in control of Darien. The militia's presence left no doubt as to who ruled McIntosh County. Moreover, the "stiff penalties meted out to the 'rioters' ... were cruel reminders of the transparent bias of Georgia's courts," even though Delegale and two of his children were acquitted. The man's influence among both races, which whites acknowledged was substantial, was part of a reality that made the coastal counties different from the rest of the state. Coastal African Americans had a history of political activity. Their solidarity was nourished by churches and a respected leadership. Black and white elites in Darien knew each other; the parties knew whom they could trust. These conditions meant, Brundage points out, that "whites lacked many of the traditional means to intimidate blacks"; they were "not dealing with a cowed and impotent population."

The black ring around the Darien jail presented a reality whites thought best not to challenge. A dead white deputy confirmed that reality. Blacks in McIntosh and other coastal counties had the means and presence to negotiate race relations that blacks in other venues did not have. In the Delegale affair, they could negotiate with a reasonable militia commander rather than simply obey. They could expect the white elite to listen. This situation did not mean blacks always trusted white authorities or basked in inter-racial tranquility. If the area yielded only thirteen lynchings between 1880 and 1930 (in a state that suffered over four hundred), those thirteen still represented a white supremacy that confronted black Georgians every day of their lives. In Darien, it was a negotiated supremacy, which meant whites did not know exactly how to explain the Delegale affair. News stories bewailed insurrection, but editorials more sensibly praised prominent blacks who had helped to resolve the crisis. Brundage points out that "bold stands" such as that in Darien suggested blacks could sometimes shun "pervasive fatalism or strict obedience even during an era of ascendant white supremacy."[25]

These four stories reveal the ethos within which Southern African Americans continued to live after the Newnan holocaust. For many whites, accusation of black men proved guilt for crimes of which the latter might even be acquitted if trials were permitted. The language of accusation, pursuit, and capture could create a crime without parallel in the universal history of mankind and birth a criminal who made Whitechapel's Jack the Ripper seem like a purse-snatcher. Whites' invention of Sam Hose before his burning surely demonstrated that fact. Inventive embellishment helped dramatize the meaning for race-partisan whites of any black man's perceived encroachment on their well-being, especially if that act could be cleverly converted into a rape. Bell's arrest made women in the area of Cedartown especially anxious, a reporter observed, and led to several incidents in which strange black men frightened them. Fear confirmed a threat that did not exist; Bell's capture immediately established his guilt. When the crowd surrounding the Cedartown jail learned no one knew what had actually happened to Mrs. Lumpkin they ignored that fact because Bell's arrest had already licensed them to kill.

The same logic applied to Mullens when Sheriff Brown told him to leave Coweta County – now! If both Bell and Mullens escaped the wrath of a crowd, furious whites still considered them fair game. The Cedartown elite knew their community well enough to prevent Bell's lynching. Sheriff Brown and the Newnan Guards acted swiftly to keep the crowd at bay until Mullens could be removed to safety. Losing Hose to a mob had sobered Brown and he refused to see another prisoner hijacked. In each case, newspapers, whose reporters usually did their best to help readers imagine the worst about any accused black man, did not have time to arouse the countryside into a fury of homicidal rectitude as they had when the hunt for Sam Hose had lasted so long.

If newspapers had had time to promise a burning and if they had sponsored symposia on a terrified countryside that existed only in whites' enflamed fantasies, surely some men intoxicated by honor would have volunteered to act as decisively as Abe Rogowski and his fellow Griffinites. But intelligence, force, courage, and the horrendous example of what had happened to Tom Wilkes allowed Cedartown's elites to prevent a lynching. Minifree's situation had been different; he was not where Leonie Smith wanted him to be. Bell was fortunate that skeptical whites realized Mrs. Lumpkin was more confused than clueless reporters imagined. Delegale represented a black community with which whites had to reckon more carefully than in Coweta County, and he was fortunate that Mrs. Hope had a reputation difficult to escape.

Each man benefitted from special circumstances, but each episode also revealed that lynching was an essential part of supremacist ethics. Sometimes lynching could be prevented, but its cultural power dominated the way in which whites thought of accused blacks and their people. At least thirty-five times in 1899, white crowds of varying sizes came together to lynch black men in Georgia.[26] Whether prevented or enacted, lynching was the default position when whites encountered or imagined signal crimes attributed to black men.

CONFLICTED "MODERATION"

The everyday life of black and white Southerners had been afflicted by violent *possibility* for a long time, but 1898 and 1899 proved vintage years, concocted of condescension, caution, suspicion, hostility, contempt, torture, and murder. The "treatment of negro soldiers," W. E. B. Du Bois pointed out in September of 1899, had been one of those significant events during the previous eleven months that had alerted African Americans to the nature of that possibility. The Atlanta University sociologist and historian had seen whites manufacture incidents such as those in Macon and Griffin that put black soldiers at risk. A more recent event, which was closer to home, had been the lynching of Sam Hose, but he also mentioned the "Wilmington Riot [and] the murder of Postmaster Baker" in the previous year. All these events had "profoundly moved these people," Du Bois announced in *The Independent*, and they had dominated discussion during two recent national conventions of African Americans.

The dispassionate tone of Du Bois' comments, however, masked his anguish, nausea, and fury during the spring of 1899. Responding to the news that Hose had killed his employer, Du Bois wrote a restrained analysis of race and violence that he was taking to *The Constitution* on April 24. Along the way, he heard that Hose had been lynched and his "blackened knuckles" exhibited in a nearby merchant's window. The report and its evocative image sickened him; in an instant he saw the reality behind a dead man's knuckles. He saw fire, cutting, contempt, and cruelty. He saw white culture as never before; it was a moment of revelation. He turned around; he could not enter the journalistic citadel of white imagination. He returned home. The cool analysis that had guided his hand was, he recalled later, not appropriate! Imagining those knuckles, he had seen "the race hatred of the whites as I had never dreamed of it before – naked and unashamed." Perhaps he imagined the mob as a force that condemned the divine before Pilate: Weeks later he would refer to Hose's death as a *crucifixion*.

Du Bois' depression plunged him further into a chasm when a few days later his little son died of diphtheria. The father watched his son's breathing "beat quicker and quicker" until it stopped and "his little soul leapt like a star that travels in the night and left the world of darkness in its train." Little Burghardt had lived a "perfect life," all "joy and love," his father later mused. "He knew no color line, poor dear – and the Veil though it shadowed him, had not yet darkened half his sun." His mother in a "simple clearness of vision" hoped he would be happy and his father, less inclined to such sentiment, also muttered to himself, "If still he be, and he be There, and there be a There, let him be happy." Burghardt had escaped the "bitter meanness" that could have sickened "his baby heart, till it die a living death," and, his father sighed, "[Now,] no taunt shall madden his happy boyhood." His parents could not lay him to rest in the poisoned red soil of Georgia, for he belonged among his family in Massachusetts. He should lie in peace "where Reverence dwells, and Goodness, and a Freedom that is free?"

Stunned and despondent, Du Bois and his wife, Nina, walked slowly behind the cart that carried their son's little casket to the railway depot as whites cried, "niggers," "niggers," "niggers." The taunting flowed naturally from the common life of black and white in Atlanta and reminded Du Bois, as he reflected on his son's death, that the child was now free. He wrote: "Well sped, my boy, before the world had dubbed your ambition insolence, had held your ideals unattainable, and taught you to cringe and bow." Little Burghardt had escaped the daily reminders of white arrogance and the possibility of dreadful violence. "Sleep, then, child" and waken "above the Veil."[27]

But that veil, which divided the world into two dimensions according to race, remained. To be sure, Newnan's everyday life seemed not to be as violent as most of Georgia between the mountains and the sea, but every once in a while something went awry. A black employee in much the same situation as that of Tom Wilkes might demand payment just as forcefully as he and also be shot by a furious employer. No one would expect an arrest, although when an elderly black man was hanged and thrown into a creek for personal reasons, two white men were jailed. The violence of night riders against peaceable and productive black families to the north of Newnan was condemned as a terrible crime that could never happen in Coweta County. Anyone there who was found to have intimidated "an upright negro without just cause" would, according to the *Herald*'s partisan editor, soon lose the respect of his neighbors and his influence in the community. No evidence was submitted. As for the mob violence in April that had been a topic for discussion from Newnan to Atlanta to London to Manila, however, the heralded white respect was absent and Newnan's chief opponent of lynching was dead.

Although the first session of the Coweta County superior court in September 1899 was awaited by the community with "decided interest," nothing happened. This meant, of course, that something unnamed had happened. Judge S. W. Harris knew he had to say something appropriate so he opened the session by addressing the grand jury. He should have called on that body to investigate the event that was on everyone's mind, but he didn't. Instead, he told a crowded courtroom that they should understand that those who had the authority legally to punish crime on behalf of the people were the "authorized agents of the government." The judge, however, managed adroitly to avoid discussing what "*un*authorized agents" had done to Tom Wilkes.

The burning should have been criminal enough to be investigated. The prosecuting attorney should have been at least as curious and determined as Louis Le Vin, but the former apparently knew enough already and as a result did not try to get an indictment. Judge Harris did disapprove punishment by most mobs because such an act, "however *just so far as the criminal was concerned* [added emphasis], was not always a vindication of the right [because it] often resulted in victimizing the innocent." Harris thus absolved the Newnan mob of responsibility and blame even as he criticized it. Everyone (white) knew Sam Hose was in fact guilty. Harris did insist that "the effort to suppress crime by committing crime is a moral absurdity." His primary concern was that mobs often killed the innocent; he implied that the Newnan mob had not done so.

Harris' understanding of mobs in general and miscreants in particular could inspire neither a legal nor a moral indictment of the mob that burned Tom Wilkes.[28] Harris spoke from within the privileged councils of Newnan's white elite; he knew what he was supposed to say; Atkinson was dead and Freeman was irrelevant. Newnan's black community – large and well informed as to the overwhelming reality of whites' sense of battered innocence – was the silent foil of Harris' self-serving homily. They knew just how much they could rely on their white neighbors' respect.

"The mob," both in general and in particular, continued to be part of Georgia's public life. African Americans continued to hear the taunts hurled at Dr. and Mrs. Du Bois. Blacks continued to be killed by individuals and mobs with impunity. The Reverend H. B. Battle of Thomson, Georgia, the home of Populist leader Thomas E. Watson and about nine counties to the east of Coweta, condemned lynching in a manner that "exasperated" whites to such an extent that he was shot to death in his cornfield a week after Harris convened superior court. No one was arrested. Two days later a mob hanged a black man in front of a black church in South Georgia for presumably facilitating the rape of a white woman. In Valdosta, even farther to the south, four hundred men marched on the jail to lynch two accused murderers but were prevented.

At about the same time in Barnesville, some sixty miles southeast of Newnan, whites claimed that blacks were on a rampage and asked for protection from the governor. Candler would have dispatched the militia under the right conditions, but he decided not to do so after he discovered that it was the blacks who needed protection.

A few days later, while addressing the Georgia legislature on the state of the state, Governor Candler conceded that there had been widespread violence in Georgia in 1899. There had also been, he claimed, a remarkable increase in crime among blacks, instigated by the "malice and hatred" of Northerners. He atypically praised a few African Americans in Darien for preventing violence, and typically condemned blacks in McIntosh County for defending the Darien jail. Ignoring what had actually happened, Candler insisted that a "reign of terror" had erupted from a "vicious criminal" class of "lawless negroes," who "assaulted white women" throughout the state. Candler did confess that there had been an instance this year of "barbarous punishment" by a white mob, but peace officers had prevented other lynching. It would be easier for authorities to keep the peace if African Americans weren't so racist. He continued to blame black people for the violence against them.[29]

Candler refused to use the occasion to explain how lynching had become part of the everyday flow of life throughout the region. Readers of newspapers knew that reports of lynching were as natural to newspapers as baseball scores and statistics. Lynching was as normal as Yankee malice, sexual scandal, religious revival, black criminality, and – if advertisements are to be believed – aging women's physical complaints. In one sense, lynching was "news" only according to its locale; generally it was what Newnan's elites denied it was: a "Southern habit."

A leading Georgia black moderate certainly believed as much, and it had shaken him. Bishop Lucious Holsey of the Colored Methodist Episcopal Church (CMEC) was one of the founders of his denomination, which had been birthed by Methodist Episcopal Church, South in 1870. Thus begat and reared in white paternalism, the CMEC was rebuked by politically active black Methodists (especially the AMEC) as the "old Slavery Church." Its bishops and ministers had long valued the "affinity" between black and white Methodists during "slavery times" and at least for a time referred to servitude as a providential school in civilization and Christianity. When white Methodists helped the CMEC establish Paine Institute in Augusta, Georgia, (1882) white paternalism seemed to be a positive force for racial progress.

As a bishop and educator, Holsey became a prominent member of the mixed-race elite in Augusta, a city which boasted a significant number of successful merchants, editors, and educators of African descent. If the city seemed to harbor amicable race relations for a while, however, during the 1890s white supremacists closed the excellent black high school, expanded segregation, and began to campaign for the disfranchisement of black men. Gradually disappointed, frustrated, and angered, Holsey finally sloughed off his apolitical deference to paternalism and condemned whites unwilling "for the race of black men to become their political equals, or occupy the same plane of freedom and citizenship, with themselves, no matter how well qualified they may be for it." Leaving Augusta for the capital city, he endorsed the Populist Party, believing it betokened a willingness on the part at least of some whites to follow policies beneficial to his people. He was mistaken, but he was optimistic. Then he learned the fate of Sam Hose.

The savagery did not cause, but it did confirm, Holsey's simmering rage with paternalism. In the late summer of 1899 he announced that African Americans must have their own government under the Constitution of the United States. White pundits such as publisher John Temple Graves of Atlanta, Holsey pointed out, were proposing complete segregation to perfect the process already begun throughout the South. Complete segregation, the bishop believed, required creation of a state or states in which blacks were in complete control. There they could elect their own leaders and fill all the offices necessary for ruling a modern state. His was a black nationalism committed to those ideals imbedded in the Declaration of Independence and the Constitution of the United States that whites were unwilling to put into practice.

Holsey's vision of Black Nationalism shared much with that of his fellow Atlantan Bishop Henry McNeal Turner of the AMEC. To be sure, Turner sited the core of his nation in Africa, but emigration of significant numbers of black people there, Turner believed, would create an ideal republic led by Africans whose praxis would consequently inspire a sense of national greatness for blacks everywhere, especially in the United States. Turner brandished the perfect metaphor of Exodus to encourage his people to flee oppression and gain sovereignty. Sovereignty and Exodus now dominated the vision of his CMEC counterpart. The details of Holsey's vision still needed to be developed four months after the burning of Tom Wilkes, but they were not as important as his demand for black autonomy. He was not defending his people or what they had done; he was testifying to the evil that surrounded them. He was revealing how moderate blacks such as he understood the world that engendered the horror of April 23, 1899.

That ferocity was not about a crime, he believed; it was about a people. And that people had, Holsey pointed out, issued a clear ultimatum to blacks: Submit, leave, or die! He had read such dictates for a long time. It is, he wrote, a "fact in history, ethnology, and science that opposite races are inherently and universally antagonistic and cannot share . . . peace and equality." If we do not leave states governed by whites we will be exterminated, he insisted. He obviously believed blacks could not submit. He had once shared the familiar dream, recently imagined by Bishop Wesley Gaines, that American Christianity could eventually bond white and black in a common faith. He was now more than skeptical; he was contemptuous. "Our so-called Christianity," he wrote, meaning that of whites, "is a failure."

Religion was everywhere "sacrificed" to white ambition. There was no reason to believe that, in the famously Christian Southland, the black man would ever be able to "rise to the dignity and possibilities of his manhood." Merit and character would never be allowed to win equality. Neither would the approach blessed by Booker T. Washington; it was "time serving and temporary." Washington's strategy would merely postpone the inevitable destruction of the race because as talented, educated, and wealthy blacks demonstrated their capacity for excellence, the oppression and killing would surge. Race for whites trumped religion and morality.

Holsey noted whites hated those they oppressed. Slavery, which the bishop had once conceded was a school for civilization, had damaged both races. You, he addressed whites, have degraded yourselves by degrading us; the rape of millions of black women reveals as much! And still you do it! He believed white men would never *quit* doing it. You will "never give the negroes the same rights, privileges, or free and full citizenship" that you yourself enjoy! You claim our leaders have concocted a crisis by creating dissension, but if that were true you would arrest them. You don't because *they* don't! They merely tell the truth. You pass laws that apply only to us and refuse to allow us to enter into "the social compact." In your world, "One must be serf to that extreme debasement where all human rights are denied and the other the single supreme and undisputed master. If this does not agree with the inexorable decrees of God it is the logic of fate and the inevitable."[30]

Holsey refused to divide blacks into two groups: 95 percent law-abiding, 5 percent criminal. He refused to divide blacks between those who deserved lynching and those who did not. He joined activists such as Ida Wells who insisted that lynching was not about black crime but rather about white power. The anger, frustration, and condemnation Holsey could no longer contain erupted from a lifetime of association with Christian white supremacists. The burning in Newnan and the response of white "Christians" combined to push him into a public declaration that was surprising to most whites who knew him. For blacks who understood how he had experienced relations with whites and who were also stunned by the burning of Sam Hose, Holsey had been an especially astute and resounding voice.

The white ministers who found it so challenging to engage the ideology and myth that justified lynching could easily imagine sex, violation, manhood, and punishment. They could not, however, imagine what it was like to be under surveillance and accusation by violent men. The black ministers, engineers, seamstresses, cooks, day-laborers, and the talented physician who cared for them in Newnan, however, knew what it meant when white clergy could not speak about lynching with the same ardor as they reserved for Sunday sales and dancing. They knew what it meant when one of their highly respected businessmen was forced by whites to proclaim his commitment to "justice" after whites took umbrage at comments they correctly inferred to be critical of the mob.[31]

Bishop Holsey was perhaps a "moderate" according to one interpretive measure, as were James Reid (by necessity) and Newnan's African American ministers, but he and they knew what castration, burning, lynching, and contempt meant. Black citizens of Newnan could understand why whites forced Reid to make his comments about justice; they had read the "poem" celebrating the divine justice of the burning; they had read the white restaurateurs' humor about a real barbecue. They were as respectable and respectful as Bishop Holsey, and they could feel the same way as he, even if they could not safely announce that fact in public. They, of course, did not know what a black college professor was feeling as he thought of blackened knuckles collected from their town, but they knew about those relics, the fire, and the stench. They knew what had happened and they would have felt its meaning as profoundly as he; he knew their souls.

ANDREW SLEDD EXPLAINS THE SAVAGE FURY; DU BOIS NAMES IT

The brutal killing of Tom Wilkes gradually slipped from public consciousness – or at least *white* public consciousness. To be sure, white citizens might have wondered how Emilio Aguinaldo could use the incident to entice black US soldiers to his cause and a few black observers could wonder why not. But the event that had seemed to match the hideous fate of Henry Smith in 1893 had apparently been forgotten or suppressed in white consciousness during the last year of the nineteenth century. Then, in July of 1902, the burning of Sam Hose was remembered once again as the symbol of white hatred through the efforts of Professor Andrew Sledd of Emory College. The man who had triggered Lundy Harris' "Austin debauch" and subsequent exile from Eden in the spring of 1898 had been on a train from Covington to Atlanta on April 23, 1899 when it stopped in Newnan.

An annoyed and frustrated Sledd discovered that the train would be delayed to allow passengers to watch the lynching of Sam Hose. He did not follow the crowd, but he knew what had happened on the killing ground, and wrote an article about the hatred that had driven whites to act. *The Independent* refused to publish the professor's essay – it was indeed rather long – and so did a distinguished Southern Methodist journal. After being seasoned for about three years, however, the piece finally appeared in *The Atlantic Monthly* for July of 1902.[32]

Sledd emphasized that the horrendous murder had not been surprising, given the fact that Southern whites generally viewed African Americans "with manifest contempt." This observation would have outraged most Southern whites, who were preternaturally proud of their "respect" for "deserving" blacks. The white mobs that terrorized blacks, he accused, sprang from the ranks of an illiterate, ignorant, brutal, and insensitive lower class. They were motivated not by respect for white women, but by lust for a "wild and diabolical carnival of blood." If he scored the lower classes, however, Sledd also pointed out that planters mistreated tenants and laborers; retailers insulted black customers; segregation punished African Americans as a race. The "average Southern community" treated the average black person with "loathing," he charged. Such people did so not because of blacks' "ignorance," "viciousness," or "offensiveness," but because of the latter's caste and color. In saying so, the scholar dismissed the most universal of white Southern bromides: The Southern white man "is the Negro's friend, and gives him even more than his just desert."

Lynching belied this claim, Sledd insisted; it was a "conspicuous expression" of white supremacy defended with lies told in the mythology of rape. The excuse that lynching counterbalanced the "impotence and delay" of legal due process was "pure pretense," Sledd observed. Everyone in the South knew African Americans at trial experienced a "sharper justice than is meted out to the white man." If lynching taught blacks anything, it was a lesson in blatant injustice; it was a lesson taught in violence that they dare not claim basic human rights. Lynching was not about justice or manhood but about the white man's craving to "gratify the brute in his own soul." The South's primary problem was "not with the negro, but with the white man!" The solution to problems whites created was to treat black and white people in exactly the same way; it would lead peace officers to shoot into lynch mobs. Sledd was clear and blunt.

The professor began his article by trying to establish his authenticity as a Southerner. He told Northerners in an unfortunate choice of words that right now "the Negro belongs to an inferior race." This meant that we need not expect "amalgamation of the races." He had apparently been reading a broad range of "scientific" studies supporting this position. Because of these comments, some black readers could have believed that with such friends as he, they deserved no enemies. Southern whites, hypersensitive to any sign of heresy in racist dogma, however, would not have been gulled by such comments because Sledd insisted that *inferiority was not innate.* Like W. E. B. Du Bois, Sledd believed African American ignorance, poverty, and debility resulted from white oppression. "Inferiority" would disappear through education, hard work, and the lapse of time as many blacks had already proved. Belief in African American progress despite whites' obstructionism was anathema to racial fundamentalists.

If African Americans' "rights and privileges" were respected there would be no "negro problem," the professor insisted. If African Americans were allowed to develop naturally under the aegis of "statute law, fairly administered," they would realize "the inherent potentialities of the race" and gain the equality to which they were entitled. That blacks had already made great progress, Sledd believed, was miraculous. If the African American were free from white terror, his future would be open (Sledd referred to the collective as a "man," "he," or "him.") Sledd concluded, "let us give him fair and favorable conditions, and suffer him to work out, unhampered, his destiny among us."[33]

Sledd should not have been surprised at the response to his article. Instead of launching a discussion of white prejudice and violence, he begat denunciation and contempt. In condemning what he believed were the lies of Southern whites, the scholar made himself a traitor to his race and section as Rebecca Latimer Felton pointed out in *The Constitution*. We do not hate African Americans, she insisted in a huff. We teach them and pay their teachers' salaries although "taxed to death" to do it.

The only place blacks were treated as the "traitor" claimed, she went on, was in a "convict camp," which was appropriate. She accused Sledd of attacking Mattie Cranford, and fumed that he had no concern for the victims of rape. Her theme was as familiar as the words to "Dixie."

Indeed, when Sledd denied most lynching was for rape, Felton blustered, he had denied what every (white) person in the South knew was the truth. If Sledd had not meant to defame the South with his lies, he'd have condemned the burning of a black criminal in Colorado, Felton crowed. By ignoring this telling incident of "Northern" brutality, Sledd was obviously trying to please those disgusting Boston "negrophilists" who had attacked her in 1897. Worse, the college professor had received money for writing his article. Strangely, she neglected to mention "thirty pieces of silver."

Newspapers throughout Georgia responded with choruses singing the same lyrics as Felton. The professor was burned in effigy in Covington, where he lived, and he spent at least one night clutching his rifle should he and his family be mobbed. In an interview, he explained his position and refused to recant. His refusal elicited even greater rage. A few furious wealthy and well-situated Methodists, some of whom he had already alienated by his commitment to academic excellence, demanded he resign. He refused, but he would, he told an intensely disturbed President James E. Dickey, be pleased to explain his views at greater length.

Because Sledd had voted against Dickey's receiving an honorary degree, it is not surprising that the latter should have replied that the issue was not "the truth," but the hue and cry from "the press and the people" of Georgia. Worse, the trustees were upset. Sledd was not surprised at this response from a man of such "amazing ignorance and the intensest bigotry." As pressure mounted, the proud professor finally yielded to his wife's pleas to resign for the sake of the family. (Her uncles despised her husband: The feeling was probably mutual. Sledd thought Judge John Candler was the personification of mediocrity.)

The Constitution announced his decision on its front page. Sledd explained he was leaving for the good of the college. To his father-in-law, Bishop Warren Candler, he pointed out that he had never been appreciated at Emory: "I feel alien and wronged. I am cramped and stunted by the atmosphere that prevails." He then accepted financial support from several sources, including Bishop Candler, to complete graduate work at Yale University and left for New Haven.[34]

Andrew Sledd, like Corra Harris, had had an experience of grace. Unlike her, he had been shamed by his inherited discomfort at interracial association in public. Her father owned slaves; his father defended the practice. By the time he wrote his article, however, he had concluded that segregation was a contrivance of racial oppression. It was but one of many such tools employed by a provincial, illiterate, uninformed electorate. The South, Sledd had written in 1901, provided a "rich soil in which all sorts of political weeds" flourished to crowd out any sensible public policy. The South's "fundamental problem" was not race but "popular [white] *ignorance*." The South's "fundamental obstacle" to solving matters of race was its hostility to education and excellence. Since politicians could not act responsibly, colleges would have to do so by producing teachers who would carry their commitment to excellence and equality into their classrooms.

Given this understanding of higher education, he may have believed his article in *The Atlantic* was merely an introductory lecture on race relations. As a professor he had wanted his students to discover the exhilaration of learning through a discourse shaped through hard questions and hard answers. He wanted to share this goal with men and women beyond the academy, but they did not want to read that Southern whites lynched blacks to sate their "lust for blood."[35] Sledd's anger at ignorance and violence had been nurtured by vexing personal experiences as a student, country teacher, and college professor. His contempt for posturing professionals and mediocre ministers and his frustration with whites who fought African American progress fed a passion familiar to anyone who has ever wanted a better world.

Sledd could not channel his passion effectively. He had been a lay preacher: He knew how to condemn sin, but not how to trigger repentance. He was a college professor: He knew how to lecture but not yet how to entice learning. Moreover, and most importantly, his readers didn't have to pass an examination. He knew the truth, but he couldn't persuade most of his readers to believe it.

Some among his audience, however, did believe him. The Emory Board of Trustees found to their dismay that their failure to allow free inquiry shamed them among some highly valued observers. Most of the Board had feared losing financial support if Sledd were retained, but they were surprised when they lost funds because he was not. The future Coca Cola magnate Asa Candler (one of his wife's censorious uncles) had to bail them out. The school had already removed President Charles E. Dowman for liberal views, and some friends of the college tried to get Sledd rehired, but negotiations broke down when he refused to recant. Dowman had been eloquent in defending a liberal education against the encroachments of a marketplace hostile to excellence. Losing another man with similar views seemed damaging to advocates of academic freedom and excellence. One man pointed out that Emory needed Sledd more than Sledd needed Emory.

Southern expatriates in the North confessed their shame at what had happened. A Southern bishop expressed dismay that a "mob spirit" should have dishonored "our humanity" and four others complained in a like manner to Candler, who had already accused the fumbling Dickey of gross incompetence. Candler thought the president had allowed Rebecca Felton and her toadies to "lynch a capable professor and banish my child from Georgia." For Candler, the institutional failure was personal; the word, "lynch," referred not simply to an act but also to an ethos.

For President John Carlisle Kilgo of Trinity College in Durham, North Carolina, the affair was a matter of principle. He wrote Candler that Georgia Methodists would have to explain why they thought it a crime to defend "poor downtrodden people at our doors," while sending missions to "Chinamen ten thousand miles away." Sledd should not have resigned, Kilgo insisted; he had made it too easy for his cowardly enemies. We need courage more than money, Kilgo wrote. If Trinity were ever challenged as Emory was, he promised Candler, he would expose the crime in such a way that "the stench" would "never cease to rise to heaven."[36] It had already risen to the North.

The father of modern American advertising, Ivy Lee, sent clippings from newspapers to his father, James, who was a Georgia Methodist minister. The commentary followed a theme suggested in a headline from the *New York Evening Post*: "Suppressing Free Speech in Georgia." It was a shame, wrote an editor of *The Independent*, that a college professor should have been punished for explaining what he thought. Other journalists pointed out that Sledd's article suggested a greater range of Southern views on race than critics realized. The writer could have mentioned a few federal judges who were trying to use the law to protect African Americans. Southern critics of Emory's Board agreed with such judges as well as Kilgo, who obviously could not be included in Sledd's wholesale condemnation. Six months before Sledd's article appeared, Trinity's president had attacked the culture of honor, which had created a damning "social sensitiveness" on sex, family, women, and class (race). White men had sculpted the white woman into a "deity" and cloaked themselves with a code that exalted lynching as justice. If Sledd thought ignorance hurt the South, Kilgo thought the fatal flaw was senseless passion fanned into a wildfire of vengeance by unscrupulous politicians and their editorial henchmen.[37]

A sampling of responses from African Americans to Sledd's article suggests the hostile scrutiny under which blacks spoke about their destiny. The expected mantra celebrating support among whites for "respectable black people" was intoned by a few wary black spokesmen. An official of Morris Brown College even claimed that Sledd had harmed black people. They had to live in the South, and "to enjoy whatever privileges [they] can" they had to avoid offending whites. Complaining that lawless whites represented the region was harmful to blacks who wished to be "respected by the white man." The fragility of that respect was all too obvious in such comments. If blacks approved a white man's criticism of racism they knew their "privileges" could be endangered; blacks had to be careful not to offend, not to complain, and not to reveal.

The desire to deflect white anger affected Bishop Gaines, too. The white people of the South were not enemies of African Americans, he told the Negro Young People's Congress meeting in Atlanta. "I believe," he announced, "that the better class of white people in this country are anxious to see the negro become a wise, intelligent, and thrifty citizen." The editor of *The Constitution* applauded Gaines' statement, but reserved comment on the views of another bishop, Henry McNeal Turner.

Turner welcomed Sledd's article despite the professor's prejudices. The essay revealed a "novel position for a southern white man" and should encourage others even more radical than he to follow in his train. Turner feared, however, that most whites did not have "the courage to speak out" if the "victim [of lynching] is black." I cannot say any more on the subject, the bishop confessed, because to do so "might diminish that friendly feeling which exists." He knew the demands of racial etiquette even as his sarcasm implied its hypocrisy. He added that Sledd meant to assist those "in need of help."[38]

Sledd's "help" eventually developed within the limited venue and slow processes of higher education. He was, after all, by temperament and commitment a scholar, not an activist. After receiving his Ph.D. from Yale University, he returned to the South, where he tried unsuccessfully as president to raise academic standards at the University of Florida. Failing to inspire academic excellence as an administrator, he was finally invited back to Emory when the college became a university. He joined the faculty at Candler School of Theology, where he taught until his death in 1939. There, he successfully mentored students who, he hoped, would undermine white racism through their own teaching and ministry.

Sledd's brief encounter with an angry constituency of professed Christians in 1902 became a subordinate clause in the story of American racism. By exposing the hypocrisy of whites' claims to respect African Americans, he dashed his hope for a broad-ranging public conversation about race. His dismissing the same "threadbare lie" about lynching that Wells had scored made no dent in the armor of white supremacists. The world that Sledd's coreligionist, Corra Harris, had imagined as dangerous to respectable white women was more acceptable to apprehensive Christian white supremacists as a description of reality than the moral miasma of contempt that Sledd condemned.[39]

Sledd represented a few white Southerners, so he was not alone even if he was safer in New Haven. It is fair to assume that Bishop Holsey was not alone, either; the restaurateur James Reid of Newnan and African Americans like him were part of a public that honored what the bishop and his AMEC counterpart, Turner, wrote and said. William Jefferson White, the African American Baptist editor, among others in Augusta, Savannah, and elsewhere in the South, agreed with the bishops and represented all those blacks who developed a narrative about Sam Hose quite different from that privileged by white Southern politicians, newspapermen, and clergy. The difference profoundly disturbed Walter Willcox of Cornell University. As a social scientist, he could place Hose within a context of "black criminality" that helped him misunderstand what happened near Palmetto and Newnan.

Sledd, the Greek scholar, described the pathology of Southern racism more clearly than the social scientist who warped Du Bois' research to defend his own position. Willcox could not understand what Tom Wilkes' world was like; he could not delve critically into the culture of white supremacy. When he thought of Hose, Willcox thought of black crime and political vengeance. When Sledd thought of Hose, he thought of white hypocrisy, ignorance, and violence. When Du Bois thought of Hose, he used a word familiar to Christians of all races, and which should have occurred to Sledd, as a student of the Bible. The word reflected the difference between the two conflicting narratives: *Crucifixion*. In an article in September of 1899, Du Bois mentioned what African Americans had experienced since the Wilmington insurrection of 1898: hostility, riot, murder, disfranchisement, and "the crucifixion of Sam Hose."[40]

Crucifixion was at the core of Christian belief and rich in symbolic power; it was a reference and an understanding that arose not from social science, but from human experience.

7

At the Altar

Crucifixion

Resolved, That the Senate

1) Apologizes to the victims of lynching for the failure of the Senate to enact anti-lynching legislation;
2) Expresses the deepest sympathies and most solemn regrets ... to the descendants of victims of lynching ...
3) Remembers the history of lynching, to ensure that these tragedies will be neither forgotten nor repeated.

U. S. Senate Resolution 39, June 13, 2005

"Woe to you, scribes and Pharisees, hypocrites. Because you build the tombs of the prophets and adorn the monuments of the righteous, and say, 'If we had lived in the days of our fathers, we would not have been partakers with them in the blood of the prophets.'"

Christian Bible KJV, Matthew, 23:29–30

*

Early one of these mornings
God's a-going to call for Gabriel,
That tall, bright angel, Gabriel;
And God's a-going to say to him: Gabriel,
Blow your silver trumpet,
And wake the living nations.

And Gabriel's going to ask him: Lord,
How loud must I blow it?

James Weldon Johnson, *God's Trombones*[1]

* * *

On the third Sunday after Easter in 1899 about forty miles southwest of Atlanta in Newnan, Georgia, a white crowd burned to death a fugitive black laborer known as Sam Hose. This atrocity blended anger, hatred, arrogance, festivity, brutality and satisfaction into a mood just beyond comprehension. "Glory!" shouted an excited man enraptured by the intensity of the moment, "Glory be to God!!" Others saw Crucifixion.

"Sam Hose was crucified."

A few weeks after the holocaust, W. E. B. Du Bois referred to it as an act at the crux of Christian consciousness. Reflecting on the burning and whites' contempt for his dead son, the professor grasped the blending of race, violence, and death as *crucifixion*. The word seemed so fitting to the event that he did not explain what he meant. Four years later, in *The Souls of Black Folk*, he once again remarked that Hose had been crucified.[2] Du Bois knew the power of symbols and evocative words. He could have written that Hose was murdered, burned, or lynched, but he used a word with connotations far beyond mere description. "Crucified" was a densely packed term and image that had long suffused Western culture; it referred to a specific execution at the beginning of a process enveloping millions of people eventually thought of collectively as *Christendom*. The word continues to drive Christian liturgy, meditation, and thought. When Du Bois imagined it in the sacrifice of Sam Hose, impassioned Southern preachers had for generations been proclaiming "Jesus Christ and Him Crucified."

The carpenter from Nazareth, it is written, had been revealed to his disciples as Christ in a blaze of Transfiguration (Christian Bible, KJV: Matt 17:1–8). To traditionalists, he was a dangerous innovator whom they delivered to Roman authorities for execution. To the Romans, he was a dangerous revolutionary who had to be put to death. To Christians, his crucifixion eventually became a sacred drama transcendent to the brutal details of trial, torture, and death. Christ's followers came to believe that he had died to pay the penalty humanity owed God for rebelling against him. As the sacrificial subject came to be understood as divine, his sacrifice had cosmic as well as personal implications for those receiving its benefits. If whites noticed Du Bois' reference at all, therefore, they would have found it offensive or blasphemous. Black criminals, they would have scoffed, were not Christ!

CRUCIFIED?

Du Bois would have expected such an objection. A stunted literalism presented Christ's crucifixion as dogma, yet it was also, Du Bois knew, a lived experience shared by generations of African Americans. Faithful whites came to believe the crucifixion had been the means of their salvation. Christian blacks sensed crucifixion as the engine of oppression and the sign of Christ's suffering with them. For whites, the cross was a positive sign; for blacks, it was ambiguous, a positive sign of God's promise, but a sign, too, of the power of evil. Christian blacks bore the cross in their imaginations because they carried it in their daily lives. Christians among them had sung in sorrow and hope, "Nobody knows the troubles I've seen. Nobody knows but Jesus." Taking on those "troubles" had led Him to the Cross.

> Were you there when they crucified my Lord?
> Oh – sometimes it causes me to tremble, tremble, tremble.
> Were you there when they crucified my Lord?

If the enslaved were *there*, their Lord was *here*! His presence and sacrifice broke the power of white oppression and promised its destruction in the end.[3]

In *The Souls of Black Folk*, Du Bois explained that Christians sang of "death and suffering and unvoiced longing for a truer world" coming through world-shattering acts when the "Trumpet sound[s] the Jubilee." In other words, "death and suffering" afflicted African Americans, but suffering was not their fate; the Trumpet would sound! If striving daily to affirm the self against everything that combined to assault it made life a theodicy, the effort nonetheless guaranteed the promise. Du Bois fully understood the ways in which the moral strength acquired by enslaved Christians could sometimes degenerate into "an infinite capacity for dumb suffering." He also knew that belief in *Christ's* suffering with the enslaved had given Christians among them hope in a hopeless world. For 300 years, Du Bois wrote, "we have called all that was best to throttle and subdue all that was worst; fire and blood, prayer and sacrifice, have billowed over this people, and they have found peace only in the altars of the God of Right."[4] At those altars lay "faith in the ultimate justice of things."

But was that faith warranted? Even after Emancipation, relations between whites and blacks, Du bois knew, had remained toxic. Blacks still faced "conflict, the burning of the body, and rending of [the] soul." In *Souls*, Du Bois moved from moral intensity to empirical data revealing the violence erupting from whites' insistence they were still masters. In exchanges such as that initiated by a reasonable request for wages, the sociologist wrote in reference to Sam Hose, blacks were always at a disadvantage. Worse, the criminal justice system was so thoroughly rigged against them that they had come to believe that every hanging was a crucifixion. The clear implication from within the ethos of the cross was that black innocence was sacrificed to the white man's power even when blacks were actually guilty of a crime.

Du Bois knew relations between the two peoples varied over time and space and he thought a few whites believed the "present drawing of the color line is a flat contradiction to their beliefs and professions." But all too often whites could not distinguish between blacks who shared their values and those who did not, between honest folk at risk through no fault of their own and a criminal class that solved problems with theft, guile, and violence. Whites were all too often obliged by their prejudice to include gifted blacks "and Sam Hose in the same despised class." Du Bois had studied black criminality, and he thought Hose had killed Cranford. Yet he did not back away from explaining the lynching as crucifixion. The mutilation, the burning, the relics, and the celebration were seared into his consciousness.

In 1920 and again in 1940 Du Bois would remember Hose's crucifixion as a revelation; in it the historian had seen "the race-hatred of the whites as I never dreamed of it before – naked and unashamed!"[5] Crucifixion carried the weight of legal oppression, religious arrogance, murderous crowds, and injustice. A few years later, as editor of *The Crisis*, he thought whites were crucifying not only blacks, but also Christ – still again.

In two similar stories, Du Bois imagined Jesus as an attractive and engaging stranger who elicits the interest of both white and black. Children and African American adults immediately recognize him. A butler cries "My Lord and my God!" A white minister thinks he has met him before – he is unsure, but the stranger replies, "I never knew you!" As the stranger converses with blacks, they become healed, but as whites gradually see him as perhaps of mixed race, they are terrified and enraged. When they see him as transcending race they realize he is "black" and – because he has come among them disregarding the rules of "race" – they crucify him. The narrative was simple, but it was not an artifact of "cultural chauvinism" or a rhetorical flourish[6] so much as a deconstruction of whites' religion.

In language familiar to both white and black believers, Du Bois emphasized that Christ comes to faithful blacks as one of them even though his "race" is ambiguous. He is of uncertain color because race is not a category that defines the divine. In the everyday imagination of the faithful he is just "black" enough to be received as Lord. For all too many whites who can feel the attraction of the racially ambiguous stranger, "race" is a category more important than "God." Thus afflicted, when gradually realizing they are confronted with a Presence for which race is not a way to engage other humans, white Christians all too often react violently. Jesus is just "black" enough to be crucified. Whites' failure to see the humanity of all humanity leads to deicide.

That Du Bois wrote in language immersed in religion did not mean he was "religious" or "Christian" or "spiritual." Rather, he understood the power of religion among both the people for whom he wrote and those whom he hoped to sway. He insisted that the teachings of Jesus addressed racial oppression in ways most white believers could not see. Those preachments, Du Bois believed, had helped nurture the collective strength of his people. He may have been agnostic about Heaven, Hell, and the Trinity, but he was not agnostic about the power of Christian narratives to supply insight into the strivings of his people and the nature of violence. He was not agnostic about the Olivet Discourse and what the preacher meant by identifying with the "least of these (Matthew 25:40)." He may have been agnostic about the last judgment as imagined in the Revelation to John of Patmos, but he was not agnostic about the evil that inspired the vision and compelled the judgment. If "God" was at times another name for *Judgment*, he did believe in "God" in his own way.

EXPIATION: FAITH IN TURMOIL

Du Bois was not alone in using language familiar to Christians in thinking about what happened near Newnan. In reporting the event in *The Constitution* the next day, a white newsman mentioned the "terrible expiation which Sam Hose was forced to pay."[7] *Expiation* and *payment* had infused Christian preaching for centuries; expiation concerned "the sinners' guilt and penalty"; the penalty had to fit the crime. The reporter was using language simultaneously sacred and secular, and he probably did not think he was making a "religious" statement when he did so. His words nonetheless reflected the moral sanction of a punitive death according to a sense of ultimate justice. The words transformed lynching from murder into sacrifice as whites insisted that the killing was supposed to accomplish something beyond punishment. Whites' defenses of the lynching fashioned meanings that ignored the stench and ashes of white savagery. The implications were familiar within a culture in which cosmic judgment affected religious discourse, sometimes furiously. God had to pay for the sins imputed to Himself within the mystery of the Trinity.

Expiation rendered to a superior power[8] could very easily shade the ways in which believers and nonbelievers alike responded to a dramatic violation of community values. Suzanne Marshall, for example, found that belief in a vengeful divinity had modeled the harsh penalties by vigilantes against their enemies in the violent Kentucky-Tennessee border-lands of the nineteenth century.[9] Shedding blood was a righteous penalty; blood was a powerful symbol for Christians. At camp meeting revivals in 1899, worshippers did, after all, sing of "pow'r, (pow'r), pow'r, (pow'r) wonderworking pow'r / In the blood (in the blood) of the Lamb." John Crowe Ransom, poet, essayist, and scholar could insist twenty years later that Southern religion must sustain its traditional message of violent denunciation and blood against a namby-pamby liberalism based on forgiveness and love.[10]

The warrant for this belief was clear to those who understood all life's calamities to be somehow "penal." Every hurt and pain betokened "God's displeasure" with human sin. Such guardians of faith as the Reverend Robert Lewis Dabney could be furious with soft-hearted heret-ics who failed to understand that "punishment of every sin is inevitable" and that Christians should share in God's wrath with sin and unbelief. A brilliant, zealous, and angry misogynist, Dabney had his critics, but such rants as his were replicated throughout the South, especially during camp meetings and revivals. It is not surprising that Christians of both races seemed compelled to say – even if many did not believe it – that Sam Hose *deserved* punishment. Men like Dabney had perfected a theology of retributive vengeance,[11] which W. J. Cash remembered as "primitive frenzy and the blood sacrifice."

Frenzy did not always mean blood; it could in some religious settings mean release and celebration. Du Bois recalled being startled by a "pythian madness" he had never before imagined while attending a black Southern worship service for the first time. Instead of the punitive obses-sion that Cash remembered, Du Bois thought such expressions elicited "supernatural joy" and *awe* at the presence of a loving God amid human suffering.[12] This insight contrasted dramatically with that of the old white man who captured the imagination of a reporter as Tom Wilkes became ash. The man was awed by a God of wrath who inflicted human suffering: "Glory," he shouted, "Glory to God!"

Expiation, blood, and punishment were not the only forces driving Southern whites' religion. "Frenzy" could be a transforming experience of having been "saved." If perfectionists and spirit-filled celebrants insisted on a rigorous authenticity, imaginative believers such as Corra Harris could defend themselves by reminding people in disarming seriousness of the precise moment when they received salvation. Corra's moment was "September 17, 1886" when a "mood of augmented excellence" settled on her during a revival. But a feeling of youthful "excellence" could not save her from a religion of vengeance when confronted by her husband's erotic rambling among black women. Responding to those offended by the burning of Sam Hose, Harris exploded at black women who had birthed monsters that menaced "every [white] home in the South."[13] Her fury encourages one to wonder how many white wives, suspicious of their menfolk's contacts with black women, displaced anger with their husbands onto black people. Personal experience with randy husbands could easily validate vengeance whenever the blending of sex, race, violation, and judgment exploded into a sensational event.

Atticus Haygood represented another Christian vision, at least for a while. In *Our Brother in Black* (1880), he denounced the fantasy of Southern innocence and whites' dread of "social equality." He urged whites to confess their sins against blacks in a surge of Christian charity to free them from the "prejudices of the past"[14] but he could not free himself from the prejudices of the present. Returning from his California exile to the solace of Southern piety, Haygood thought African Americans were becoming more dangerous. Disturbed by the savagery of the lynching in Paris, Texas, he, nonetheless, concluded that such an act by Christian people could have resulted only from their having been afflicted by a temporary and justifying insanity. Haygood knew white Southerners were Christians; they were no less moral than Yankees.[15] Both white and black critics attacked him. Ida B. Wells was especially eloquent! She had long attacked the lies of white supremacy, but her "facts" were useless in a culture that encouraged even Christian ministers to believe manhood trumped law and adapted Christian faith to reality.

Reality became especially dangerous, whites believed, when black US troops were stationed in Georgia during the Spanish American War. The "burning of Sam Hose" began long before Tom Wilkes asked for his wages and a brief respite. The event was far more complicated than a simple illegal act of retribution and "justice." It was framed within the context of white anxiety and alarm at anomalous blacks. As the vindicating responses to Hose's immolation revealed, something other than rapists and violated women stirred the minds of Southern patriots. Newnan's guardians, defensive ministers, outraged editors, Governor Candler, former Governor Northen, and the killers of Elijah Strickland all agreed that lynching was a righteous response to "rape and murder." But it was far more than that. The terse excuses for burning Hose were to cow black criminals, threaten educated blacks, and teach blacks their civic duty. The murderers of the Reverend Elijah Strickland meant to terrorize blacks and taunt the "enemy." They pinned a message to the minister's corpse and addressed a "New York" newspaper, emphasizing what Southern men could do despite the censure of Yankee scolds. Strickland's body was an obscene gesture for the minister's killers. It proclaimed that this is what *we* think of *you*!

Such taunts, of course, were foreign to Christian ministers, but many seemed to be confused as to what they should be saying publicly about the burning of Sam Hose. Some, like Dr. Broughton, denounced the violence; others matched Governor Allen Candler's attack on African Americans as a racist people by scolding black leaders to teach their people to behave. Popular religious leaders affected by the stories of sexual danger from blacks simply ignored the actions of savage whites and held African Americans responsible for lynching. Andrew Sledd personified those who could not agree. He believed whites not blacks needed lectures on Christian morality. He was joined by people such as W. W. Landrum, Wilbur Thirkield, John Kilgo, and the women affected by the plight of black women and "The Man with the Hoe." A welcome change of perspective would require white Christians to imagine black people as being wronged by whites generally, as Sledd insisted, and not merely by mobs. Whites thinking about lynching would have to empathize not only with white victims of an imagined rape, but also with the victims of white savagery.

LYNCHING JESUS AND CRUCIFYING SAM HOSE: SACRIFICE

Christians would have to rethink how they understood lynching within the ethos of the Cross. They would have to identify black victims with Christ, whose death within the traditional understanding of atonement satisfied divine justice. Atonement somehow had to be understood within a context of injustice as well as justice, or so argued at least one white minister. Christ had to be understood as suffering with the victims of collective violence because he, too, had been lynched. In 1905, the pastor of the First Presbyterian Church of Newport News, Virginia, Edwin Talliaferro Wellford, made the case in *The Lynching of Jesus.*

The minister did not confront the traditional understanding of atonement directly; rather, he tried to change the emphases associated with it by first calling attention to the lynching of black men throughout the South, which he called a "reign of Terror." He condemned state authorities for contributing to this "disastrous state of affairs." The bloodletting would continue, the minister warned, until Christians understood the similarity between lynching African Americans and lynching Jesus. Like Du Bois, he understood lynching as crucifixion and insisted it could not be justified by any imaginable provocation. Believers had to realize that God was on the side of the victims rather than the victimizers. He implied something far more radical: In the sacrificial drama, God was a victim.

Identifying lynched blacks as "Innocents" struck most Southern whites at the time as outrageous, but the minister did so anyway. He reassured his audience: "The lynching of Jesus excels in brutality and in the slaughter of the innocent, all succeeding offences." But he also wanted readers to understand those "succeeding offences" were criminal, and he entitled his chapter about them "The Slaughter of the Innocents." Wellford transformed Christ's crucifixion from a necessary sacrifice within the metaphysics of *fall-and-redemption* into the greatest crime in human history. By emphasizing the *injustice* of Christ's sacrifice, he was attempting to transfer empathy for the crucified Christ to modern lynch victims. Christ had been lynched by the "insatiate passion of a misguided multitude!" The implication was clear. Blacks were being lynched in the same way! The clergyman ended his lesson by linking the reader with Christ and Christ, in turn, with current "victims of injustice."[16]

No evidence suggests how the clergyman's congregation and audience received his book. He did not spark an anti-lynching crusade, but he may eventually have found some conversations about African Americans among his communicants to be more empathic. Wellford's booklet is an important cultural artifact; it contains a dissenting voice in the Christian conversation about race in the South at the time. By insisting that Christians see the crucifixion as lynching, Wellford had tried to transform the metaphysical mystery of cosmic justice and divine wrath into a moral challenge to Christian discipleship. His essay was radically different from the confused defensiveness of public Christian discourse after the burning of Sam Hose. The minister did not mention manhood or provocation.

Such mischievously imagined tropes could not justify lynching blacks because they could not justify lynching Jesus. Lynching was not about sex but injustice!

W. E. B. Du Bois' reference to a "crucified" Hose had been confirmed in at least one white man's mind. The insight did not change popular discourse dominated by supremacist ideology, but it did appeal to white Christians to think about lynching not as *deserved* but as the functional equivalent of killing God. Du Bois and Wellford captured in the conjoined words, "lynching-and-crucifixion," a way to judge the moral confusion of many Christians and to appreciate the moral clarity of a few others.

Skeptics may point out that much lynching was triggered by anger, fear, or private vengeance lacking community warrant. Other deaths that may be claimed as outside the realm of sacrifice may be the result from mistake or accident. The simple dispatch of a criminal without the "sanction" of ritual may also be said to be absent sacrifice until actors justify what they did according to values shared within the community. Justifying death is a sacrifice to those values, especially if one believes that human life is sacred. Because intentionally committed killings always require justification, which in turn, requires rationalization, it is always important to consider the mental contexts within which they occur. Du Bois' understanding of context included African Americans' experience of oppression and a flawed criminal justice system. Wellford's understanding of context was shaped by his understanding of the Cross; he wanted white Christians to see themselves as the mob.

Critics may insist that reference to Sam Hose's death as a crucifixion was a homiletic device, dramatic hyperbole, or tendentious judgment useless to historical understanding. They may warn that because lynchers did not say they were sacrificing Wilkes, they were not doing so. The rituals of offering, blood, and fire, however, suggest that they did believe they were engaged in a purifying sacrifice even if they could not call it that. Actions shriek when words fail.

In carrying Wilkes back and forth through the center of Newnan the crowd sensed that each intersection was an altar at which something meaningful had to happen. Later, the vanguard cut and mutilated Wilkes before crafting a slow death by fire. Those shouting approval, feeling the heat, and smelling the conversion of a man into ash and relics were sharing in acts of spiritual union. Each act reflected power and dominion. Lynchers lived in a culture that had sent crowds seasonally to religious meetings to feel the ecstasy of being transported beyond themselves within the tradition of the Shout. Members of the crowd in Newnan were also transported beyond themselves. Torture and pain changed the universe at the altar on which they were inflicted; participants transferred attention from what Hose *did* to what they claimed him to *be*. "Glory!" shouted an old man as the fire died, "Glory to God!"

Thirty years later, Walter White, the secretary of the National Association for the Advancement of Colored People (NAACP), reflected on the white religious impulse that ignited such a shout. In *Rope and Faggot*, which was a *Biography of Judge Lynch*, he wrote that white Southerners' religion had created a "particular fanaticism" that led to lynching. When he thought of the "Christian South" he imagined an "insane rage" exploding from an emotional and ignorant people – the same images that arrested Cash. Christian history, White recalled, had been littered with the bodies of Jews, heretics, witches, and Africans. Each belonged to a class that could become sites of all the violence accumulated within the true community and sacrificed because they were alien to it. No people were more alien than Jews, whom Christians slaughtered in the fourteenth century to stop the Black Death. The mechanism that allowed Christ to take on the sins of the world turned Jews into sacrificial victims. Having Jews to blame in the high middle ages modeled having African Americans to blame within the sacred precincts of segregation.[17]

Trudier Harris agreed in a much better analysis in 1984. In *Exorcising Blackness*, she exposed lynching as a scapegoating mechanism analyzed long ago by Sir James Frazer in *The Golden Bough*. The rite in modern America was a way, Harris observed, for whites violently to project "their basest fears and desires onto other groups" and thus elevate themselves above those thus despised. Cutting and burning also purified.[18] Recently, Orlando Patterson also argued the case for sacrifice and the sacred in *Rituals of Blood*, but he believes that only a "minority of lynchings qualify as ritual or sacrificial murder." His view is quite unlike that of Rene Girard, who believed that "there is hardly any form of violence that cannot be described in terms of sacrifice." The acts that Patterson had in mind, however, were those in which large numbers of people were involved, as in the burning of Sam Hose. Patterson developed a model based on the classic study of sacrifice by Henri Hubert and Marcel Mauss. In the torture, blood, pain, drama, solemnity and celebration of each event he, like many others, finds elements of human sacrifice.[19]

Theologian James Cone insists that black writers made the explicit connection between the "lynching tree" and the cross before ministers and scholars did. No one, Cone points out, focused on this theme with more passion and insight than Du Bois, but Du Bois had learned it from listening to his people. And the burning of Sam Hose engraved it on his memory. The idea was so familiar in the 1930s that a group of white savages could mock their black victim with the placard, "King of the Jews." That simple act exposed a shameful reality. Poet Langston Hughes may have dismissed Christ as an "object of black faith" in 1932, as one critic observes, but the Black Christ who had appeared in Hughes' poetry in the 1920s reappeared during the 1950s. At the end of the twentieth century, it still seemed natural for a book about suffering and Christian faith to be covered by the image of a crucified African American. Cone asks Christians to understand the cross and lynching tree as closely "linked to Jesus' spiritual meaning for black and white life together" in America. The two images are "not literally the same – historically or theologically," Cone writes, but he believes that they belong together as Americans engage who they have been, who they are, and who they shall become.[20]

Sam Hose's burning seized W. E. B. Du Bois' attention as a revelation. He had been in Germany studying after having graduated from Harvard when Henry Smith was burned alive in 1893. He was much closer in time and space to the atrocity in Newnan in 1899. He learned of it through a rumor coupling the burning with Atlantans' celebration of the cutting and the torture only thirty-five miles away. Whites had chanted, "nigger" as he and his wife followed their child's coffin to the train that would take him to "freedom." "Crucified!" The word came naturally to him in writing about the impact of the burning in the fall of 1899. And he carried this awareness into his essays on *The Souls of Black Folk*.

He began an essay on the "Dawn of Freedom" with poet James Russell Lowell's reflections on the power of the crucifixion. Lowell had conceded that Truth was ever on "the scaffold" and "Wrong forever on the Throne." Yet – as Christian history had demonstrated, Lowell believed, "that scaffold sways the future." Du Bois noted that blacks had been sacrificed on "the altar of national integrity" in their "swaddling clothes" of citizenship when the nation valued reconciliation with the South more highly than the rights of black people. If God were "keeping watch above His own," as Lowell had written, however, "His own" were neither passive nor helpless. No Americans had believed more fervently than they in equality, liberty, and justice; none had striven more consistently to achieve them. "Someday the Awakening will come," he wrote, and we "shall sweep irresistibly toward the Goal, out of the Valley of the Shadow of Death." As for white Americans, he appealed to a "headstrong, careless people to despise not Justice, Mercy, and Truth, lest the nation be smitten with a curse."[21]

These words came much later. In the wake of the burning, it was difficult to imagine that the "Awakening" would come. But even after the fire had died, the smoke had cleared, and Tom Wilkes had disappeared in ash, relics, and smoke, African Americans in the area surrounding Newnan had discovered something that symbolized their grit and determination. Sam Hose had kept his Voice; the act profoundly offended whites and especially their clergy. He had transcended white viciousness; he had borne witness to the resolve of his people to endure. Offended whites had been outraged that blacks could see his silence and transcendence as martyrdom. A few white observers, enveloped in the stench of death, had even seen his silence and grit as courage; one even said as much for public consumption. Faced with obliteration, he defied white terror.

Black defiance, whites believed, was dangerous enough to justify violence. That is what whites thought they faced from Palmetto to Macon to Griffin to Newnan in the spring of 1899. In response, whites demanded victims! A popular cliché of liberal sympathy, when it comes to evaluating the role of poverty and desperation in producing criminals, insists that critics of the poor and desperate "blame the victim." This is supposed to be a demystifying insight, but it is not sufficient. Victims are created as a class so they may in fact be blamed; that is what victims are for[22]; that is why blacks fought against treatment as victims. That is why Tom Wilkes shrieked in *silence*. If, in the sanctity of segregation, whites made a class available for sacrifice, Du Bois pointed out that that class was striving motivated by their own conception of sacrifice to claim justice. They refused to be victims. Perhaps they were consigned to the scaffold by white supremacy for the present, but DuBois believed that James Russell Lowell was right, that that scaffold swayed the future. This conviction was not a plan; it was the determination to emerge victorious from the "whirl and chaos of things" to make America *America* as it pretended to be.[23]

REMEMBERING SAM HOSE: THEN AND NOW

Such a vision, of course, was beyond the imagination of most Americans in 1899. The "whirl and chaos of things," as far as white Southerners were concerned, erupted from the acts of unruly blacks whom white crowds continued to kill with impunity. The burning near Newnan sobered a few community leaders, to be sure, but criticizing what happened there continued to arouse the fury of Georgians. Andrew Sledd learned that lesson three years later. Flawed though his criticism was, it was inaccessible even to "progressives" who continued to believe that violence against blacks resulted from a "Negro problem."

The Reverend Edgar Gardner Murphy certainly believed as much. The Episcopal priest had been profoundly troubled by Sam Hose's fate. The savagery of whites had shocked him, but the "problem" he imagined was not white; it was a "Negro problem." As a result, he convinced friends and associates to invite a few prominent white men conversant with the "Negro problem" to Montgomery, Alabama, to discuss the issue in a public meeting. He told a Northern audience that Southerners could solve their problems if Yankees stopped fussing about social equality and African American voting. He ignored the fact that Southerners could not stop fussing about such things, which they had fashioned into the symbols of pollution and danger. He complained that educated blacks had offended whites and that black ministers claimed lynching black criminals had martyred them. Too many blacks had a bad attitude. He did concede, however, that it was difficult for African Americans to receive justice in the South. The problem was that juries were made up of "unthinking" elements.

When "thinking" elements arrived in Montgomery, however, they didn't do any better. To be sure, a former Federal official argued white "savagery" could not "save our civilization," but he understood why lynching occurred and thus endorsed it. Somehow white "savagery" had become a "Negro Problem." Courts did not meet often enough, the orator said; worse, "the Negro" was not civilized enough. Such a statement merely repeated what lynching partisans had been saying *pro forma* for years. Most speakers in Montgomery who thought to mention mob violence at all said much the same thing. The primary target of public discussion at the meeting, however, was not white violence but African American voting. The consensus was that blacks shouldn't do it. If they insisted – announced one of the chief plotters of the 1898 Wilmington, North Carolina, massacre – he had the solution. The violence he had led was the appropriate model of white policy.

One of the few speakers to honor black people was the Very Reverend J. R. Slattery of the Roman Catholic St. Joseph's Seminary of Baltimore, who had criticized Atticus Haygood in 1893 for blaming lynching on the "moral insanity" of good people. African Americans who attended the meeting were not scheduled to speak because its sponsors believed they had nothing to say that whites wanted to hear. They were the problem. They would have offended whites. Murphy and his people thought whites had to solve the "Negro problem," which was of course what lynch mobs claimed to be doing. The organizers wanted harmony; they settled for cliché, platitude, banality, and self-righteousness.

The Montgomery meeting was important to Murphy, who went on to devote his life to Southern progress. He thought the event was a success. Booker T. Washington tepidly praised Murphy's motives, adding, no doubt with a whiff of sarcasm, that a public exchange on race by enemies as well as friends of black people was to be valued. The New England press criticized Southern whites' commitment to denying blacks' civil rights.[24]

The conference enhanced Gardner's reputation among white Southerners as a progressive but it was a monumentally irrelevant response to the burning of Sam Hose. Participants ignored the attack on the constitutional right of "due process," the carnival of violence, the fire. They ignored the black people in attendance; most – not all – personified white supremacy. "The Negro" wanted too much to suit Southern whites – equity, respect, education, amity, and citizenship. Father Slattery had said as much when criticizing Haygood years earlier. Whites saw danger in such desire, as Louis Le Vin discovered after interviewing whites in the Newnan area. There, the killers of Tom Wilkes insisted that they had responded appropriately to rape and homicide as well as to blacks' insolence, education, and alliance with Northern "niggers."[25]

Tom Wilkes was not highly educated or insolent and knew no Northern blacks; he found it difficult to look white men in the eye and speak to them. Ritually killed, he became a "scapegoat" who represented all young insolent, unhappy, and dangerous black men: members of the mob said so. Before Hose disappeared into the mythology of black criminality and provocation, he continued to bob-up now and then in white Southern discourse. His sacrifice suggested to the famed Southern writer Thomas Nelson Page that authorities should legalize burning at the stake. Another writer thought his being burned by "church going people" was a natural and therefore moral result of living in a biracial society. A Northern sociologist knew his readers would recognize Sam Hose when in 1907 he used his lynching as an example of misplaced punishment better applied to railroad magnates. In 1908 Hose still personified the "Negro problem" in Alfred Stone's *Studies in the American Race Problem*.[26]

For many Georgia whites, lynching remained the default position for punishing serious crimes by African Americans. Even the horrendous Atlanta Race Riot of 1906 could not change the culture. That violence did, however, affect former Governor William J. Northen. In response, the man who defended the burning of Sam Hose to the people of Boston in May of 1899 tried, in 1906 and 1907, to organize an anti-lynching campaign. He approached associates who shared his religious enthusiasm and faith in business as a guarantor of progress to help him stop the violence. He toured ninety counties to organize law-and-order "legions" of religious, civic, business, and professional elites. He "modeled his vision of elite leadership," David Godshalk writes in a definitive article, "on the patriarch's role as guardian of his wife's and daughters' sexual purity." Northen failed. The "legions of honor" sank into the quicksand of white supremacy. Christian ministers failed to enlist; they insisted that prohibition would stop mob violence. There was no need to join a crusade explicitly against lynching.[27] If the horror of the 1906 riots could not shame whites into action against lynching, the savagery of burning one man to death could change very little.

African Americans remembered the lynching as one event in a long history of savagery. Ida Wells-Barnett had stoked blacks' memories with the findings of Louis Le Vin and dispatched thousands of anti-lynching circulars as a result. Pamphleteer Irenas Palmer explained American history as the *Black Man's Burden* that led inexorably through slavery, civil war, and white violence to a white Georgian's decision to "defraud" a "colored man out of his wages" and to kill him when he complained. Palmer prayed for the rule of law lest the world conclude that the US government could not protect its citizens. For Mary Church Terrell, Sam Hose's fate had been the natural result of a society ruled by men who inherited values grounded in the "brutalizing effect of slavery." Southern leaders had confirmed such ethics in segregation, disfranchisement, and peonage; they secured the ethic by violence.

Terrell, an activist from the African American elite, told readers of the *North American Review* that the "best people" of the South were responsible for the things that shocked civilized people. "The great concourse of Christians who had witnessed the tragedy" and scavenged for relics had been promised a burning many days before it happened. Those who insisted on purging their world of evil by fire were encouraged by newsmen who were the "best citizens" of Atlanta. Because the "best people" controlled due process, it seemed illogical to encourage lynching, but Terrell knew logic would not prevail against the "rising tide of barbarism." The tide was a force so natural to the region that Christians there were overwhelmed by it and the US government was powerless to stop it.[28] Terrell's analysis represented the view of highly educated, relatively affluent, and activist African Americans. Sam Hose's fate, Terrell insisted, was not an astonishing example of Southern culture, but a commonplace one. For Du Bois it was nonetheless shocking. He remembered the event as a revelatory moment for well over fifty years. He didn't always remember the details of what had happened, but he could not forget the message.

In 1900 in New Orleans, Robert Charles remembered the burning of Sam Hose, too; he was in fact fixated on its message. Charles' fury led to what should have been a minor exchange shortly after eleven o'clock on the hot and muggy evening of Monday, July 23, 1900. A white policeman approached Charles and a friend at 2815 Dryades Street. There was a problem, August Mora believed: Charles and Lenard Pierce were black and they were sitting on a white family's stoop. Mora asked why the men were there and didn't like the answer. Charles got up, Mora brandished his pistol and fired at the black man, who shot Mora in the thigh and fled. Discovered at home after dressing his own wound, Charles killed two police officers. By 7:00 a.m. the next day, most New Orleans policemen had surrounded his rooming house, but he wasn't there and crowds were beginning to gather.

Racial tensions might have birthed a riot sometime that summer absent Charles' exploits, but they erupted now. News of the killings spread quickly among New Orleans blacks, many of whom applauded what Charles had done. In response, the police began to arrest anyone noticeably pleased with the killings and this action encouraged white gangs to begin attacking both blacks and those whites who tried to protect them. Newsmen claimed "hundreds of negroes" had known Charles was a "dangerous agitator" who hated whites, a charge that transformed all Crescent City African Americans into prey.

The police were now charged with the twin tasks of stopping a riot and arresting Charles. Late Friday afternoon they found him. Five thousand people arrived at the site to watch while Charles killed two more policemen and a white civilian. Finally, he was cut down and his body riddled with bullets. Hundreds of whites later paraded through the municipal morgue to view his tattered body. Property-owning blacks were relieved that his death would prevent further rioting; many others were dismayed that Charles had killed only four policemen. Soon they were gathering to sing "the Robert Charles song" and praise the man. A famous New Orleans musician later recalled that the song-fest had been brief. Safety demanded it.[29]

Charles' exchanges with peace officers before arriving in Louisiana had already prompted his animosity toward whites. The cutting and burning of Sam Hose, however, depressed him to the point of imagining a violent response. He carried a .32 caliber revolver and owned a Winchester rifle, but instead of using those weapons, he opted at first for something less perilous. He wrote to Bishop Henry McNeal Turner of Atlanta requesting appointment as an agent for the *Voice of Missions*, Turner's monthly magazine. The bishop's tone and ideas captured Charles' imagination and he began delivering the publication and creating a network of contacts interested in leaving the US for Africa. This was a modest achievement but one nonetheless positive as a service to his people. He was of course angry; he carried a speech encouraging those opposing Conservative rule to "*oil up their Winchesters* and prepare for a fight." The obsession with Hose had diminished, but then a little over a year after the burning, as he was resting on a stoop, he was shot by a policemen. Charles erupted. He was not alone when he and his friend were challenged by three policemen; Bishop Turner and Sam Hose were there, too.

If Sam Hose was a name conjuring the "Negro problem" for whites in Newnan, Montgomery, and Atlanta, his was also a name eliciting black fury. The name exposed white savagery, encouraged blacks' solidarity, and drove some African Americans to think in a burst of resentment: "No More!" The savagery that claimed Sam Hose did not, to be sure, specifically cause the New Orleans riots; it did not force Robert Charles to shoot August Mora; it did not inspire the "Robert Charles song," but it did provide a name to the remarkably long list of savaged blacks. Names can be potent. They can elicit feelings far removed from their source but rich in meaning: John Wilkes Booth, Lee Harvey Oswald, Sirhan Sirhan, James Earl Ray, Emmett Till, Michael Brown, Tamir Rice, Trayvon Martin. For Charles, the name was "Sam Hose."

The name and the burning became well-known for a short while at the beginning of the twentieth century until other names were added to the list to eclipse his. Rebecca Felton, Andrew Sledd, W. E. B. Du Bois, and Robert Charles remembered the name differently. Corra Harris probably forgot it, but she became a minor figure in popular American fiction and culture because the name had signified interracial coupling. Sex and race have been dangerous enough within American culture when kept separate, but when fused in hysterical accusation and public discourse they have been absolutely catastrophic for safety, reason, and common sense. Felton, newsmen, and the Cranford family knew how to enlist that fusion in service to vengeance and white supremacy.

Historians have not forgotten Tom Wilkes' pseudonym. Joel Williamson joined William Ivy Hair in linking Hose to Robert Charles. Fitzhugh Brundage described how whites transformed a day laborer into "a ravenous beast undeserving of human sympathy," and Leon Litwack did the same in his monumental study of black Southerners in the age of Jim Crow. In his brief account of white Americans' enacting "Popular Justice," Michael Berg points out that spectacular lynchings, such as the one suffered by Sam Hose, were meant to emphasize that there were *no limits* to what whites would do to blacks. The best study of spectacle lynching is Amy Louise Wood's book, but as an exposure of America's love affair with violence and condign punishment it is far more than that. Americans love spectacle and violence. Grace Elizabeth Hale discussed the burning of Sam Hose in the context of "deadly amusement."

The burning was memorable enough for Philip Dray to begin his comprehensive book on "the lynching of Black America" by describing it at some length. He believed that Hose may have committed "some kind of sexual assault," an ambiguous phrase appropriate to the event. If a black man inadvertently touched a white woman or even gazed at her in some venues and times, the act qualified as "sexual assault." In the emotional whirlwind of Alfred's death the Cranford family knew Truth not as a dispassionate report, but homicide, violation, torture, and fire. Mary Louise Ellis ended her dissertation on the lynching in 1992 by observing that it "was not about the truth" but rather about the "Ultimate Southern Truth": white supremacy.[30]

In 2009 Edwin T. Arnold explained the lynching of Sam Hose and the "cultural memory" flowing from it. Arnold claims not to examine the "practice of lynching," but his study is nonetheless a significant contribution to precisely that end. He tells stories with a careful attention to individuals involved, their context, and details grounded in the area from Palmetto to Griffin. He corrects errors, uncovers bias, and chides postures he claims violate scholarly standards. He discusses the differing stories of what happened to Mattie Cranford and how difficult it is to translate them into history. Memory is shaped by ideology, experience, value, and identity. Memory of traumatic experience is shaped by pain, loss, and fear; none of these matters ensures accuracy. Memory, as Arnold points out, is "magical," and the same should be said of newspaper accounts in the spring of 1899.

In the early twenty-first century, however, local whites, Arnold points out, believe the stories about the lynching as told in *The Constitution* and the *Atlanta Journal*. They focus on the Cranford family and what happened to Mattie; they do not probe white violence. Those stories, however, were challenged by a group of activists who had recently memorialized innocents lynched in 1946 at Moore's Bridge near Monroe, Georgia. They wanted to raise a monument in Newnan to victims of lynching throughout the state and they wanted to include "Sam Hose." Venerating an alleged rapist, however, was not an easy sell. A member of the Cranford family sensibly doubted "barbarous acts of a lynch mob" could be made more atrocious by insisting its subject was "innocent." Resulting public exchanges in Newnan about memory, race, and lynching led to a series of lectures, discussions, and newspaper articles as well as an essay contest on "racial Justice and Reconciliation." There is no monument. A few Newnanites feared Arnold's book would stigmatize the community; one feared it would become a "racial story," when it wasn't "that simple." Arnold points out, however, that in all its complexity, it was, nonetheless, "a racial story."[31]

That story, Walter Willcox of Cornell had insisted, was divided into two: one "black" and one "white." Arnold agrees that one set of stories was sympathetic to Hose and one was sympathetic to the Cranford family and white Newnan. The "Negro" story, sketched by Louis Le Vin, he writes, shapes the flawed and inaccurate accounts of "revisionist historians" who get details wrong and ignore "individual or community motives, however misguided, other than the basest desire for revenge, punishment, and carnival horrors." Arnold resists joining revisionists, but he cannot show how "individual or community motives" led to anything other than the "horrors" historians exposed. He is understandably annoyed that Grace Hale transformed Mattie Cranford – who lay prostrate on the edge of consciousness – into a "vengeful, manipulative" liar. As a literary scholar, Arnold is at his best when following Hose's "ghost" beyond the New Orleans riots into Southern fiction. He discusses Erskine Caldwell, William Faulkner, Thomas Dixon, and Margaret Mitchell.

Arnold's familiarity with Southern culture, however, also leads him into unexpected twists, as when he recalls W. E. B. Du Bois' response to the display of knuckles in Atlanta. He faults Du Bois for failing to understand that the knuckles were actually those of pigs, which butchers had displayed as those of Sam Hose as an "advertising gimmick."[32] Du Bois did not get the joke.

Hawking food as if seasoned by human remains, however, suggests something beyond humor even if white butchers laughed. That the burning of a human being should qualify as the source of humor in a sales-pitch suggests why William Northen failed to recruit white Georgians for his anti-lynching crusade. Blacks understood white humor; they knew who was laughing; they knew why. Atlanta grocers thought "pigs' knuckles" and sales. Du Bois thought crucifixion and sacrifice. The difference between "knuckles" and "sacrifice" is beyond reckoning. The two images exist in different dimensions, but they were both meaningful in April of 1899. The event that made "knuckles" significant was not the butchery of pigs but of a human being; they represented not the market but vengeance and sacrifice. Why would anyone laugh?

The immolation of Sam Hose changed very little. US Representative George Henry White of North Carolina, the only African American in Congress, introduced a bill in January 1900 to make lynching a federal crime; it was referred to committee and vanished. In 2005, the US Senate apologized for failing to pass such legislation and offered sympathy to victims' descendants, but took no action to redress the lasting effects of supremacist culture that had nourished lynching. As for Newnan, silence and suppression settled on the town; Jessica Ruckheim found African Americans in Newnan who remembered slavery through their grandparents' stories, but who never apparently volunteered anything about the lynching.[33] The conversations initiated by the attempt to memorialize Hose in 2007 may have stirred some citizens to think of things they'd rather have ignored, but it was easier to believe the past was "complicated." A grandchild of someone living in Newnan when the burning happened could have "remembered" emotions incited by the event and shared them within the family but not with anyone outside it.

The generation of Newnan's citizens born in the 1890s included at least one woman who helped organize the Association of Southern Women for the Prevention of Lynching (ASWPL). Mrs. W. A. Turner, who lived on Greenville Street with her physician husband, worshiped in the Presbyterian Church. She was active in projects backed by the General Federation of Women's Clubs before joining the ASWPL executive committee.[34] The ASWPL was successor to the Interracial Women's Committee that Carrie Parks Johnson chaired for the Commission on Inter-Racial Cooperation (CIC). The Committee morphed into the ASWPL under the leadership of Jessie Daniel Ames in 1930. At the founding conference, Will Alexander of the CIC confessed his distress that someone such as he, raised within the hothouse of Southern piety, had never been alerted to the evil of lynching. The women now met to fill that void: They proposed to displace the supremacist-authorized narrative of lynching. They told politicians to stop using "race as a political bludgeon"; they denounced the lie that "lynchings are for protecting women." They shared Alexander's shame.

Newnan's Turner pointed out that framing an agenda would help people understand the difficulties they faced and guide them to their goal. The women agreed that they would have to work with local law enforcement to prevent lynching, and they had to speak out because silence had endorsed the mob. Having learned to act through lobbying within their respective religious communities, they could be imagined as acting as "Christians," but they acted because Christians before them had failed and most of them still did. They had failed to challenge the most obvious evil festering in the culture of white supremacy.[35] Association women did not necessarily oppose segregation, but they were nevertheless different. They hoped to belie the ideological props of white supremacy. Whereas Edgar Gardiner Murphy and his convention, like slaveholders, wanted blacks to behave, Association women like Mrs. Turner wanted *whites* to behave. They learned soon enough, of course, that the past and failure cast lingering and sinister shadows.

AT THE ALTAR

Hose's killing was one among thousands of similar incidents in the United States. It was savage and without the sanction of law or the ethics of any religious community nestled within American culture. It was nonetheless a dramatic instance of a long American tradition of populist violence and racial contempt. When W. E. B. Du Bois pointed out that African Americans viewed even legal killings by whites as "crucifixions," he knew his people understood killing within a religious ethos. When Walter White of the National Association for the Advancement of Colored People wondered in 1929 how whites, in their most spectacular lynchings, could do what they did to blacks, he condemned a "Christian South" immersed in a religiosity of race and rage. Will Alexander of the CIC objected to this comment before conceding in the same breath that White had told the truth. Alexander was profoundly ashamed. Whites before him had condemned lynching and then succumbed to the fantasies of female vulnerability, black criminality, and manly duty. Whites like Corra Harris could cower before the "savage fury" that destroyed black men but imagine it as just vengeance for the hurt done to themselves. Logic was irrelevant.

Christians like Atticus Haygood condemned lynching but could surrender their opposition briefly and without shame when *provocation* inflicted a momentary insanity. The excuse confirmed the justice and therefore the "sanity" of torture, mutilation, and fire. This comment may be offensive, but five years after Hose's burning, white Methodists in Statesboro, Georgia, could not agree that a recent lynching was "un-Christian." After the minister expelled two men for participating in populist violence, twenty-five members left with them.[36] The issue was beginning to disturb various locales, to be sure, but lynching was still "Christian" for many of the faithful in 1904. Corra Harris' essays condemning black mothers came from a woman who had married a preacher, taught Sunday school, and would find fame by writing about the religion of ordinary [white] folk. An outspoken Christian woman such as Rebecca Felton defended lynching eloquently, and blacks understood it as crucifixion. The "burning of Sam Hose" was immersed in religion.

On reflection, the burning seemed to have been enacted on a sacrificial altar with such intensity that it was disturbing that anyone curious about Southern religious culture should have ignored it. White Christians had crafted the institutions of oppression while offering the hope of a blessed life to the enslaved *after* the one they now endured. To most evangelical whites, sin and imputed guilt had been defeated when God entered history through a sacrificial death that set the Universe aright for believers. Salvation had been "purchased" in blood: "In the cross of Christ I glory, Tow'ring o'er the wrecks of time." Salvation had already happened, but black Christians knew better.

The cross was raised not only nineteen centuries ago on Golgotha, but near Palmetto and Newnan in 1899. The Cross was existentially contemporary. "Were you there when they nailed him to the tree?" was not only a question about the past; it was also a promise for the future. Accept his sacrifice as he accepts yours and follow him to victory! Evil had yet to be overcome; the chosen had yet to escape Egypt; the captives still waited to be freed; Christ still had to come again. He would vindicate them: "King Jesus rides on a milk-white horse; no man can hinder Him." Du Bois knew blacks awaited the trumpet; Gabriel asks, "How loud must I blow it?"

Two different Christianities flowed from the Pentecost of evangelical imagination and white supremacy. White Christianity had merged with slavery, violence, segregation, and the Lost Cause to create a syncretic blending of white dominion and salvation. The fusion of purity and danger, which Lillian Smith exposed, sustained belief in the threat to civil society from African Americans. While Tom Wilkes was being tracked in a long and well-publicized hunt, newsmen and vigilantes schooled the public in the nature of that threat. They claimed that the African American community harbored criminals, planned reprisals, and protected rapists. White men punished the fugitive for a specific crime, to be sure, but publicists and politicians explained that the crime was vastly more evil than rape and homicide. The violence in Alfred Cranford's back yard became desecration of white perfection and thus represented an attack on all white people. Punishment therefore had to represent the ultimate in white power.

In his transformation from fugitive to sacrifice, Tom Wilkes was lost. Sam Hose remained: a symbol of threat and danger for whites, and a symbol of white savagery and martyrdom for Du Bois and blacks such as Robert Charles. African Americans' claim – or insight – profoundly offended whites because it seemed to make Hose innocent, but "martyr" means "witness." In failing to yield to his pain and white contempt and in keeping his voice, Wilkes had *belied* the justice of his fate and the legitimacy of white dominion. He bore witness to the evil done him. He had borne witness to how blacks endured life in a white world – through courage, defiance, and transcendence. That witness Du Bois understood as crucifixion, which led him eventually to imagine a Black Christ lynched by whites when they beheld his true nature. A white minister tried to impress on his people that in lynching blacks, whites were committing deicide. The idea was lost among whites but not African Americans.

The religion of white Southerners did not cause them to join mobs similar to that before Pontius Pilate but it did not prevent them either. The reticence of white ministers other than the likes of Wilbur Thirkield, W. W. Landrum, and Andrew Sledd to condemn and to rally their people against illegal white collective violence was, as Will Alexander confessed, shameful. A religious aura permeated communal lynching because the act occurred within the context of a sacred order designed to sustain holiness. Holiness demands purity and purity was sustained in the segregated South by avoidance, margins, distances, aloofness, strict classification, and racial contempt. The logic and holiness of segregation was the logic of white supremacy and was sustained by the lessons Lillian Smith had learned as a child about the purity of being white. A religion that could imagine the death of God as just in its most extreme forms could not raise serious objections to the justice of terrible punishment for terrible crimes. Sam Jones – who demanded in revivals throughout the South that men "quit their meanness" and be manly Christians – personified the failure of his brand of evangelical Christianity to engage racial contempt or even the most dramatic forms of the violence that erupted from it. Christian whites were more comfortable thinking about a "Negro problem" than a white one.

Popular Southern Christianity was not fertile ground for self-critical thinking about race, white supremacy, or lynching. The same could be written for the religions of the entire nation. The religious who presumably believed lying was sinful believed the lies of white supremacy because supremacists had enlisted them in their cause. Popular Christianity lent its rectitude to those who claimed that a pervasive black criminality and a dangerous sexually aggressive generation of young black men threatened white civilization. The symposium printed on the day whites burned Sam Hose represented the best that "informed" public critics could do. If most participants opposed lynching, they, nonetheless, embraced the lie about white vulnerability and black hostility that supremacists such as Rebecca Felton preached.

Religion, however, was not absent when the crowd burned Tom Wilkes. Participants lived it; they enacted it; they shouted it. The burning was not merely a spectacular punishment; it was a sacrifice. Wilkes was *not* Christ, but his burning as Sam Hose was supposed to resolve matters far beyond homicide and rape: black equality, black autonomy, or black defiance. The torture and the fire were a shocking revelation to anyone who would see evil – that is, reality – in breathtaking clarity. Religion and lynching had melded on the altars of a savage faith drenched in blood and consumed by fire.

Glory!

Notes

Introduction

1 Brian K. Smith, "Capital Punishment and Human Sacrifice," *Journal of the American Academy of Religion*, 68 (March 2000): 3–25; Robert Jay Lifton and Greg Mitchell, *Who Owns Death? Capital Punishment, the American Conscience, and the End of Executions* (New York: HarperCollins Publishers, 2000, 2002), 230.

2 See Gail Bederman, *Manliness and Civilization: A Cultural History of Gender and Race in the United States, 1880–1917* (Chicago: University of Chicago Press, 1993), 1–44.

3 Daniel F. Littlefield, *Seminole Burning: A Story of Racial Vengeance* (Jackson: University Press of Mississippi, 1996), 4–7.

4 Thank you David Ball, Leslie Banner, Sylvia Hoffert, Katie Lofton, and Betsy.

5 Donald G. Mathews, "Crucifixion—Faith in the Christian South," in *Autobiographical Reflections on Southern Religious History*, ed. John B. Boles (Athens: University of Georgia Press, 2001).

6 The Wesleyan Methodist Church split from the Methodist Episcopal Church in the early 1840s on two grounds. To be a Wesleyan Methodist was to be opposed to slavery and committed to achieving "Christian Perfection." My grandfather's father was a Wesleyan. See: Donald G. Mathews, "Orange Scott: the Methodist Evangelist as Revolutionary" in *The Antislavery Vanguard: New Essays on the Abolitionists* (Princeton: Princeton University Press, 1965), 71–101.

7 Scholars of lynching point out that, according to definition, one may not survive a lynching. The mob, however, that beat my father's father had tried to kill him. Robert W. Thurston defines lynching in this way: "[In] essence the word means that a group, acting with a [professed] goal of service to the public, puts someone to death outside the bounds of the law. How death is delivered does not matter." See Robert W. Thurston, *Lynching:American Mob Murder in Global Perspective* (Burlington, VT: Ashgate Publishing Company, 2001, © by Robert W. Thurston.): 1. Also Christopher Waldrep, "War of Words: The Controversy over the Definition of Lynching, 1899–1940," *The Journal of*

Southern History, 66 (February 2000): 75–100; Waldrep, *The Many Faces of Judge Lynch: Extralegal Violence and Punishment in America* (New York: Palgrave Macmillan, 2002).

8 Students interviewing African Americans in Mississippi found that knowledge of lynching *as a fact of life* was widespread and personal. Kim Lacy Rogers, *Life and Death in the Delta: African American Narratives of Violence, Resilience, and Social Change* (New York: Palgrave Macmillan, 2006), 24–25: "Almost all of the narrators interviewed by Delta Project staff had heard stories of lynchings or even recalled lynching stories from their own families." The great number of studies of lynching over the past twenty years suggests this memory is extensive. See footnotes to discussions of lynching in *Journal of American History*, 101 (December 2014): 832–860. See also Kidada E. Williams, *They Left Great Marks on Me: African American Testimonies of Racial Violence from Emancipation to World War I* (New York: New York University Press, 2012). See Barbara Whitmer, *The Violence Mythos* (Albany: State University of New York Press, 1997), 186–188 on how trauma is transferred from generation to generation.

9 Gustaf Aulen, *Christus Victor: An Historical Study of the Three Main Types of the Idea of Atonement* (New York: Macmillan and Company, 1951).

10 Anthony W. Bartlett, *Cross Purposes: The Violent Grammar of Christian Atonement* (Harrisburg: Trinity Press International, 2001), 75. Bartlett calls Anselm's work a "Master-Text of Divine Violence." See also Timothy Gorringe, *God's Just Vengeance: Crime, Violence and the Rhetoric of Salvation* (Cambridge: Cambridge University Press, 1996).

11 The "pogroms" were known as Whitecapping; see William F. Holmes, "Whitecapping: Agrarian Violence in Mississippi, 1902–1906," *Journal of Southern History*, 35 (May 1962): 165–185; Holmes, "Moonshining and Collective Violence: Georgia 1889–1895," *Journal of American History*, 67 (December 1980): 589–611.

12 The phrase is famously that of Paul Tillich, whose theology is explained in David H. Kelsey's *The Fabric of Paul Tillich's Theology* (New Haven: Yale University Press, 1967). Kelsey explains the content of the "biblical picture of Jesus as Christ" and revelation. Revelation, Kelsey quotes Tillich, "is a manifestation of what concerns us ultimately" and this ultimate concern "determines our being or not-being." The "manifestation" of being is not information but "the ecstatic manifestation of the Ground of Being in events, persons, and things." These have "shaking, transforming and *healing power*." Those who privilege race in conceiving the self, receive it as the "healing power" of their "being": that is, they privilege race above Christ. They "sacrifice" in the name of what they value most in their being, i.e., race. See pages 25–32, especially page 26.

13 James S. Hirsch, *Riot and Remembrance: The Tulsa Race War and its Legacy* (Boston: Houghton Mifflin Company, 2002).

14 See Paul W. Kahn, *Out of Eden: Adam, and Eve and the Problem of Evil* (Princeton: Princeton University Press, 2007), 116, 118, 128, 134–135, 138–142. On page 129, Kahn writes: "The evil person cannot live with the acknowledgment of his own death that lies implicit in the recognition of the

other as a subject. His response to this is murderous. His actions are guided by a Ptolemaic psychology that places his own self at the center of the universe." He does not imagine "himself as an object" and thus cannot "imagine his own death."

15 Mrs. L. H. Harris, "A Southern Woman's View," *The Independent* (May 18, 1899): 1354–1355.

16 Wilbur J. Cash, *The Mind of the South* (New York: Random House [Vintage Books], 1969), 58; Donald G. Mathews, "'We Have Left Undone Those Things Which We Ought to Have Done': Southern Religious History in Retrospect and Prospect," *Church History*, (June 1998): 19.

17 Charles Reagan *Wilson, Baptized in Blood: The Religion of the Lost Cause 1865–1920* (Athens: University of Georgia Press, 1980).

18 W[illiam] Fitzhugh Brundage, *Lynching in the New South: Georgia and Virginia 1880–1930* (Urbana: University of Illinois Press, 1993); Jacquelyn Dowd Hall, *Revolt against Chivalry: Jessie Daniel Ames and the Women's Campaign Against Lynching* (New York: Columbia University Press, 1979); Timothy Gorringe, *God's Just Vengeance: Crime, Violence and the Rhetoric of Salvation* (Cambridge: Cambridge University Press, 1996).

Chapter 1

1 Jacqueline Goldsby, *A Spectacular Secret: Lynching in American Life and Literature* (Chicago: University of Chicago Press, 2006), 12–42.

2 Edward L. Ayers, *The Promise of the New South: Life after Reconstruction* (New York: Oxford University Press, 1992), 153–159; W[illiam] Fitzhugh Brundage, *Lynching in the New South: Georgia and Virginia 1880–1930* (Urbana: University of Illinois Press), 41–48, 49–85; Jacquelyn Dowd Hall, *Revolt against Chivalry: Jessie Daniel Ames and the Women's Campaign Against Lynching* (New York: Columbia University Press, 1979), 141, 147–49; Paula J. Giddings, *Ida: A Sword Among Lions, Ida B. Wells and the Campaign Against Lynching* (New York: Amistad, HarperCollins Publishers, 2008), 207–208; Martha Hodes, *White Women, Black Men: Ilicit Sex in the 19th century South* (New Haven: Yale University Press, 1997), 154, 187–190; Glenda Elizabeth Gilmore, *Gender and Jim Crow: Women and the Politics of White Supremacy in North Carolina, 1896–1920* (Chapel Hill: UNC Press, 1996), 85; Neil R. McMillen, *Dark Journey: Black Mississippians in the Age of Jim Crow* (Urbana: University of Illinois Press, 1989), 14–19, 224–253; Diane Miller Sommerville, *Rape and Race in the Nineteenth Century South* (Chapel Hill: University of North Carolina Press, 2004), 165–69, 173; Joel R. Williamson, *The Crucible of Race:Black-White Relations in the American South Since Emancipation* (New York: Oxford University Press, 1984); Daniel W. Stowell, "'We Have Sinned, and God Has Smitten Us!' John H. Caldwell and the Religious Meaning of Confederate Defeat," *Georgia Historical Quarterly*, 78 (Spring 1994): 1–32.

3 The quotation is from Elizabeth Fox-Genovese and Eugene D. Genovese *The Mind of the Master Class: History and Faith in the Southern Slaveholders' Worldview* (New York: Cambridge University Press, 2005), 89. For the

different Souths, see Lacy K. Ford, *Deliver Us from Evil: The Slavery Question in the Old South* (New York: Oxford University Press, 2007), 4, 5–10, 503–536.

4 Bertram Wyatt Brown, *Southern Honor: Ethics and Behavior in the Old South* (New York: Oxford University Press, 1982), 15, 369, 371, 380–91, 397, esp. 440; Gary M. Ciuba, *Desire, Violence, and Divinity in Modern Southern Fiction* (Baton Rouge: Louisiana State University Press, 2007), 21. See also Dickson D. Bruce, *Violence and Culture in the Antebellum South* (Austin: University of Texas Press, 1979), 3–20, 69.

5 Stephen M. Stowe, *Intimacy and Power in the Old South: Ritual in the Lives of the Planters* (Baltimore: The Johns Hopkins University Press, 1987), 1–49; [Bishop] Wesley John Gaines, *The Negro and the White Man* (Philadelphia: The A[frican]. M[ethodist]. E[piscopal] Publishing House, 1897), 45; Jon Pahl, *Empire of Sacrifice: The Religious Origins of American Violence* (New York: New York University Press, 2010), 15, 16–18.

6 This paragraph is based on Sommerville, *Rape and Race*, 53; Hodes, *White Women, Black Men*, 157, 161–162; Walker Brooks to Iverson Brooks [Father], November 3, 1849 in Iverson Brooks Papers, Southern Historical Collection, University of North Carolina at Chapel Hill; Georgia Narratives in *American Slavery: A Composite Autobiography*, ed. George P. Rawick, (Westport, CN: Greenwood Publishing Company [Greenwood Electronic Media], 2002.); Eugene D. Genovese's classic, *Roll, Jordan, Role: The World the Slaves Made* (New York: Pantheon Books of Random House, 1974), 37–38, 67–73, 271–272, 378–379, 619–620, 632–635.

7 This paragraph is based on Lillian Smith, *Killers of the Dream*, (New York: W. W. Norton & Co., 1961 [1949]), 101. [Thomas Smyth] "The Divine Appointment and Obligation of Capital Punishment," *Southern Presbyterian Review*, 3 (December 1847): 21; Edgar Young Mullins, *The Christian Religion in its Doctrinal Expression* (Nashville: Sunday School Board of the Southern Baptist Convention, 1917), 323; Enoch M. Marvin, *The Work of Christ; or, The Atonement* (St Louis: Southwestern Book and Publishing Company, 1872), 68, 87–91; Thomas N. Ralston, *Elements of Divinity* (Nashville: Cokesbury Press, 1924), 235; Robert Lewis Dabney, "Vindicatory Justice Essential to God" [*Southern Pulpit*, April, 1881] reprinted in *Discussions of Robert Lewis Dabney, D.D., Ll. D.*, ed. C. R. Vaughn, 2 vols. (Richmond: Presbyterian Committee of Publication, 1890), 1: 466, 467. William Walker, *The Southern Harmony and Musical Companion* (Philadelphia: E. W. Miller, 1847), 25, 26, 32, 45, 46, 55.

8 Albert J. Raboteau, *Canaan Land: A Religious History of African Americans* (New York: Oxford University Press, 1999), 45; Raboteau, *Slave Religion: The 'Invisible Institution' in the Antebellum South* (New York: Oxford University Press, 1978); Donald G. Mathews, *Religion in the Old South* (Chicago: University of Chicago Press, 1977), Chap. 5.

9 Wilbur J. Cash, *The Mind of the South* (New York: Random House [Vintage Books], 1969 [Alfred Knopf, 1941]), 58. After the trial of John Scopes for teaching "evolution," John Crowe Ransom wrote a defense of the South's "stern and inscrutable" God against the liberals' "amiable and understandable

God." See *God without Thunder: An Unorthodox Defense of Orthodoxy* (New York: Harcourt Brace and Company, 1930), 1–25, 49–51. For the violence inherent in traditional theology, see [Rene Girard,] *The Girard Reader*, ed. James G. Williams (New York: Crossroads Publishing Co., 196), 9–29; Girard, *Job: The Victim of His People* (Stanford: Stanford University Press, 1987), 10–13, 34, 122–123, 140; Williams, *The Bible, Violence and the Sacred: Liberation from the Myth of Sanctioned Violence* (San Francisco: HarperSanFrancisco, 1991), vii-ix, 1–20, 25–31.

10 Sally E. Haddon, *Slave Patrols: Law and Violence in Virginia and the Carolinas* (Cambridge: Harvard University Press, 2001); Manfred Berg, *Popular Justice: A History of Lynching in America* (Chicago: Ivan R. Dee, 2011), 11–13.

11 Leon F. Litwack, *Been in the Storm So Long: The Aftermath of Slavery* (New York: Alfred A. Knopf, 1979), 167–386; Jennifer Ritterhouse, *Growing Up Jim Crow: How Black and White Southern Children Learned Race* (Chapel Hill: University of North Carolina Press, 2006), 3–7, 22–54.

12 Adam Fairclough, "'Scalawags,' Southern Honor and the Lost Cause: Explaining the Fatal Encounter of James H. Cosgrove and Edward L. Pierson," *The Journal of Southern History*, 77 (November 2011): 803–804 and 799–826.

13 Allen W. Trelease, *White Terror: The Ku Klux Klan Conspiracy and Southern Reconstruction* (Baton Rouge: Louisiana State University Press, 1971, 1999). Hannah Rosen, *Terror in the Heart of Freedom: Citizenship, Sexual Violence, and the Meaning of Race in The Post-Emancipation South* (Chapel Hill: University of North Carolina Press, 2009), 179–221; Hodes, *White Women, Black Men*, 162, 159–165; Herbert Shapiro, *White Violence and Black Response: From Reconstruction to Montgomery* (Amherst: University of Massachusetts Press, 1988), 30–63.

14 Michael Fellman, *In the Name of God and Country: Reconsidering Terrorism in American History* (New Haven: Yale University Press, 2009, 2010): 69, 73, and 67–74.

15 George C. Rable, *But there was no Peace: The Role of Violence in the Politics of Reconstruction* (Athens: University of Georgia Press, 1984), 80–170; Eric Foner, *Reconstruction: America's Unfinished Revolution 1863–1877* (New York: Harper and Row, Publishers, 1988), 171–175; LeeAnna Keith, *The Colfax Massacre: The Untold Story of Black Power, White Terror, and the Death of Reconstruction* (New York: Oxford University Press, 2008); Charles Lane, *The Day Freedom Died: The Colfax Massacre, The Supreme Court, and the Betrayal of Reconstruction* (New York: Henry Holt and Company, 2008).

16 Martha Hodes, "The Sexualization of Reconstruction Politics: White Women and Black Men in the South after the Civil War," in *American Sexual Politics: Sex, Gender, and Race since the Civil War*, eds. John C. Fout and Maura Shaw Tantillo (Chicago: University of Chicago Press, 1993), 59–74, esp 61; William Cohen, *At Freedom's Edge: Black Mobility and the Southern White Quest for Racial Control 1861–1915* (Baton Rouge: Louisiana State University Press, 1991); Jane Dailey, "Deference and Violence in the Postbellum

Urban South: Manners and Massacres in Danville, Virginia," *The Journal of Southern History*, 63 (August, 1997): 555–564; Foner, *Reconstruction*, 281–411; Rable, *But there was no Peace*, 1–33. Rosen, *Terror in the Heart of Freedom*, 122–131, 141.

17 The previous two paragraphs rely on Lawrence Goldstone, *Inherently Unequal: The Betrayal of Equal Rights by the Supreme Court, 1865–1903* (New York: Walker & Company, 2011), 97, 118–129; Mark Elliott, *Color-Blind Justice: Albion Tourgee and the Quest for Racial Equality from the Civil War to Plessy v. Ferguson* (New York: Oxford University Press, 2008), 262–263, 268–269, 285–286; Lane, *Day Freedom Died*, 227–248; Foner, *Reconstruction*, 529–530, 569; Richard Kluger, *Simple Justice: The History of Brown v. Board of Education and Black America's Struggle for Equality* (New York: Vintage Books Random House, 1975 and 1977), 60–61, 64–66, 68, 71, 77, 86, 120.

18 Douglas A. Blackmon, *Slavery by Another Name: The Re-Enslavement of Black Americans from the Civil War to World War II* (New York: Anchor Books, Random House, Inc., 2009), 52, 54–57, 63–66, 68–151; Howard N. Rabinowitz, *Race Relations in the Urban South 1865–1890* (New York: Oxford University Press, 1978), 31–60; Cohen, *At Freedom's Edge*; J. William Harris, *Deep Souths: Delta, Piedmont and Sea Island Society in the Age of Segregation* (Baltimore: The Johns Hopkins University Press, 2001), 57–66.

19 Leon F. Litwack, *Trouble in Mind: Black Southerners in the Age of Jim Crow* (New York: Alfred A. Knopf, 1998), 123–142; Cohen, *At Freedom's Edge*, 248–273.

20 Elliott, *Color-Blind Justice*, 9–36.

21 *The [Newnan, Georgia] Herald and Advertiser*, July 8, 1892; Perman, *Struggle for Mastery*, pp. 48–50; Rayford W. Logan, *The Betrayal of the Negro from Rutherford B. Hayes to Woodrow Wilson* (New York: Collier Books of Collier-Macmillan Ltd, 1965 [originally published in 1954 as *The Negro in American Life and Thought: The Nadir 1877–1901* by Dial Press of New York]), 64–65.

22 Perman, *Struggle for Mastery*, 37–90; see also Harris, *Deep Souths*, 57–66.

23 Ayers, *Promise New South*, 52–54, 146–149, 269, 175–178, 289–290, 298–299, 304–309, 409–413; Fellman, *God and Country Terrorism*, 99, 106–142.

24 Ibid., 248–309; Jane Dailey, *Before Jim Crow: The Politics of Race in Post-emancipation Virginia* (Chapel Hill: University of North Carolina Press, 2000); *Jumpin' Jim Crow: Southern Politics from Civil War to Civil Rights*, eds. Jane Dailey, Glenda Elizabeth Gilmore, and Bryant Simon (Princeton: Princeton University Press, 2000), 88–114; Helen G. Edmonds, *The Negro and Fusion Politics in North Carolina 1894–1901* (New York: Russell & Russell, 1951); Lawrence Goodwyn, *Democratic Promise: The Populist Moment in America* (New York: Oxford University Press, 1976); Sheldon Hackney, *From Populism to Progressivism in Alabama* (Princeton: Princeton University Press, 1966); Barton C. Shaw, *The Wool-Hat Boys: Georgia's Populist Party* (Baton Rouge: Louisiana State University Press,

1984; C. Vann Woodward, *Tom Watson, Agrarian Rebel* (New York: Oxford University Press, Galaxy Book, 1963, orig. The Macmillan Company, 1938).

25 The following is based on Dailey, *Before Jim Crow*, 32, 43; Michael Perman, *Pursuit of Unity: A Political History of the American South* (Chapel Hill: University of North Carolina Press, 2009), 142–156.

26 Ibid., 44, 47, 51–53; Jane Dailey, "The Limits of Liberalism in the New South: The Politics of Race, Sex, and Patronage in Virginia, 1879–1883" quoting William Mahone on page 92 in Dailey et al., *Jumpin' Jim Crow*.

27 Jane Dailey, "Deference and Violence in the Postbellum Urban South: Manners and Massacres in Danville, Virginia," *The Journal of Southern History*, 63 (August 1997): 553–590, quotation from 582; Dailey, "Limits of Liberalism," 95–105; Dailey, *Before Jim Crow*, 103–131, 135–154, 157–165; J. Douglas Smith, *Managing White Supremacy: Race, Politics, and Citizenship in Jim Crow Virginia* (Chapel Hill: University of North Carolina Press, 202), 19–23.

28 Ayres, *Promise New South*, 239: The sub-treasury plan was to have the US government build warehouses in certain specified counties to allow farmers to store their agricultural commodities for sale until they could fetch a reasonable profit.

29 Woodward, *Tom Watson*, 226–227, 238–243; Ayres, *Promise New South*, 251; Shaw, *The Wool-Hat Boys*, 63–77, 109–119.

30 Shaw, *Wool-Hat Boys*, 155–156; *The* [Atlanta] *Constitution*, November 27, 1894; February 19, May 4, July 17 and 23, 1895; March 8 and 16, August 2 and 25, September 20, October 3, 1896.

31 Joe Creech, *Righteous Indignation: Religion and the Populist Revolution* (Urbana and Chicago: University of Illinois Press, 2006), 87, and 41–91.

32 Ibid., 122–138; Edmonds, *The Negro and Fusion Politics*, 25–37.

33 Edmonds, *Negro and Fusion Politics*, 41, 62–64.

34 Creech, *Righteous Indignation*, 163–165.

35 This and the previous paragraph are based on Gilmore, *Gender and Jim Crow*, 82–89, 102–105; *The* [Raleigh] *News and Observer*, January 9 and 16; March 12, June 4, August 3, 6, 7, 11, 18, 19, 20, 24, 25 and 28, September 8, 9 and 18, November 8 and 27, 1898; *The* [Raleigh, North Carolina] *Morning Post*, January 5–8, 11–15, 1899; Perman, *Struggle for Mastery*, 148–149; *Democracy Betrayed: The Wilmington Riot of 1898 and Its Legacy*, eds. David S. Cecelski and Timothy B. Tyson (Chapel Hill: University of North Carolina Press, 1998): 3–41, 113–224; Robert Howard Wooley, "Race, and politics: The Evolution of the White Campaign of 1898 in North Carolina" (Ph.D. diss., University of North Carolina at Chapel Hill, 1977); Gilmore, *Gender and Jim Crow*, 91–118, 173–244, 270–320; H. Leon Prather, Sr., *We Have Taken a City: Wilmington Racial Massacre and Coup of 1898* (Wilmington NC: NU World Enterprises, 1984 and 1998); Ayers, *Promise New South*, 52–53, 146–149, 289–299, 304–309, 409–413.

36 Mary Douglas, *Purity and Danger An Analysis of Concepts of Pollution and Taboo* (Baltimore: Penguin Books, Inc., 1970), 136–153.

37 C. Vann Woodward, *The Strange Career of Jim Crow* (New York: Oxford University Press, 1974).

38 Goldstone, *Inherently Unequal*, 128–129; Jonathan Haidt, *The Righteous Mind: Why Good People are Divided by Politics and Religion* (New York: Vintage Books of Random House, 2012), 32–108 discusses the basis of moral judgments defended by "confirmatory" reasoning. See also Philip Alexander Bruce, *The Plantation Negro as a Freeman: Observations on His Character, Condition, and Prospects in Virginia* (Williamstown: Corner House Publishers, 1970 of the 1889 edition), 45–46, 48, 49.

39 Cohen, *At Freedom's Edge*, 214–215; Woodward, *Strange Career*, 67–109; Ayres, *Promise New South*, 67–68, 121–127, 136–146, 429, 433–434; Rabinowitz, *Race Relations 1865–1890*: 152–183, Rosen, *Terror in the Heart of Freedom*, 122–131, 141; Foner, *Reconstruction*, 373; Philip Alexander Bruce, "Evolution of the Negro Problem," *Sewanee Review*, 19 (October, 1911): 385–399, reprinted as "In Defense of Southern Race Policies" in *The Development of Segregationist Thought*, ed. I. A. Newby (Homewood: The Dorsey Press, 1968), 70–78; Bruce, *The Plantation Negro as a Freeman*, 41–49; Douglas, *Purity and Danger*; Emile Durkheim, *The Elementary Forms of Religious Life*, Tr. Karen E. Fields (New York: The Free Press, 1995 [original publication as *Les Formes elementaires de la vie religieuse: Le system totemiqoe en Australie*, Paris, by F. Alcan, 1912]), 303–329.

40 Foner, *Reconstruction*, 364–371; Litwack, *Trouble in Mind*, 229–230; Ayres, *Promise New South*, 135–136.

41 Rabinowitz, *Race Relations 1865–1890*, 106–121; Williamson, *Crucible of Race*, 149–156; Giddings, *Ida, A Sword*, 55–68.

42 Gilmore, *Gender and Jim Crow*, 62–63, 75–89; Kevin K. Gaines, *Uplifting the Race: Black Leadership, Politics and Culture in the Twentieth Century* (Chapel Hill and London: University of North Carolina Press, 1996), 1–9, 19–46; Goldsby, *Spectacular Secret*, 51–60; see comments by a black spokesman in Perman, *Struggle for Mastery*, 248.

43 Giddings, *Ida, A Sword*, 136–137.

44 Goldstone, *Inherently Unequal*, 162.

45 Elliott, *Color-Blind Justice*, 283–284 for quotations; also 262–271, 280–290.

46 Kluger, *Simple Justice*, 74, 78–81.

47 Goldstone, *Inherently Unequal*, 167.

48 Ibid., 108–110, quoted on page 110; Kluger, *Simple Justice*, 81–83.

49 Ibid., 171–176.

50 Litwack, *Trouble in Mind*, 278; he quotes a comment by Sterling Brown, *The Collected Poems of Sterling Brown* (New York: Harper & Row, 1980), 170.

51 Litwack, *Trouble in Mind*, 258–270.

52 Pahl, *Empire of Sacrifice*, 15.

53 George M. Fredrickson, *Racism: A Short History* (Princeton: Princeton University Press, 2002), 23–27, 43–47, 51–63; Willie James Jennings, *The Christian Imagination: Theology and the Origins of Race* (New Haven: Yale University Press, 2010), 22–38. See also William McKee Evans, *Open Wound: The Long View of Race in America* (Urbana and Chicago: University of Illinois Press, 2009), 13–62. For an analysis of the Enlightenment and racism, see Colin Kidd, *The Forging of Races: Race and Scripture in the Protestant Atlantic World 1600–2000* (Cambridge: Cambridge University Press,

2006):79–120, esp. 120. See also Peter Gay, *The Cultivation of Hatred* [Volume 3 of *The Bourgeois Experience: Victoria to Freud*] (New York: W. W. Norton & Company 1993), 71–73.

54 Kidd, *Forging of Races*, 121–167, especially 137–140. See also William Sumner Jenkins, *Pro-Slavery Thought in the Old South* (Chapel Hill: University of North Carolina Press); Elizabeth Fox-Genovese and Eugene D. Genovese, *The Mind of the Master Class: History and Faith in the Southern Slaveholder's Worldview* (Cambridge: Cambridge University Press, 2005), 505–27; Mathews, *Religion in the Old South*.

55 Mark M. Smith, *How Race is Made: Slavery, Segregation and the Senses* (Chapel Hill: The University of North Carolina Press, 2006), 47.

56 Charles Carroll, *The Negro Not the Son of Ham: or, Man Not a Species Divisible into Races* (Chattanooga: Times Printers, 1898), 45, 46; Carroll, *"The Negro a Beast:' or In the Image of God* (N.p.: n. p: 1900), 29–30, 89–102, 223, 227–266; Carroll, *The Tempter of Eve, or: The Criminality of Man's Social, Political, and Religious Equality with the Negro and the Amalgamation to which these Crimes Inevitably Lead* (St Louis: The Adamic Publishing Co., 1902), 497–499.

57 Glenda E. Gilmore, "Murder, Memory, and the Flight of the Incubus," in *Democracy Betrayed: The Wilmington Race Riot*, 73–93.

58 I. A. Newby, *Jim Crow's Defense: Anti-Negro Thought in America 1900–1930* (Baton Rouge: Louisiana State University Press, 1965), 2–102; George M. Fredrickson, *The Black Image in the White Mind: The Debate on Afro-American Character and Destiny, 1817–1914* (Hanover: Wesleyan University Press, 1987 [original copyright Harper & Row, 1971]), 256–275; William Benjamin Smith, *The Color Line: A Brief in Behalf of the Unborn* (New York: McClure, Phillips & Co., 1905), ix, 29–74, 111–157, quotations from 165 and 178.

59 Gregory A. Wills, *Democratic Religion: Freedom, Authority, and Church Discipline in the Baptists South, 1785–1900* (New York: Oxford University Press, 1997; Ted Ownby, *Subduing Satan: Religion, Recreation, and Manhood in the Rural South 1865–1920* (Chapel Hill: University of North Carolina Press, 1990), 194–212; Waldrep, *Night Riders*, 115.

60 W. Harrison Daniel, "The Effects of the Civil War on Southern Protestantism," *Maryland Historical Magazine*, 69 (1974): 44–63; Ayers, *Promise New South*, 498–500; Hunter Dickinson Farish, *The Circuit Rider Dismounts: A Social History of Southern Methodism 1865–1900* (Richmond: The Dietz Press, 1938), 63–105; Paul Harvey, *Redeeming the South: Religious Cultures and Racial Identities among Southern Baptists 1865–1925* (Chapel Hill: University of North Carolina Press, 1997), 24–31, 80; Ernest Trice Thompson, *Presbyterians in the South; Volume Three: 1890–1972* (Richmond: John Knox Press, 1973), 3: 28–70; Ownby, *Subduing Satan*, 122–164; Beth Barton Schweiger, *The Gospel Working Up: Progress and the Pulpit in Nineteenth-Century Virginia* (New York: Oxford University Press, 2000).

61 Robert Lewis Dabney, "The Public Preaching of Women" originally published in the *Southern Presbyterian Review* October, 1879 in *Discussions of Robert*

Lewis Dabney, ed. C. R. Vaughn, 2 vols. (Richmond: Presbyterian Committee of Publication, 1891), 2: 96–97.

62 John Patrick McDowell, *The Social Gospel in the South: The Woman's Home Mission Movement in the Methodist Episcopal Church, South, 1886–1939* (Baton Rouge: Lousiana State University Press, 1982), 6–35; Harvey, *Redeeming the South*, 77–106; Regina D. Sullivan, *Lottie Moon: A Southern Baptist Missionary to China in History and Legend* (Baton Rouge: Louisiana State University Press, 2011), 74–87. The Methodists also celebrated Moon's work in China: "Extract from letter of Miss Lottie Moon." *Woman's Missionary Advocate*, 2 (May 1881): 2–3.

63 See Joe L. Coker, *Liquor in the Land of the Lost Cause: Southern White Evangelicals and the Prohibition Movement* (Lexington: The University Press of Kentucky, 2007), 199–209; Charles R. Israel, *Before Scopes: Evangelicalism, Education, and Evolution in Tennessee 1870–1925* (Athens: University of Georgia Press, 2004). The rhetoric of temperance campaigns enlisted white "church people" in support of white supremacy: see Frederick A. Bode, *Protestantism and the New South: North Carolina Baptists and Methodists in Political Crisis 1894–1903* (Charlottesville: University Press of Virginia, 1975); *The* [Raleigh, North Carolina] *News and Observer*, May 24, 1908; Mrs. J. J. Ansley, *History of the Georgia Women's Christian Temperance Union from its Organization 1883 to 1907* (Columbus: Gilbert Printing Company, 1914); Paul Isaac, *Prohibition and Politics: Turbulent Decades in Tennessee, 1885–1920* (Knoxville: University of Tennessee Press, 1977); James Benson Sellers, *The Prohibition Movement in Alabama 1702 to 1943* (Chapel Hill: University of North Carolina Press, 1943); Daniel Jay Whitener, *Prohibition in North Carolina 1715–1945* (Chapel Hill: University of North Carolina Press, 1946).

64 Hall, *Revolt against Chivalry*, 145–175.

65 Durkheim, *Elementary Forms*, 208. 209, 213, 215, 216; Robert G. Hamerton-Kelly, *Sacred Violence: Paul's Hermeneutic of the Cross* (Minneapolis: Fortress Press, 1992), 15; Williams, *The Bible, Violence and the Sacred*, 16–17.

66 Mary Douglas, *Purity and Danger*, 15, 33.

67 Durkheim, *Elementary Forms*, 216.

68 Charles Reagan Wilson, *Baptized in Blood: The Religion of the Lost Cause* (Athens: University of Georgia Press, 1980).

69 David W. Blight, *Race and Reunion: The Civil War in American Memory* (Cambridge: Belknap Press of Harvard University Press, 2001), 254–299; Rayford W. Logan, *Betrayal of the Negro*. For Davis as Christ, bleeding from a "crown of thrones for his people," see *The* [Newnan, Georgia] *Herald and Advertiser*, December 13, 1889.

70 Philip J. Lee, *Against the Protestant Gnostics* (New York: Oxford University Press), 117.

71 Studies on which this interpretation rests were primarily the critical analysis in Dickson D. Bruce, Jr., *And They All Sang Hallelujah: Plain-Folk Camp-Meeting Religion, 1800–1845* (Knoxville: University of Tennessee Press, 1974); John Boles, *The Great Revival 1787–1805: The Origins of the Southern Evangelical Mind* (Lexington: University Press of Kentucky, 1972); Anne C. Loveland,

Southern Evangelicals and the Social Order 1800–1860 (Baton Rouge: Louisiana State University Press, 1980); Mathews, *Religion in the Old South*; Ownby, *Subduing Satan*, 103–166; Snyder, *Protestant Ethic and Punishment*; Howard Thurman, *The Luminous Darkness: A Personal Interpretation of the Anatomy of Segregation and the Ground of Hope* (Richmond: Friends United Press, 1989, copyright 1965 by Thurman), 62–65.

72 See the statement by the anonymous Southern Baptist intellectual, as reported in Harold Bloom, *The American Religion* (New York: Simon & Schuster, 1992): 203–204; Mathews, *Religion in the Old South*; Lee, *Protestant Gnostics*, 101–114. The boorish comment is from William Hooper Haigh, Diary, August 14, 18, 1844, Southern Historical Collection, University of North Carolina at Chapel Hill. The theologian is Snyder in *Protestant Punishment*, 69.

73 See Mary Douglas, *Purity and Danger*, 17–40.

74 John W. Cell, *The Highest Stage of White Supremacy: The Origins of Segregation in South Africa and the American South* (New York: Cambridge University Press, 1982), 134; Cohen, *At Freedom's Edge;* Woodward, *Strange Career of Jim Crow.*

75 Bruce, *The Plantation Negro as a Freeman*, 48–49, 93–110, esp. 97; Bruce, "Evolution of the Negro Problem"; Douglas, *Purity and Danger*, 145.

76 Cash, *The Mind of the South*, 116–120; Hall, *Revolt against Chivalry*, 112, 129, 145–157; Diane Miller Sommerville, "The Rape Myth in the Old South Reconsidered," *Journal of Southern History*, 61 (August 1995): 481–518.

77 Douglas, *Purity and Danger*, 67.

78 Smith's comment in "A Report from Lillian Smith on Killers of the Dream." An editorial in *The* [Atlanta] *Constitution* referred to Smith as "the ex-missionary" who "purposely sets out to debase the South, with a fury that continually overleaps itself." See Lillian Smith Papers 1283A, University of Georgia Library, Box 30. See also Fred Hobson, *Tell About the South: The Southern Rage to Explain* (Baton Rouge: Louisiana State University Press, 1983): 321: By emphasizing segregation, Hobson writes, she missed "much of what else the South was and had been."

79 Lillian Smith, *Killers of the Dream*, 83, 88–90, 101, 224–252. See Smith to Paul Tillich November 17, 1959, letter quoted in Anne C. Loveland, *Lillian Smith: A Southerner Confronting the South; a Biography* (Baton Rouge: Louisiana State University Press, 1986), 172 and 97–105.

80 Williamson, *Crucible of Race*, 285–323. He writes on page 308: "In their frustration white men projected their own worst thoughts upon black men, imagined them acted out in some specific incident, and symbolically killed those thoughts by lynching a hapless black man. Almost any vulnerable black man would do."

81 Thurman, *The Luminous Darkness*, 3, 5, 7, 9, 23–32, 48.

82 *Remembering Jim Crow: African Americans Tell about Life in the Segregated South*, ed. William H. Chafe, Raymond Gavins, Robert Korstad, et al. (New York: The New Press and Lyndhurst Books of the Center for Documentary Studies of Duke University, 2001), 7–12, 18, 27–29, 88, 152–204, 268; *The* [Atlanta] *Constitution*, May 15, 1899.

83 See Bruce, *Plantation Negro as a Freeman*, 1–60, 46–47, 93–110, 113–116, 126–142, 246; Williamson, *Crucible of Race*, 117–141, esp 118; William Patrick Calhoun, *The Caucasian and the Negro in the United States* (New York: Arno Press, 1977 [Reproduction of edition published by R. L. Ryan Company of South Carolina, 1902); Smith, *The Color Line*; Alfred Holt Stone, *Studies in the American Race Problem*, intro. William F. Willcox (New York: Doubleday, Page & Co., 1908); the [Newnan, Georgia] *Herald and Advertiser*, February 22, 1895; *Griffin Daily News*, February 27, March 2 and 10, June 18 and 21, 1901.

84 Mary de Young, "Folk Devils Reconsidered," in *Moral Panic and the Politics of Anxiety* ed. Sean P. Hier (London: Routledge, Taylor & Francis Group, 2011), 120–122.

85 The previous ten paragraphs are based on Christopher Waldrep, *The Many Faces of Judge Lynch: Extralegal Violence and Punishment in America* (New York: Palgrave Macmillan, 2002), 20–37, 112–114, map between pages 132 and 133. See also the chart in Amy Kate Bailey and Stewart E. Tolnay, *Lynched: The Victims of Southern Mob Violence* (Chapel Hill: University of North Carolina Press, 2015), 11; also Stewart E. Tolnay and E. M. Beck, *Festival of Violence: An Analysis of Southern Lynchings 1882–1930* (Urbana: University of Illinois Press, 1995), 30, 157, 157–160; NAACP, *Thirty Years of Lynching* (New York: National Association for the Advancement of Colored People) and Supplements (1919–1928); Arthur Raper, *The Tragedy of Lynching* (Chapel Hill: The University of North Carolina Press, 1933), 25; W[illiam] Fitzhugh Brundage, "Lynching in the New South: Georgia and Virginia, 1880–1930" (Ph.D. diss., Harvard University, 1988), 69–72, 78; more accessible is his book based on the dissertation, *Lynching in the New South*, 17–85, 103–139; Hall, *Revolt against Chivalry*, 144–149; Hall, "The Mind that Burns in Each Body: Women, Rape, and Racial Violence," in *Powers of Desire: The Politics of Sexuality*, eds. Ann Snitow, Christine Stansell, and Sharon Thompson (New York: Monthly Review Press), 331; Terence Robert Finnegan, "'At the Hands of Parties Unknown' Lynching in Mississippi and South Carolina, 1881–1940" (Ph.D. diss., University of Illinois at Urbana-Champaign, 1993), 94–98, 264, 280–301, 308–309 and 314–315, 325; Roberta Senechal de la Roche explains the importance of relational differences between the victim and the crowd in "The Sociogenesis of Lynching" in *Under Sentence of Death: Lynching in the South*, ed. Fitzhugh Brundage (Chapel Hill: University of North Carolina Press, 1997), 48–76, esp. 52–55, 63–64. See also McMillen, *Dark Journey*, 14–19, 224–253; Cynthia Skove Nevels, *Lynching to Belong: Claiming Whiteness Through Racial Violence* (College Station: Texas A & M Press, 2007); Gilles Vandal, *Rethinking Southern Violence: Homicides in Post-Civil War Louisiana, 1866–1884* (Columbus: Ohio State University Press, 2000): 91–93; Elliot Jaspin, *Buried in the Bitter Waters: The Hidden History of Racial Cleansing in America* (New York: Basic Book, 2007); James W. Loewen, *Sundown Towns: A Hidden Dimension of American Racism* (New York: The New Press, 2005); Kimberly Harper, *White Man's Heaven: The Lynching and Expulsion of Blacks in the Southern Ozarks, 1894–1909* (Fayetteville: University of

Arkansas Press, 2010); William F. Holmes, "Whitecapping: Agrarian Violence in Mississippi, 1902–1906,) *Journal of Southern History*, 35 (May 1962): 165–185; Holmes, "Moonshining and Collective Violence: Georgia 1889–1895," *Journal of American History*, 67 (December 1980): 589–611; *Southwestern Christian Advocate*, January 5, August 30, September 6, 1888; February 10, March 24, 1898; February 23, March 9, September 7, 1899; *The* [Atlanta] *Constitution*, November 10 and December 23, 1894; January 2 and 13, 1895.

86 Mary Elizabeth Hines, "Death at the Hands of Persons Unknown: The Geography of Lynching in the Deep South 1882 to 1910" (Ph.D. diss., Louisiana State University, 1992), 121; Finnegan, "At the Hands of Parties Unknown," 102–103; Williamson, *Crucible of Race*, 186; Stephen David Kantrowitz, *Ben Tillman and the Reconstruction of White Supremacy* (Chapel Hill: University of North Carolina Press, 2000); Francis Butler Simpkins, *Pitchfork Ben Tillman, South Carolinian* (Baton Rouge: Louisiana State University Press, 1944); Stephen D. Kantrowitz, "White Supremacist Justice and the Rule of Law: Lynching, Honor, and the State in Ben Tillman's South Carolina," in *Men and Violence: Gender, Honor, and Rituals in Modern Europe and America*, ed. Pieter Spierenburg (Columbus: The Ohio State University Press, 1998), 213–239.

87 *The* [Atlanta] *Constitution*, October 3 1896 as cited in Shaw, *The Wool-Hat boys*, 156, see also 155–157; *The* [Atlanta] *Constitution*, November, 27 and 28, 1894; January 6 and 9, February 19, May 5, June 15, 1895; February 2, March 6 and 8, 1896; November 11, 1899; *The* [Newnan, Georgia] *Herald and Advertiser*, July 22 and 29, October 14 and 28, 1892, and April 28, 1899; *The* [Atlanta] *Constitution*, April 24, 1899; *The Atlanta Journal*, April 24, 1899.

Chapter 2

1 T[heophilus]. G[ould]. Steward, "The Reign of the Mob," *The Independent*, 51 (May 11, 1899): 1296–1297; Albert G. Miller, *Elevating the Race: Theophilus G. Steward and the Making of an African American Civil Society* (Knoxville: University of Tennessee Press, 2003), 128.

2 "Our Attitude to the Negro Problem," *The Independent*, 51 (December 14, 1899): 3376.

3 H. H. Proctor, "Public Sentiment and Lynch-Law in Georgia, and a Suggestion," *The Independent*, 49 (August 26, 1897): 4.

4 Editorial, no title, *The Independent*, 51 (March 30, 1899): 914; Editorial, no title, *The Independent*, 51 (May 4, 1899): 1252.

5 Mrs. L. H. Harris, "A Southern Woman's View," *The Independent*, 51 (May 18, 1899): 1354–1355.

6 Ibid. On the matter of interracial sexual relations, see the discussion by Nell Irvin Painter in "Introduction: The Journal of Ella Gertrude Clanton Thomas: An Educated White Woman in the Eras of Slavery, War, and Reconstruction" in [Ella Gertrude Clanton Thomas] *The Secret Eye: The Journal of Ella*

Gertrude Clanton Thomas 1848–1889, ed. Virginia Ingraham Burr (Chapel Hill: University of North Carolina Press, 1990), 55–66.

7 Editorial in *The Independent*, 51 (June 22, 1899): 1703–1704; Harris, "Negro Womanhood," *The Independent*, 51 (June 22, 1899): 1687–1689; Hamilton Holt to Mrs. L. H. Harris June 29, 1899, Corra White Harris Papers, Woodruff Library Special Collections, Emory University; Corrie [Mrs. L. H.] Harris to [Bishop] Warren Akin Candler, June 27, 1899, Warren Akin Candler Papers, Woodruff Library Special Collections, Emory University.

8 Harris, "The Negro Child," *The Independent*, 51 (October 26, 1899): 2884–2886; Harris, "A Southern Woman's View": 1355; Catherine Oglesby, *Corra Harris and the Divided Mind of the New South* (Gainesville: University Press of Florida, 2008).

9 Crystal N. Feimster, *Southern Horrors: Women and the Politics of Rape and Lynching* (Cambridge: Harvard University Press, 2009), 90; See also Jacquelyn Dowd Hall, *Revolt against Chivalry: Jessie Daniel Ames and the Women's Campaign against Lynching* (New York: Columbia University Press, 1979); Jacqueline Goldsby, *A Spectacular Secret: Lynching in American Life and Literature* (Chicago: University of Chicago Press, 2006), 49–60; Paula J. Giddings, *Ida: A Sword Among Lions: Ida B. Wells and the Campaign against Lynching* (New York: Amistad, HarperCollins Publishers, 2008), 122–229.

10 Robert Howard Wooley, "Race and Politics: The Evolution of the White Supremacy Campaign of 1898 in North Carolina" (Ph.D. diss., University of North Carolina at Chapel Hill, 1977); George Howard to Henry G. Connor, November 4, 1898, Henry G. Connor Papers, Southern Historical Collection, University of North Carolina at Chapel Hill; Richard L. Watson, "Furnifold Simmons: 'Jehovah of the Tar Heels'?" *North Carolina Historical Review*, 44 (Spring 1967): 166–187.

11 *The Richmond Planet*, November 11, 1899; also *Southwestern Christian Advocate* July 13, 1899; "Negro Immorality," *The Independent*, 51 (June 22, 1899): 1703.

12 *The [Atlanta] Constitution*, September 17, 1886 as quoted in Feimster, *Southern Horrors*, 73, 74. These two paragraphs are based on Feimster's study, 62–86. See also Leslie K. Dunlap, "The Reform of Rape Law and the Problem of White Men: Age of Consent Campaigns in the South, 1885–1910," in *Sex, Love, Race: Crossing Boundaries in North American History*, ed. Martha Hodes (New York: New York University Press, 1999), 352–372.

13 Rebecca Latimer Felton, "The Rescue Work in Relation to Womanhood and Temperance" in Rebecca Latimer Felton Papers, University of Georgia Hargett Library Manuscripts Division, as quoted in Feimster, *Southern Horrors*, 83.

14 *The [Atlanta] Constitution*, August 20, 1897. The narrative here relies on Crystal N. Feimster, in her *Southern Horrors*.

15 Rebecca Latimer Felton as quoted from "'Mrs. Felton vs Manly' in the Rebecca Latimer Felton papers, University of Georgia Library, reel 13 in LeeAnn Whites, "Love, Hate, Rape, Lynching: Rebecca Latimer Felton and the Gender Politics of Racial Violence," in *Democracy Betrayed: The Wilmington Race Riot of*

1898 and Its Legacy, eds. David S. Cecelski and Timothy B. Tyson (Chapel Hill: University of North Carolina Press, 1998), 159.

16 *The* [Atlanta] *Constitution*, August 20, 1897.

17 Corra Harris, *My Book and Heart* (Boston: Houghton Mifflin Co., 1924), 174.

18 W[illiam]. P. Lovejoy, D. D., "Georgia's Record of Blood," *The Independent*, 51 (May 11, 1899): 1297–1300. See William Pope Harrison, *The Gospel Among the Slaves* (Nashville: Publishing House of the Methodist Episcopal Church, South, 1893), 393–394.

19 Lundy Howard Harris to Warren Akin Candler, March 8, 1886 in Candler Papers, Emory University.

20 John E. Talmadge, *Corra Harris: Lady of Purpose* (Athens: University of Georgia Press, 1968), 1–3; Oglesby, *Corra Harris*, 27.

21 Oglesby, *Corra Harris*, 26–27. The book is *A Circuit Rider's Wife* (Philadelphia: Henry Altemus Company, 1910); R. F. Burden to Warren Akin Candler, April 21, 1882; Lundy Howard Harris to Warren Akin Candler, April 22, 1882; Harris to Candler, March 8, 1886; Atticus Greene Haygood to Warren Akin Candler, December 31, 1888; Haygood to Candler June 3, 1889, all in the Candler Papers, Emory University. See also Lundy Howard Harris to "My Dear Grandma," September 8, 1882, Burge Family Papers, Emory University; *The Emory Phoenix*, 2 (June 1888): 3; Corra Harris, *Book and Heart*, 127.

22 Polly Stone Buck, *The Blessed Town: Oxford, Georgia, at the Turn of the Century* (Chapel Hill: Algonquin Books, 1986); Corra and Lundy Harris' comments are in *Book and Heart*, 129–130, 136, 150.

23 This and the previous two paragraphs rely on Mark Auslander, *The Accidental Slaveowner: Revisiting a Myth of Race and Finding an American Family* (Athens: University of Georgia Press, 2011), 68–94, 171–173, 201, 325.

24 Harris, *The House of Helen* (New York: George H. Doran Co., 1923), 241–256.

25 Harris, *Book and Heart*, 134.

26 Harris, "A Southern Woman's View," 1355.

27 Hunter Dickinson Farish, *The Circuit Rider Dismounts: A Social History of Southern Methodism 1865–1900* (New York: De Capo Press, 1969 [1938]); Daniel W. Stowell, *Rebuilding Zion: The Religious Reconstruction 1863–1877* (New York: Oxford University Press, 1998); Paul Harvey, *Redeeming the South: Religious Cultures and Racial Identities Among Southern Baptists 1865–1925* (Chapel Hill: University of North Carolina Press, 1997; Rufus B. Spain, *At Ease in Zion: A Social History of Southern Baptists 1865–1900* (Tuscaloosa: University of Alabama Press, 2003, reprint of original publication by Vanderbilt University Press in 1967).

28 Regina D. Sullivan, *Lottie Moon: A Southern Baptist Missionary to China in History and Legend* (Baton Rouge: Louisiana State University Press, 2011); Admissions papers and reports of deaconesses in Scarritt College Papers. Methodist Center, Drew University.

29 Sam P. Jones, *Sam Jones' Own Book: A Series of Sermons* (Cincinnati: Cranston & Stowe, 1887 [Paperback edition published by The University of South Carolina Press, Columbia], 2009), 77.

30 Warren Akin Candler to General [and Reverend] Clement A. Evans October 9,
   1883; Evans to Candler, October 11, 1883; Mrs. John Jay Cohen to
   "Mr Candler," October 31, 1883; A J Goodloe to Candler September 15,
   1885; Clipping from Nashville newspaper on the "Abbott Affair," Box 2.2;
   Warren A. Candler "The Church vs the Theater" (Nashville: Southern Methodist Publishing House, 1887), pamphlet, all in the Candler Papers, Emory
   University. Dancing had bedeviled Methodists from the middle of the eighteenth century when they began to form within the Church of England. After the
   Civil War some of the laity were dancing and conservatives were aghast. See for
   example, *Wesleyan Christian Advocate*, February 22, 1879; Farish, *The Circuit
   Rider Dismounts*, 342–347.

31 H. Stokes to "My Dear Mrs Moore," March 12, 1892; Warren Akin Candler
   to Mrs. [John] Sibley, May 2, 1892; Candler to "Dear Doctor"[W. W. Evans],
   February 14, 1894, and Evans to Candler February 15: Candler told Professor
   Henry Scomp that "bawdy houses [were] one of the channels through which
   Woman suffrage would work in the lower grades of society." Candler Papers,
   Emory University. See also *The* [Atlanta] *Constitution* July 15, 1894.

32 The previous two paragraphs rely on J.O.A. Clark to "My darling child,"
   November 22, 1893, James Osgood Andrew Clark Papers, Emory University;
   Christopher H. Owen, *The Sacred Flame of Love: Methodism and Society in
   Nineteenth Century Georgia* (Athens: University of Georgia Press, 1998),
   154–165, 172–176; Harvey, *Redeeming the South*, 91–102; Joe Creech, *Right-
   eous Indignation: Religion and the Populist Revolution* (Urbana: University of
   Illinois Press, 2006), 11–20, 143–146, 178–186; Randall J. Stephens, *The Fire
   Spreads: Holiness and Pentecostalism in the American South* (Cambridge:
   Harvard University Press, 2008), 15–55, 62–68.

33 A. B. Stark, "The Light of Asia," *Methodist Quarterly Review*, 2(April 1880):
   253–264. [T O Summers], "One of the Great Topics of the Day," *Methodist
   Quarterly Review*, 3 (January 1881): 135–137; A. B. Stark, "Carlyle's Remin-
   iscences," *Methodist Quarterly Review*, 3 (July 1881): 409–21; John B. Robins,
   "Methodistic Philosophy," *Methodist Quarterly Review*, 4 (January 1882):
   59–67; G. W. Horn, "Christian Culture," *Methodist Quarterly Review*, 4 (July
   1882): 428–440; William Harrison, "Unconscious Orthodoxy," *Methodist
   Quarterly Review*, 6 (April 1884): 245–267; T J Dodd, "Methodism and
   Advanced Thought" *Methodist Quarterly Review*, 9 (October 1890): 39–60;
   William F. Warren, "Methodist and Pre-Methodist Principles of Education in
   New England," *Methodist Quarterly Review*, 9 (January 1891): 380–394,
   especially 387; Wilbur Fisk Tillett, "A Wesleyan Arminian Confession of
   Faith," *Methodist Quarterly Review*, 10 (July 1891): 282–299;
   M. B. Chapman, "Evolution as a Method of Creation," *Methodist Quarterly
   Review*, 17 (November–December 1894): 224–231; Wilbur Fisk Tillett, "The
   Higher Criticism," *Methodist Quarterly Review*, 17 (January–February 1895):
   321–332; O. E. Brown, "A Comparative Study of Methodist Theology,"
   Methodist Quarterly Review, 18 (May–June 1895): 193–203; Wilbur Fisk
   Tillett, "Some Currents of Contemporaneous Theological Thought," *The
   Methodist Review* [The MQR renamed] 27 (July–August, 1901): 483–495;
   Harold Mann, *Atticus Haygood: Methodist Bishop, Editor and Educator*

(Athens: University of Georgia Press, 1965): 121–122, 162–166. George Gilman Smith [former Confederate chaplain] to Young John Allen December 13, 1891? [Box 16]; Smith to Allen, January 23, 1896; Smith to Allen, June 10, 1903. Mollie Yarborough Haygood to Y. J. Allen, April 30, 1903: She had heard a minister dismiss traditionalists as not quite civilized. Y. J. Allen Papers, Emory University; Charles Dowman to Davis Gray January 13, 1881, Burge Family Papers, Emory University; Owen, *Sacred Flame of Love*, 130–187.

34 Harris, *Book and Heart*, 23–24, 32, 156–159; Unidentified Manuscript, Box 102, folder 18, Corra White Harris Papers, University of Georgia Library; Harris, *As A Woman Thinks* (New York: Houghton Mifflin Co., 1925), 173–174, 177, 206; Harris, *The Happy Pilgrimage* (Boston: Houghton Mifflin Co., 1927), 90–95, 111, 135, 194; Harris, *Widow*, 74.

35 M. Landrum, "The Christian College," *The Emory Phoenix*, 2(November 1887): 2–3. "Christ in College," *The Emory Phoenix*, 5 (November 1890): 20.

36 Comments by the editor of *The Emory Phoenix*, 3 (November 1888): 2–4, 6; Comments by the editor of *The Emory Phoenix*, 3 (January 1889): 1. An essay on the religious life of Emory students in April 1890 reported that three fourths of the students were "consistent Christians"; 90 percent were "moral"; and they uttered few "oaths." Students boarded in Christian homes; there were "no theatres, germans [dancing clubs], bar-rooms, or gambling dens" in Oxford, see *The Emory Phoenix*, 4 (April 1890): 6; Mel R. Colquitt to Warren Akin Candler, December 2, 1888, insisted Emory students were no better behaved than those at the state university, Candler Papers, Emory University.

37 Lundy Howard Harris, "Speech of Professor Lundy H. Harris," *The Emory Phoenix*, 5 (March 1891): 11, 13.

38 Lundy Howard Harris, "Christ and Christmas," *The Emory Phoenix*, 10 (December 1895): 1–3.

39 Corra Harris, *Happy Pilgrimage*, pp. 90–95, 194.

40 Lundy Howard Harris, "Bishop Haygood," *The Emory Phoenix*, 10 (February, 1896): 5–6; Harris, "Second Paper on Bishop Haygood," *The Emory Phoenix*, 10(May 1896): 4–6.

41 Mann, *Haygood*, 37, 45, 150–210; *Teach the Freeman: The correspondence of Rutherford B. Hayes and the Slater Fund for Negro Education*, ed. Louis D. Rubin, 2 vols. (Baton Rouge: LSU pr, 1959), 1: 70–74.

42 Ibid 142–145, 189–196; Atticus Greene Haygood to Warren Akin Candler, August 30, 1882, and September 11, 1883, in Candler Papers, Emory University; "Service of Dedication of the Warren Akin Candler Memorial Library, September 5, 1947," in Warren Akin Candler Memorial Library Box; George E. Clary, Jr., "Biographical Notes on … Morgan Calloway"; E. C. Peters, "Dr. George Williams Walker, Pioneer [Second President]," Biographical Files, Paine College Archives.

43 The previous four paragraphs are based on Mann, *Haygood*, 125, 130–142 especially 142, and 187–199; Atticus G. Haygood, "A Thanksgiving Sermon" [at Emory], *Wesleyan Christian Advocate*, December 25, 1880; Atticus Greene Haygood, *Our Brother in Black: His Freedom and His Future* (New York: Phillips and Hunt, 1881): 58–72, 115–116, 158–219, especially 184, 185 and 187–195; Haygood, *Jack-Knife and Brambles* (Nashville: Publishing

House Methodist Episcopal Church South, 1893), 40, 291; Haygood, *The Monk and the Prince* (Atlanta: Foote & Davies, 1895), 299. See Haygood to "My Dear Warren [Warren Akin Candler]," September 11, 1883 and September 26, 1883, Candler Papers, Emory University. See also the following in the Young John Allen Papers, Emory: Haygood to Young John Allen, September 25, 1881 and March 21, 1882 and May 30, 1882; Eugene R. Hendrix to Allen, February 10, 1882, July 1, 1882, and January 21, 1896; Atticus Greene Haygood to Allen May 30, 1882. See also Francis J. Grimke, *The Negro: His Rights and Wrongs, The Forces For Him and Against Him* (Washington DC: Fifteenth Street Presbyterian Church, 1898), 63–64.

44 Atticus Greene Haygood to [former President of the United States] Rutherford B. Hayes, 12 June 1885, in Rubin, *Teach the Freeman*, 1: 149–152.

45 J. B. Eustis, "Race Antagonism in the South," *Forum*, 6 (October 1888): 144–154.

46 *Southwestern Christian Advocate*, August 30, September 6, 1888.

47 Atticus G. Haygood, "Senator Eustis on the Negro Problem," *The Independent*, 40 (8 November 1888): 1426–1427.

48 See for example the comments of F. C. Woodward, "The Freedman's Case in Reality," *Methodist Quarterly Review*, 7 (January 1885): 3–16; I. E. Shumate, "A Novelist out of His Element," *Methodist Quarterly Review*, 8 (April 1886): 193–214.

49 Ralph E. Luker, *The Social Gospel in Black and White: American Racial Reform, 1885–1912* (Chapel Hill: University of North Carolina Press, 1991), 69–71; Joel Williamson, *The Crucible of Race: Black-White Relations in the American South Since Emancipation* (New York: Oxford University Press, 1984), 104–107. George Washington Cable, *The Silent South [Together with `The Freedman's Case in Equity* (Montclair: Patterson Smith, 1969 originally published by Charles Scribner's Sons in 1889), 10, 16, 208; Lundy Howard Harris, "Speech of Professor Lundy H. Harris," *The Emory Phoenix*, 5 (March 1891): 11, 13.

50 William H. Baskervill to George Washington Cable, January 8, 1890; Cable to Baskervill January 14, 1890 [Copy], George Washington Cable Collection, Tulane University.

51 Mann, *Atticus Haygood* 192–196; Haygood to Young John Allen May 30, 1882, Allen Papers, Emory University; Haygood to "My Dear Warren," September 11 and 26, 1883, Candler Papers, Emory University; Haygood, *Jack-Knife and Brambles*, 40, 291; Haygood, *The Monk and the Prince*, 1895), 299.

52 Atticus G. Haygood, "The Black Shadow in the South," *Forum*, 13 (October 1893): 167, 168; *The Independent*, 15 (1 February 1889): 1–3. For his celebration of a utopian Christian "brotherhood" see "The Chief Characteristics of our Century," *Methodist Quarterly Review*, 15 (October 1893): 49–57. See also Ida B. Wells, *A Red Record: Lynchings in the United States* (Chicago: Wells 128 Clark Street, 1894): 25–26. The "Record" is reprinted in *Southern Horrors and Other Writings: The Anti-Lynching Campaign of Ida B. Wells, 1892–1900*, ed. Jacqueline Jones Royster (Boston: Bedford Books, 1997) and Ida Wells-Barnett, *On Lynchings* (New York: Arno: The New York Times, 1969).

53 *The Christian Recorder*, November 30, 1893.
54 The previous four paragraphs are based on Haygood, "The Black Shadow in the South": 167–174 and Wells, "A Red Record: Lynchings in the United States": 25–26. The books that revealed Haygood in another, more recognizable mood were *Jack-Knife and Brambles*, esp. 121, 131, 291, 277–300, and *Monk and Prince*, esp. 96.
55 Henri Hubert and Marcel Mauss, *Sacrifice: Its Nature and Function*, tr. W. D. Hall (London: Cohen & West, 1964, first published in French in 1898), 53, 55.
56 Wells, "A Red Record: Lynchings in the United States": 21–32, esp. 31; *The* [Baltimore] *Sun*, February 2, 1893; *Chicago Daily News*, February 2, 1893; Williamson, *Crucible of Race*, 186–192.
57 L[ogan]. E[dwin]. Bleckley, "Negro Outrage No Excuse for Lynching," *Forum*, 13 (November 1893): 300–302; J[ohn]. R[ichard]. Slattery, "The South in the Saddle," *The Independent*, 45 (16 November 1893): 5–8. For discussion of Father Slattery's evangelization of African Americans, see Stephen J. Ochs, *Desegregating the Altar: The Josephites and the Struggle for Black Priests, 1871–1960* (Baton Rouge: Louisiana State University Press, 1990), 4–5, 49–134. Slattery was too conservative for black Catholics, but he was not gulled by defenders of lynching. His attempt to recruit more than three black priests for the Roman Catholic Church in the United States was a failure: He was compromised by his ambivalent paternalism and the Church's racism. See also E. L. Godkin, "Southern Lynching," *The Nation*, 57 (November 2, 1893): 322–323.
58 Atticus Greene Haygood to Rutherford B. Hayes March 30, 1885 in Rubin, *Teach the Freeman*: 1: 139.
59 Atticus G. Haygood, "The Chief Characteristics of Our Century, *Methodist Quarterly Review*, 15 (October 1893): 49–57.
60 Atticus G. Haygood, "Lynching by Wholesale," *The Independent*, 46 (June 28, 1894): 1.
61 E. E. Hoss, "Lynch Law and the Southern Press," *The Independent*, 46 (February 1, 1894): 1–2; Atticus G. Haygood, "The Chief Characteristics of Our Century"; J. C. Galloway, "Lynching in the South," *The Independent*, 46 (February 1, 1894): 2–3; Haygood, "A Christmas Letter from the South," *The Independent*, 48 January 9, 1896): 2–3; Haygood to Warren Akin Candler, September 11, 26, 1883, December 31, 1888; J. D. Hammond to Candler, 6 March 1893; J. L. Pierce to Candler, January 9, 1894; H. L. Ellis to Candler, January 10, 1895; W. W. Duncan to Candler, February 5, 1895, Candler Papers, Emory University; Mann, *Atticus Haygood*, 205–256. W[illiam]. P. Lovejoy, D. D., "Georgia's Record of Blood," *The Independent*, 51 (May 11, 1899): 1297–1300.
62 Lundy H. Harris, "Bishop Haygood," *The Emory Phoenix*, 10 (February 1896): 5–6; Harris, "Second Paper on Bishop Haygood," *The Emory Phoenix* 10 (May 1896): 4–6.
63 Mark K. Bauman, *Warren Akin Candler: The Conservative as Idealist* (Metuchen: The Scarecrow Press, 1981), 71; Warren Akin Candler to "My Dear Brother [T. Y. Ramsey], April 11, 1895; W. P. Patillo to Candler February 8,

1893, Candler Papers, Emory University; *The* [Atlanta] *Constitution*, July 11 and 15, 1894.

64 Henry Stiles Bradley to Mrs. L. H. (Corra) Harris, October 3, 1910, Harris Papers, University of Georgia; Elam Dempsey to his Parents, November 28, 1897 in Elam Dempsey Papers, Emory University Library; Lundy Howard Harris, "Speech of Professor Lundy H. Harris," *The Emory Phoenix*, 5 (March 1891): 11, 13; Harris, "Christ and Christmas," *The Emory Phoenix*, 10 (December 1895): 1–3; Note in *The Emory Phoenix*, 9 (January 1895): 14; Corrie Harris to Warren Akin Candler, 17 and 24 June 17, 24, 1898, Candler Papers, Emory University. The party is mentioned in *The Emory Phoenix*, 12 (June 1898): 371. See also Talmadge, *Corra Harris*, 16. John E. Talmadge interviewed Charles J. Harrell who reported the note.

65 Corrie Harris to Warren Akin Candler, June 12, 18, and 19 [?], Candler Papers, Emory University; "Dr. Moore's Successor," *The Emory Phoenix*, 12(December 1897): 97. Sledd met with the Latin Club every Thursday beginning in February. Note in *The Emory Phoenix*, 12 (February 1898): 187. See Terry Lee Matthews, "The Emergence of a Prophet: Andrew Sledd and the 'Sledd Affair of 1902'" (Ph.D. diss., Duke University, 1989): 76–89.

66 Corrie Harris to Warren Akin Candler, June 12, 17, 18, 24 and July 1, 8, 22 1898; Harris to Bishop and Mrs. Candler July [15], 1898, Candler Papers, Emory University.

67 Luke G. Johnson to Warren Akin Candler, June 16 and 22, 1898; Corrie Harris to Candler, June 12, 17, 18, 24 and July 1 and 8, 1898; William Albinus Harris to Candler, June 22, 1898; Henry Harris to Candler June 26, 1898; William P. Lovejoy to Candler, June 21, 1898; Nath[an] Thompson to Candler June 23, 1898; Lundy Harris to Candler June 28, 1898 and October 29, 1899, Candler Papers, Emory University.

68 Lundy Harris Notebook, Box 99.12, Harris Papers, University of Georgia.

69 Corra Harris, *Justice* (New York: Heart's International Library, 1915), 17–63; Harris, *Eve's Second Husband* (Philadelphia: Henry Altemus Company, 1910), esp. 304–6; Harris, *In Search of a Husband* (Garden City: Doubleday, Page & Company, 1913); Harris, *House of Helen* (New York: George Doran Company, 1923). At the end of the book there is a confrontation between the wife and her husband's dark, arrogant, and beautiful mistress.

70 Lundy Harris to Warren Akin Candler October 31, 1899; Corrie Harris to Mrs. Candler, October 29, 1899, Candler Papers, Emory University; Mrs. L. H. [Corra] Harris, "Negro Womanhood," *The Independent*, 51 (June 22, 1899): 1687–1689.

71 See for example: *Mary Chesnut's Civil War*, ed. C. Vann Woodward (New Haven: Yale University Press, 1981), 29–31; [Gertrude Clanton Thomas], *Secret Eye*, 166–169.

72 Harris, *Book*, 23–25.

73 Corrie Harris to Warren Akin Candler, June 17, 18, 24 1898, Candler Papers, Emory University; Harris, *As A Woman Thinks*, 81. Harris, *The Happy Pilgrimage*, 111.

74 Corrie Harris to Warren Candler, June 24, 1898 and July 1, 1899; Harris to Candler, June 29 1899; see also William J. Lovejoy to Candler, 27 July 1898, Candler Papers, Emory University.

75 Corra Harris to William Hayes Ward, March 17, 1900 and February 5, 1903 in Corra White Harris Papers, University of Virginia Library.

76 Mrs. Lundy H. Harris [Corra] to Paul Elmer More, July 12 and 13, 1901, Paul Elmore More papers, Princeton University, available on microfilm in the University of Georgia Microfilm Collection.

77 Corra Harris to William Hayes Ward, February 5, 1903, Harris Papers, University of Virginia Library.

78 In a speech manuscript, Harris confessed that her "prejudices have died down" and that her "Nordic conceit is fading out." She trashed the idea that one race was "superior to other people of other races." See Corra Harris, "Black and White," manuscript article in box 74.12, Harris Papers, University of Georgia.

79 Hall, *Revolt against Chivalry*, 86–99; Carrie Parks [Mrs. Luke] Johnson was an activist within the missionary societies of the Methodist Episcopal Church, South; she was committed to the Scarritt School for Christian Workers that trained women for various kinds of missionary work, mostly within the United States. Her family had been active in Georgia Methodism for over 120 years. Her pedigree made her appear to be more conservative than she actually was. See Scarritt College Papers. Methodist Center, Drew University, 1381–1384-2 Box 9b/ Folder "Mrs. Luke Johnson."

Chapter 3

1 Ann Taves, *Fits, Trances & Visions: Experiencing Religion and Explaining Experience from Wesley to James* (Princeton: Princeton University Press, 1999), 107, 113–117, 239–240; Christopher H. Owen, *The Sacred Flame of Love: Methodism and Society in Nineteenth-Century Georgia* (Athens: University of Georgia Press, 1998), 162.

2 William James, *The Varieties of Religious Experience: A Study in Human Nature* (New York: Random House, The Modern Library, Copyright by William James, 1902), 53–76; Carol Zaleski, "Speaking of William James to the Cultured Among His Despisers," in *The Struggle for Life: A Companion to William James' The Varieties of Religious Experience*, eds. Donald Capps and Janet L. Jacobs (Princeton: Society for the Scientific Study of Religion and Princeton Theological Seminary, 1995), 50–51 and 40–60. See also Emile Durkheim, *The Elementary Forms of Religious Life*, tr. Karen E. Fields (New York: The Free Press, 1995. Original printed as *Les Formes elementaries de la vie religieuse: Le systeme totemique en Australie*, Paris, F. Alcan, 1912), 217–218.

3 William Walker, *The Southern Harmony & Musical Companion*, ed. Glenn Wilcox (Philadelphia: E. W. Miller, 1854 reissued in 1987 by the University Press of Kentucky), 36–39, 40–41, 81–85, 89, 118, 123, 139, 181; Dickson D. Bruce, *And they All Sang Hallelujah: Plain-Folk Camp-Meeting Religion 1800–1845* (Knoxville: University of Tennessee Press, 1974), 103–107;

Walter White, *Rope and Faggot: A Biography of Judge Lynch* (New York: Arno Press and the New York Times, 1969 reprint of the 1929 edition), 40–53. Mark Wallace, in *Figuring the Sacred: Religion, Narrative, and the Imagination* (Minneapolis: Fortress Press, 1995) notes that the shout of "Glory!" should be understood as testimony affirming the Infinite. See also Robert Lewis Dabney, "Vindicatory Justice Essential to God" [*Southern Pulpit* April 1881], *Discussions of Robert L. Dabney D. D., LL. D.*, ed. C. R. Vaughn, 3 vols. (Richmond: Presbyterian Committee of Publication, 1890), 1: 466–481, esp. 467, 468, 469, 479. See also *The* [Atlanta] *Constitution*, January 31, 1898.

4 Orlando Patterson, *Rituals of Blood: Consequences of Slavery in Two American Centuries* (Washington, DC: Civitas/Counterpoint,1998); James G. Williams, *The Bible, Violence and the Sacred: Liberation from the Myth of Sanctioned Violence* (San Francisco: HarperSan-Francisco, 1991); Rene Girard, *Violence and the Sacred* (Baltimore: The Johns Hopkins University Press, 1972); Susan L. Mizruchi, *The Science of Sacrifice: American Literature and Modern Social Theory* (Princeton: Princeton University Press, 1998), 52–76; Henri Hubert and Marcel Mauss, *Sacrifice: Its Nature and Function*, tr. W. D. Hall, (London: Cohen & West, 1964, first published in French in 1898), 17–49, 77–98.

5 The quotation is from Jon Pahl, *Empire of Sacrifice: The Religious Origins of American Violence* (New York: New York University Press, 2010), 15. See also *The* [Atlanta] *Constitution*, April 27, 28, 1899.

6 See for example, Ralph C. Wood, *Flannery O'Connor and the Christ-Haunted South* (Grand Rapids: William B. Eerdmans Publishing Company, 2004), 153, 265, 265n.18; also Susan Ketchin, *The Christ-Haunted Landscape: Faith and Doubt in Southern Fiction* (Jackson: University Press of Mississippi, 1994). For the Bible and slavery, see Donald G. Mathews, *Religion in the Old South* (Chicago: University of Chicago Press, 1977), chap. 4.

7 *The* [Atlanta] *Constitution*, February 21, 1898.

8 "Report on Temperance," in *Minutes of the Forty-Eighth Anniversary of the Georgia Baptist State Convention, Held at Newnan, April 22d, 23d, and 25th, 1870* (Atlanta: Franklin Steam Printing House, 1870), 13, referenced in Joe L. Coker, *Liquor in the Land of the Lost Cause: Southern White Evangelicals and the Prohibition Movement* (Lexington: The University Press of Kentucky, 2007), 19–36, esp. 34. Peter Gay, *The Bourgeois Experience Victoria to Freud, Volume 1: Education of the Senses* (New York: Oxford University Press, 1984), esp. 278–327.

9 J[ames]. H[enley]. Thornwell, *Report on the Subject of Slavery* (Columbia: Steam-Power Press of A. S. Johnston, 1852), 4–5; Ted Ownby, *Subduing Satan: Religion, Recreation and Manhood in the Rural South, 1865–1920* (Chapel Hill: The University of North Carolina Press, 1990).

10 Coker, *Liquor and Lost Cause*, 37–173.

11 See for example the [Newnan, Georgia] *Herald and Advertiser* July 8, 1892; Michael Perman, *Struggle for Mastery: Disfranchisement in the South 1888–1908* (Chapel Hill: University of North Carolina Press, 2001), 48–50; Joel Williamson, *The Crucible of Race: Black-White Relations in the American South Since Emancipation* (New York: Oxford University Press,

1984), 113; Rebecca Latimer Felton, "The Rescue Work in Relation to Womanhood and Temperance" in Rebecca Latimer Felton Papers, University of Georgia Library Manuscripts Division, as quoted in Crystal N. Feimster, *Southern Horrors: Women and the Politics of Rape and Lynching* (Cambridge: Harvard University Press, 2009), 83.

12 The [Newnan, Georgia] *Herald and Advertiser*, August 19, September 2, 1887; October 26, 1888; February 24, 1893; December 16, 1898; January 6, 20, 27, and March 31, 1899; See also, *The* [Atlanta] *Constitution*, April 23, 27, 28 1899; see columns devoted to religion in *The Constitution* every week for the first eight months of 1899.

13 *The* [Atlanta] *Constitution*, June 5, 1898.

14 Drew Gilpin Faust, *The Creation of Confederate Nationalism: Ideology and Identity in the Civil War South* (Baton Rouge: Louisiana State University Press, 1989), 22–40 esp. 17 and 26; David B. Chesebrough, *"God Ordained this War": Sermons on the Sectional Crisis, 1830–1865* (Columbia: University of South Carolina Press, 1991), 208; Robert Lewis Dabney, *A Defence of Virginia and through Her of the South* (New York: E J Hale & Son, 1867), 22, 356; Charles Reagan Wilson, *Baptized in Blood: The Religion of the Lost Cause, 1865–1920* (Athens: University of Georgia Press, 1980), 55, 76.

15 The previous three paragraphs rely on *The* [Newnan, Georgia] *Herald and Advertiser*, August 5 and 19, 1887; David W. Bright, *Race and Reunion: The Civil War in American Memory* (Cambridge: Harvard University Press, 2001), 38.

16 Ibid., August 5 and 12, 1887; March 18, May 18, July 20 and 27, 1888; November 3, 1893; April 12 and August 23, 1895; July 2, 1897; May 13 and October 7, 1898.

17 Numan V. Bartley, *The Creation of Modern Georgia* (Athens: University of Georgia Press, 1990), 161 and 45–74; Donald L. Grant, *The Way it Was in the South: The Black Experience in Georgia* (Athens: University of Georgia Press, 1993), 113–136; Elizabeth Studley Nathans, *Losing the Peace: Georgia Republicans and Reconstruction, 1865–1871* (Baron Rouge: Louisiana State University Press, 1968), 127–132. Paul A. Cimbala points out that when the Federal government established the Freedman's Bureau to protect Georgia's freedpeople, Conservatives responded with subterfuge and violence. The Bureau tried to protect African Americans at times, but all too often failed. Of the 341 complaints of white violence in 1868, only 71 could be resolved. Conservatives easily seized control of the local bureaucracy in order to serve planters not African Americans. See *Under the Guardianship of the Nation: The Freedman's Bureau and the Reconstruction of Georgia, 1865–1870* (Athens: University of Georgia Press, 1997), 196 and 208; also 50–165, 193–216. See also Steven Hahn, *A Nation Under Our Feet: Black Political Struggles in the Rural South from Slavery to the Great Migration* (Cambridge: Harvard University Press, 2003), 288–294.

18 The best discussion of Reconstruction is Eric Foner, *Reconstruction: America's Unfinished Revolution, 1863–1877* (New York: Harper & Row Publishers, 1988). Specific material referred to here is on page 113. See also

308 *Notes to pages 102–106*

Grant, *The Black Experience in Georgia*, 115, 106–126; Daniel W. Stowell, *Rebuilding Zion: The Religious Reconstruction of the South, 1863–1877* (New York: Oxford University Press, 1998), 152–156, 185.

19 Jacqueline Jones, *Soldiers of Light and Love: Northern Teachers and Georgia Blacks, 1865–1873* (Chapel Hill: University of North Carolina Press, 1980) and Joe M. Richardson, *Christian Reconstruction: The American Missionary Association and Southern Blacks, 1861–1890* (Athens: The University of Georgia Press, 1986). See also Stephen Ward Angell, *Bishop Henry McNeal Turner and African American Religion in the South* (Knoxville: University of Tennessee Press, 1992), 33–107; Grant, *The Black Experience in Georgia*, 92, 105, 118, 130–132; Allen W. Trelease, *White Terror: The Ku Klux Klan Conspiracy and Southern Reconstruction* (Baton Rouge: Louisiana State University Press, 1971, 1999), 318–335. See also Barton C. Shaw, *The Wool-Hat Boys: Georgia's Populist Party* (Baton Rouge: Louisiana State University Press, 1984), 63, 69–74, 82–88, 132–138. Historians agree with Jacquelyn Hall's statement that "private, collective violence in support of white supremacy was embedded in southern political culture" by 1877. See Jacquelyn Dowd Hall, *Revolt against Chivalry: Jessie Daniel Ames and the Women's Campaign against Lynching* (New York: Columbia University Press, 1979), 131.

20 W. Fitzhugh Brundage, *Lynching in the New South: Georgia and Virginia 1880–1930* (Urbana: University of Illinois Press, 1993), 72–74. See also the classic Bertram Wilbur Doyle, *The Etiquette of Race Relations in the South: A Study in Social Control* (Chicago: University of Chicago Press, 1937).

21 *American Slavery: A Composite Autobiography*, George P. Rawick, General Editor. Greenwood Electronic Media (Westport: Greenwood Publishing Company, 2002.): Interviews in Georgia: Mattie Fannen, Newnan, Georgia; *The* [Newnan, Georgia] *Herald and Advertiser*, July 20, 1888, April 7, 1899; John H. Caldwell, *Slavery and Southern Methodism: Two Sermons Preached in the Methodist Church in Newnan, Georgia* ([Probably LaGrange, GA]: John H. Caldwell, 1865), iii–x, 16–21, 23–29, 32–43, 49–80; Daniel W. Stowell, "'The Negroes Cannot Navigate Alone' Religious Scalawags and the Biracial Methodist Episcopal Church in Georgia, 1866–1876," in *Georgia in Black and White: Explorations in the Race Relations of a Southern State, 1865–1950*, ed. John C. Inscoe (Athens: University of Georgia Press, 1994), 74 for quotation, and 65–90; Stowell, "'We Have Sinned, and God Has Smitten Us!' John H. Caldwell and the Religious Meaning of Confederate Defeat," *Georgia Historical Quarterly*, 78 (Spring 1994): 1–32. Editors of the *Southwestern Christian Advocate*, April 13, 1899 recalled Caldwell fondly.

22 James Gilligan, *Violence: Our Deadly Epidemic and Its Causes* (New York: George. P. Putnam's Sons, 1996), 185; Jeanette Anderson Good, *Shame, Images of God and the Cycle of Violence* (Lanham: University Press of America, Inc., 1999), 17–22, 23–27.

23 *The* [Newnan, Georgia] *Herald and Advertiser*, October 18, 1898.

24 Ibid., December 13, 1889 and October 7, 1898.

25 *The* [Atlanta] *Constitution*, March 20, 1898, [Charles Hudgins]; August 21 [E. P. Davis], September 4 [T. M. McConnell], October 30 [A. V. Boone], November 20 [R. V. Atkinson], 1899.

26 *The* [Newnan, Georgia] *Herald and Advertiser*, May 31 and July 14, 1889, July 29, 1893, August 23, 1895, April 8, July 29, and also December 16 and 30, 1898; January 13 and 20, and February 10,1899; Warren A. Candler "The Church vs. the Theater" (Nashville: Southern Methodist Publishing House, 1887), pamphlet, in Warren Akin Candler Papers, Woodruff Library Special Collections, Emory University; Kathleen Minnix, *Laughter in the Amen Corner: The Life of Evangelist Sam Jones* (Athens: University of Georgia Press, 1993), 123.

27 John Shackford Collection, Methodist Center Archives, Drew University.

28 *The* [Atlanta] *Constitution*, June 26 [George Lofton], August 21 [E. P. Davis], September 11 [S. J. Heaton] and 18 [Thornton Whaling], October 2 [W. W. Landrum] and 23 [John Mathews], December 4, 1899 [W. O. Cochrane].

29 Cash, Wilbur J., *The Mind of the South* (New York: Random House [Vintage Books], 1969 [1941, Alfred Knopf]), 58; Allen Tullos, *Habits of Industry: White Culture and the Transformation of the Carolina Piedmont* (Chapel Hill: University of North Carolina Press, 1989), 91: "God was a 'Fearful God.' I don't remember anything about His mercy and compassion and forgiveness."

30 *The* [Atlanta] *Constitution*, December 25, 1899 [John C. Kilgo, President of Trinity College, Durham, N.C.] Harris, *A Circuit Rider's Wife*, 77; Bishop O. P. Fitgerald, *Fifty Years: Observations – Opinions – Experiences* (Nashville: Publishing House of the Methodist Episcopal Church South, 1903), 50–51, 184–187; John Andrew Rice, *I Came out of the Eighteenth Century* (New York: Harper and Brothers, 1942), 54–58, 154, 161–163, 176.

31 Harris, *A Circuit Rider's Wife*, 289–290.

32 These two paragraphs are based on *The [Newnan, Georgia] Herald and Advertiser*, July 22 and 29, 1898; see also December 16 and 30, 1898; January 13 and 20, and February 10, 1899. See also Christopher H. Owen, "By Design: The Social Meaning of Methodist Architecture in Nineteenth Century Georgia," *Georgia Historical Quarterly*, 75 (Summer 1991): 221–253.

33 Mrs. Juliana Hayes at the "world's Missionary Conference" as reported in the *Woman's Missionary Advocate*, 9 (November 1888); see also W. Winston Skinner, *A Centennial History of Central Baptist Church Newnan, Georgia* (Franklin TN: Providence House Publishers, 1997); see also for previous quotations and reference to commerce *The* [Newnan, Georgia] *Herald and Advertiser*, October 15 and December 11, 1897; May 6, 1898. For Baptist women, see Regina D. Sullivan, *Lottie Moon: A Southern Baptist Missionary to China in History and Legend* (Baton Rouge: Louisiana State University Press, 2011).

34 *The* [Newnan, Georgia] *Herald and Advertiser*, October 15 and 29, November 12 and 26, 1897; April 29, May 27, July 8 and 22, August 5 and September 16, 1898; January 6 and 20, and February 3, 1899. One writer explained on January 20, 1899, "Our commercial and political interests as well as our religious duty demand that we should give [Roman Catholic countries] the enlightenment and stimulus that come from an open Bible."

35 Haygood's attempts to convince ministers to accept blacks as "brothers" had to contend with a ministerial obsession with sex. See, for example,

W. M. Leftwich, "The Race Problem in the South," *Southern Methodist Review*, 6 (April 1889): 88–89. "Mr. Cable," the minister wrote, "is a renegade Southron ... feeding Northern fanaticism and in turn being fed by Northern flattery and money."

36 Belle Harris Bennett, "Miss Bennett's Address," *Our Homes*, 6 (January 1897) and also issues in February, June, August, September 1897; April, May, July, 1899. See Mrs. R. W. [Tochie] Macdonell, *Belle Harris Bennett: Her Life and Work* (Nashville: Board of Missions, Methodist Episcopal Church, South, 1928). To understand how Methodist women embraced womanhood to spearhead progress in the Methodist Episcopal Church, South, see Hall, *Revolt against Chivalry*, 57–77.

37 See http://en.wikipedia.org/w/index.php?title=The_Man_With_the_Hoe& printable=yes. Quotations from the poem and Markham's response are in Edwin Markham, *The Man with the Hoe* (New York: Doubleday and McClure Company, 1900), 39.

38 [Mary Helm], "Restoration or Retribution, Which?" *Our Homes*, 8 (July 1899), 1.

39 *The* [Atlanta] *Constitution*, August 27, ("The Man with the Hoe") and September 3, November 19, 1899 (Speech by W. H. Council). See also *The* [Sparta, Georgia] *Ishmaelite*, November 24, 1899.

40 These four paragraphs are based on Stephen Ward Angell, *Bishop Henry McNeal Turner and African American Religion in the South* (Knoxville: University of Tennessee Press, 1992), 260–274; Andre E. Johnson, *The Forgotten Prophet: Bishop Henry McNeal Turner and the African American Prophetic Tradition* (Lanham: Lexington Books, 2012); Wesley John Gaines, *The Negro and the White Man* (Philadelphia: AME Publishing House, 1897), 124, 129, 142–145; *Star of Zion*, June 13, 1889, March 28 and April 14, 1898; *The Georgia Baptist*, esp. January 19 and 26, 1898; December 1, 1898; January 19, February 9, April 20, 1899.

41 *The Georgia Baptist*, December 1, 1898 and April 20, 1899.

42 *The* [Newnan, Georgia] *Herald and Advertiser*, October 7, 1887; May 24, 1889; July 14 and October 13, 1893; September 28, 1894; May 31 and October 4, 1895; January 31, 1896; April 15 and July 22, 1898.

43 Ibid., January 19, 1894; April 19, 1895; October 1, 1897; November 26, 1897.

44 For these two paragraphs, ibid., September 17 and 24, October 9, 22, and 29, November 5, 1897; February 11, 1898.

45 Jessica Hendrickson Ruckheim, "Defining a Celebrated Community: Newnan, Georgia African American Residents in Pinson Street 1920–1940," (M. A. Thesis, State University of West Georgia, 2002), 7–24.

46 Twelfth Census of the United States. Schedule One – Population. Georgia, Coweta County, Newnan City, Fifth District outside the City; Newnan City Militia District 646; Newnan City Fourth District, 647; Newnan City Militia District 753; Newnan City Hurricane District 755; Newnan City Militia District 691. See also Newnan-Coweta Historical Society, *A History of Coweta County, Georgia* (Roswell: W. H. Wolfe Associates, 1988), 5–12; *The* [Newnan, Georgia] *Herald and Advertiser*, August 5 and 19, 1898 and April 28, 1899.

47 *The* [Newnan, Georgia] *Herald and Advertiser*, April 9, 1897.

48 Ibid., July 29, 1887; November 6, 1891; October 21 and December 16, 1892; January 27 and March 3, 1893; February 9, and May 4, 1894; January 11, May 10, September 27, and October 11, 1895; January 15 and 22, March 5, April 9, and October 11, 1897; July 22 and 29, August 5, 1898; May 19 and August 4, 1899.

49 Ibid., May 19, also August 4, 1899.

50 Shaw, *The Wool-Hat Boys*, 67–90, 124–126, 136–138, 140–157. For context, see *The* [Atlanta, Georgia] *Constitution*, June 1 to June 30, August 26 and 30, October 14 and 26, 1894; *The* [Newnan, Georgia] *Herald and Advertiser*, April 30 and May 24, 1889; November 7 and December 5, 1890; August 5, 1892; March 23, 1894.

51 For previous two paragraphs, see ibid., 136–138; *The* [Newnan, Georgia] *Herald and Advertiser*, December 6, 1895; November 6, 1896; August 13 and 20, 1897; *The* [Atlanta, Georgia] *Constitution*, November 4 and December 18–30, 1894; January 1, February 5 and December 4, 5, 9, 11, 1895; October 28, 1897; "Southern Protests Against Lynching," *The Century*, 55 (January 1898): 476.

52 *The* [Newnan, Georgia] *Herald and Advertiser*, May 21, August 8, 13 and 20, 1897; *The* [Sparta, Georgia] *Ishmaelite*, August 6 and 27, 1897.

53 Pahl, *Empire of Sacrifice*, 13–34. Kathleen Taylor, *Cruelty: Human Evil and the Human Brain* (New York: Oxford University Press, 2009), 6, makes two points about cruelty: It is usually done by normal people; and the "difference between someone hurling verbal abuse at an immigrant [or African American] and someone beating an immigrant [African-American] to death is a difference of degree, not a difference in kind." See also *The* [Atlanta] *Constitution*, November 16 and 21, 1893; November 10, 19 and December 23, 1894; January 13, April 2, 11, 12, 1895; March 17 and 19, 1896. William F. Holmes, "Moonshining & Collective Violence: Georgia 1889–1895, *Journal of American History*, 67 (December 1980): 589–611.

54 *The* [Newnan, Georgia] *Herald and Advertiser*, December 7, 14, 21, 1894; March 8, 1895.

55 Ibid., June 18, 25, July 23 and 30, 1897; Amy Louise Wood, *Lynching and Spectacle: Witnessing Racial Violence in America, 1890–1940* (Chapel Hill: University of North Carolina Press, 2009), 27–33, 276n30; Michael A. Trotti, "The Scaffold's Revival: Race and Public Execution in the South," *Journal of Social History*, 45 (Number One, 2011): 195–224.

56 Irene Quenzler Brown and Richard D. Brown, *The Hanging of Ephraim Wheeler* (Cambridge: Harvard University Press, 2003), 232, 290, and 230–290. See also Brian K. Smith, "Capital Punishment and Human Sacrifice," *Journal of the American Academy of Religion*, 68 (March 2000), 3–25; Elizabeth D. Purdum and J. Anthony Paredes, "Rituals of Death: Capital Punishment and Human Sacrifice" in *Facing the Death Penalty: Essays on a Cruel and Unusual Punishment*, ed. Michael L. Radelet (Philadelphia: Temple University Press, 1989), 139–155; Michael Taussig, "Transgression," in *Critical Terms for Religious Studies*, ed. Mark C. Taylor (Chicago: U of Chicago Press, 1998), 349–364; Georges S. Bataille, *Eroticism Death and Sensuality*,

tr. Mary Dalwood (San Francisco: City Lights Books, 1986 of a book original published in 1957 as *L'Eroticisme*, par Les Editions de Minuit, Paris), 17–22, 89–93, 120–121; Michael Foucault, "A Preface to Transgression" in Michel Foucault, *Religion and Culture*, ed. Jeremy R. Carrette (New York: Routledge, 1999), 57–71; Katerina Clark and Michael Holquist, *Mikhail Bakhtin* (Cambridge: Belknap Press of Harvard University Press, 1984), 299–303; the [Newnan, Georgia] *Herald and Advertiser*, July 23, 30, 1897.

57 The *[Newnan, Georgia] Herald and Advertiser*, December 7, 14, 21, 1894; March 8, 1895; Trotti, "The Scaffold's Revival."

58 Michel Foucault, *Discipline and Punish: The Birth of the Prison*, tr. Alan Sheridan (New York: Random House Vintage Books, 1995), 8, 9.

59 Wood, *Lynching and Spectacle*, 29–30, 38.

60 Annulla Linders, "The Execution Spectacle and State Legitimacy: The Changing Nature of the American Execution Audience, 1833–1937," *Law & Society Review*, 36 (Number 3, 2002): 610–612,623–626, 630.

61 The [Newnan, Georgia] *Herald and Advertiser*, August 20, 1897.

62 Maggie Nelson, *The Art of Cruelty: A Reckoning* (New York: W. W. Norton & Company, 2011), 10, 31, 32, 35, 63, 268, 269. Psychologist Stanley Milgram enlisted the aid of middle class people in an experiment in which "authority" told subjects to administer severe electrical shocks to victims: "sixty four of the eighty contestants were willing to deliver shocks that could have killed their recipients had there been any actual receivers (35)."

63 Eric G. Wilson, *Everyone Loves a Good Train Wreck: Why We Can't Look Away* (New York: Sarah Crichton books of Farrar, Straus & Giroux, 2012), 10, 10l, 106–108, esp. 107, also 109–117, 163, 164–186; Bataille, *Eroticism*, 89–108, esp. 101, and 118–146.

64 Brundage, *Lynching in the New South*, 271–273. In January 1899, The [Newnan, Georgia] *Herald and Advertiser* carried a story based on statistics made available by the *Chicago Tribune*. The *Herald* listed numbers for murder, suicide, fire, storm, explosion, drowning, but not lynching.

65 This and the preceding paragraphs are based on The [Newnan, Georgia] *Herald and Advertiser*, November 29, 1895; August 12 and November 4, 1898; February 10, 1899; The [Atlanta, Georgia] *Constitution*, November 21, 1894 to January 2, 1895 for vigilantism; December 23, 1894 to January 1, 1895; October 31 and December 6, 1895; June 2 and 3, September 19 and December 6, 1896; July 26, 1897.

66 The [Sparta Georgia] *Ishmaelite*, November 22, 1901.

67 The [Newnan, Georgia] *Herald and Advertiser*, November 4, 1898.

68 Ibid., April 15 and July 8, 1898.

69 Stuart Creighton Miller, *"Benevolent Assimilation:" The American Conquest of the Philippines, 1899–1903* (New Haven: Yale University Press, 1982), 9, 11; Kristin L. Hoganson, *Fighting for American Manhood: How Gender Politics Provoked the Spanish-American and Philippine-American Wars* (New Haven: Yale University, 1998), 15–16, 18–35, 45–49, 66; Michael Hunt, *Ideology & U. S. Foreign Policy* (NewHaven: Yale University Press, 1987), 59–63.

70 The *Georgia Baptist*, March 31, April 7, 21 and 28, May 5, 19 and 26, July 21 and 28, August 11, 1898; February 9 and April 20, 1899.

71 *The* [Newnan, Georgia] *Herald and Advertiser*, August 19, 1898. John Hay christened the war as "splendid" and "little," quoted in Miller, *Benevolent Assimilation*, 12.

72 *The* [Newnan, Georgia] *Herald and Advertiser*, November 4, 1898: "Our Reunited Country."

73 Ibid., May 20, 1898.

74 *The* [Atlanta] *Constitution*, May 6, 12, 29; June 8, 13–16; July 17; September 26; October 25 and December 5, 21–23, 27, 1898; *Chicago Daily Tribune*, February 6 and March 30, 1899 for Minnesota volunteers who tried to lynch a white merchant in Augusta for killing one of their comrades. See also John E. Lewis to the Editor of the Illinois Record, June 5, 1898 in *"Smoked Yankees" and the Struggle for Empire: Letters from Negro Soldiers, 1898–1902*, ed. Willard B. Gatewood, Jr. (Fayetteville: University of Arkansas, 1987), 30–33, esp. 31.

75 *The Georgia Baptist*, March 31 and April 7 and 14, 1898. N. C. Bruce to the Editor of the *News and Observer*, May 7, 1898 in Gatewood, *Letters of Negro Soldiers*, 106–108.

76 The *Colored American*, October 15, 1898; March 18 and June 24, 1899.

77 The previous three paragraphs rely on: "Ham" to Editor of the Richmond *Planet*, September 24 and November 28, 1898; A Black Man to Editor of the Richmond *Planet*, December 1 and 13, 1898; C. W. Cordin to H. C. Smith, Editor of the Cleveland *Gazette*, December 17 21, 1898, February 5 and 14, 1899; Allen S. Peal to Smith March 15, 1899 in Gatewood, *Letters of Negro Soldiers*, 125–126, 138, 140–144, 147–150, 157–160, 171–175; *The* [Atlanta] *Constitution*, October 30, November 17 and 25, and December 23, 1898.

78 *The* [Atlanta] *Constitution*, March 7, 1899; *The Macon Telegraph*, February 4–11, 1899.

79 Ibid., December 29, 1898; January 6, 11, 12, 25, 1899; February 1–5 and 11, 1899; *The Macon Telegraph*, February 2, 4, 7–11, 1899.

80 The previous two paragraphs are based on *The Macon Telegraph*, March 7–9, 1899; *The* [Atlanta] *Constitution*, March 9–11, and 15, 1899; *The* [Newnan, Georgia] *Herald and Advertiser*, August 12, 1898; *Los Angeles Times*, March 9, 1899; *Louisville Courier-Journal*, March 9, 1899; *Nashville American*, March 9, 1899; *New York Times*, March 9, 1899; *Savannah Tribune*, March 11, 1899 *The Washington Post*, March 10, 1899.

81 *The* [Atlanta] *Constitution*, March 17 and 18, 1899; *Louisville Courier-Journal*, March 18, 1899; *New York Times*, March 17, 1899; *The* [Newnan, Georgia] *Herald and Advertiser*, March 31, 1899.

82 *The* [Newnan, Georgia] *Herald and Advertiser*, February 3, March 17, 24, 31, 1899. William J. White of *The Georgia Baptist* (March 3, 1899) called Cotton a "worthless colored youth."

Chapter 4

1 *The* [Atlanta] *Constitution*, April 4, 5, 9, 16, 1899.

2 Ida B. Wells-Barnett, *Lynch Law in Georgia* (Chicago: Chicago Colored Citizens, 1899), Kindle Edition; see also http://memory.loc.gov/cgi-bin/query/r?ammem/murray:@field (FLD001+91898209+):@@@REF based on the

same pamphlet in the Daniel A. P. Collection, 1818–1907; see also *The Richmond Planet*, October 14, 1899.

3 *The* [Newnan] *Herald and Advertiser*, April 17, 1899.

4 Wells-Barnett, *Lynch Law in Georgia*; see also *The Richmond Planet*, October 14, 1899.

5 Jacquelyn Dowd Hall, *Revolt against Chivalry: Jessie Daniel Ames and the Women's Campaign against Lynching* (New York: Columbia University Press, 1979), 149–157; Philip Dray, *At The Hands of Persons Unknown: The Lynching of Black America* (New York: Random House, 2002), 9–16 begins his book with the lynching of Sam Hose. No one should believe that black men did not rape white women; they did. Hose, however, probably didn't.

6 *The* [Atlanta] *Constitution*, April 24, 1899; *The* [Newnan] *Herald and Advertiser*, April 28, 1899. Also Dray, *At the Hands of Persons Unknown*, 16. As Dray makes clear, there is no way to know with absolute certainty what happened to Mrs. Cranford, but she was devastated. The first full report of the crime, *The* [Atlanta] *Constitution*, April 13, 1899, reports that Wilkes "assaulted" Mrs. Cranford, which could mean he laid hands on her. The *Herald* reported that Mrs. McLeroy accused Wilkes of having wronged her daughter by killing Alfred. *The Constitution* early reported that "There is great excitement over the murder." The nationally known statistician, Walter F. Willcox, received a letter from Governor W. Y. Atkinson, which Willcox interpreted as confirming the report of rape. African American leaders who trusted Atkinson were reported to have told him Hose was "guilty"; but they did not mention rape. See Willcox's comments in "Negro Criminality," in Alfred Holt Stone, *Studies in the American Race Problem*, Intro. William F. Willcox (New York: Doubleday, Page & Company, 1908), 463–468.

7 The previous five paragraphs are based on *The* [Atlanta] *Constitution*, March 19, 22, 25 and April 16, 25, 1899.

8 The *Atlanta Journal*, April 21 and 22, 1899. Johnston's version of what was happening was apparently the basis for a later interpretation of events by Walter Willcox, in "Negro Criminality" in Stone, *Studies in Race*, 443–475.

9 *The* [Atlanta] *Constitution*, April 13 to April 23 is the source for the previous 14 paragraphs. See also parallel reports in the *Atlanta Journal* and *The Macon Telegraph* for April 25, 1899.

10 *The* [Atlanta] *Constitution*, March 26 and June 8, 1897; February 15, October 11, and 21–22, 1898; January 3 and 29, February 10, March 1 and April 23, 1899; see also W. E. Burghardt DuBois, *On Sociology and the Black Community*, eds. Dan S. Green and Edwin D. Driver (Chicago: University of Chicago Press, 1978), 154–164. Du Bois reported that blacks who cleared fifty dollars in a year were the most successful; most lived in servile debt. Quoted segments are from W. E. Burghardt Du Bois, *The Souls of Black Folk* [1903] in W. E. B. Du Bois, *Writings*, ed. Nathan Huggins (New York: Literary Classics of the United States, Inc., 1986), 447–448, 450, 452,454.

11 The previous five paragraphs are based on *The* [Atlanta] *Constitution*, May 19, June 21 and 27, 1897; February 11 and December 5 and 11, 1898; April 23, 1899. Northen as governor had in May 1892 offered a reward for the

arrest of men who had lynched prisoners at Clarksville – to no avail. In October he asked the General Assembly for laws that would encourage sheriffs to protect prisoners. See *The New York Times*, May 22 and October 28, 1892.

12 *The* [Atlanta] *Constitution*, July 17 and 23, 1895; February 2, March 6 and 8, August 2, September 13 and 20, 1896; January 3 and 4, February 18, August 9, 1897; April 25, 1898; January 8 and April 23, 1899. The comments by the Reverend J. B. Hawthorne of Nashville are covered in *The Constitution*, December 19, 22, 23, 29, 30, 1898.

13 These six paragraphs are based on *The* [Atlanta] *Constitution*, April 23, 1899.

14 The previous six paragraphs are based on: *The Constitution*, April 23 and 25, 1899; the *Atlanta Journal*, April 24, 1899; *The Macon Telegraph*, March 23, 1899 and April 24, 1899.

15 Ida B. Wells-Barnett, *Lynch Law in Georgia* (Chicago: Chicago Colored Citizens, 1899), Kindle Edition; see also http://memory.loc.gov/cgi-bin/query/ r?ammem/murray:@field (FLD001+91898209+):@@@REF based on the same pamphlet in the Daniel A. P. Collection, 1818–1907; see also *The Richmond Planet*, October 14, 1899. The next section is developed from stories in *The Macon Telegraph*, April 24, 1899; the *Atlanta Journal*, April 24, 1899; *The* [Atlanta] *Constitution*, April 24, 25; the [Newnan] *Herald and Advertiser*, April 28, May 5, 1899.

16 *The Washington Post*, April 24, 1899; *The* [Atlanta] *Constitution*, April 25, 1899.

17 *The* [Newnan] *Herald and Advertiser*, April 28, 1899 reported one "special train," but Professor Andrew Sledd's experience in Newnan suggests there were in fact two trains. One of these was packed with men and boys from Griffin and one was carrying passengers who had boarded the train before it arrived in Griffin.

18 Le Vin reported William Pinson, Clair Owens, and William Potts of Palmetto; W. W. Jackson, H. W. Jackson, Peter Howson, and T. Vaughn of Newnan; John Hazlett, Pierre St. Clair, and Thomas Lightfoot of Griffin. There was a W. Jackson from Newnan in the 1900 census, but the rest were absent. The detective may have written the names incorrectly. See Wells-Barnett, *Lynch Law in Georgia* (Kindle Edition).

19 Amy Louise Wood, *Lynching and Spectacle: Witnessing Racial Violence in America 1890–1940* (Chapel Hill: University of North Carolina Press, 2009), 7, and 5–8; HistoricMapWorks: Residential Genealogy. Georgia, Newnan 1900, Plates 4–9, Sanford Map Company 1900: www.historicmapworks .com>Browse >United States>Georgia, hereinafter cited as HistoricMap-Works: Residential Genealogy. Georgia, Newnan 1900. On "outsiders'" participation in lynching, see Cynthia Skove Nevels, *Lynching to Belong: Claiming Whiteness through Racial Violence* (College Station, TX: Texas A&M Press, 2007). On lynching and masculinity see Kris DuRocher, "Violent Masculinity: Learning Ritual and Performance in Southern Lynchings," in *Southern Masculinity: Perspectives on Manhood in the South Since Reconstruction*, ed. Craig Friend (Athens: University of Georgia Press, 2009), 46–64. See also Sigmund Freud, *Civilization and Its Discontents*, tr. James Strachey

(New York: W. W. Norton & Company, 1962), 33–38, 41–45, 64–69; Peter Gay, *Freud: A Life for Our Time* (New York: W. W. Norton & Company, 2006), 543–553, esp. 547–553.

20 The narrative from the train station to the court house square is based on *The* [Newnan] *Herald and Advertiser*, April 21 and 28, 1899; *The Baltimore Sun*, April 24, 1899; *The Chicago Tribune*, April 24, 1899; *The New York Times*, April 24, 1899; the *Atlanta Journal*, April 24, 1899; HistoricMapWorks: Residential Genealogy. Georgia, Newnan 1900, Plates 1–9. The contrast between Dean's and Delk's executions and the lynching of Sam Hose was suggested by Michael Trotti's research, explained in both conversation and written product: See Michael A. Trotti, "The Scaffold's Revival: Race and Public Execution in the South," *Journal of Social History*, 45 (Number One, 2011): 195–224. See also Bertram Wyatt-Brown, *Southern Honor: Ethics and Behavior in the Old South* (New York: Oxford University Press, 1982), 435–461.

21 Mark Curriden and Leroy Phillips, Jr., *Contempt of Court: The Turn of the Century Lynching that Launched 100 Years of Federalism* (New York: Faber and Faber, Inc., 1999), 205, 206, 211; Richard Gambina, *Vendetta: A True Story of the Worst Lynching in America* (Garden City: Doubleday & Company, Inc., 1977), 80–81; Steve Oney, *And the Dead Shall Rise: The Murder of Mary Phagan and the Lynching of Leo Frank* (New York: Pantheon, 2003), 566–68; Michael Fedo, *The Lynching in Duluth* (St. Paul: Minnesota Historical Society Press, 1993), 128–129.

22 Hilary B. P. Bagshaw, *Religion in the Thought of Mikhail Bakhtin: Reason and Faith* (Farnham, Surrey, England: Ashgate Publishing Limited, 1988), 93; Mikhail Mikhailovich Bakhtin, *Rabelais and His World*, tr. Tvorchestvo Fransua Rable (Bloomington: University of Indiana Press, 1984), 196–277, esp. 213; Katerina Clark and Michael Holquist, *Mikhail Bakhtin* (Cambridge: Harvard University Press [The Belknap Press], 1984), 295–320.

23 Wood, *Lynching and Spectacle*, 45–47, 94–98; *The* [Atlanta] *Constitution*, any edition during the late 1890s; Ruth Coates, *Christianity in Bakhtin: God and the Exiled Author* (Cambridge: Cambridge University Press, 1998), 127; Ray Stannard Baker, *Following the Color Line: An Account of Negro Citizenship in the American Democracy* (Williamstown: Corner House Publishers, 1973. Original copyright S. S. McClure, 1904, 1905, 1908), 181–191.

24 *The Macon Telegraph*, April 24, 1899 reported that Mrs. Cranford and her mother were staying at the home of E. M. Hudson.

25 Paul W, Kahn, *Sacred Violence: Torture, Terror, and Sovereignty* (Ann Arbor: University of Michigan Press, 2008), 30, but also 21–41. On page 30 he writes: "Every act of torture is a competition between the power of the torturer to demand confession and the power of the victim to refuse and die as a martyr to his own sovereign." References to "sovereignty" derive from my understanding of Kahn.

26 Michel Foucault, *Discipline and Punish: The Birth of the Prison*, tr. Alan Sheridan (New York: Vintage Books Random House, 1977), 3–9, 11; James Gilligan, *Violence: Our Deadly Epidemic and Its Causes* (New York: G.P. Putnam's Sons, 1996), 93, 113–114; My understanding of Wilkes'

actions is based not only on *The Constitution* and the *Atlanta Journal* for April 24, but also through the report of Louis Le Vin as published in Wells-Barnett, *Lynch Law In Georgia* and *The Richmond Planet*, October 14, 1899.

27 Clifford Geertz, "Notes on a Balinese Cockfight" in *The Interpretation of Cultures* (New York: Basic Books, 1973), 432, 433, 436, 448–453; Hall, *Revolt against Chivalry*, 149–152; Mircea Eliade, *The Sacred and the Profane: The Nature of Religion*, tr. Willard R. Trask (New York: Harcourt, Brace & World, Inc., 1959), 30.

28 William Faulkner, *Light in August* (New York: The Modern Library [Random House, Inc.,], 1968), 439; Hannah Arendt, *Eichman in Jerusalem: A Report on the Banality of Evil* (New York: The Penquin Group, 2006, [original copyright by Hannah Arendt 1963 and 1964]), 12.

29 Jacqueline Goldsby, *A Spectacular Secret: Lynching in American Life and Literature* (Chicago: University of Chicago Press, 2006), 12–15; Daniel F. Littlefield, Jr., *Seminole Burning: A Story of Racial Vengeance* (Jackson: University Press of Mississippi, 1996); Michael J. Pfeifer, *The Roots of Rough Justice: Origins of American Lynching* (Urbana and Chicago: University of Illinois Press, 2011), Appendix.

30 Jill Lepore, *New York Burning: Liberty, Slavery, and Conspiracy in Eighteenth Century Manhattan* (New York: Knopf, 2005), 219, also see 201, 198–220 and Appendix; Mark Fearnow, "Theatre for an Angry God: Public Burnings and Hangings in Colonial New York," *The Drama Review*, 40 (Summer 1996): 15–36; Maureen Flynn, "Mimesis of the Last Judgment: The Spanish *Auto de fe*," *Sixteenth Century Journal*, 22 (Number 2): 281–297; J. R. Reinhard, "Burning at the Stake in Medieval Law and Literature," *Speculum*, 16 (Number 2): 186–209; Francisco Bethencourt, "The *Auto de fe*: Ritual and Imagery," *Journal of the Warburg and Courtland Institutes*, 55 (1992): 155–168; Roland Bainton, *Hunted Heretic: The Life and Death of Michael Servetus 1511–1553* (Boston: Beacon Press, 1953).

31 Fearnow, "Theatre for an Angry God;" Rene Girard, *Violence and the Sacred*, tr. Patrick Gregory (Baltimore: The Johns Hopkins University Press, 1977), 1–3; Girard, *Things Hidden since the Foundation of the World*, trs. Stephen Bann and Michael Metteer (Stanford: Stanford University Press, 1987), 30–47, 126–158, 224–237; Robert Jay Lifton and Greg Mitchell, *Who Owns Death? Capital Punishment, the American Conscience, and the End of Executions* (New York: HarperCollins Publishers, 2000, 2002), 230.

32 Susan Sontag, *Regarding the Pain of Others* (New York: Picador Farrar, Straus and Giroux, 2003), 114.

33 Kathleen Taylor, *Cruelty: Human Evil and the Human Brain* (New York: Oxford University Press, 2009), 6, 7–11, 55, 223, 264.

34 Wilkes' cry to "Jesus" came at the *beginning* of his ordeal. James H. Cone, in his brilliant theological discussion of *The Cross and the Lynching Tree* (Maryknoll: Orbis Books, 2011, © James H. Cone), 161, claims the scream was his last word. Cone rests this on the mistaken assumption of Leon F. Litwack in his brilliant *Trouble in Mind: Black Southerners in the Age of Jim Crow* (New York: Alfred Knopf, 1998), 281. The mistake is understandable and in no way casts doubt on either author's work. But, *The* [Newnan] *Herald and*

Advertiser, April 28, 1899 provides ample citations to demonstrate that whites at the end of the lynching drama observed that Wilkes (Hose) had died in silence. Moreover, the widespread anger of whites at how blacks used what everyone agreed was his silence bears witness to his grit and self-possession and validates the argument here.

35 Elaine Scarry, *The Body in Pain: The Making and Unmaking of the World* (New York: Oxford University Press, 1985), 48–56.

36 The narrative from the court house square to the site of holocaust is based on *The* [Newnan] *Herald and Advertiser*, April 28, 1899; *The Baltimore Sun*, April 24, 1899; *The Chicago Tribune*, April 24, 1899; *The New York Times*, April 24, 1899; *The Atlanta Journal*, April 24 and 25, 1899; *The* [Atlanta] *Constitution*, April 24 and 25, 1899. In the iconography of Christianity such control could characterize a saint. Javier Moscoso observes that an altarpiece depicting the martyrdom of George of Cappadocia represents him as showing no "sign of fear, pain, or doubt. His passivity serves as proof of his supernatural resistance." See Javier Moscoso, *Pain: A Cultural History*, trs. Sarah Thomas and Paul House (New York: Palgrave Macmillan, 2012), 13. See also Foucault, *Discipline and Punish: The Birth of the Prison*, 3–9, 11; Gilligan, *Violence: Our Deadly Epidemic*, 93, 113–114.

37 The discussion of Elijah Strickland is based especially on *The Macon Telegraph*, April 25, 1899. See also *The* [Atlanta] *Constitution*, April 24, 25, 1899; the *Atlanta Journal*, April 24, 1899; *The Baltimore Sun*, April 24, 1899; *The Chicago Tribune*, April 24, 1899; *The* [Newnan] *Herald and Advertiser*, April 28, 1899.

Chapter 5

1 The first two paragraphs are based on the experience of John Mathews' family and Edwin T. Arnold, *"'What Virtue There Is in Fire': Cultural memory and the Lynching of Sam Hose* (Athens: University of Georgia Press, 2009), 192–193; Cathy Caruth, *Unclaimed Experience: Trauma, Narrative, and History* (Baltimore: The Johns Hopkins University Press, 1996), 91–92.

2 *The* [Atlanta] *Constitution*, July 25–27, 1899.

3 Brian K. Smith, "Capital Punishment and Human Sacrifice," *Journal of the American Academy of Religion*, 68 (March 2000): 3–25; Robert Jay Lifton and Greg Mitchell, *Who Owns Death? Capital Punishment, the American Conscience, and the End of Executions* (New York: HarperCollins Publishers, 2000, 2002), 230; Paul W. Kahn, *Out of Eden: Adam and Eve and the Problem of Evil* (Princeton: Princeton University Press, 2007), 68, emphasis added; Henri Hubert and Marcel Mauss, *Sacrifice: Its Nature and Function*, tr. W. D. Hall, (London: Cohen & West, 1964, first published in French in 1898): 53, 55.

4 *The* [Newnan] *Herald and Advertiser*, April 28, May 5, and 12, 1899; *The Dalton* [Georgia] *Argus*, July 31, 1899.

5 *The Atlanta Journal*, April 24, 1899; author's emphases.

6 Heyworth's hosts knew he had served in the Union army and supervised thousands of freedmen in Louisiana. See George H. Hepworth, *The Criminal;*

the Crime; the Penalty (Boston: Walker, Fuller and Company, 1865), esp. 30–31; Susan Hayes Ward, *George H. Hepworth: Preacher, Journalist, Friend of the People: The Story of His Life* (New York: E. P. Dutton and Company, 1903), 72–74, 262. The previous six paragraphs are based on an article in *The* [Atlanta] *Constitution*, May 15, 1899 and *The* [Baltimore] *Sun*, May 29, 1899: "Dr. Heyworth Roasted."

7 See *The* [Newnan] *Herald and Advertiser*, April 28, 1899; *The* [Atlanta] *Constitution*, May 7, 1899; H. C. Dennis to Wilbur P. Thirkield, April 30, 1899 in the Wilbur P. Thirkield Papers 1883–1899 in microfilm records at Gammon Theological Seminary 1833–1940, Reel 3; *The Boston Evening Transcript*, April 27, 1899; *The Chicago Daily Tribune*, May 1, 1899. George Hepworth told Walter F. Willcox about his meeting. See Willcox's on "Negro Criminality" in Alfred Holt Stone, *Studies in the American Race Problem*, intro Walter F. Willcox (New York: Doubleday, Page & Company, 1908), 468 and also 463–70.

8 James Weldon Johnson, *The Autobiography of an Ex-Colored Man* in James Weldon Johnson, *Writings*, ed. William L. Andrews (New York: Literary Classics of the United States, 2004, distributed by Penguin Putnam, Inc.), 113–114.

9 *The* [Newnan] *Herald and Advertiser*, April 28 and May 5, 1899; *The Georgia Baptist*, April 20, 1899. The Reverend H. R. Bennett was the pastor and well-known to leading whites in the city. See also *The* [Atlanta] *Constitution*, May 7, 1899. The reference to "Sackcloth" is quoted in the last paragraph of chapter 4 in Andre E. Johnson, *The Forgotten Prophet: Bishop Henry McNeal Turner and the African American Prophetic Tradition* (New York: Lexington Books 2012); *The Dalton* [Georgia] *Argus*, July 31, 1899.

10 *The Georgia Baptist*, April 27, May 4 and 11, 1899; *The Savannah Tribune*, April 29, 1899; *The Southwestern Christian Advocate* [of New Orleans], April 27, May 4 and 11, 1899. See also *The Washington Bee*, April 29, 1899.

11 W. E. Burghardt DuBois, *The Souls of Black Folk* (New York: The New American Library, 1969 edition of a book of essays published in 1902), 79, 80. The essay had appeared earlier as "Of Mr. Booker T. Washington and Others."

12 The previous three paragraphs are based on *The Booker T. Washington Papers*, ed. Louis R Harlan et al., 12 vols. (Urbana: IL, 1972–1989), 3: 583–587; David Silkenat, "The Civilizing Mission of Booker T. Washington," *Journal of Southern History*, 73 (May 2007): 323–362; David Levering Lewis, *W. E. B. DuBois: Biography of a Race, 1868–1919* (New York: Henry Holt and Company, 1993), 259; Bishop Turner's comments were recorded in *Addresses and Proceedings of the Congress on Africa … in connection with the Cotton States and International Exposition December 134–15, 1895*, ed. John Wesley Edward Bowen (Atlanta: Gammon Theological Seminary, 1896), 196–197; *The [Atlanta] Constitution*, September 19, 20, 24, 1899. Bishop Turner was not alone in condemning Washington. *The Washington Bee* was only one of many papers that opposed the Wizard of Tuskegee: see its edition of April 29, 1899. Bishop Petty insisted the nation owed blacks "freedom without restraint" because they had already earned the right to "civil equality." See *The* [Indianapolis] *Freeman*, January 25, 1896.

13 *The New York Times*, April 26 and May 11, 1899. See also *Washington Papers*, vol. 5, 91, text and note 2. Paula Giddings implies she does not believe Fortune – she calls his interview "bizarre," and Fortune may indeed not have been recording "history" so much as myth. Washington may not have written anything; his reaction was probably unprintable enough to allow Fortune to suggest he tried. Washington was many things, but he was not stupid or impervious to white atrocities. Paula J. Giddings, *Ida: A Sword Among Lions, Ida B. Wells and the Campaign Against Lynching* (New York: Amistad, HarperCollins Publishers, 2008), 407.

14 Wesley John Gaines, *The Negro and the White Man* (Philadelphia: A[frican] M[ethodist] E[piscopal] Publishing House, 1897), 4–19, 43, 145.

15 The six paragraphs are based on *The* [Atlanta] *Constitution*, May 15, 1899; the next day *The Constitution* praised Gaines for supporting lynching. *The Louisville Courier-Journal*, May 16, 1899 lied that "Mob Law is Approved" by Bishop Gaines. The brief reference to racial destiny is based on Michelle Mitchell, *Righteous Propagation: African Americans and the Politics of Racial Destiny after Reconstruction* (Chapel Hill: University of North Carolina Press, 2004), especially 3–15. See also Mia Bay, *The White Image in the Black Mind: African American Ideas about White People, 1830–1925* (New York: Oxford University Press, 2000), 41. Saint Paul's words are in the Christian Bible, King James Version, Epistle to the Ephesians 6: 11, 12. See esp. W. E. Burghardt Du Bois, *The Souls of Black Folk* in W. E. B. Du Bois, *Writings*, ed. Nathan Huggins (New York: Literary Classics of the United States, Inc., 1986), 505.

16 The paragraph is based on the ideas developed by Diane Miller Sommerville in her *Rape and Race in the Nineteenth-Century South* (Chapel Hill: University of North Carolina Press, 2004), 219–259; Leslie K. Dunlap, "The Reform of Rape Law and the Problem of White Men: Age-of-Consent Campaigns in the South, 1885–1910," in *Sex, Love, Race: Crossing Boundaries in North American History*, ed. Martha Hodes (New York: New York University Press, 1999), 352–372. See also *The Constitution* April 23, 1899 and Mrs. L. H. Harris, "A Southern Woman's View," *The Independent*, 51 (May 18, 1899): 1354–5.

17 *The [Newnan] Herald and Advertiser*, May 5, 1899; *The Chicago Tribune*, April 12, 1899. *The* [Atlanta] *Constitution*, September 27, October 13, November 8 and 14, December 9, 1898; April 25, 28, 30, 1899.

18 Orra Moore Gray Langhorne, *Southern Sketches from Virginia, 1881–1901* (Charlottesville: University of Virginia Press, 1964 original published 1902).

19 The previous two paragraphs are based on *The Boston Evening Transcript*, May 6, 1899; *The Colored American*, June 17, 1899; *The* [Atlanta] *Constitution*, April 25, 28, 30, 1899; *The* [Newnan] *Herald and Advertiser*, April 28, May 5, May 12, 1899; *The New York Times*, April 25 and 30, 1899; Edgar Gardner Murphy, "The Georgia Atrocity and Southern Opinion," *The Outlook*, 62 (May 20, 1899): 179; [Anon], "Lynching and Southern Sentiment," *The Outlook*, 63 (May 27, 1899): 200. See also *The* [Sparta] *Ishmaelite*, April 28, 1899.

20 The previous two paragraphs rest on *The* [Atlanta] *Constitution*, April 25, 1899; *The Star of Zion*, June 22, 1899.

21 Jacqueline Goldsby, *A Spectacular Secret: Lynching in American Life and Literature* (Chicago: University of Chicago Press, 2006), 67.

22 *The Chicago Daily Tribune*, August 8, 1899.

23 The previous four paragraphs are based on *The Boston Evening Transcript*, April 24–26; *The* [Atlanta] *Constitution*, April 25, 1899; *The Chicago Daily Tribune*, April 26 and July 25, 1899; *The Los Angeles Times*, April 25 and 30, 1899; *The New York Times*, April 30, May 4, 17 and 24, 1899; [Anon], "Worse than Lynching," *The Outlook*, 62 (May 6, 1899): 8. The *Boston Globe* and the *New York Tribune* were also cited by *The* [Atlanta] *Constitution*. See E. L. Godkin, "Southern Lynching," *The Nation*, 57 (November 2, 1893): 322–323 for his early dismissal of all charges of rape; and also his "A Parochial Affair," *The Nation*, 68 (April 27, 1899): 306; "Secretary Long's Defence," *The Nation*, 68 (May 4, 1899), 326–327; and "Savagery as a Civilizer," *The Nation*, 68 (May 11, 1899), 347.

24 David W. Blight, *Race and Reunion: The Civil War in American Memory* (Cambridge: Belknap Press of Harvard University Press, 2001), 216–217, 222; Rayford W. Logan, *The Betrayal of the Negro from Rutherford B. Hayes to Woodrow Wilson* (New York: Collier Books, 1965, original copyright 1954), 242–275.

25 The previous two paragraphs are based on *The* [Atlanta] *Constitution*, April 26 and 30, 1899; *The* [Newnan] *Herald and Advertiser*, May 12, 1899; Estelle B. Freedman, *Redefining Rape: Sexual Violence in the Era of Suffrage and Segregation* (Cambridge: Harvard University Press, 2013), 119–124; *Southern Horrors and Other Writings: The Anti-Lynching Campagn of Ida B. Wells*, ed. Jacqueline Jones Royster (Boston: Bedford Books, 1997), 143–148; Giddings, *Ida, Sword*, 330–341.

26 These two paragraphs are based on Walter F. Willcox, "Negro Criminality," an address before the American Social Science Association at Saratoga, New York, September 6, 1899, in Alfred Holt Stone, *Studies in the American Race Problem*, 443–475; W. E. Burghardt Du Bois, "Two Negro Conventions," *The Independent*, 51 (September 7, 1899).

27 Three of Ida Wells' pamphlets are available in Wells (Royster), *Southern Horrors*. See also Kidada E. Williams, *They Left Great Marks on Me: African American Testimonies of Racial Violence from Emancipation to World War I* (New York: New York University Press, 2012) Chapters 1–3; also Amanda K. Frisken, "'A Song without Words': Anti-Lynching Imagery in the African American Press, 1889–1898," *The Journal of African American History*, 97 (Summer 2012), 240–269; *The Daily* [Chicago] *Inter-Ocean*, March 17, 1899.

28 *The Chicago Daily Tribune*, May 1, 1899; see also *The Colored American*, April 29, 1899; *The Washington Bee*, April 29, 1899.

29 Ida B. Wells-Barnett, *Lynch Law in Georgia* (Chicago: Anti-Lynching Bureau, 1899), 7–12, in the Daniel A. P. Murray Collection 1818–1907 in the Library of Congress, accessed through: http://memory.loc.gov/cgi-bin/query/r?ammem/murray:@field(FLD001+91898209+)@@@REF. See also *The Daily* [Chicago] *Inter-Ocean*, June 4–5, 1899.

30 Wells (Royster), *Southern Horrors*; see also Freedman, *Redefining Rape*, 73–124.

31 For a discussion of class and race among African American writers, see Kevin K. Gaines, *Uplifting the Race: Black Leadership, Politics, and Culture in the Twentieth Century* (Chapel Hill: University of North Carolina Press, 1996).

32 These two paragraphs are derived from Pauline E. Hopkins, *Contending Forces: A Romance Illustrative of Negro Life North and South* (Boston: The Colored Co-operative Publishing Co., 1900), 271, 299 as reprinted in a publication by the same title by Oxford University Press in 1988 in the series, The Schomburg Library of Nineteenth-century Black Women Writers. See also Freedman, *Redefining Rape*, 104–124 and William Councill's comments in "The Race Problem: A Symposium," *The Arena*, 21 (April, 1899): 433–434. See also J[ohn] E[dward] Bruce, *The Blood Record. A Review of the Horrible Lynchings and Burning of Negroes by Civilized White Men in the United States* (Albany: The Argus Company, 1901). See also *The Christian Recorder*, April 27, 1899: "Whereas we have no toleration for that class of depraved creatures among us, who are equally reckless in their invasion of divine rights of priceless life and sacred virtue, and who have done more to place the race in universal disfavor, if not contempt ... Resolved, that we pray that God's gospel light may reach [Southern] regions of lawlessness." See also a resolution by Newnan black ministers from *The Herald and Advertiser*, May 12, 1899: "We have no toleration for those who heap disgrace upon our race by the commission of crime," and who "defile women."

33 *Star of Zion*, April 10, 1885; November 2, 1893; September 20, and October 4, 1894, March 24, September 29, October 27, November 10 and November 17, and December 8, 1898; April 20, May 11 and May 25, 1899; *The* [Indianapolis] *Recorder*, April 1, 1899; Giddings, *Ida, Sword*, 187–208; Goldsby, *Spectacular Secret*, 67, 71–88.

34 On the previous three paragraphs, see, for example, *Star of Zion*, April 20 and 27, May 4, 11 and 25, 1899; also *The Chicago Tribune*, May 13, 1899; *The New York Times*, May 4 and 11, 1899. See also the editorial on "The Lynching Evil" and the sermon by an AMEC minister delivered in Indianapolis: *The Indianapolis Recorder*, April 1 and June 10, 1899; *The* [Richmond] *Planet*, May 25, 1895; December 17, 1898; November 11 and December 10, 1899; *The Washington Post*, April 27, 1899; John Edward Bruce in *The Colored American*, May 27, 1899. For Glessner's comment, see *The* [Atlanta] *Constitution*, April 28, 1899.

35 *The Washington Post*, April 27, 1899; see also *The Colored American*, May 20, 1899.

36 Kristin L. Hoganson, *Fighting for American Manhood: How Gender Politics Provoked the Spanish-American and Philippine-American Wars* (New Haven: Yale University Press, 1998), especially the first three chapters; P. C. Pogue to Editor of the Cleveland *Gazette*, February 3, 1900 in Willard B. Gatewood, Jr., *"Smoked Yankees" and the Struggle for Empire, Letters from Negro Soldiers 1898–1902* (Fayetteville: University of Arkansas Press, 1887), 258–259; Paul A. Kramer, *The Blood of Government: Race, Empire, the United States & the Philippines* (Chapel Hill: University of North Carolina Press, 2007), chapter 2; Stuart Creighton Miller, *"Benevolent Assimilation:" The American Conquest of the Philippines, 1899–1903* (New Haven: Yale University Press, 1982), 72–78, 88, 250–251; Nerissa S. Balce, "Filipino

Bodies, Lynching, and the Language of Empire," *Positively No Filipinos Allowed: Building Communities and Discourse*, eds. Antonio T. Tiongson, Jr., Edgardo V. Gutierrez and Rocard V. Gutierrez (Philadelphia: Temple University Press, 2006), 43–60; Cynthia L. Marasigan, "'Between the Devil and the Deep Blue Sea': Ambivalence, Violence, and African American Soldiers in the Philippine-American War and its Aftermath" (Ph.D. diss., University of Michigan, 2010: UMI Dissertation Publishing, ProQuest LLC, 2011), 318–324, 353–368.

37 Giddings, *Ida, Sword*, 410–423.

38 Ida Wells-Barnett," Lynch Law in America," *Arena* (January, 1900): 15–24 as printed in Ida B. Wells, *The Light of Truth: Writings of an Anti-Lynching Crusader*, ed. Mia Bay (New York: Penguin Books 2014), 394–403.

39 These two paragraphs are based on *The* [Atlanta] *Constitution*, April 25, 1899; *The New York Times*, April 24 and May 2, 1899; *The* [Sparta, Georgia] *Ishmaelite*, April 28, 1899; W[illiam]. P. Lovejoy, D. D., "Georgia's Record of Blood," *The Independent*, 51 (May 11, 1899): 1297–1300.

40 The previous 12 paragraphs on the speeches by Northen and Arnett are based on *The Boston Evening Transcript*, May 23 and 24, 1899; *The* [Atlanta] *Constitution*, May 18, 23–25, 1899; *The* [Nashville,TN] *Christian Advocate*, June 1, 1899; *The Georgia Baptist*, June 8, 1899; *The* [Louisville KY] *Courier-Journal*, May 23, 1899; *The New York Times*, May 23 and 24, 1899; *The Savannah Tribune*, May 27, 1899. The quotation about Mrs. Cranford's rape was creatively edited by pro-lynching partisans. See William Patrick Calhoun, *The Caucasian and the Negro in the United States* (New York: Arno Press, 1977 edition of a publication from R. L. Bryan Company of Columbia South Carolina, 1902), 97–98. A few blacks criticized Arnett for defending segregation but they weren't paying attention. Before Arnett spoke, Northen read to the audience a telegram in which a prominent white woman from Georgia promised to educate black youngsters. After basking in the warmth of white benevolence, she backed down: The task was too degrading. See *The Columbus* [Georgia] *Enquirer-Sun*, May 24, 1899. Explanation here has also been guided by Celeste Michelle Condit and John Louis Lucaites, *Crafting Equality: America's Anglo-African Word* (Chicago: University of Chicago Press, 1993), 69–100.

41 *The New York Times*, July 29, 1899; *The* [Atlanta] *Constitution*, May 24–30, July 28 and 29, 1899. One of the best statements confirming these paragraphs was printed in *The* [Newnan] *Herald and Advertiser*, September 1, 1899. African Americans were told not to believe anything Yankees and Republicans told them because they lied.

42 *The* [Atlanta] *Constitution*, August 1 and 14, 1899; *The Chicago Tribune*, August 1, 1899; the [Newnan] *Herald and Advertiser*, August 11, 1899; *The Washington Post*, August 1, 1899; "Governor Candler Once More," *The Independent*, 51 (August 10, 1899): 2171.

Chapter 6

1 *The* [Atlanta] *Constitution*, April 24, 1899.

2 Ibid., March 21, 1898 for names; also April 24–25, 27, 1899; the *Atlanta Journal*, May 1, 1899; *The Georgia Baptist*, May 19, 1899.

3 The previous five paragraphs are based on *The* [Atlanta] *Constitution*, April 25 and 28, May 1, June 6, August 8, 1899; *The Savannah Tribune*, June 3, 1899; Broughton thought blacks had "no political conscience" whatsoever, possibly because they supported William Y. Atkinson who was insufficiently "dry," see *The New York Times*, August 14, 1899; for the Northern Presbyterians, see the *Times* for May 25, 1899. See also the letter from W. P. Thirkield to W. E. B. Du Bois, October 14, 1902, W. E. B. Du Bois Papers, Special Collections and University Archives, University of Massachusetts Amherst Libraries.

4 Characterization of Broughton is based on *The* [Atlanta] *Constitution*, April 25 and 28, 1899; June 6, 1899; July 24, 1899; August 17, 1899; February 2 and 4, 1900; July 19 and 23, 1900.

5 Kathleen Minnix, *Laughter in the Amen Corner: The Life of Evangelist Sam Jones* (Athens and London: University of Georgia Press, 1993), 75, 80, 102; Chad Gregory "Sam Jones: Masculine Prophet of God," *The Georgia Historical Quarterly*, 86 (Summer 2002): 231–252, esp. 233–234, 238; Sam P. Jones, *Sam Jones' Own Book: A Series of Sermons* (University of South Carolina Press, 2009 edition of the cloth edition of 1887 published by Cranston & Stowe of Cincinnati, Ohio), 66, 187–199, 238, 264, 293–305. See his celebration of masculinity and his attack on spineless preachers, *The* [Atlanta] *Constitution*, September 14, 1898 and June 26, 1899. See also George R. Stuart, *Famous Stories by Sam P. Jones* (New York: Fleming H. Revell Company, 1908), Kindle edition, locations 1402–1409, 1640–1647. The call for a "sinewy religion" is in Theodore M. Smith, *Sermons by Reverend Sam P. Jones with a History of His Life* (Philadelphia: Scammell, 1886), 37, as cited by Kathryn E. Lofton, "Queering Fundamentalism: John Balcom Shaw and the Sexuality of a Protestant Orthodoxy," *Journal of the History of Sexuality*, 17 (September 2008): 447; Lofton's comment about "grotesque gender minstrelsy" is on page 468. See also Lofton, "The Preacher Paradigm: Promotional Biographies and the Modern-Made Evangelist," *Religion and American Culture: A Journal of Interpretation*, 16 (Winter 2006): 95–123, 103–104.

6 Minnix, *Laughter Amen*, 103; *The* [Atlanta] *Constitution*, February 21 and 22 (Jones approved the letter in which the "rape" charge was made). See also Richard L. Wilson, "Sam Jones: An Apostle of the New South," *The Georgia Historical Quarterly*, 57 (Winter 1973): 264–269. The Gatling gun was antecedent to the modern machine gun.

7 Darren E. Grem, "Sam Jones, Sam Hose, and the Theology of Racial Violence," *The Georgia Historical Quarterly*, 90 (Spring 2006): 35–61, esp. 47–48, 51–52.

8 Ibid., 58, quoting Jones from the *Atlanta Journal*, August 19, 1899.

9 Ibid., 54–61. Two days after the burning, *The* [Atlanta] *Constitution* printed a long article based on the assumption that women were the moral "citadel" of the Anglo-Saxon race, see *The* [Atlanta] *Constitution*, April 25, 1899.

10 *The* [Newnan] *Herald and Advertiser*, April 28, 1899 quoting a Macon, Georgia newspaper. See also article by Judge L. E. Bleckley taken from *The Forum* of November 1893 and printed in the [Newnan] *Herald and Advertiser*,

August 13, 1897; Christopher Waldrep, "Word and Deed: The Language of Lynching, 1820–1953," in *Lethal Imagination: Violence and Brutality in American History*, ed. Michael A. Bellesiles (New York: New York University Press, 1999), 241–243; Bertram Wyatt Brown, *Southern Honor: Ethics & Behavior In the Old South* (New York: Oxford University Press, 1982), 306, 388–389. See press responses to the murder of Sam Hose by a mob in Newnan, Georgia April 23, 1899 in the *Herald and Advertiser*, April 28, 1899; also E. L. Godkin, "Southern Lynching," *The Nation*, 57 (November 2, 1893): 322–323. See also Donald G. Mathews, "Lynching is Part of the Religion of Our People," in *Religion in the American South: Protestants and Others in History and Culture*, eds. Beth Barton Schweiger and Mathews (Chapel Hill: University of North Carolina Press, 2004), 153–194, esp. 159–165.

11 Jones, *Sam Jones' Own Book*, 70–72, 145, 264, 307. The reference to "noble men" was in an article in the *Sunny South*, an Atlanta magazine that denounced ministers' criticism of lynching in early July. See also *The* [Nashville] *Christian Advocate*, July 13, 1899; S. J. Heaton's sermon emphasizing that Christianity had "exalted women and made the home the vestibule of heaven" in *The* [Atlanta] *Constitution*, September 11, 1899 . Two days after the lynching, *The* [Atlanta] *Constitution* printed a long article based on the assumption that women were the moral "citadel" of the Anglo-Saxon race, see *The* [Atlanta] *Constitution*, April 25, 1899.

12 [Thomas Smyth], *Complete Works of Rev. Thomas Smyth, D.D.*, ed. J. William Flinn, 6 vols. (Columbia: R. L. Bryan Company, 1909), 6:103, 109. In a sermon at the Central Baptist Church in Nashville, Tennessee, June 25, 1899, the Reverend George A. Lofton pointed out as an aside: "The atonement on the cross was a judicial vindication of law." God's justice was revealed in Christ's death.

13 James Baldwin, *The Cross of Redemption*, ed. Randall Kenan (New York: Vintage International, 2011), 198.

14 *The* [Atlanta] *Constitution*, April 25, 28, and 30, May 18 and 26, 1899; *The Christian Advocate* [Nashville, Tennessee], April 6, May 4, June 1 and 15, July 13, 1899; *The Presbyterian Standard* [North Carolina], May 4, June 29, July 6, 1899; *The Southern Presbyterian* [South Carolina], May 4, 18, and 25, 1899; Manuscript Lecture to African American students of the North Carolina Mechanical and Agricultural College, Greensboro, North Carolina, May 25, 1899 in Julian Shakespeare Carr Papers in the Southern Historical Collection, University of North Carolina at Chapel Hill; John W. Stagg, "Race Problem in the South," *The Presbyterian Quarterly*, 14 (July 1900): 317–348, especially 317 and 341–342; *Western Christian Advocate*, April 26, May 3, 1899; Robert F. Campbell, *Some Aspects of the Race Problem in the South* (Asheville: The Citizen Company, 1899); W[illiam]. P. Lovejoy, "Georgia's Record of Blood," *The Independent*, 51 (May 11, 1899): 1297–1300. Reference to *The State* is in "Lynching and Southern Sentiment," *Outlook*, 62 (May 27, 1899): 200.

15 *The* [Newnan] *Herald and Advertiser*, May 12, 19 and 26; June 2, 9, 16, 23 and 30; July 7 and August 11, 18, and 25, 1899; *The* [Atlanta] *Constitution*, May 6, 10, 22, 23, 1899; June 3, 6, 13, 16, 18, 26, 1899.

16 *The* [Newnan] *Herald and Advertiser*, August 11, 18, and 25, 1899; *The* [Atlanta] *Constitution*, August 9 and 10, 1899. William Jefferson White was less than enthusiastic about Atkinson, who had failed to mobilize black troops during the Spanish-American War, see *The Georgia Baptist*, May 5, 1898 and August 17, 1899.

17 The three previous paragraphs rely on *The* [Atlanta] *Constitution*, May 25 and 30; June 5, 12–16; July 22, 26–28, 1899; *Louisville* [Kentucky] *Courier-Journal*, July 26, 1899.

18 *The* [Atlanta] *Constitution*, July 22–27, 1899; *The Chicago Daily Tribune*, July 29 and 30, 1899; *Louisville Courier-Journal*, July 26, 1899; *New York Times*, July 22, 27, and 30, 1899.

19 *The* [Atlanta] *Constitution*, June 6–12, July 22, 25–27, August 3–5, 12, and 22, September 8 and 15, October 22, November 19–25 and 29, December 7 and 19, 1899; *The* [Newnan] *Herald and Advertiser*, July 26, August 18 and 25, 1899. See also W. Fitzhugh Brundage, "The Darien 'Insurrection' of 1899: Black Protest During the Nadir of Race Relations," *The Georgia Historical Quarterly*, 74 (Summer 1990): 234–253.

20 *The* [Atlanta] *Constitution*, May 6, 10, 22, 23, 1899; June 3, 6, 13, 16, 18, 26, 1899; *The* [Newnan] *Herald and Advertiser*, June 9, 1899. The false fabrication of black lynch mobs here does not mean that there were none; see Karlos K. Hill, "Black Vigilantism: The Rise and Decline of African American Lynch Mob activity in the Mississippi and Arkansas Deltas, 1883–1923," *Journal of American History*, 95 (Winter, 2010): 26–43.

21 *The* [Atlanta] *Constitution*, June 4–8 and 10, 1899; see also Ida B. Wells-Barnett, "Lynch Law in America," originally published in *Arena* in January 1900, but reprinted in Ida. B. Wells, *The Light of Truth: Writings of an Anti-Lynching Crusader*, ed. Mia Bay (New York: Penguin Books, 2014), 397.

22 *The* [Atlanta] *Constitution*, June 4–8; W. A. Harris, "A Georgia Negro's Acquittal," *The Outlook*, 62 (August 5, 1899): 816.

23 *The* [Atlanta] *Constitution*, August 2–4 and September 12–15, 1899; the [Newnan] *Herald and Advertiser*, September 8 and 15, 1899. The report was supposed to be humorous: a frightened black man was funny.

24 W[illiam] Fitzhugh Brundage, "The Darien 'Insurrection' of 1899: Black Protest During the Nadir of Race Relations," *The Georgia Historical Quarterly*, 74 (Summer 1990): 234–253. All the material on Delegale is based on this thoroughly researched article.

25 Ibid., 249–252; see also *The* [Atlanta] *Constitution*, August 27 and September 2, 1899; "Delegal [sic] Riots in Georgia," *The Independent*, 51 (September 7, 1899): 2443 .

26 Brundage reports at least one white man and fifteen black men were executed by mobs after April 23, 1899, for a total of twenty-five for the year. Brundage, *Lynching in the New South*, 273. In addition, a black man, Alf Thurman, was reportedly killed by black men for informing on their gang.

27 The previous four paragraphs are based on W. H. [Sic: E.] Burghardt Du Bois, "Two Negro Conventions," *The Independent*, 51 (September 7, 1899): 2425–2427; David Levering Lewis, *W. E. B. Du Bois: Biography of Race*

1868–1919 (New York: Henry Holt and Company, 1993), 225–232; Du Bois, *The Souls of Black Folk* (New York: The New American Library A Signet Classic,1969 [originally published in 1903), 231–232; Du Bois, *Darkwater: Voices from within the Veil*, Intro. Marable Manning (Mineola: Dover Publications, Inc., 1999, originally published in 1920), 11; Du Bois, *Dusk of Dawn, An Essay toward an Autobiography of a Race Concept* (Brunswick: Transaction Publishers, 1984, original publication by Harcourt, Brace & World, Inc., 1940), 67–69.

28 *The* [Atlanta] *Constitution*, September 6, 1899.

29 Ibid., September 13, 15; October 17, 18, 21,25, 26; November 2, 1899.

30 Ibid., August 30, September 25 and 29, 1899; Glenn T. Eskew, "Black Elitism and the Failure of Paternalism in Postbellum Georgia: The Case of Lucius Henry Holsey," in *Georgia in Black and White: Explorations in the Race Relations of a Southern State 1865–1950*, ed. John C. Inscoe (Athens: The University of Georgia Press, 1994), 106–140; Edwin S. Redkey, *Black Exodus: Black Nationalist and Back-to-Africa Movements, 1880–1910* (New Haven: Yale University Press, 1969), 24–46.

31 *The* [Newnan] *Herald and Advertiser*, April 21, 28, 1899; see the text associated with note number 6 of Chapter 5.

32 Matthews, "Emergence of a Prophet," 120–122.

33 The previous three paragraphs are based on Andrew Sledd, "The Negro: Another View," *The Atlantic Monthly*, 90(July 1902): 65–73. See also Khalil Gibran Muhammad, *The Condemnation of Blackness: Race, Crime, and the Making of Modern Urban America* (Cambridge: Harvard University Press, 2010), especially pp.1–87. See also Aldon D. Morris, *The Scholar Denied: W. E. B. Du Bois and the Birth of Modern Sociology* (Berkeley: University of California Press, 2015), 41.

34 The previous five paragraphs are based on *The* [Atlanta] *Constitution*, August 3, 5, 6, 7, 9, 1902; Matthews, "Emergence of a Prophet,"120–137, 160–201, 320; Andrew Sledd to Warren Akin Candler August 27, 1902, Candler Papers, Emory University; Ralph E. Reed, Jr., "Emory College and the Sledd Affair of 1902: A Case Study in Southern Honor and Racial Attitudes," *The Georgia Historical Quarterly*, 72 (Fall, 1988): 463–492.

35 Andrew Sledd, "Illiteracy in the South," *The Independent*, 53 (17 October 1901): 2471–4; Matthews, "Emergence of a Prophet," 50–64, 175.

36 Matthews, "Emergence of a Prophet," 87–89, 160–228; Charles E. Dowman, "The Responsibility of the Educated Man," *The Emory Phoenix*, 17 (October 1902): 2, 7; James W. Lee to Warren Akin Candler, August 23, 1902; Robert J. Bigham to Candler, August 24, 30 1902; Charles Foster Smith to Candler, August 25, 1902; Bishop Eugene R. Hendrix to Candler August, 27, 1902; James E. Dickey to Candler November 26 and December 1, 1902 and January 2, 1903; Copy of Candler to Dickey November 28, 1902; Andrew Sledd to Candler, September 1 1902, November 8 1902; E. E. Hoss to Candler, September 25, 1902; Candler to Dickey January 5, 1903; J. D. Hammond to Candler January 14 1903, all in Candler Papers, Emory University; John C. Kilgo to Warren Akin Candler, August 14 1902, John C. Kilgo Papers, Duke University Archives [*not* Special Collections].

37 Matthews, "Emergence of a Prophet," 202–213; John Carlisle Kilgo, "An Inquiry Concerning Lynching," *South Atlantic Quarterly*, 1 (January 1902): 2–7; Brent J. Aucoin, *A Rift in the Clouds: Race and the Southern Federal Judiiciary, 1900–1910* (Fayetteville: University of Arkansas Press, 2007).

38 *The* [Atlanta] *Constitution*, August 6–9, 1902.

39 Philip Alexander Bruce, *The Plantation Negro as a Freeman: Observations on His Character, Condition, and Prospects in Virginia* (Williamstown: Corner House Publishers, 1970 of the 1889 edition), 1–60, 46–47, 93–142.

40 Walter F. Willcox, "Negro Criminality," September 6, 1899, in Alfred Holt Stone, *Studies in the American Race Problem*, (New York: Doubleday, Page & Company, 1908), 443–475; W. E. Burghardt Du Bois, "Two Negro Conventions."

Chapter 7

1 James Weldon Johnson, *God's Trombones: Seven Negro Sermons in Verse* (New York: Penguin Books, 1927 [Grace Nail Johnson, 1955), 53.

2 W. E. Burghardt Du Bois, *The Independent*, September 7, 1899; Du Bois, *The Souls of Black Folk* in W. E. B. Du Bois, *Writings*, edited by Nathan Huggins (New York: Literary classics of the United States, Inc., 1986), 365, 439–447.

3 Margaret Washington Creel, *"A Peculiar People:" Slave Religion and Community-Culture Among the Gullahs* (New York: New York University Press, 1988), 260–261, 263–266; Lydia Parrish, *Slave Songs of the Georgia Sea Islands* (Athens: University of Georgia Press, 1992), 161, 165–166, 178. See also Albert J. Raboteau's "The Blood of the Martyrs is the Seed of the Faith," in *The Courage to Hope: From Black Suffering to Human Redemption*, eds. Quinton Hosford Dixie and Cornell West (Boston: Beacon Press, 1999), 22–39; Riggins R. Early, Jr., *Dark Symbols Obscure Signs: God, Self & Community in the Slave Mind* (Maryknoll: Orbis Books, 1993); Howard Thurman, *Jesus and the Disinherited* (Nashville: Abingdon Press, 1949).

4 John Lovell, Jr., *Black Song: The Forge and the Flame* (New York: The Macmillan Company,1972), 321, 322; Du Bois, *The Souls of Black Folk*, (Huggins) *Writings*, 499–501, 538–545. On literalism, see Du Bois, William Edward Burghardt, 1868–1963, "My Sunday School Class, ca. 1895." W. E. B. Du Bois Papers, Special Collections and University Archives, University of Massachusetts Amherst Archives.

5 Du Bois, *The Souls of Black Folk*, (Huggins) *Writings*, 369, 468, 486–492; Du Bois, *Darkwater: Voices from within the Veil*, intro. Marable Manning (Mineolo, NY: Dover publications, Inc., 1999, published by Harcourt, Brace, 1920), 11; Du Bois, *Dusk of Dawn: An Essay toward an Autobiography of a Race Concept* (Piscataway: Transaction Publishers, 1984, originally published by Harcourt, Brace, and World, Inc., 1940), 67–68.

6 W. E. B. Du Bois, *Darkwater*, 60–62, 70–77: "The Second Coming," and "Jesus Christ in Texas." See also typescript of "Jesus Christ in Georgia," ca, 1911 in Du Bois, W. E. B. (William Edward Burghardt) 1868–1963, Special Collections and University Archives, University of Massachusetts Amherst

Libraries. David Levering Lewis, *W. E. B. Du Bois: The Fight for Equality and the American Century, 1919–1963* (New York: Henry Holt and Company, 2000), 19.

7 *The* [Atlanta] *Constitution*, April 24, 1899.

8 J. Denny Weaver, *The Nonviolent Atonement* (Grand Rapids: William B. Eerdmans Publishing Company, 2001), 16; Timothy Gorringe, *God's Just Vengeance: Crime, Violence, and the Rhetoric of Salvation* (Cambridge: Cambridge University Press, 1996), 54. See also David Garland, "Durkheim's Theory of Punishment: A Critique," in *Power to Punish*, eds. David Garland and P. Young (Aldershot: Ashgate, 1992), 37–61.

9 Suzanne Marshall, *Violence in the Black Patch of Kentucky and Tennessee* (Columbia: University of Missouri Press, 1994), 43 (32–43), 89–91, 99–100. See also Christopher Waldrep, *Night Riders: Defending Community in the Black Patch 1890–1915* (Durham: Duke University Press, 1993), 15–17, 50–51, 67.

10 John Crowe Ransom, *God without Thunder: An Unorthodox Defense of Orthodoxy* (New York: Harcourt Brace and Company, 1930), pp. 1–25, 49–51. "There is Power in the Blood," Words and Music by Lewis E. Jones, 1899, See http://members.tripod.com/~Synergy_2/lyrics/power.html.

11 Robert Lewis Dabney, *Christ Our Penal Substitute*, ([Davidson College Divinity Lectures, Otis Foundation, Second series, 1897] Richmond: The Presbyterian Committee of Publication, 1898), 32, 38, 64; Dabney, "Vindicatory Justice Essential to God," *Discussions of Robert Lewis Dabney*, ed. C. R. Vaughn, 3 vols. (Richmond: Presbyterian Committee of Publication, 1890), 1: 469–72; Dabney. "The Christian's Duty towards His Enemies," in Vaughn, Discussions, 1:706–721. See as well, Timothy Gorringe, *God's Just Vengeance*, 140; Philip Greven, *Spare the Child: The Religious Roots of Punishment and the Psychological Impact of Physical Abuse* (New York: Vintage Books [Random House], 1992 [first edition 1990]); Jeanette Anderson Good, *Shame, Images of God and the Cycle of Violence* (Lanham: University Press of America, Inc., 1999).

12 Du Bois, *Souls of Black Folk*, (Huggins) *Writings*, 493–495.

13 Mrs. L. H. Harris, "A Southern Woman's View," *The Independent*, 51 (May 18, 1899): 1354–1355. See also Philip Alexander Bruce, *The Plantation Negro as a Freeman: Observations on His Character, Condition, and Prospects in Virginia* (Williamstown: Corner House Publishers, 1970 of the 1889 edition), 41–49, 93–116, 126–142.

14 Atticus G. Haygood, "A Thanksgiving Sermon" [at Emory], *Western Christian Advocate*, December 25, 1880; Haygood, *Our Brother in Black: His Freedom and His Future* (New York: Phillips and Hunt, 1881), 58–72, 115–116, 158–219, especially 184, 185, and 187–195.

15 See for example, Atticus Greene Haygood "Governor Altgeld's Crime," *The Independent*, 45 (July 20, 1893): 969–970; Haygood, "The Chief Characteristics of Our Century," *Methodist Quarterly Review*, NS 15 (October 1893): 49–57; Haygood, "The Black Shadow in the South." *Forum*, 16 (October 1893): 167–75; Haygood, "The Negro Problem: God Takes Time – Man Must," *Methodist Quarterly Review*, NS 19 (September–October 1895): 40–53.

16 Edwin Talliaferro Wellford, *The Lynching of Jesus: A Review of the Legal Aspects of the Trial of Christ* (Newport News: The Franklin Printing Company, 1905), 12–15, 18–19, 88–91, 104; Dabney, *Christ Our Penal Substitute*, 32.

17 Walter White, *Rope and Faggot: A Biography of Judge Lynch* (New York: Arno Press and The New York Times, 1969, originally published in 1929), 40–53, esp. 40–44, 48, and 52; Kenneth Robert Janken, *White: The Biography of Walter White, Mr. NAACP* (New York: The New Press, 2001), 122–126.

18 Trudier Harris, *Exorcising Blackness: Historical and Literary Lynching and Burning Rituals* (Bloomington: Indiana University Press, 1984), 1, 12, 17, 95, and 95–128, 195. See also William F. Pinar, *The Gender of Racial Politics and Violence in America: Lynching, Prison Rape and the Crisis of Masculinity* (New York: Peter Lang, 2001), 126–131.

19 Orlando Patterson, *Rituals of Blood: Consequences of Slavery in Two American Centuries* (Washington, DC: Civitas/Counterpoint, 1998), 179, 182–214; Rene Girard, *Violence and the Sacred* (Baltimore: The Johns Hopkins University Press, 1977), 1; W. Fitzhugh Brundage, *Lynching in the New South: Georgia and Virginia 1880–1930* (Urbana: University of Illinois Press, 1993), 17–48; Henri Hubert and Marcel Mauss, *Sacrifice: Its Nature and Function*, tr. W. D. Hall (London: Cohen & West, 1964, first published in French in 1898). See also Andrew S. Buckser, "Lynching as Ritual in the American South," *Berkeley Journal of Sociology: A Critical Review*, 37 (1992): 11–28.

20 James H. Cone, *The Cross and the Lynching Tree* (Maryknoll: Orbis Books, 2011), 42, 101–108, 165–166; Michel Foucault, *Discipline and Punish: The Birth of the Prison*, tr. Alan Sheridan (New York: Vintage Books, Random House, Inc., 1995 [© 1977 by Sheridan]), 32–69; W. Jason Miller, *Langston Hughes and American Lynching Culture* (Gainesville: University Press of Florida, 2011), 56–64, 86–88; Anthony B. Pinn, *Why Lord?: Suffering and Evil in Black Theology* (New York: Continuum, 1999); Brian K. Smith, "Capital Punishment and Human Sacrifice," *Journal of the American Academy of Religion*, 68 (March, 2000): 3–25; Eric J. Sundquist, *To Awaken the Nations: Race in the Making of American Literature* (Cambridge: Harvard University Press, 1993), 591–594;

21 Du Bois, *Souls of Black Folk*, (Huggins) *Writings*, 359, 363–365, 493–505, 545, 547, but especially 500–505. Du Bois often referred to the "spiritual world" about which he was writing as "the Negro church." This practice led scholars, heedless of the fallacy of misplaced concreteness, ironically to think of the world expressed also as superstition, worship, aspiration, song, community, and the ideals of Right and Just, as an institution. For correction, see Kathryn Lofton, "The Perpetual Primitive in African American Religious Historiography," in *The New Black Gods*, ed., Edward E. Curtis and Danielle Brune Sigler (Bloomington: Indiana University Press, 2009), 171–191.

22 The *Oxford Universal Dictionary* begins the definition of "victim" thus: "A living creature killed and offered as a sacrifice to some deity or supernatural power."

23 Du Bois, *Souls of Black Folk*, (Huggins) *Writings*, 545.

24 These four paragraphs are based on Edgar Gardner Murphy, *The White Man and the Negro of the South* (Philadelphia: n.p., 1900), 10–18, 20–21, 31, 40–45; *Race Problems of the South: Report of the Proceedings of the First Annual Conference Held Under the Auspices of the Southern Society for the Promotion of the Study of the Race* (Richmond: B. F. Johnson Publishing Company), 11–12, 29, 30–32, 39, 48, 83, 109,134, 151, 152, 160–165, 193, 203; Hugh C. Bailey, *Edgar Gardner Murphy Gentle Progressive* (Coral Gables: University of Miami Press, 1968), 49–50.

25 [Ida B. Wells,] *The Light of Truth: Writings of an Anti-Lynching Crusader*, ed. Mia Bay (New York: Penguin Books, 2014), 328–329.

26 Thomas Nelson Page, *The Negro: The Southern's Problem* (New York: Charles Scribner's Sons, 1904), 105–106, 213; William Patrick Calhoun, *The Caucasian and the Negro in the United States* (Columbia: R. L. Bryan Company, 1902), 125–134, esp. 131–132; Edward A Ross, *Sin and Society: An Analysis of Latter-Day Iniquity* (Boston: Houghton, Mifflin & Company, 1907), 5–11, 33–39, 88, 89; Stone, *Studies in the American Race Problem*, 443–474.

27 David F. Godshalk, "William J. Northen's Public and Personal Struggles against Lynching," in *Jumpin' Jim Crow: Southern Politics from Civil War to Civil Rights*, eds. Jane Dailey, Glenda Elizabeth Gilmore, Bryant Simon (Princeton: Princeton University Press, 2000), 140–161, especially 146.

28 Irenas J. Palmer, *The Black Man's Burden: The Horrors of Southern Lynchings*, edited by Michael L. Goines, Sr., (See www.mgoines.com: Irenas J. Palmer, 1902), 46–53, 55–56; Mary Church Terrell, "Lynching from A Negro's Point of View," *The North American Review*, 178 (June 1, 1904): 853–868, especially 859–868.

29 William Ivy Hair, *Carnival of Fury: Robert Charles and the New Orleans Race Riot of 1900* (Baton Rouge: Louisiana State University Press, 1976), 110–120, 125–127, 147, 155, 166, 171, 178–179.

30 Manfred Berg, *Popular Justice: A History of Lynching in America* (Chicago: Ivan R. Dee, The American Ways Series, 2011), 93; Brundage, *Lynching in the New South*, 83; Philip Dray, *At the Hands of Person's Unknown: The Lynching of Black America* (New York: Random House, 2002), 3–16; Mary Louise Ellis, "'Rain Down Fire': The Lynching of Sam Hose," (Ph.D. diss., The Florida State University, 1992), 240; Grace Elizabeth Hale, *Making Whiteness: The Culture of Segregation in the South, 1890–1940* (New York: Pantheon [Random House], 1998), 209–215; Leon F. Litwack, *Trouble in Mind: Black Southerners in the Age of Jim Crow* (New York: Alfred A. Knopf, 1998), 180–183; Joel Williamson, *The Crucible of Race: Black-White Relations in the American South Since Emancipation* (New York: Oxford University Press, 1984), 201–204; Amy Louise Wood, *Lynching and Spectacle: Witnessing Racial Violence in America, 1890–1940* (Chapel Hill: University of North Carolina Press, 2009).

31 Edwin T. Arnold, *"What Virtue There Is in Fire": Cultural Memory and the Lynching of Sam Hose* (Athens: University of Georgia Press, 2009), 184–202.

32 Ibid., 171–172.

33 Jessica Hendrickson Ruckheim, "Defining a Celebrated Community: Newnan, Georgia African American Residents in Pinson Street 1920–1940" (M. A. Thesis, State University of West Georgia, 2002).

34 Inference made from information regarding Mrs. W. A. Turner of Greenville Street in Newnan during the 1930s and 40s. See *The* [Atlanta] *Constitution*, January 5, 1930, February 2, 1930, November 22, 1931 (photograph of the leadership of the Association of Southern Women for the Prevention of Lynching [ASWPL]). See also Minutes of the Anti-Lynching Conference of Southern White Women, Atlanta, November 11, 1930 and Minutes of Round-Table Discussion Executive Session, ASWPL, 1939, both in the microfilm of the Papers of the Association of Southern Women for the Prevention of Lynching accessed in the University of North Carolina at Chapel Hill.

35 Report of the Association of Women of the South for the Prevention of Lynching, January–April, 1931; Minutes Anti-Lynching Conference of Southern White Women, Atlanta, Georgia, November 1, 1930; Minutes of Meeting, Commission on Study of Lynching, Atlanta, Georgia, September 5, 1930, Papers of the Association of Southern Women for the Prevention of Lynching accessed in the University of North Carolina at Chapel Hill.

36 Ray Stannard Baker, *Following the Color Line: An Account of Negro Citizenship in the American Democracy* (Williamstown: Corner House Publishers, 1973; copyright 1908 by Doubleday, Page & Company), 188–190.

Index

abolitionists, 66
Abu Ghraib, 125
African Americans, 186
  betrayal of, by Federal Government,
    208–209
  Broughton on, 224, 232
  capitalism and, 100
  Christianity and, 18–19, 77, 82–83, 95–96,
    113
  citizenship of, 21, 24–25, 31, 187
  as commodities, 100
  criminality of, 202–203
  criminalization of, 23, 37, 48
  in Cuba, 207
  debt of, 149–150
  Democrats and, 101–102
  derogatory terms for, 200–201
  dialect of, 200–201
  disfranchisement of, 24–25, 31
  education of, 102
  emancipation of, 15–16, 20
  Felton on, 253–254
  Harris, C., on, 57, 223
  Hepworth and, 185
  historical justice for, 212–218
  Holsey on, 250–251
  humanity of, 184
  Jones, S., on, 232
  Landrum on, 232
  Le Vin on, 205
  literacy of, 102
  manhood of, 169
  middle class, 34
  missions to, 109
  in Newnan, 99–100, 114, 251
  after Newnan holocaust, 243–244
  in the North, 203–204
  patriotism of, 130
  progress of, 77
  Protestantism and, 112–113
  punishment of, 180–181
  on rape, 191, 206
  after Reconstruction, 101–102
  rights of, 253
  self-consciousness of, 112
  self-worth of, 212
  Sledd and, 252–253, 257
  soldiers, 128–138
  in the South, 189–190
  in Spanish American War, 265–266
  Thirkield on, 222, 232
  voting rights of, 21, 24, 114–115
  women, 87, 90–91, 206
African Methodist Episcopal Church
    (AMEC), 186–187, 189–190, 213
African Methodist Episcopal Zion (AMEZ),
    207
Afro-American Council, 203–204, 207, 210
Aguinaldo, Emilio, 251–252
  on Hose, 210
Alexander, Will, 90, 279–280, 282
Allen, Dixon E., 153
Allen, Lela, 153
AMEC. *See* African Methodist Episcopal
    Church
American exceptionalism, 209

American Red Cross, 150
Ames, Jessie Daniel, 279
AMEZ. *See* African Methodist Episcopal Zion
Andrew, James Osgood, 65–66
Anselm (Archbishop of Canterbury), 6–7
ante-bellum times, 99–100, 102–103
Anti-Lynching Bureau, Wells as head of, 211
anti-Semitism, 38
Arnett, Benjamin W., 213
Arnold, Edwin T., 277–278
Arp, Bill, 228–229
The Art of Cruelty (Nelson), 125
Association of Southern Women for the Prevention of Lynching, 111–112, 279
Atkinson, William Yates, 27, 53, 56–57, 118, 127, 159
   Candler, A. D., and, 127–128, 233
   in Democratic Party, 27
   funeral of, 233–234
   Herald on, 233–234
   on Hose, 159
   Howell and, 233–234
   on lynching, 119–120, 182–183, 194, 199
   Turner, H., on, 234
The Atlanta Compromise, 188–189
Atlanta Evangelical Ministerial Association, 222
The Atlanta Journal, 183
Atlanta University, 234
The Atlantic, 252, 255
Atlantic slave trade, 38–39
atonement, 7, 224, 267
Augusta, 27–28, 74, 195, 249
Aycock, Charles Brantley, 30–31
Ayres, Edward, 50

Bakhtin, Mikhail, 163–164
   on carnival, 164
Baptists, 10–11, 18, 41, 221
   Central Baptist Church, 108
   Newnan Baptist Church, 103
   Southern Baptist Convention, 212–213
   women as, 41
   Zion Hill Baptist church, 114
Barnett, Ferdinand L., 204
   on punishment, 230
Baskervill, William H., 77–78
Bataille, Georges, 126

Battle of Santiago, 116
Beatitudes, 106–107
Beck, E. M., 51
Bell, Grant, 238–239
   arrest of, 239
   Candler, A., on, 239
   trial of, 239–240
Bennett, Belle Harris, 110
Bennett, H. L., 114, 116
Berg, Michael, 276–277
Bethel Houses, 110
the Bible, 43–44, 71
   Genesis, book of, 71
   slavery and, 96
Black Christ, 269–270
Black Codes, 20, 23
Black Man's Burden (Palmer), 274
Black Nationalism
   of Holsey, 249–250
   of Turner, H., 249–250
Blackmon, Douglas, 23
Bleckley, Logan Edwin, 81, 119
Blount, Thomas B., 241–242
   on mobs, 242
Boas, Franz, 40
born again, 43–44
Boston Evening Transcript, 62, 197–198
Bright, David, 100–101
Brotherhood, 77–83
brotherly love, 101–102
Broughton, Leonard, 105–106
   on African Americans, 224, 232
   on Hose, 221
   on law, 221–222
Brown, Henry Billings, 36
Brown, Joseph, 157–158, 240
Bruce, Phillip Alexander, 32–33, 44–45, 48
Brundage, W. Fitzhugh, 50–52, 241–242
   on Darien, 242–243
Bryan, Mary E., 152
burning, 169–170
   as *auto da fe*, 171–172
   of Hose, 171, 181, 270, 275–276
   as sacrifice, 170–171

Cable, George Washington, 78
   Haygood and, 77–78
Caldwell, John H., 103
Calvin, Jean, 170
Calvinism, 18

Candler, Allen D., 53–54, 70, 128, 136–137,
    156, 187–188
  Atkinson and, 127–128, 233
  on Bell, 239
  Jones, S., and, 225–226
  on lynching, 53, 131–132, 195, 216–217,
    248, 265–266
  on mobs, 235
  on Newnan Holocaust, 212
  on peace, 217–218
  as politician, 234
  Proctor on, 218
  on violence, 248
  Washington and, 189
Candler, Asa, 70, 255–256
Candler, John, 254
Candler, Warren Akin, 64, 72, 76, 106, 254
  Harris, C., and, 85
  Harris, L., on, 69
  at Oxford, 64–65
  on religion, 69–70
  Scomp and, 83
capitalism
  African Americans and, 100
  race and, 134–135
  slavery and, 100
carnival, 163, 199
  Bakhtin on, 164
carpet-baggers, 200
Carroll, Charles, 39–40
Caruth, Cathy, 179
Cash, W. J., 10, 229–230, 264
  on punishment, 264–265
  on sacrifice, 106–107
Central Baptist Church, 108
Charles, Robert, 275
Chattanooga, 132
Chesnut, Mary Boykin, 87
Chicago Daily Tribune, 197–199, 218
Chickamauga, 130–131
Christian Advocate, 76
Christian Recorder, 114
Christianity, 6–7. *See also specific types*
  African Americans and, 77, 82–83, 95–96,
    113
  discipline and, 96–97
  Du Bois on, 260–261, 269–270
  Gaines on, 191, 250
  Godkin on, 197
  hatred and, 7
  of Haygood, 70–71, 265

  Holsey on, 250
  identification of, 108
  Jones, S., on, 227
  lynching and, 8–9
  manhood and, 72
  Mathews, J. D., and, 8–9
  in Newnan, 108–109
  punishment and, 18–19
  slavery and, 7–8, 39
  Sledd on, 258, 266
  in the South, 10, 99, 282–283
  superiority and, 39
churches. *See also specific churches*
  lynching and, 106
  membership of, 41, 96
  as moral institutions, 97
  in Newnan, 108
  Zion Hill Baptist, 114
CIC. *See* Commission on Interracial
    Cooperation
citizenship, 26, 130
  of African Americans, 21, 24–25, 31, 187
Ciuba, Gary, 16–17
Civil Rights Act (1875), 22–23, 32
Civil Rights Cases, 22–23, 35–36
Civil War, 40–41, 190
Clark, J. O. A., 70
clergy
  on equality, 232
  on Hose lynching, 231
  laity and, 164–165
  on lynchings, 204
  public roles of, 108
  words of, 222
Colored Citizens Convention, 26
Colored Methodist Episcopal Church, 74,
    248
Commission on Interracial Cooperation
    (CIC), 90–91, 279
Cone, James, 269–270
Confederate constitution, 99
confession, punishment and, 167
Constitution, U.S.
  Fifteenth Amendment, 21–22
  Fourteenth Amendment, 22, 35–36,
    101–102
  Thirteenth Amendment, 20, 35–36,
    101–102
The Constitution (newspaper), 145–146
  on Hose, 157, 196
  on Northen, 216

The Constitution (newspaper) (cont.)
　on rape, 193
　reward given by, 177
contagion, 117–118, 173–177
Contending Forces (Hopkins), 206
convict lease system, 23
Cotton States Exposition, 210–211
Coweta, 108–109, 120, 141–142, 228
　court in, 246–247
　lynching in, 240–241
Cranford, Alfred, 14–15, 47–48, 51, 138,
　155
　death of, 179–180
　Felton on, 179–180
　Hose and, 139–140
　murder of, 16, 93–94, 141, 144
Cranford, Mattie McLeroy, 150, 154,
　160–161, 201, 277
　alleged rape of, 141–142, 156–157, 215
　Hepworth and, 183
　Hose and, 165
　trauma of, 179
Creech, Joe, 29
crucifixion, 7, 19, 43–44, 95, 99, 113, 229,
　258, 261–263
　Du Bois on, 261, 268, 282
　of Hose, 245, 268
cruelty, 172–173
Cruikshank, William J., 22
Cuba, 116, 129
　African Americans in, 207
　revolution in, 128
culture, public execution as, 126

Dabney, Robert Lewis, 264
Dailey, Jane, 25
dancing, 106
Daniels, Josephus, 30–31
Darien, 241–242, 248
　Brundage on, 242–243
Davis, Jefferson, 43, 132, 183, 188
Davis, Winnie, 103–104
de Sade, Marquis, 173
Dean, Joe, 120, 125, 172
　hanging of, 120–123, 161
death
　punitive, 124–125
　sexuality and, 126
debt
　of African Americans, 149–150
　peonage, 23–24

Declaration of Independence, 131, 216
Delegale, Henry, 241–242, 244
Deliverance, 114
Delk, Tom, 125, 172
　hanging of, 121–122, 161
democracy, 185–186, 202–203
　in Georgia, 126–127
　hanging and, 122
Democrats, 29, 53–54, 182–183
　African Americans and, 101–102
　Atkinson in, 27
　Jones, S., on, 226
　prohibition and, 98
Deus homo, 6–7
Dickey, James E., 254
discipline, Christianity and, 96–97
discourse, 203
disfranchisement, of African Americans,
　24–25. *See also* voting rights, of
　African Americans
Dougherty County, 149–150
Douglas, Mary, 42–43, 45, 170–171
Dray, Philip, 277
Dreyfus, Alfred, 211
Du Bois, W. E. B., 10–11, 188, 191–192,
　220, 234, 267
　at Atlanta University, 234
　on Christianity, 260–261, 269–270
　on crucifixion, 261, 268, 282
　depression of, 245–246
　on God, 264–265
　on Hose, 245, 258, 262, 270
　on Jesus Christ, 262
　on lynching, 262
　on race relations, 261–262
　on religion, 263
　son's death, 245–246
　on violence, 245
due process, 151, 153
Duncan, Adolphus, 28–29, 53–54, 152–153
Durkheim, Emile, 42, 94–95
　on religion, 42–43

Eden, 63–67
education
　of African Americans, 102
　Washington on, 210–211
"Egypt of the Confederacy," 149–150
Elementary Forms of Religious Life
　(Durkheim), 94–95, 122
Ellis, Mary Louise, 277

Emancipation, 46, 57–58, 196
Emancipation Proclamation, 6, 20
   whites' reaction to, 20–21
Emerson, Ralph Waldo, 70–71
Emory College, 63–64, 67, 73–74, 76,
      87–90
   Sledd leaving, 254–256
Enforcement Act (1870), 22
Episcopalians, 44–45, 105
equality, 25, 93
   clergy on, 232
   discouragement of, 32–33
   rape and, 30
   Turner, H., on, 188–189
   Washington, B., 188–189
Eucharist, 78
Europe, racism in, 38
Eustis, John B., 76
   Haygood and, 76–77
Evangelical Ministerial Association, 105
Evangelicals, 43–44, 66–69, 73, 75, 95–98,
      105, 164–165, 215–216, 227, 229, 281
   sexuality and, 44
Evans, Clement, 96, 225–226
exceptionalism, American, 209
executive clemency, 152–153
Exorcising Blackness (Harris, T.), 269
expiation, faith and, 263–266

Fairburn, 146
faith, 118
   expiation and, 263–266
   hope and, 19
   vengeance and, 181–182
   white supremacy and, 99–105
Farmers' Alliance, 26, 29–30
Faulkner, William, 168–169
Fearnow, Mark, 170–171
Federal Government
   African Americans betrayed by, 208–209
   Fortune on, 208–209
   on lynching, 279
   Walters on, 208–209
Fellman, Michael, 21
Felton, Rebecca, 60–63, 72–73, 156–157,
      193, 221
   on African Americans, 253–254
   on Cranford, A., 179–180
   on lynching, 152
   Manly on, 62
   on rape, 180

   on Scomp, 83
   on women, 60–61
Felton, William H., 60
Ferguson, John, 35–36
A Festival of Violenc;e, 163
Fifteenth Amendment, 21–22
Fitzgerald, O. P., 107
Flanagan, Edward G., 153
Floyd, Silas X., 113–114
Force Bill, 24–25
Fort Haskell, 132–135
Fortune, Thomas, 208
   on Federal Government's actions, 208–209
The Forum, 119
Foucault, Michel, on punishment, 123,
      166–167
Fourteenth Amendment, 22–23, 35–37,
      101–102
fraud, prevention, 29–30
Frazer, James, 269
Fredrickson, George, 38
Freedman's Bureau, 74–76
freedom, 209–210
Freeman, Alvan D., 159, 233
   on Hose, 159
   on lynching, 182, 194, 199
frenzy, 7, 10, 19, 153–154, 198, 236,
      264–265
Freud, Sigmund, 96–97, 126
Fusionists, 31

Gaines, Wesley John, 112, 189–193, 206,
      257
   on Christianity, 191, 250
   on lynching, 191–192
   on slavery, 190
Gammon Theological Seminary, 143, 222
Geertz, Clifford, 168
General Assembly, of Georgia, 28–31,
      118
Georgia, 30, 78–79
   democracy in, 126–127
   elections in, 27
   General Assembly of, 28–31, 118
   Ku Klux Klan in, 102
   lynchings in, 50, 216–217
   mobs in, 247–248
   public execution in, 120–121
   rape in, 149–150
   religion in, 105–106
   violence in, 120

The Georgia Baptist, 113–114, 187
Giddings, Paula, 210–211
Girard, Rene, 170–171
  on violence, 269
Glessner, Douglas, 159, 208
Glory, 55–56, 68–69, 92, 95, 165, 173–174,
    268–269, 283
  Hose and, 168
  as religious expression, 94
God, 2, 88–89, 264
  as black, 112
  Du Bois on, 264–265
  Harris, C., on, 89, 107
Godkin, E. L., 81, 197
  on Christianity, 197
Godshalk, David, 273–274
The Golden Bough (Frazer), 269
Goldsby, Jacqueline, 198–199, 203–204
Goldstone, Lawrence, 35–36
Golgotha, 43, 281
Gordon, Loulie, 149
Graves, John Temple, 249
Gregory, Chad, 225
Griffin, 127, 135–138, 146, 155
  episode, 135–137, 140, 148, 155, 205,
    234–236
Griffin Rifles, 135–136
guilt, punishment and, 18–19

Hale, Grace Elizabeth, 276–278
Hall, Jacquelyn, 168
Hampton Institute, 188
hanging
  of Dean, 120–123, 161
  of Delk, 121–122, 161
  democracy and, 122
  as diversion, 124
  public, 108
  as sacred, 122
Hardy, Thomas, 126
Harlan, John Marshall, 36–37
Harmon, John, 186–187
Harris, Corra, 10, 57–59, 62, 71, 147–148
  on African American women, 58–59,
    86–87
  on African Americans, 57, 223
  Candler, W. A., and, 85
  on God, 89, 107
  Harris, L., and, 84–88
  Haygood and, 83, 93
  on lynching, 89, 280–281

  on marriage, 64
  at Oxford, 67
  religion and, 87–90, 265
  on sexuality, 193
Harris, Faith, conversion of, 88–89
Harris, Lundy, 63–64
  as academic fraud, 84–85
  Austin debauch of, 85
  Candler, W., on, 69
  Harris, C., and, 84–88
  Haygood and, 64, 83
  infidelity of, 86
  on manhood, 72
  in Oxford, 76
  as professor, 83–84
  religion and, 88
Harris, S. W., 233, 246–247
  on mobs, 247
Harris, Trudier, 269
Harrison, Benjamin, 24, 204
Haskins, Sara Estelle, 90
hatred, Christianity and, 7
Havana, Cuba, 128
Haven, Gilbert, 222
Haygood, Atticus Greene, 63, 73–74, 77,
    220–221, 227–228
  Cable and, 77–78
  Christianity of, 70–71, 265
  death of, 82–83
  Eustis and, 76–77
  Harris, C., and, 83, 93
  Harris, L, and, 64, 83
  on John L. Slater Fund, 81–82
  on lynching, 79, 81–82, 272–273, 280–281
  on racism, 74, 82
  on rape, 80
  on Reconstruction, 74–75
  Slattery on, 273
  Wells on, 81–82, 265
Helm, Mary, Markham and, 111
Hemphill, William, 144
Hepworth, George, 183, 201–202, 219–220
  African Americans and, 185
  Cranford, M., and, 183
  on lynching, 183–184
  in Newnan, 183
The Herald and Advertiser (newspaper),
    114, 116, 118–119, 126, 128–129
  on Atkinson, 233–234
  on lynching, 114, 181–182
  on rape, 192–193

Hodes, Matha, on manhood, 21
Hoffman, Frederick L., 48
Hoganson, Kristin, 129, 209–210
Holiness reformers, 69–71, 73, 107
Holsey, Lucious, 248–249, 258
 on African Americans, 250–251
 Black Nationalism of, 249–250
 on Christianity, 250
 on oppression, 250
 on paternalism, 249
honor, 16, 41–42
 punishment and, 19–20
 slavery and, 16–17
 violence and, 17
 Wyatt Brown on, 16–17
Hope, Lugenia, 90
Hope, Matilda Ann, 241–242, 244
Hopkins, Pauline, 206
 on punishment, 230
Hose, Sam, 4, 10, 39–40, 50, 52, 62, 166,
 222
 Aguinaldo on, 210
 Atkinson on, 159
 blood of, 168–169
 Broughton on, 221
 burning of, 171, 181, 270, 275–276, 279
 capture of, 154–166
 clergy on lynching of, 222–223, 231
 The Constitution on, 157, 196
 countryside terror and, 149–154
 Cranford, A., and, 139–140
 Cranford, M., and, 165
 Cranford's murder and, 16
 crucifixion of, 268
 cruelty inflicted upon, 172–173
 Du Bois on, 245, 258, 262, 270
 Freeman on, 159
 Glory and, 168
 guilt of, 153–154
 humanity of, 175
 Jesus Christ and, 266–271
 Jones, J. B, capture of, 154–155
 lynching of, 10–11, 14–15, 86, 93, 95,
 201, 231–233, 252
 as martyr, 174–175, 282
 punishment of, 223, 230
 pursuit of, 141–149
 recognizing, 154–155
 remembering, 271–280
 as sacrifice, 168, 266–271, 273, 282
 silence of, 174–175, 202, 211, 271

 Sledd on lynching of, 252
 Strickland and, 145, 156
 as symbol, 162, 164, 276
 sympathy with, 190
 Terrell on, 274
 transmutation of, 178–179
 trauma of death of, 179
 Turner, H., on, 187
 voice of, 174, 211, 271, 282
 Washington on, 189
 White, W. J., on, 187
 Willcox on, 258
Howell, Clark, 131, 144, 171–172, 201
 Atkinson and, 233–234
 on Newnan, 223
Hubert, Henri, 181, 269
Hughes, Langston, 269–270
humanity, 7, 198
 of African Americans, 184
 of Hose, 175

The Independent, 86–87, 93, 256–257
Ingersoll, Robert, 181–182
insanity, 79–80
International Sunday School Convention,
 221
interracial marriage, 26, 32, 75, 213
Interracial Woman's Committee, 90–91

James, William, 94–95
Jeffries, Jim, 3
Jennings, W. J., 38–39
Jesus Christ, 6–7, 18–19, 41
 Du Bois on, 262
 Hose and, 266–271
 sacrifice of, 43
 suffering and, 113
Jews, 7, 38, 269
Jim Crow laws, 47
Joan of Arc, 170
John L. Slater Fund, 73–74, 76
 Haygood on, 81–82
John of Patmos, 263
Johnson, Jack, 3
Johnson, James Weldon, 185–186
Johnston, Hal, 144, 147, 149, 156, 171–172
 on conspiracies, 149
 on lynching, 148
Jones, John B., 154, 158–159
 compensation of, 177
 Hose captured by, 154–155

Jones, Sam, 106, 224
  on African Americans, 232
  Candler, A., and, 225–226
  on Christianity, 227
  on Democrats, 226
  on lynching, 226–227, 230–231
  on manhood, 224–225, 227–228
  on punishment, 228–230
  on rape, 228–229
  on religion, 231
  on sexuality, 225
  on theology, 224
Jordan, John Henry, 115–116
Jung, Carl, 125–126
justice, 198
  for African Americans, 212–218
  lynching and sense of, 118–119, 126–127
  race and, 36

Kahn, Paul, 181
Kilgo, John C., 107, 266
  Sledd and, 256
Killers of the Dream (Smith, L.), 45
Kincaid Manufacturing Company, 234–235
King, Porter, 151
Kitty, 66–67
Ku Klux Klan, 21, 28, 213
  in Georgia, 102

laity, clergy and, 164–165
Landrum, W. W., 220–221, 266
  on African Americans, 232
  on lynching, 282
Langhorne, Orra, 194
law
  Broughton on, 221–222
  against lynching, 117–118
  race and, 37
  Reid on, 185
  segregation as, 31–38
  as violence, 37–38
Lawton, Alexander, 242
Le Vin, Louis, 160, 204–206, 247, 274
  on African Americans, 205
LeConte, Joseph, 107
Lee, Ivy, 256–257
Leigh, A. B., murder of, 120
Lepore, Jill, 170
Lewis, David Levering, 188
liberalism, 26
Life of Jesus (Renan), 107

Lifton, Robert Jay, 2, 170–171
Linders, Annulla, 123–124
literacy, of African Americans, 102
Litwack, Leon, 37–38, 277
the Lost Cause, 42–44, 100–101, 109–110
  sacrifice and, 124–125
Louisiana, 35–36
Lovejoy, William P., 62–63, 85, 88–89
Lowell, James Russell, 270–271
Lumpkin, J. C., 239–240, 244
lunacy, 79–80
Lynch, Charles, 49
lynching, 51, 151. *See also* hanging
  Atkinson on, 119–120, 182–183, 194, 199
  aversion of, 237–244
  Candler, A. D., on, 53, 131–132, 195,
    216–217, 248, 265–266
  as carnival, 163
  Christianity and, 8–9
  church and, 106
  clergy on, 204
  in Coweta, 240–241
  as custom, 119
  as diversion, 124
  Du Bois on, 262
  Federal Government on, 279
  Felton on, 152
  in Florida, 237
  Freeman on, 182, 194, 199
  as fun, 127
  Gaines on, 191–192
  in Georgia, 50, 216–217
  Harris, C., on, 89, 280–281
  Haygood on, 79, 81–82, 272–273, 280–281
  Hepworth on, 183–184
  Herald on, 114, 181–182
  of Hose, 10–11, 14–15, 86, 93, 95, 201,
    231–233, 252
  of innocent people, 118, 267
  Johnston on, 148
  Jones, S., on, 226–227, 230–231
  justice and, 118–119, 126–127
  justification of, 93
  Landrum on, 282
  laws against, 28, 117–118
  legislation against, 28
  mass crowds, 51
  Mims on, 151–152
  motivations for, 197
  narratives around, 173–174
  in Newnan, 119–120, 124, 127, 160–162

Northen on, 53, 150–151, 212–215,
265–266
origins of, 49
in Palmetto, 138, 142–143
political theology of, 217–218
posses, 51
private, 51
public acceptability of, 51
rape allegations and, 14–15, 45, 80,
180–181
religion and, 10, 127
Sledd on, 252–254, 256–257, 282
of Smith, H., 80–81
of Strickland, 232–233
terrorist, 51
Thirkield on, 223, 282
types of, 51
as violence, 119–120
Walters on, 207
Washington on, 189
as way of life, 48–54
Wells on, 237–238
whites' understanding of, 82–83
Willcox on, 202
The Lynching of Jesus (Wellford), 266–267

Macon, 132–134
Macon Telegraph, 135
Mahone, William, 25
"The Man with the Hoe" (Markham),
110–112
manhood, 41–42
of African Americans, 169
Christianity and, 72
Harris, L., on, 72
Hodes on, 21
of Jones, S., 224–225, 227–228
provocation and, 228
sobriety and, 97–98
voting, 21
Manly, Alex, 30, 59
Felton, R. on, 62
Markham, Edwin, 110–111
Helm and, 111
Marshall, Suzanne, 264
Marshallville, 145, 154
Martinet, Louis, 35
martyrs, 131, 167
Hose as, 174–175, 282
masculinity. *See* manhood
master-slave relationship, 66–67

Mathews, John Demarest, 4, 179
Christianity and, 8–9
Mathews, Leo, 5
Mathews, Lula, 5
Mathis, A. A., 120–123
Mauss, Marcel, 181, 269
McIntosh County, 241
McKinley, William, 128, 208–209
McLeroy, Pitt, 142, 165
Methodist Episcopal Church, South
(MECS), 73–74, 110
Methodist Woman's Missionary Council, 90
Methodists, 10, 63, 65–66, 71–72, 74
African American, 113
women as, 41
middle class, 33
African Americans, 34
Milledgeville, 117
Millett, Jean-Francois, 110
Mims, Sarah Harper, on lynching, 151–152
The Mind of the South (Cash), 10
Minfree, Harvey, 237–238, 244
Minnix, Katherine, 226–227
missionaries, 75, 82–83
missions, 108–109
to African Americans, 109
commercial advantages of, 109
maternalism of, 109
in Newnan, 111–112
mobs, 119, 176
Blount on, 242
Candler, A., on, 235
demographics of, 160–161
in Georgia, 247–248
Harris, S. W., on, 247
as madness, 194
in Newnan, 127
Moon, Charlotte Digges, 41, 68–69
Moore's Bridge, 277–278
Mora, August, 275–276
moral panic, 48
morality, church and, 97
morbid curiosity, 123–126, 172
Wilson on, 126
Moses, 18–19
Mullens, John, 240–241, 244
multiplier effects, 6
Murphy, Edgar Gardner, 194, 202–203,
272, 279–280
Washington on, 273
myth, 100–101

NAACP. *See* National Association for the Advancement of Colored People
NACW. *See* National Association of Colored Women
Napier, J. C., 78
National Association for the Advancement of Colored People (NAACP), 49, 269, 280
National Association of Colored Women (NACW), 210
  Wells in, 210–211
Native Americans, 38
"*the Negro, a Beast*," 39–40
The Negro and the White Man (Gaines), 189–190
"Negro Domination," 24–26, 29, 98
  Conservative campaign against, 30
"negro law," 37–38
"Negro Problem," 272
Nelson, Maggie, 125–126
New Orleans, 275–276
New Woman, 34
New York Herald, 183
New York Times, 198, 212
Newnan, 95, 98–99, 114–119, 137
  African Americans after holocaust, 243–244
  African Americans in, 99–100, 114, 251
  Christianity in, 108–109
  churches in, 108
  dramas in, 119–128
  Hepworth in, 183
  holocaust, 212, 243–244
  Howell on, 223
  lynching in, 119–120, 124, 127
  merchants in, 116
  middle class in, 116
  missions in, 111–112
  mobs in, 127
  punishment in, 119–128
  religion in, 105–106
  suppression in, 279
noblesse oblige, 17–18
the North
  African Americans in, 203–204
  the South and, 43, 193–194
North Carolina, 29–30, 256
Northen, William J., 27, 117–118, 150–151, 213
  Constitution on, 216
  on firearms, 150–151

on lynching, 53, 150–151, 212–215, 265–266
on race relations, 213
on rape, 215
re-election of, 53
on the South, 213–214

Olivet Discourse, 263
Open Letter Club, 77–78
Our Brother in Black (Haygood), 74, 77–78, 83
Outlook (magazine), 195
Ownby, Ted, 97–98
Oxford, 65, 67
  Candler, W. A., at, 64–65
  Harris, C., on, 67
  Harris, L., in, 76

Page, Thomas Nelson, 273
Pahl, Jon, on violence, 17
Paine Institute, 74, 81–82
Palmer, Irenas, 274
Palmetto, 137, 149
  arsons, 138
  lynching in, 138, 142–143
  militia in, 208
  race relations in, 143
Panic of 1893, 98–99, 116
Paris, Texas, 78–80, 82
Parks Johnson, Carrie, 90–91, 279
paternalism, 249
  Holsey and, 249
  of whites, 206
Patillo, Sallie Chase, 151–152
patriotism, 130
Patterson, Orlando, 269
peace, Candler, A., on, 217–218
People's Party, 26–27, 29–30, 117
Petty, C. C., 188–189
Philemon, 7–8
Philippines, 209–210
piety, 99, 104
  in the South, 96
Pilate, Pontius, 7, 282
Plessy, Homer Adolphe, 35–36
Plessy v. Ferguson, 37
populism, 25–31
Populists, 27–28, 43, 249
poverty, 112–113
prisoners, leasing of, 23
private lynching, 51

Proctor, Henry H., 56, 72–73
  on Candler, A., 218
prohibition, 41–42, 46
  Democrats and, 98
  Protestantism and, 98–99
  Republicans and, 98
prohibitionism, 98
Protestantism, 65–66
  African Americans and, 112–113
  prohibition and, 98–99
provocation, 81, 119, 160–161, 197, 201,
  227–228, 230–231, 236, 280–281
  manhood and, 228
public execution, 123. *See also* hanging
  as cultural manifestation, 126
  in Georgia, 120–121
  as sacrifice, 170–171
public opinion, on violence, 201–202
punishment
  of African Americans, 180–181
  Barnett, F., on, 230
  Cash on, 264–265
  confession and, 167
  death as, 124–125
  Foucault on, 123, 166–167
  guilty and, 18–19
  honor and, 19–20
  Hopkins on, 230
  of Hose, 223, 230
  Jones, S., on, 228–230
  justification of, 230
  in Newnan, 119–128
  of rape, 223
  sexuality and, 19
  of sin, 264
  as spectacle, 123
  Wells on, 230

R. D. Cole Manufacturing Company, 108
Rabelais and His World (Bakhtin), 163–164
Rable, George, 21
Raboteau, Albert, 18–19
race
  capitalism and, 134–135
  as Idol, 8
  interracial marriage, 26, 32, 75, 213
  justice and, 36
  law and, 37
  rape and, 60–63
  in the South, 77
  violence and, 40

race relations
  Du Bois on, 261–262
  Northen on, 213
  in Palmetto, 143
  slavery and, 195–196
  white women and, 109–110
  Willcox on, 202–203
racism, 38
  in Europe, 38
  Haygood on, 74, 82
  Sledd on, 258
railway travel, 33–34
  segregation of, 34–35, 196
  Wells and, 34
Ransom, John Crowe, 264
rape, 142
  of African American women, 206
  African Americans on, 206
  alleged, of Cranford, M., 141–142,
    156–157, 215
  Constitution on, 193
  equality and, 30
  Felton on, 180
  in Georgia, 149–150
  Haygood on, 80
  Herald on, 192–193
  Jones, S., on, 228–229
  lynching victims and allegations of, 14–15,
    45, 80, 180–181
  Northen on, 215
  punishment of, 223
  race and, 60–63
  Reconstruction and, 21
  in trials, 193
  Wells on, 59, 204
  white supremacy and,
    193–194
Readjuster Party, 25–26
rebellion, 142–143
Reconstruction, 15–16, 20–25, 43
  African Americans after, 101–102
  in Georgia, 101–102
  Haygood on, 74–75
  perceived failure of, 200
  rape and, 21
  resistance to, 21
  sexuality and, 21
  Supreme Court in, 22
Red Record (Wells), 199–200, 204
redemption, 122–123
Reece's Opera House, 106

Reid, James, 116, 185, 196–197, 251, 258
  on law, 185
religion, 2. *See also* Christianity
  Candler, W. A., on, 69–70
  defining, 2, 42
  Du Bois on, 263
  Durkheim on, 42–43
  in Georgia, 105–106
  Glory as expression of, 94
  Harris, C., and, 87–90, 265
  Harris, L., and, 88
  Jones, S., on, 231
  Lost Cause and, 43, 104, 124–125, 213
  lynching and, 10, 127
  in Newnan, 105–106
  pain in, 18–19
  segregation and, 38–48
  transcendence and, 42
Renan, Ernst, 107
Republicans, 29–30, 101
  prohibition and, 98
Revelation of St. John, 171
Rituals of Blood (Patterson), 269
Roche, Roberta Senechal de la, 52
Rogowski, Abraham, 146–147, 158–160,
  172, 244
Roman Catholics, 105
Rope and Faggot (White), 269
Rosen, Hannah, 21–22
Ruckheim, Jessica, 279
Ryder, W. L., 118–119

the sacred, 181
  hanging as, 122
  segregation and, 46–47
sacrifice, 2, 9–11
  burning as, 170–171
  Cash on, 106–107
  Hose as, 168, 266–271, 273, 282
  of Jesus Christ, 43
  the Lost Cause and, 124–125
  public execution as, 170–171
  salvation and, 6–7
sadism, 172–173
salvation, 99, 281
  sacrifice and, 6–7
Santiago, 132–133
The Savannah Tribune (newspaper), 187–
  188
Scarritt Bible and Training School, 110
Scarry, Elaine, 174

segregation, 22–23, 31, 152
  Evil and, 46–47
  as law, 31–38
  pollution and, 32–33, 40, 44,
    95–96
  prohibition of, 32
  of railway cars, 34–35, 196
  religion and, 38–48
  in rural environments, 33
  the sacred and, 46–47
  sex and, 45
  Smith, L., on, 45–46
  Supreme Court on, 114–115
  in urban environments, 33
  violence and, 47
  Wells on, 33–35
self-discipline, 68
Seminole, 9
Separate Car Law, 35–37
  constitutionality of, 36
Sermon on the Mount, 232
Servetus, Michael, 170
sex, segregation and, 45
sexuality
  death and, 126
  Evangelicals and, 44
  Harris, C., on, 193
  Jones, S., on, 225
  punishment and, 19
  Reconstruction and, 21
Shivarees, 162–163
Slater Fund. *See* John L. Slater Fund
Slattery, John Richard, 81–82, 272–273
  on Haygood, 273
Slaughterhouse Cases, 22, 35–36
slaves and slavery
  Atlantic slave trade, 38–39
  the Bible and, 96
  capitalism and, 100
  Christianity and, 7–8, 39
  Gaines on, 190
  honor and, 16–17
  obedience under, 16
  race relations and, 195–196
  violence and, 17–18
  virtue and, 75
  wealth and, 16–17
  whites and, 17
Sledd, Andrew, 84–85, 251–258
  African Americans and, 252–253, 257
  article by, 252–254

on Christianity, 258, 266
on Hose lynching, 252
Kilgo and, 256
leaving Emory, 254–256
on lynching, 252–254, 256–257, 282
on racism, 258
Turner, H., on, 257
Smith, Henry, 78–79, 169–170, 200, 238, 244, 270
lynching of, 80–81
Smith, Leonie, 237–238
Smith, Lillian, 18, 45, 229–230, 281
on segregation, 45–46
Smith, Mark, 39–40
sobriety, 98
manhood and, 97–98
social equality, 75–76
Sontag, Susan, 172
The Souls of Black Folk (Du Bois), 10–11, 260–261
the South, 40–41, 68
African Americans in, 189–190
Christianity in, 10, 99, 282–283
family in, 4
the North and, 43, 193–194
Northen on, 213–214
piety in, 96
race in, 77
Washington on, 189
South Carolina, 208–209
Southern Baptist Convention, 212–213
Southern Evangelical Protestantism, 67–68
Southern Horrors (Wells), 204
Spanish American War, 131, 209
African Americans in, 265–266
A Spectacular Secret (Goldsby), 198–199
Speer, Emory, 194
Stacy, James, 106
The State (newspaper), 231
Steward, T. G., 55–56, 72–73
Stone, Alfred, 273
Stowe, Harriet Beecher, 214
Strickland, Elijah, 147, 154–156, 165–166, 175–177, 196
death of, 220–221
Hose and, 145, 156
innocence of, 205
lynching of, 232–233
murder of, 265–266
torture of, 176–177

Studies in the American Race Problem (Stone), 273
Supreme Court, 35
in Reconstruction, 22
on segregation, 114–115
syncretism, 9

Taylor, Kathleen, 172–173
temperance, 41–42
Woman's Christian Temperance Union, 41–42, 60, 69, 72–73
women and, 96–97
Tennessee, 34–35
Tenth Immune Regiment, 135, 138
Terrell, Mary Church, 210, 274–275
on Hose, 274
terrorist lynching, 51
Tharpe, J. W., 143
Thirkield, Wilbur P., 143, 222, 266
on African Americans, 232
on lynching, 223, 282
Thirteenth Amendment, 20, 35–37, 101–102
Thomas, W. W., 145, 175
Thornwell, James Henley, 97
threadbare lie, 34, 61, 203–211, 258
Thurman, Howard, 46–47
on violence, 47
Tillman, Ben, 53
Tolnay, Stewart E., 51
The Tongue of Fire, 70
torture, 125
of Hose, 168–169
of Strickland, 177
Tourgee, Albion, 35–36
transcendence, religion and, 42
transgression, 6, 122–123, 126, 158–161, 177, 180–181, 199
trials, rape in, 193
Trinity College, 107, 256
Trotti, Michael, 123
Turner, Henry McNeal, 112, 143
on Atkinson, 234
Black Nationalism of, 249–250
on equality, 188–189
on Hose, 187
on Sledd, 257
Turner, Mrs. W. A., 279
Tybee Island, 152

Uncle Tom's Cabin (Stowe), 214
United Daughters of the Confederacy, 103–104
United States v. Cruikshank, 22, 35–36
urban environments, segregation in, 33
USS *Maine*, 128

Vance, Myrtle, 79–81
    murder of, 200
Vandal, Gilles, 52
The Varieties of Religious Experience (James), 94–95
vengeance, faith and, 181–182
victim-blaming, 271
vigilantism, 52
violence
    Candler, A., on, 248
    defiance and, 271
    Du Bois on, 245
    in Georgia, 120
    Girard on, 170–171, 269
    honor and, 17
    law as, 37–38
    lynching as, 119–120
    Pahl on, 17, 37–38
    public opinions on, 201–202
    race and, 40
    segregation and, 47
    slaves and, 17–18
    Thurman on, 47
    of whites, 187
Violence and the Sacred (Girard), 170–171
Virginia, 25
voting rights, of African Americans, 21, 24, 114–115

Waddell, Alfred Moore, 30–31
Waldrep, Christopher, 48–49
Walters, Alexander, 207, 209
    on Federal Government's actions, 208–209
    on lynching, 207
Ward, William Hayes, 89
Washington, Booker T., 188, 192–193, 273
    Candler, A., and, 189
    on education, 210–211
    on equality, 188–189
    on Hose, 189
    on lynching, 189
    on Murphy, 273
    on the South, 189

Watson, Thomas Edward, 27, 247–248
wealth, slavery and, 16–17
Wellford, Edwin Talliaferro, 266–268
Wells, Ida B., 62, 79, 149, 197, 204, 236–237
    in Anti-Lynching Bureau, 211
    on Haygood, 81–82, 265
    on lynching, 237–238
    in NACW, 210–211
    on punishment, 230
    railway car incident, 34
    on rape, 59, 204
    on segregation, 33–35
    Willard and, 199–200
Wesley, John, 69–70
Wesley Community Houses, 110
Wheeler, Joseph, 130–131
whiskey, 61, 97
White, George Henry, 279
White, Walter, 269, 280
White, William Jefferson, 113, 258
    on Hose, 187
white supremacy, 8, 21, 30, 44, 50, 94–99, 104–105, 138, 142, 216–217, 238, 242, 273, 279–280, 282
    faith and, 99–105
    paranoia and, 208
    rape and, 193–194
Whitecappers, 52
whites
    alleged assaults on, 236–237
    lynching as understood by, 82–83
    paternalism of, 206
    power of, 186–187
    reaction to Emancipation Proclamation, 20–21
    slaves and, 17
    violence of, 187
whiteness, 6, 9, 14–15
    women, 90–91
Wilkes, Tom. *See* Hose, Sam
Willard, Frances, 200
    Wells and, 199–200
Willcox, Walter F., 48, 201–203, 219–220, 258, 278
    on Hose, 258
    on lynching, 202
    on race relations, 202–203
Williams v. Mississippi, 37
Williamson, Joel, 228
Wilson, Charles Reagan, 99
Wilson, Eric, 125–126

Withrow, C. H., 136
Woman's Christian Temperance Union,
    41–42, 60, 69, 72–73
Woman's Missionary Union, 41
women
    African American, 87, 90–91, 206
    as Baptists, 41
    Felton, R., on, 60–61
    Harris on, 58–59
    as Methodists, 41
    temperance and, 96–97
    white, 90–91
    white, race relations and, 109–110

Women's Christian Temperance Union,
    97–98, 199–200
Women's Home Missionary Society,
    110–112
Women's Missionary Society, 117
Wood, Amy, 160–161, 164–165,
    276–277
"A Word to the Negroes" (Gordon),
    150
Wyatt Brown, Bertram, 16, 162–163
    on honor, 16–17

Zebulon, 121